# THE GRECO-ROMAN WORLD

## OF THE NEW TESTAMENT ERA

### Exploring the Background of Early Christianity

## JAMES S. JEFFERS

**InterVarsity Press**
Downers Grove, Illinois

*InterVarsity Press*
*P.O. Box 1400, Downers Grove, IL 60515*
*World Wide Web: www.ivpress.com*
*E-mail: mail@ivpress.com*

*InterVarsity Press® is the book-publishing division of InterVarsity Christian Fellowship/USA®, a student movement active on campus at hundreds of universities, colleges and schools of nursing in the United States of America, and a member movement of the International Fellowship of Evangelical Students. For information about local and regional activities, write Public Relations Dept., InterVarsity Christian Fellowship/USA, 6400 Schroeder Rd., P.O. Box 7895, Madison, WI 53707-7895.*

*Cover photograph: The Granger Collection, New York*

*ISBN 0-8308-1589-9*

*Printed in the United States of America*

**Library of Congress Cataloging-in-Publication Data**

*Jeffers, James S., 1956-*
     *The Greco-Roman world of the New Testament era: exploring the*
  *background of early Christianity/James S. Jeffers.*
          *p.      cm.*
     *Includes bibliographical references and index.*
     *ISBN 0-8308-1589-9 (pbk.: alk. paper)*
     *1. Bible.  N.T.—History of contemporary events. 2. Church*
*history—Primitive and early church, ca. 30-600.     I. Title.*
*BS2410.J44      1999*
*225.9'5—dc21*
                                                                      *99-37146*
                                                                         *CIP*

| 22 | 21 | 20 | 19 | 18 | 17 | 16 | 15 | 14 | 13 | 12 | 11 | 10 | 9 | 8 | 7 | 6 | 5 | 4 |
|----|----|----|----|----|----|----|----|----|----|----|----|----|---|---|---|---|---|---|
| 17 | 16 | 15 | 14 | 13 | 12 | 11 | 10 | 09 | 08 | 07 | 06 | 05 | 04 | | | | | |

*This book is dedicated to ministers*
*and lay Christians who,*
*in the midst of ministry challenges*
*and hectic schedules,*
*still make the time to understand*
*what the New Testament means*
*in the various contexts in which*
*its parts were written,*
*and who believe*
*that a Christian*
*never need fear the pursuit of truth.*

# Contents

# List of Figures

# List of Maps

# List of Tables

# Preface

Most Christians and others interested in the New Testament would love to be able to read it and understand what it means without having to read other books. Of course, one can always read some kind of meaning into a verse of Scripture. But those who understand that the books of the New Testament were written to specific people, in specific places, nearly two thousand years ago, know that this is not a good idea. If the New Testament texts were written to make sense to people in the first century, then we must try to put ourselves into their places in order to determine what the writers of the New Testament intended their readers to understand by what they wrote.

If we try to make sense of the Bible with no knowledge of the people who wrote it, those who read it and the society in which they lived, we will be inclined to read into the Scriptures our own society's values and ideas. This would be a major mistake since our culture is very different from that of the ancient Romans.

This book is written with the nonscholar in mind. It uses technical terms only when necessary to make the point, and then explains them clearly. This does not mean, however, that the book is not suitable for the serious student. I am convinced that one does not have to sacrifice accuracy to make a work understandable to the inexpert.

Many Bible background books have been written over the years, but few have addressed thoroughly what the student of the New Testament needs to know about Greco-Roman societies and cultures of the time. Still fewer have been written by someone with expertise in both Roman history and early Christianity.

The birthplace of Christianity was a very complex and complicated place in the first century. Chapter one introduces the cultural and political milieu by means of a fictional dinner in Jerusalem. For those who want a fuller account, appendix A presents the Roman and Hellenistic historical background, with attention to themes and events such as the conquest of the eastern Mediterranean that will help place the early church in the Greco-Roman context. Chapter two tries to give the reader a sense of what it was like to live in the first century with a look at how the people of the day worked, played, traveled, ate, clothed themselves and attended to the deceased.

Although most of the population of the day lived in the countryside, Christianity arose in the cities of the Empire. So chapter three focuses on the city and city life in the Greco-Roman world and its impact on the early churches. Consult chapter thirteen for descriptions of the various cities and Roman provinces and their significance in the New Testament era. Chapter four looks at how the early Christians organized themselves within the cities and considers to what extent the synagogue, the Roman voluntary association, and Roman household structures may have affected the development of early church organization.

Religion was a very important element of life in the ancient world. Chapter five presents a brief overview of the key religions of the day. It shows how the Romans and others looked at religion, and how this affected Judaism and Christianity.

The next two chapters look at how the Romans ruled the Empire they assembled. Chapter six describes how Rome governed its provinces, with special attention to Palestine and the Near East. Chapter seven examines some of the key tools that the Romans used to control and administer their empire: taxes, the legal system and the military.

We cannot understand the connection between Christianity and Greco-Roman society until we realize the importance of honor and respect in the social order. The next several chapters address the various issues that contributed to a person's social standing and how these issues affected Christians of the New Testament era. Chapter eight looks at social class and the complex way in which status was measured. Chapter nine examines the importance of citizenship, chapter ten presents the position of the Jews in the cities of the Empire, and chapter eleven shows the significance of slavery to ancient society and how its presence affected the first Christians.

An understanding of how peoples in the Roman Empire organized themselves privately also sheds light on the early Christian congregations. Chapter twelve surveys the family, the place of women, and education in the Roman world. It examines how New Testament comments about these topics relate to Roman ideas and practices.

Appendix B is a timeline of the events and persons described in this book. An index of Scripture passages is supplied to help the reader find comments related to a Bible passage he or she may be studying.

This work uses the phrases "New Testament era" and "first century A.D." (or simply "first century") to refer to the same period. Something also needs to be said about how I use the term *Greco-Roman*. Scholars generally use this term to refer to the interaction of Roman culture and society with Greek/Hellenistic culture and society, a process that began several centuries before the time of Christ. Sometimes this was a blending of ideas; other times it involved sharp opposition of ideas. But by the first century A.D., the Romans were in firm control of the eastern (as well as western) Mediterranean basin. So when we talk about the New Testament era in that area, we are talking about a society still influenced by Hellenistic ideas, customs, religion and language but dominated by Roman law, governmental forms, ideas of class and status, and the military. It was beginning to be influenced by Roman cultural values as well. So this book does not present a full-blown account of Hellenistic society and culture; rather it tries to present this society within the context of Roman control, hopefully in the way that Christians in the first century would have experienced it.

I would like to thank my editor at InterVarsity Press, Daniel G. Reid, for his invaluable help and support during the editing process. I am also in the debt of Craig S. Keener for his timely suggestions and enthusiasm about the manuscript. J. P. Moreland offered me the encouragement of a true friend and the insights of a gifted scholar. Finally, I want to thank my wife, Bonnie, for helping me think through this project at every point from its inception some five years ago.

*James S. Jeffers*

# *Chapter 1*

# Historical
# Background
# to the
# New Testament Era

IF YOU SUDDENLY FOUND YOURSELF IN FIRST-CENTURY JERUSALEM,[1] IN THE
home of a member of the Jewish ruling class, you might be surprised by
what you discover. You would soon learn that your host speaks Greek and
some Latin as well as Aramaic.[2] He dresses in Hellenistic clothing, pos-
sesses Roman citizenship and claims to worship the God of the Jews, but he
does not follow Jewish dietary regulations very closely. In fact, the dinner he
serves you seems more like a banquet in Athens or Rome than the meal of a
devout Jew. The dinner table groans with various delicacies, some of which do
not fit what you know of Jewish dietary regulations. The gleam of silver is
everywhere, fine wine flows freely, and slaves bustle around you, each with his
or her unique task.

His home is decorated with art from around the Mediterranean, and his
library contains the works of a number of pagan authors. When he talks politics,
he talks about the influence of the Jewish Sanhedrin, but also about the looming
threat of Roman power. He speaks in hushed tones of Jewish desires for
independence, as if afraid he might be overheard.

What has led to this situation, you ask your host. Why is his life such an
amazing patchwork quilt of cultural and political influences? His answer leads
you step by step into a world very different from ours, but in its own way

equally complex and bewildering to an outsider.

Your host begins by telling you what you already know from reading the Jewish Scriptures—that Judea was once a prosperous, independent kingdom under David and his successors. Following conquests by the Assyrians and Babylonians, the Jewish people began a long history of varying levels of subservience to greater powers, and they gradually adopted some of those powers' customs and ideas. They were allowed by their new overlords, the Persians, to rebuild the Jewish temple in Jerusalem, which the Babylonians had destroyed.

He tells you that Judea was still a client kingdom of the Persians when Alexander the Great and the Greeks arrived, conquering everything in sight. One of Alexander's successors set up the Seleucid kingdom in the Near East, and another successor, Ptolemy, took control of Egypt. Ptolemy and his successors also ruled Judea for many years. Throughout Palestine the Hellenistic rulers built Hellenistic cities such as the cities of the Decapolis. Anyone doing business with them had to learn their language, Greek, and could not help but be influenced by their culture. Hellenistic culture, he adds, has much to offer the educated Jew. When you raise your eyebrows, he assures you that one can dismiss the idolatrous elements of Hellenism and still appreciate its philosophies and much of its culture. He adds that Egypt lost Palestine to the Seleucids in 198 B.C., so one way or another the destinies of the Jews were not theirs to control for nearly two centuries.

Then, with an air of pride, he says that an astonishing thing followed: the Jews successfully revolted from the Seleucids and set up an independent kingdom for the first time in centuries. It was not easy, and the Jews certainly benefited from the weakening state of the Seleucids, but it was a genuine victory against a despised regime. For the next century, Judea would pursue its own course—not without difficulties or infighting, but its own course nonetheless.

Your host becomes more subdued as he tells you that Rome came on the scene a little over a century ago. It had been chipping away at the old Hellenistic kingdoms in the eastern Mediterranean for a number of years, but finally, in the person of General Pompey, it came to Judea. Seeing that the Romans were too strong to resist, Judea voluntarily allied itself with Rome, becoming a semi-independent client state of what was now an empire in all but name. This protected Judea from domination by the more powerful states around it—the Seleucid and Ptolemaic empires at first and later the Parthian Empire to the east. Judea has remained a part of the Roman Empire, either as a client state or as a Roman province. Your host glances around as though he does not trust his slaves and quickly adds that, while Judea is not entirely free, the union with

Figure 1.1.  View of the Mediterranean from the medieval crusader fortress (outer wall to the right) at Lindos on the island of Rhodes. The apostle Paul is said to have stopped here (Acts 21:1).

Rome has brought great benefits to the Jewish people and is certainly a gift from God.

You must know something about the Roman people to understand the world we live in, your host says. The Romans arose some eight centuries ago on the Italian peninsula in the western Mediterranean. They were heavily influenced by Greek culture early on; consequently, the civilization of the Romans, at least in the eastern Mediterranean, is as much Greek as it is Roman. Rome was first ruled by kings, but the wealthy and powerful among them threw off their king and established a republic influenced by Greek ideas. The citizens of Rome elected the various officials of the Republic, but you must understand that much of the true power lay with the senate, a semiofficial body made up of the most wealthy and powerful men of the state who largely inherited their positions from their fathers.

In fact, the politics of Rome, like its religion and other institutions, was driven in part by an ancient institution: the patron-client relationship. This model, which grew out of Rome's tribal origins, allowed aristocrats of the new republic to exercise power as patrons through their clients. A client, who was a Roman with less power and status than his patron, was expected to show honor to his patron, and to support him in any political action the patron took. The patron in turn owed his client legal protection and at times financial assistance. As Rome expanded, it would see the world through the lens of this relationship. Its generals would become the patrons first of their own soldiers, then of those people they conquered—even of entire nations in the case of great generals like Sulla, Pompey and Julius Caesar. This dynamic would weaken the power of the senate, as true power shifted from them to the generals. This power shift would help cause the transition from republic to empire.

Like a number of great civilizations of our past, Rome arose by gradually conquering the peoples around it. But unlike many other kingdoms, the Romans incorporated the conquered peoples into their society. They continue this practice today, he tells you, which helps explain why he is a Roman citizen. It was difficult at first for the Romans to accept the idea of sharing power with former enemies, but two things won them over. First, the Romans learned from dealing with their own people and the Italians they initially conquered that a small group of leaders can hold power only so long as the people let them do so. It took a series of uprisings in Italy to teach them this. Second, they learned that they could convince the upper classes of conquered peoples to buy into their system, partly out of greed and partly out of a sense of self-preservation. Your host adds, the Roman system offers great rewards to those locals who support it, as he himself has learned.

The Romans first took control of most of the Italian peninsula. After a series of bloody battles, many of which they lost, the Romans conquered their great rival in the West, Carthage in North Africa. This allowed them to dominate the western Mediterranean and freed them to pursue conquests in western Europe to their north. It also demonstrated an important lesson, your host says, which some of his countrymen tend to ignore to their grave peril: the Romans never give up. They can be bested in battle, even lose whole armies, but they are never beaten, for they refuse to admit defeat.

Then Rome turned its attention in a serious way to the east. They first defeated the kingdom of Macedonia and took control of Greece as well. Then they handed the Seleucids a series of defeats, which weakened them enough so that they could not prevent the establishment of an independent temple-state in Judea, under the rule of the high priest. By 143 B.C., Judea had voluntarily allied itself with Rome and thereby gained a number of important rights. To begin with, its religion was officially recognized by Rome. Later, when the odious cult of emperor worship was instituted, Jews were not required to participate, and Jews across Rome were allowed the unprecedented right to pay their annual tax to support the Jewish temple.

After dealing with a number of civil wars and revolts over the next century, it became clear that Rome had become an empire that could no longer be governed effectively by a large body of aristocrats. At the same time, these wars had made the generals of Rome even more powerful. Wars among them led to the emergence of a single leader, Julius Caesar, who seemed on the way to declaring himself king when he was killed by fellow senators. After more civil wars, his nephew, Octavian, used his uncle's influence to take power as emperor in all but name. When he died early in the first century, Romans could call the Mediterranean "our sea." Roman power in this part of the world was virtually unchallenged, and under the firm control of a single leader.

Your host turns to you with a half smile. So, he says, if you were in my place, what would you do? Would you try to fight against a power vastly superior to yours that you know has so far been unbeatable by anyone? Would you resist a people that, while at times insensitive to your beliefs and practices, for the most part allows you to pursue them in peace, a peace never known in this part of the world except perhaps at the height of King David's power? Would you refuse out of principle to adopt those elements of Roman culture that are not necessarily in conflict with Jewish beliefs and values? Only if you are a fool, he says with a laugh.

# Chapter 2

# Life & Death
# in the First Century

*I'll teach him a trade—a barber's or auctioneer's or indeed a lawyer's,*
*for that's what the devil alone can take away from him.*
PETRONIUS *SATYRICON 46: A POOR MAN THINKING OF HIS SON'S FUTURE*

*What race of men would you call more wretched than traders and shippers?*
*They sail about seeking markets ill-supplied, dealing with local agents*
*and petty retailers, borrowing at unholy rates and risking their heads.*
PHILOSTRATUS *LIFE OF APOLLONIUS OF TYANA 4.32*

*But we exhort you, brethren, to do so more and more,*
*to aspire to live quietly, to mind your own affairs, and to*
*work with your hands, as we charged you; so that you may command*
*the respect of outsiders, and be dependent on nobody.*
1 *THESSALONIANS 4:10-12*

THE ANCIENTS LOOKED AT LABOR AND OCCUPATIONS DIFFERENTLY than the way we do on a number of counts. For example, they gave the greatest honor to those wealthy persons whose income came from agriculture. They respected the work of the lawyer as honorable in itself and as a main route to higher public service.

Some jobs and professions that we esteem they regarded with contempt. They knew that a lot of money could be made in trade, but the elite believed it was a dirty business. Any job typically done by a slave was despised. Professions that we regard highly, such as doctor, artist, and scientist, were part of the private realm, not qualifying one for service to the state. Because doctors and artists often were skilled slaves or former slaves, the upper classes did not esteem their work as much as we do. Figure 2.1 shows a medical procedure being performed by what appears to be a slave.

Figure 2.1. A bas-relief sculpture showing a medical procedure (removal of a spear), Herculaneum, Italy.

## Food Production

In general, and much like the modern world, foodstuffs were produced in the country, and finished goods were manufactured in the city. Perhaps 90 percent of the Empire's workers were engaged in farming and herding. The New Testament, especially the Gospels, depicts this more fully than does most of the other literature of the day.

Small, private farms were tended by the owning family, with perhaps some help from a couple of wage laborers or slaves. These independent farmers generally worked about 100 days a year. Often a wealthy landowner leased out five- to ten-acre plots of his land to tenant farmers (Mt 21:33-41; Mk 12:1-9; Lk 20:9-16). These farms may seem very small to us, but vegetables and cereals could be grown profitably on such small farms. At busy seasons, peasants would help each other with chores or hire extra workers by the day. Wealthy landowners, of course, could afford to add day workers (Lk 15:17, 19). Such day laborers waited in a public place each morning to be hired and were paid at the end of the day (Mt 20:1-16). James considers it sinful to withhold their wages (Jas 5:4).

Major landowners, especially in Italy, often farmed their lands with gangs of slaves under the supervision of slave or freed stewards. The use of slave gangs may have been a more efficient way to cultivate olives and grapes or to tend large flocks of sheep, goats or pigs. By the time of Jesus, this approach had become much more common among Roman aristocrats than was the practice of leasing land to tenants. This was because slaves could not be drafted into the army and thus lost to farming. In addition, slaves could be worked twice as many days as tenant farmers normally worked. Once the slaves finished the work in one field, they were simply rotated to another crop in another place.

Farmers with small holdings typically brought their own surplus to market. On carts and wagons they transported their goods to the city gates or to the town's central market. Here they sold their olive oil, wine, grain, fruit and homemade wares.[1]

Herding meant caring for sheep, goats, pigs or cattle. Sometimes the owners *shepherd* cared for their own livestock, and sometimes they entrusted this work to their sons, slaves or hired hands (Jn 10:12-13). It was the custom in Palestine for shepherds to lead their flocks (Jn 10:4), but elsewhere it was more common to drive the flocks from behind. Shepherds protected the flock from predatory animals and thieves (Jn 10:1). At night they led the sheep to a place of shelter and protection, such as a field or a natural enclosure, where they counted them to see that none had strayed (Lk 15:3-7). In the New Testament, Christ declares himself the Good Shepherd who is known by his sheep and will one day be shepherd over all of God's redeemed (Jn 10:11-16; cf. Heb 13:20; 1 Pet 2:25; 5:4). The leaders of New Testament churches are compared to shepherds in that they should feed and protect their human flocks (Acts 20:28-31). The same commission is repeated by Peter (1 Pet 5:1-4), who suggests that elders are undershepherds of Christ as Chief Shepherd. This metaphor is used in the tradition of the Old Testament (1 Chron 11:2).

In general, Greeks and Romans looked down on shepherds, who were thought of as dirty and smelly since they spent most of their time out of doors with animals. Aristotle said that among men, the "laziest are shepherds, who lead an idle life, and get their subsistence without trouble from tame animals; their flocks having to wander from place to place in search of pasture, they are compelled to follow them, cultivating a sort of living farm" (*Politics* 1.8).

Many Romans believed that shepherds practiced highway robbery as well. The metaphor of Christ as the Good Shepherd, one of the central metaphors of

Christianity, would have made no sense to them apart from an understanding of Old Testament images of God and King David as loving, responsible shepherds. It would have seemed to Romans to confirm the disreputable nature of Christianity, what the Roman writer Suetonius called "a novel and mischievous superstition" (*Vita Neronis* 16).

*fishermen* The commercial fishing industry in Palestine used cast nets and dragnets. The cast net, or circular throwing net, was about fifteen feet in diameter, made of fine mesh and weighted with leaden sinkers (Mk 1:16). It was used in shallow water. The dragnet was a large net used with two boats. Once they came to the fishing area, the net was loaded half into one boat and half into the other. The boats then separated, letting out the net as they went. As they both sailed toward the shore, they pulled in the net on both sides and eventually dragged the net and its contents onto the shore (Mt 13:47-48). At times they just dragged the fish into the boats (Lk 5:6-9). Peter protested Jesus' instruction to fish at night (Lk 5:5), probably because he knew the fish at that time would be in deep water and his cast net would be useless. Fishermen had to keep their nets mended (Mk 1:19). They also had to salt down and sell their fish.

An independent fisherman could make a living, but the initial cost and maintenance of the nets, boats and other equipment was high. The Gospels imply that fishermen on the Sea of Galilee, like Simon and the sons of Zebedee, formed small cooperatives that also hired additional help (Lk 5:1-11; Mk 1:20). Some scholars believe that the Zebedee family, the family of the apostles James and John, who were able to employ hired servants (Mk 1:20), had a concession for selling fish in Jerusalem. This could explain how the high priest knew the unnamed apostle with Peter, if he was in fact John as many believe (Jn 18:15-16).

### Trade
Those with money to invest and the willingness to take great risks could make large fortunes in commerce. Because shipping involved many hazards, from shipwreck to piracy, if successful it paid off very well. Roman aristocrats considered trade to be a dirty business in which no self-respecting member of the upper class would be involved. The old-fashioned source of income for the elite was farming, but many aristocrats, enticed by the profits, did engage in trade or had slave or freed agents do so on their behalf. Jesus speaks in a parable of a master who went on a long journey and expected his servants to make a profit by trading (Mt 25:14-16). Below the aristocracy, people of all classes and statuses took part in trade. Those who enjoyed great success in trade were the main class of upwardly mobile persons in this period.

Trade did involve many risks, and the risks did not always pay off, as the

Philostratus quote at the beginning of this chapter shows. Many lost their investments when a ship sank or a merchant was robbed. A Roman epitaph from the era says, "Whoever hopes he may grow rich by trade will be fooled in his hopes" (*Corpus inscriptionum latinarum* 6.9659).

Those engaged in trade did not form companies as we think of them today. When they formed partnerships with others in an investment, each partner remained personally liable for his investment and the partnerships usually were temporary.

The sale and transport of grain was normally a matter of private enterprise, but the cities usually took on the responsibility of making sure that an adequate supply was available for the urban population. Food normally was not transported very far, but large cities at times had to import grain from overseas. Aside from these special importations of grain, only specialty wines, exotic dried fruits, spices and other small luxury items such as jewels were regularly shipped long distances. We read in Matthew of a pearl merchant (Mt 13:45).

**Banking and Debt**

People in the New Testament era sought various ways to protect their savings. Many deposited their money in temples, hoping that the god would protect their money (Juvenal *Satires* 14). This helped a number of major temples across the Empire become important banking concerns. Some people buried their treasure in fields, risking the danger of having it discovered by a stranger (Mt 13:44). People often put at least part of their money and precious objects in strongboxes or hidden places in the safest room of their home (Mt 6:19; 12:29; 13:52; 24:43; Mk 3:27; Lk 11:21-22; 12:39; Jas 5:1-6). Excavations of large houses in the Italian city of Pompeii have uncovered strongboxes containing small fortunes of one thousand to two thousand denarii. Bankers' records from Pompeii show deposits of up to ten times this amount. Probably many of the rich kept a small portion of their wealth at home, but deposited most of it at interest in the bank.

Wealthy Roman families all practiced some moneylending, at times using one or more slaves to operate a small, private bank. Usually, they lent money to the tenants on their properties, to their clients or to fellow members of the upper class. Those aristocrats whose clientele included entire cities or kingdoms sometimes made large loans to them.

The Empire also included professional bankers. Some operated small deposit and lending businesses. Among them were the "moneychangers" in the Court of the Gentiles of the Jerusalem temple (Mt 21:12; Mk 11:15). They provided a service to visiting Jews. They changed foreign money for the half shekels required of each Jew, living in Judea or not, as the temple tax on the Day of Atonement (Ex 30:11-15). This was necessary because Jewish coins were the only ones fit to be presented as an offering to God. Roman coins bearing the images of the deified emperors were considered idolatrous. Because of the absence of silver money with Hebrew inscriptions, however, the half shekel was paid in Tyrian silver coins. Jesus overthrew the tables of these moneychangers, not because they were changing money but because they were dishonest and charged exorbitant fees (Mt 21:13). These moneychangers also functioned as banks, receiving money at fixed rates of interest and lending it out to other borrowers (Mt 25:27; Lk 19:23).

Large-scale bankers included tax farmers *(publicani)* doing private business (see the discussion of the collection of taxes in chapter seven). Among their customers were government officials in the provinces who cashed government bills of exchange with them. Women were excluded from banking.[2]

Lenders often charged interest, as the Gospels indicate (Mt 25:27; Lk 19:23). A number of lenders, especially among the upper classes, did not charge interest. However, they could demand payment of their loans at any time.

Those who lent money, either formally or informally, were well protected from default. Under Greek, Roman and Near Eastern law, creditors could bind into permanent slavery or temporary debt bondage those debtors who did not pay up. The parable of the unmerciful servant illustrates this (Mt 18:23-25). When the servant cannot repay his loan, the king threatens permanent slavery. In turn, the servant threatens to place in temporary debt bondage another servant who owes him money. The law courts cooperated in enforcing this type of temporary debt bondage (Mt 5:25-26; Lk 12:58-59). Some Christians would later sell themselves into bondage in order to ransom fellow believers, or sell themselves into outright slavery in order to raise money for the churches in Rome.

### Crafts and Manufacturing

Manufacturing in the ancient world was for the most part in the hands of small business and individuals. Large factories were rare, and every small business had to compete with many similar businesses. Because of this, one rarely became rich in manufacturing.

The upper classes scorned those employed in crafts. Since many who did this work were slaves, the work itself was deemed slavish by both Greeks and Romans. The Roman orator Cicero once said that a workshop does not befit the honor of a free person (*On Duty* 1.42.150). In addition, the elite typically considered artisans uneducated and lacking in virtue. Paul appears to respond to this attitude when he says that his labor has enslaved and humiliated him (1 Cor 9:19; 2 Cor 11:7). Paul was sometimes in financial need, suggesting that either his trade was not always profitable or that he was not able to practice it consistently (2 Cor 11:9; Phil 4:12).

The streets of ancient cities were lined with the shops of weavers, potters, fullers, barbers, bakers, butchers, book sellers, grocers, cobblers, auctioneers, money lenders and many others. They worked from sunrise to sunset, with a couple of hours off at midday for a siesta. They were proud of their work and trained their children to follow in their footsteps. In fact, throughout the Empire we find inscriptions of families in business together.

Like today, such merchants were known by their occupations. The New Testament describes Jesus as "the carpenter's son" or the "carpenter" (Mt 13:55; Mk 6:3), Matthew as a tax collector (Mt 10:3), Simon as a tanner (Acts 9:43), Cornelius as a centurion (Acts 10:1) and Lydia as a seller of purple (Acts 16:14).[3]

Workshops were found in a room of the artisan's home, on the ground floor of an apartment building or in a separate building. Most workshops were located near the city's marketplace to facilitate the purchase of supplies and the

Figure 2.2. Exterior of the Flavian Amphitheater (Colosseum), Rome, Italy

sale of finished goods. A tentmaker's shop, like that of Paul or Aquila and Priscilla, would have been quieter and less dirty than that of, for example, a smith or a sculptor.[4] Shops of a certain trade tended to locate on the same street. Unlike much of the modern world, the small business atmosphere of that day seems to have been one more of amiable cooperation than of cutthroat competition.

**Types of Manufacturing**
Countless products were manufactured in the ancient world, but we must not imagine them being produced in modern factories on assembly lines. Most goods were made by artisans working alone, or with one or two slaves. The few factories that existed were tiny by modern standards. Potters made dishes and vases for everyday use, fullers and weavers produced cloth, workers in leather sewed shoes and awnings, blacksmiths made farm implements and artisans' tools, carpenters made furniture and wagons, and sculptors made statues and decorative reliefs. They usually used raw materials available nearby and sold their finished wares in their own workshops.

Weaving was the most widespread and economically the most important industry of the ancient world. A number of the early Christians were involved in this clothing manufacture. The Roman Empire traded with Parthia, India and China to obtain silk, fine linen and other special cloth.

In Roman cities, bakeries ground the grain and provided finished bread. In the rural economy of the Gospels, however, breadmaking seems to have been confined to the individual household (Mt 13:33; 24:41).

Studies of the pottery industry of Arretium in central Italy during the New Testament period show us how such industries were organized. The high-quality pottery from this region was produced in nearly a hundred small factories. Small numbers of skilled slave artisans, under ten at most locations and around sixty at the largest three, produced the bowls with the assistance of others who dug and cleaned the clay and tended the kilns. As the market for these products grew, the Romans built new small factories rather than expand existing ones.

The engraver carved or chiseled stone, gems, ivory, bone and metals to produce jewelry, seals, scarabs and various images (Acts 17:29). Silversmiths refined their metal and made silver vessels and jewelry. They also repaired silverware by heating the object until it became sufficiently softened for reworking. Then they soldered on any missing parts, such as legs or handles. Next they filled in holes and cracks with silver solder and hammered out any deformities or dents. Like most other artisans, they usually performed their work while squatting on the ground. Demetrius, who made silver shrines of the goddess Artemis at Ephesus (Acts 19:24), apparently belonged to a guild of silversmiths or artisans in that city. Paul mentions a coppersmith by the name of Alexander, who had done him great harm (2 Tim 4:14).

A fuller was a man or woman who cleaned cloth (Mk 9:3), the ancient equivalent of a dry cleaner. Newly woven material ("unshrunk cloth"; Mt 9:16; Mk 2:21) had to be cleansed of natural oils or gums before dyeing. The cloth was steeped in water mixed with a cleansing substance, stamped and felted, bleached with fumes of sulphur, and then pressed in the fuller's press. Because this work caused foul odors, it typically was done outside of the city.

Since most persons in the ancient world lived at or just above a subsistence level, very few people could afford luxury items. The main market for such goods was the upper classes in the cities. However, itinerant merchants also brought luxury items to the various annual fairs held in celebration of the local patron deities in the smaller towns of the Empire. In this way fine silks from the Orient, or the linens for which Tarsus was famous in the second century A.D., were brought to less wealthy customers.

Fine dyes, often transported over long distances, could provide a lucrative income. Acts mentions Lydia, a merchant of such dyes (Acts 16:14, 40). She came from Thyatira in Asia Minor and was a prosperous resident of Philippi. The purple dye that Lydia handled was a pigment removed from the glands of mollusks. After treatment, it became light or dark purple. The Phoenicians kept the process secret for centuries.

### Tentmaking and the Apostle Paul

Both men and women engaged in tentmaking, as the New Testament example of Aquila and Priscilla indicates (Acts 18:2-3). About his trade, Paul himself tells us only that he works with his hands (1 Cor 4:12). Acts tells us that Paul is a tentmaker (Acts 18:3). The meaning of the word translated "tentmaker" *(skenopoios)* is obscure, leading translators and scholars over the centuries to interpret it differently.

Since Paul came from Tarsus in Cilicia, he may have been trained to make tents from the wool or hair of Cilician goats. Tentmakers who worked with cloth first had to weave the tent cloth on their looms. In Palestine, camel hair and goat hair were used; these yielded a dark brown, almost black material. Then the long, narrow, loomed strips were sewn together. Cords attached to the cloth were tied to stakes when the tent was pitched.

Paul may have been a leatherworker who specialized in tentmaking, since most tents in this era were made of leather. This does not mean that he engaged in tanning leather. Rather, he would purchase leather from tanners or traders.

Tanning was a complicated and smelly business. The hides of animals were tanned using tannic acid, which was extracted from lime, from the juice of certain plants, or from the bark of trees. Tanners often worked by the seashore to facilitate the disposal of chemicals and because they used salt water in the tanning process. Because of the very unpleasant odors the work generated, its practice was not allowed within cities.

Tanning was not held in favor among the Jews because the work with dead animals was ceremonially defiling. However, Simon the tanner was accepted among Christians (Acts 9:43; 10:6, 32). Peter stayed in Simon's home in Joppa. Clearly Peter was becoming more liberal-minded about ceremonial rules.

Based on evidence from apprentice contracts of the era, Paul would have begun his apprenticeship around age thirteen and would have spent most days in the workshop. After two or three years of demanding training, he would have been as skilled as his trainer. He would have learned the various tools and techniques for cutting leather. Paul may have been given a set of tools at the end of his apprenticeship. Since the tools were fairly small and few, his was a readily portable trade.[5] A tentmaker's shop would have required a stool, a table, a sharpening stone for the tools, oil and blacking for treating the leather, and places to store leather material and finished goods. These things could be borrowed when the tentmaker came to a new town.

Paul says that in Thessalonica he worked "night and day" (1 Thess 2:9). That is, Paul began his work before sunrise and continued it during much of the day. Apprentice contracts usually specified sunrise to sundown as the expected workday. He would likely have followed the Mediterranean custom of taking off several hours in the middle of the day for rest and a meal. He may have used this time to minister, as well. We know that Paul taught during the middle of the day at Ephesus, but we do not know if this was true elsewhere. He also described his work as "labor" and as "toil and hardship" (1 Cor 4:12; 2 Cor 11:27). The work of an artisan like Paul never paid well and could only lead to a measure of success if the artisan's reputation exceeded that of his fellows. For an artisan like Paul, always on the move and thus never able to build a reputation, the self-sufficiency Paul describes could have come only from long days of very hard work (Phil 4:12).

A number of passages depict Paul plying his occupation during his three missionary journeys ([1] 1 Thess 2:9; 1 Cor 4:12; 9:6; [2] Acts 18:3; [3] Acts 19:11-12; 20:34; 2 Cor 12:14). We have no direct testimony that he made tents during his earlier missionary efforts in Damascus, Syria and Cilicia. It seems likely that Paul used his workshop when possible to carry out missionary activity. The relatively quiet nature of leatherwork would have made possible discussions with fellow workers and customers. For example, the Bereans who examined the Scriptures daily in order to verify Paul's claims may have met in his workshop (Acts 17:11).[6]

## LEISURE AND GAMES

Baths, wine and love-making destroy our bodies, yet love-making, wine and baths make life worth living.
COMMON ROMAN GRAFFITO

Now the spring races are on: the praetor's dropped his napkin
And sits there in state (but those horses just about cost him
The shirt off his back) one way and another; and if
I may say so without offense to that countless mob, all Rome
Is in the Circus today.
JUVENAL *SATURNALIA* 11

Do you not know that in a race all the runners compete, but only one receives the prize? So run that you may obtain it. Every athlete exercises self-control in all things. They do it to receive a perishable wreath, but we an imperishable. Well, I do not run aimlessly, I do not box as one beating the air; but I pommel my body and subdue it, lest after preaching to others I myself should be disqualified.
1 CORINTHIANS 9:24-27

The Greeks and Romans were like modern Westerners in that they took their leisure time seriously. Those of independent wealth might exercise daily in the gymnasia of Greek cities. The gymnasium was considered by many Greeks to be just as important a part of civilized urban life as the temple. Usually built and maintained at public expense, the gymnasium was essentially a courtyard surrounded by a colonnade. Most athletic events occurred in the open-air courtyard. Rooms under the colonnade were used to instruct children in all areas of education and for bathing.

The public bath was a basic requirement of any self-respecting Roman city. In fact, the city of Rome alone had over two hundred public baths by the time of Paul. Life in an ancient Mediterranean city was often hot and dusty. After working in the morning, a Roman might exercise and meet business associates and friends in the baths for several hours in the afternoon. This public socializing was part of what it meant to be civilized to the Romans. Among the first structures Romans added to an Eastern city they occupied was the public bath. Observant Jews would have found the baths offensive.

**Figure 2.3.** Interior of the Flavian Amphitheater (Colosseum), Rome, Italy. The horizontal line at the middle of the photo shows where the arena's wooden flooring once rested. Below the flooring were many storage rooms and holding areas for animals, human victims and combatants.

Gentiles considered it foolish and wasteful of Jews to devote every seventh day to forced leisure, but they took time off from work periodically, usually during religious festivals. In fact, the holidays observed by the Romans exceed the number of our holidays and weekends combined. The weekend as we know it began to come into existence only in the fourth century, when Constantine the Great made Sunday a holiday.

Urban dwellers would lean out an exterior or courtyard window to gossip with neighbors, or chat with customers or the shopkeeper next door. They would recline for a proper business lunch with colleagues at a restaurant, or sit on a tavern stool to drink wine and chat with friends. Or they might just sit in the public square and watch the passing crowd. Dinner came several hours before sunset and was an occasion to visit and entertain. Ancient literature tells us about a number of dinner parties that went on long into the night, but most people tended to go home early since the streets in most towns were not safe. Those out at night risked being mugged by robbers or beaten up by a police patrol.

Special occasions offered relief from the normal routine. Dignitaries might celebrate the assumption of a new office or the dedication of a new public building by inviting their fellow citizens to a banquet. Aristocratic families might observe the coming-of-age of their sons, or the marriage of a child, by inviting the whole family to a party or by sending gifts of money to all the residents of their town. The practice got out of hand at times. In fact, a second-century governor asked the emperor Trajan if he should end the practice (Pliny the Younger *Letters* 10.116). This kind of special feast probably was more popular with the unemployed poor, who had nothing better to do, than with prosperous farmers and merchants (Mt 22:2-14; Lk 14:16-24).

Religious festivals also varied the pattern of daily life. On the day of a deity's annual festival, the people decorated and opened the temple, made sacrifices and held parades. The event resembled a modern country fair.

## The Games of Greece and Rome

The New Testament, especially the Pauline letters, make a number of allusions to athletics and games. These allusions refer to both Greek and Roman styles. The games of Greek cities were very popular. Some were held purely for locals, but others, which offered large prizes or were connected to an important religious observance, brought prestige to the city and attracted competitors from far away. In fact, some amateur competitors from the upper classes traveled from town to town to compete in the various games. Often the prize was very simple: a crown of greenery, usually olive or laurel leaves, as Paul notes (1 Cor 9:25). But the victor would return home to a hero's welcome.

The chief sacred games of the Greeks, the Olympics, were held in the Greek town of Olympia every four years in honor of the god Zeus. The competitions included athletic, equestrian and musical contests. The second most prestigious games, the Isthmian games at Corinth, were held in a grove sacred to the god

Poseidon in the second and fourth years of each Olympiad. The Greeks favored games of athletic skill, such as foot races, wrestling, throwing the discus and the javelin, and boxing. Greek athletes traditionally competed in the nude. Romans frowned on this practice and refused to adopt it.

Paul's references to running and boxing in 1 Corinthians 9:25-27, and the fact that he addresses the believers in Corinth, indicate that he has in mind the Greek Isthmian games held only a few miles from his readers. He says that self-discipline and playing by the rules are necessary to winning. Hebrews 12:1 alludes to spectators watching a Greek foot race, in which Jesus Christ is the lead runner. The New Testament talks in a number of passages about life and ministry as a course to be run (Acts 13:25; 20:24; Phil 3:14; 2 Tim 2:5; 4:7). It also speaks of running in vain (Gal 2:2) and running well (Gal 5:7).

The major Roman games were also the oldest: the Ludi Romani, celebrated in honor of Jupiter. In addition, the Romans held the Ludi Plebes, which included drama; the Ludi Cereales, in honor of the goddess Ceres; the Ludi Apollinares, in honor of Apollo; the Ludi Megalenses, in honor of the Great Mother; and the Ludi Florales. The games were intimately connected with Roman religion, and priests frequently directed the games. Admission to the public games was free to Roman citizens. Slaves and free noncitizens were not allowed to attend.

The Roman games usually were held in an amphitheater or stadium. Some were wooden and temporary, while others have survived for two thousand years nearly intact. The largest stadium, the first-century B.C. Circus Maximus in Rome, allowed 150,000 to 180,000 spectators to view horse and chariot races. Chariots usually were pulled by four horses, but at times by even more. The chariot course was seven laps (almost 5.25 miles). The average racing day consisted of twenty-four fifteen-minute races. Four companies, identified by the colors white, red, green and blue, competed. Spectators identified fanatically with one or another of these companies, betting on and fighting over their favorites.[7]

The circular arena, or amphitheater, was designed for the combats of gladiators and wild beasts and was first used in Italy. By the time of Jesus and Paul, every large town had an amphitheater. The twenty-thousand-seat amphitheater in Pompeii probably could have seated the entire city, a testament to the popularity of the games. We know of more than seventy such theaters across the Empire, including famous ones at Corinth, Pergamum, Antioch and Alexandria. One of the most famous was the Flavian Amphitheater, known commonly as the Colosseum (see figures 2.2 and 2.3). It was 158 feet high and seated around fifty thousand people. In this arena large groups engaged in mock battle and humans fought wild animals. At times the arena was flooded to allow re-creations of famous naval battles. Contrary to the views of some modern authors, we have no evidence that Christians were persecuted in the Colosseum. It was not opened to the public until A.D. 80, long after the persecutions under Nero in A.D. 64.

Gladiatorial shows, probably the oldest form of Roman games, were held at irregular intervals. Although less popular than chariot races, they attracted huge crowds. Even the Greek cities of the East built or remodeled facilities for them. Skilled gladiators were almost always professional fighters, not amateurs, and some were quite popular. Most were slaves, often captured enemy soldiers. They specialized in one of several forms of fighting, and the crowd followed with avid interest their skills as they hunted wild beasts imported from exotic locales or fought in equally matched pairs. The blood, the odors and the threat of death gave the games a unique excitement for Romans.[8]

One or more executions of people convicted of capital crimes might be included in the gladiatorial program. Typically this consisted of an armed gladiator or soldier quickly killing an unarmed criminal. Since Romans did not find this very entertaining, such executions were scheduled at midday, when most left the arena to eat and take a nap. At times more imaginative executions were staged. For example, convicted persons might be thrown unarmed into the arena to be devoured by hungry, wild beasts. They might be dressed in animal hides or left naked. At times they were dressed as mythological characters and forced to enact in reality a brutal death from literature. During his A.D. 64 persecution, the emperor Nero executed Christians convicted of participating in a conspiracy to burn Rome by dressing them in animal hides and having them torn apart by wild dogs. Some of these displays occurred in the Circus Maximus. About this, the Roman historian Tacitus says:

> Despite their guilt as Christians, and the ruthless punishment it deserved, the victims were pitied. For it was felt that they were being sacrificed to one man's brutality than to the national interest. (*Annals* 15.44)

Theatrical performances also were popular but could not compete in popularity with the races and gladiators. The two main types of performances were comedies with stereotyped characters and the *mimus,* a clown burlesque made up of songs and crude jokes laced with sexual comments. Open sexual expression was a widespread theme in plays, dances and art, and in the private lives of Rome's leaders.

Games might be hosted by a city or an individual. Games dedicated to the gods usually were funded from the public treasury. As the games grew in duration and grandeur, major cities around the Empire found their locally hosted games to be a significant financial drain. Individuals or organizations also hosted private games to commemorate births, marriages and funerals. Private games might be held as fundraisers that required payment for admission. At times, privately sponsored games would be opened to the public as a way to gain good will.

Roman leaders, especially in the city of Rome, used the games to neutralize the emotions of the populace. As the mime Pylades reportedly said to Augustus about the games, "It is to your advantage, Caesar, that we keep the public occupied." During the Empire, since the emperors did not allow public political meetings, the games were the only mass assemblies of the Roman population. Sixty-five days of games per year were held in the city of Rome by the end of the Republic, and 135 by the end of the second century A.D. The city of Rome hosted far more games than the other cities of the Empire because of the wealth of its leaders and the desire to pacify a large and potentially unruly population.

Because they used the games to win the favor of the people, Roman leaders could be forced occasionally to give in to the people and release the hero of the moment. The classic story of this, although probably mythical, is that of Androcles and the lion. A runaway slave, Androcles, was captured and condemned to death by wild beasts. But the lion sent to kill him recognized him as the man who had once removed a thorn from his paw, and thus the lion refused to kill him. Once the spectators learned the circumstances, they demanded the release of both Androcles and the lion, and the emperor Claudius agreed.

While Paul seems to have Greek games in mind in his 1 Corinthians 9 passage, as noted above, he has Roman-style games in mind when he refers to fighting wild beasts in Ephesus in 1 Corinthians 15:32. The references to athletics in 2 Timothy could be to either Greek or Roman games (2 Tim 2:5; 4:7-8).

## TRAVEL

Three times I have been shipwrecked; a night and a day I have been adrift at sea; on frequent journeys, in danger from rivers, danger from robbers, danger from my own people, danger from Gentiles, danger in the city, danger in the wilderness, danger at sea, danger from false brethren; in toil and hardship, through many a sleepless night, in hunger and thirst, often without food, in cold and exposure.
2 CORINTHIANS 11:25-27

Residents of the Roman Empire during the New Testament era frequently traveled the Mediterranean region, by both land and sea. In fact, the area had never known such extensive travel and would not again until the nineteenth century. Ronald Hock has calculated that Paul traveled nearly ten thousand miles during his reported career, sharing the roads with "government officials, traders, pilgrims, the sick, letter-carriers, sightseers, runaway slaves, fugitives, prisoners, athletes, artisans, teachers, and students"[9] (see maps 4 and 5).

Two circumstances made such travel possible. The first was the travel *loods* infrastructure built by the Romans. That infrastructure included a strategic network of roads connecting the entire empire and myriads of ships plying the waters of the Mediterranean, as described below.

The second was the peace brought about and maintained by the Roman Empire, the *Pax Romana*. The *Pax Romana* resulted from Rome's firm control of the various peoples of the Mediterranean. It meant that one could travel without stumbling into the middle of a regional war. Rome had by the first century B.C. greatly reduced the threat of piracy. It also maintained some control over bandits on land. One could usually avoid bandits by keeping to the main roads.

But we must not imagine modern travel, with its air-conditioned ocean liners and comfortable automobiles, in the ancient world. By our standards, travel was arduous, miserable and long. It also was not without dangers. Brigandage and piracy, shipwreck, and the many minor hardships of travel on the road still existed. On back roads in troubled provinces, a traveler might well be accosted by thieves, as the parable of the good Samaritan illustrates (Lk 10:29-37). Paul, who frequently left the main roads to pursue his mission, knew this all too well. He says that he had to deal with floods, robbers, shipwreck, sleeplessness, hunger, thirst and cold (2 Cor 11:25-27).

The impact of Greco-Roman culture, at least on the cities of the Empire, meant that an experienced traveler would have little trouble negotiating the streets of a new city. Although not as safe as credit cards or travelers checks today, the Empire's coinage would be accepted anywhere. And language did not present a problem. Travelers who knew both Greek and Latin, and even those who knew only Greek, could expect to be understood in any city of the Empire.

**By Land**

Rome built and maintained hundreds of miles of roads for the sake of its military. These roads connected all the provinces and cities of the Empire, enabling Rome to respond quickly to uprisings from within or invasions from without. The roads were paved to withstand the wear of hobnail boots and loaded wagons. Engineers designed them to allow the transport of heavy wagons over mountain passes by means of switchbacks, and over rivers by wagons over mountain passes by means of switchbacks, and over rivers by means of fords, ferries or bridges. Though built for the army, these roads were open to all people and so provided a great benefit to travelers.

Most who traveled by land had to walk, but those who could afford it might ride a donkey, horse, or camel. The well-to-do traveler, like the Ethiopian eunuch (Acts 8:26-31), used chariots or carriages pulled by mules or horses. Persons traveling long distances, such as the apostles, would carry a sack with food, a change of clothes and perhaps the tools of their trade. They would buy food in towns or from farmers along the way. When the apostle Paul stayed in a town for under a week, he probably spent more time in travel than in ministry.

The traveler between cities looked for the inns and way stations constructed for the imperial messengers. He could find such stations about ten miles apart along the major communication roads of the Empire. Here couriers could change horses and ordinary travelers could find food and rest. But those on government service had first claim to such facilities, as well as to the ships of the Roman navy. This included messengers bearing official dispatches, ambassadors from cities or client kingdoms delivering petitions, provincial governors going out to their provinces or moving about in them, or soldiers marching from one post to another. If a way station was full or nowhere in sight, the traveler could find many towns along the road offering places to eat and lodging to suit a range of budgets.

Those who could do so, from all social classes, stayed with friends or relatives when they traveled. This usually meant that the rich stayed with rich friends and the poor with poor friends, who might find it very straining to entertain guests, but in that culture one was expected to show hospitality to visitors, regardless of circumstances. Paul often stayed in private homes (Acts 16:12-15; 17:5; 21:16; 28:7, 14; cf. Philem 22).[10]

Who traveled the Empire besides government workers and apostles? Another important group was merchants: shippers, entrepreneurs and their agents, who traveled about making contracts and supervising the shipment of goods. Itinerant merchants also frequently shuttled back and forth, buying goods in one spot and selling them in cities and towns across the seas.

Slaves might be entrusted with a message to deliver or assigned by their masters to supervise some business enterprise abroad. It would not have been uncommon to see a strange slave traveling, by himself or with a few others, on his master's business. Thus, a runaway slave like Onesimus (Philem 10-18) probably would not attract attention. Other travelers included touring companies of actors, athletes and pilgrims headed to a religious festival or shrine, and wandering philosophers,

One of the most important east-west highways was the "common route." It crossed Asia Minor from Ephesus past Tralles, up the Maeander valley to Laodicea, to Apameia, Pisidian Antioch, Philomelium, across Lycaonia to Iconium, down by Laranda and the Cilician Gates to Tarsus, then either to Syrian Antioch or across to Zeugma on the Euphrates River. Most of these names will be familiar to those who have studied the apostle Paul's missionary journeys, suggesting that Paul sought to plant churches where they could have the greatest influence.

Farther west, the major communication between Rome and the East was the Via Egnatia or Egnatian Way. It began at the Adriatic coast of Greece in two branches, one from Dyrrhachium (in modern Albania), the other from Apollonia to the south. Then it ran up the valley of the Genusos, crossing the river to Candavia, skirting the northern side of Lake Lychnitis to Lychnidos, across the mountains to Heraclea, Edessa, down the valley of the Ludias, across the Axius to Thessalonica, and on to Philippi's port, Neapolis. Two of the most important settings for Pauline churches, Thessalonica and Philippi, were key points on the Egnatian Way.[11]

## By Sea

The extensive shipping on the Mediterranean meant that ships that could carry passengers were more readily available than ever before. Travel by sea was faster and cheaper than travel by land. A ship could travel about a hundred miles a day, while the imperial messenger service, using fresh horses at regular intervals, could manage only twenty-five to thirty miles a day. Ordinary travelers by land, like Paul and his associates, probably covered at best fifteen to twenty miles a day (see in figure 3.3 a photograph of the port city of Herculaneum).[12]

Sea travel in the first century was safer than it had ever been, and even fairly safe by our standards, if one had an experienced crew and a seaworthy vessel and avoided the winter months. The Roman presence kept the threat of piracy low. The greatest risk by this time was shipwreck caused by storms or shallow waters.

The safest weather in which to travel occurred between May and October. Even then rough weather could swamp the ships of the first century. Ships normally were taken out of service between mid-November and mid-February to avoid the winter storms (Acts 20:3, 6; 28:11; 1 Cor 16:6; 2 Tim 4:21; Tit 3:12). A month before and after this period were considered somewhat dangerous times to travel because storm clouds were apt to hide the sun and stars and thus obscure navigation (Acts 27:9-13).

Well-known seaports in the first century included Seleucia near Antioch, Ephesus, Cenchrea (the port of Corinth; cf. Acts 18:18), Alexandria, Puteoli, Ostia (the port of Rome), and Caesarea Maritima (a harbor built by Herod the Great). Paul came to the port of Caesarea at the end of his second missionary journey (Acts 18:22) and sailed from it on his journey to Rome (Acts 23:33; 27:2). Myra, on the southern coast of Asia Minor, was a major port of the Alexandrian grain fleet. Paul and his guards boarded the grain ship here (Acts 27:5).

In Paul's day the best seafaring service was between Alexandria and Rome, the route of the great ships transporting grain from Egypt. With favorable winds, the trip from Rome to Alexandria took as little as ten days, but the return trip could take up to two months. Unfavorable head winds frequently caused ships to travel from Alexandria to Rome by first heading northeast to Syria and Asia Minor. Paul's trip to Rome followed this route (Acts 28:11).

Ships carrying official Roman government cargo during the first century A.D. commonly weighed between three hundred and four hundred tons, while private vessels were usually much smaller. The ships of Rome's grain fleet were the largest of all, weighing up to twelve hundred tons and measuring up to two hundred feet long. They did nothing but travel back and forth between Egypt and Italy, bringing hundreds of tons of grain to the masses in the city of Rome. Grain ships had a great square mainsail, a raked foremast and a small square sail (Acts 27:40). Such merchant vessels had anchors, a sounding bell, rudders and sails (Acts 27:28, 29, 40). The grain ship that transported Paul on his trip to Rome had as its figurehead the images of the gods Castor and Pollux, the "Twin Brothers" of Roman mythology (Acts 28:11). The "boat" mentioned in Acts was the ship's lifeboat (27:16, 30, 32).

While primarily cargo ships, these large grain ships often carried passengers. Josephus says he once sailed to Rome on a ship carrying 600 passengers (*Life* 3). Many if not most of the 276 persons on board Paul's ship to Rome would have made up the crew. Passengers normally provided their own mattresses, blankets, clothes, materials for washing, food and cookware.

## DINING

Four things are required for a good dinner: pleasant guests, well-chosen time and place, and good preparation. Guests should be neither too talkative nor too dumb. . . . Moreover, the host must aim not so much at extravagance in his dinner as at an absence of meanness.

AULUS GELLIUS, *NOCTES ATTICAE* 13, 11, 3-4

Food will not commend us to God. We are no worse off if we do not eat, and no better off if we do. Only take care lest this liberty of yours somehow become a stumbling block to the weak. For if any one sees you, a man of knowledge, at table in an idol's temple, might he not be encouraged, if his conscience is weak, to eat food offered to idols?
1 CORINTHIANS 8:8-10

Prosperous Romans had three main meals. Breakfast was a simple affair, usually featuring bread and cheese. Lunch was not much more elaborate, often bread, cold meat, fruit and wine. Dinner was the main meal of the day, served in the afternoon or evening. For those who could afford it, it consisted of three courses. The first course might include egg dishes, vegetables, salad, salt fish, shellfish, other hors d'oeuvres and wine mixed with honey. The second or main course included wine with boiled or roast meat or poultry. The third course featured fruit, sweets and more wine.

Romans ate while reclining on couches, usually situated in a U shape (called a *triclinium*) around a low table. The triclinium had places for nine to twelve

**Figure 2.4.** A *popina* or stand-up food counter in Herculaneum, Italy, c. first century A.D. The openings in the counters are the tops of clay pots, which held the food being served.

guests, including a place of honor (Lk 14:8-10). Diners supported themselves on their left elbows and ate with their right hands. The ancients did not have forks, only knives and spoons. In any event, seated in this position it was more convenient to eat with one's fingers. The New Testament often refers to guests reclining at table (Lk 7:36; 11:37; 17:7; Jn 13:12). This posture explains how Mary could anoint Jesus' feet (Jn 12:3) and how the disciple could lean on Jesus' breast at the Last Supper (Jn 13:23, 25).

The banquet was very important to prosperous Romans. Banquets marked virtually every special occasion. They provided Romans a way to show off their wealth and to reward their clients and friends for their service. Romans had a great appreciation for good food that was served well.

The lower classes tried to imitate this interest of the rich in several ways. Those who had gained wealth in their lifetimes hosted their own great parties. The famous *Banquet of Trimalchio* is the writer Petronius's satirical re-creation of such a party. The banquet's coarseness and overwrought extravagance (it includes sixty-two separate dishes) is intended to show how the newly rich can imitate the opulence of the elite, but not their sophistication. The poor at times pooled their resources to stage a banquet. As noted in chapter twelve, burial associations used part of the dues contributed by their poor members to host banquets when a member died.

In general, however, lower-class Romans could not afford such sumptuous fare. In fact, many who lived in the apartment houses of the cities did not have indoor cooking facilities. They might cook on an outdoor charcoal brazier or purchase hot food from one of the many *popinae*, something like modern fast-food restaurants (see figure 2.4).[13]

At banquets in Palestine, guests were received with a kiss as a matter of courtesy (Lk 7:45). When it was time for the banquet to begin, the host would close the door, and no more guests would be allowed to enter (Lk 13:25). This is the basis for the parable of the five foolish virgins who are excluded from the marriage feast (Mt 25:10). Guests had their feet washed (Lk 7:36, 44) and at weddings were given garments to wear for the occasion (Mt 22:11-12). Typical entertainment included music and dancing (Mk 6:22; Lk 15:25).

## Food

The ancients enjoyed many of the same foods that we do, but they seasoned and cooked them very differently. For example, the Romans loved to mix sweet and sour tastes in the same dish. They enjoyed fresh fish, but they might cook it in plum or apricot sauce. They loved mushrooms, which they cooked in honey. They might cook poultry in a sauce of oil, vinegar, honey, wine, mint, pepper and other seasonings. Sugar was unknown to the Mediterranean peoples; they used honey and fruit as sweeteners. The seasoning they used the most, *garum,* would be the hardest for us to stomach. It was made from fish and fish entrails left to ferment in the sun; then it was strained to create a very potent liquid that they might add to virtually any dish.

Among the staples of every household, by the New Testament era, was a variety of breads. Vegetables included broad beans, lentils, chickpeas, lettuce, cabbage, mushrooms, and leeks. Artichokes and asparagus were rare and enjoyed only by the rich. The most common fruits were apples, pears, cherries, plums, apricots, grapes and dates. Citrus fruits were not introduced from the East until the fourth century A.D. Olives were an important part of the Roman diet. They were eaten and their oil was used for cooking. In addition, people used olive oil for personal hygiene, applying oil before exercising and in the baths. Some oil was used as a perfume. Olive oil also fueled lamps. When olive oil was unavailable, people cooked in butter or lard. Poorer Egyptians used vegetable oil for cooking and personal hygiene.[14]

Meats favored by Romans included some we still eat: beef, pork, venison and wild birds. They also enjoyed meat that we no longer eat, such as wild ass, flamingo, stork, crane and peacock. Their favorite meat, however, was fish. The lower classes could only afford small fish preserved in brine. Wealthy Romans favored rare fish such as turbot, mullet and sturgeon.[15]

Wine was the staple drink of the Mediterranean peoples. Although Romans and Greeks did not drink beer, it was a favorite drink in northern Europe, Egypt and Ethiopia.

Jews were not the only people who abstained from eating pork. For example, Cappadocians and others in Asia Minor, many in Syria, Arabs and Indians all refused to eat pork. Egyptians, with few exceptions, would not eat lamb. Vegetarianism was practiced by followers of Pythagoras, who taught that souls transmigrate at death from humans to animals, and vice versa. Others refrained from meat for a variety of reasons.[16]

The New Testament does not enumerate the dietary restrictions of the Jewish Scriptures. According to Acts, the apostles in Jerusalem instructed Gentile Christians not to eat meat sacrificed to idols or the meat of animals who had been strangled and not to drink the blood of animals (Acts 15:29; 21:25). But Paul does not repeat these prohibitions in his letters. Paul takes up the issue of meat sacrificed to idols in 1 Corinthians. Priests of the temples of the Empire were allowed to sell to the public meat that had been sacrificed to their deity. People could buy that meat at a discount. Paul tells the Corinthian Christians that it is not sinful to eat such meat. He reasons that, since the meat has been

offered to a god that does not exist, eating the meat does not involve identification with another god (1 Cor 8:4-13; 10:25-33). On the other hand, the
Christian must consider the negative influence eating this meat might have on
those who do not feel free to eat it; at times it would be best for the Christian to
voluntarily refrain.

### Attire and Fashions

*Roman clothing and hair styles.* Rank was asserted in the clothing that people
wore. From Augustus on, only senators and their sons were allowed to wear a
white toga with a broad purple stripe. The signs of the equestrians, the second
level of the Roman elite, were a gold ring and a toga with a narrow purple stripe.
The emperor Tiberius attempted to prevent members of the lower ranks from
wearing gold rings in imitation of the equestrians.

The toga, the characteristic garment of male Roman citizens, was a massive
semicircular piece of white woolen cloth. A complicated folding and draping
process virtually immobilized one arm, so it was more ceremonial than daily
wear, especially by the first century A.D. A tunic, a knee-length, short-sleeved,
shirtlike garment, was worn under the toga. Freed male citizens wore a special
toga to mark their status (the toga *praetexta*).

It is likely that, by the New Testament era, the average male Roman citizen
outside of Italy did not wear the toga. This seems true for Paul since no one is
able to identify him by sight as a Roman citizen (e.g., Acts 16:35-39). The toga
was the dress of male citizens; women never wore it. A woman's tunic was
similar in design to a man's, but longer, reaching to the ankles. The traveling
cloak of Paul referred to in 2 Timothy 4:13 may have been a Roman garment,
the *paenula,* a circular cape used for protection against stormy weather.[17]

The Romans normally did not cover their heads. However, to indicate piety,
especially during prayer and sacrifice, they would lift their togas over the backs
of their heads. Paul may want Christians to avoid any imitation of this pagan
practice when he says that a man's head must remain uncovered in worship
(1 Cor 11:3).

Peasants and soldiers wore leather shoes with nailed soles and uppers slit
into strips. The enclosed Roman boot had uppers of soft leather and a gaiterlike
leg over the anklebone.

The traditional dress of Roman women was a tunic reaching to the ankles,
covered by the *stola,* a gown belted at the waist. Roman women also wore
leather sandals or shoes, veils, bonnets, and jewelry such as earrings (worn in
pierced ears), bracelets, brooches and rings.[18]

Roman men wore long hair until the third century B.C. but came to consider long hair old-fashioned or barbaric. By contrast, Greeks typically wore their hair long. Greeks who wore their hair long at times felt contempt for fellows who cut their hair short in imitation of the Romans. Long-haired recruits to the Roman auxiliary army were given a haircut. Freeborn boys in Egypt in this period typically wore their long hair in braids. Women's hair styles changed rapidly, often following the styles of the women in the imperial family.

Most Roman men gave up the custom of wearing beards in the second century B.C. They shaved with only water and a blade. At times young Romans wore small beards, to the consternation of their elders. For three centuries, Romans took a beard or long hair as the sign of a foreigner. Beards became popular again with Romans in the second century A.D.[19]

*Near Eastern attire.* Wool and linen (made of flax) were the favorite materials for clothing in Palestine (Mk 14:51; 15:46). The usual color was the natural white of the material, or white resulting from the bleaching process of fullers. However, dyeing was also popular from early times. Gold and silver thread were used in the clothing of royalty and the upper classes (Acts 12:21). John the Baptist, like others in the prophetic mold, wore rough garments. John's clothing was made of camel's hair, a course woven cloth (Mt 3:4).

Men and women wore the same basic articles of clothing in Palestine. The distinction between the two was more in the color and other details. The quality of the fabric of these garments indicated the wealth of the owner. The tunic or shirt, similar to that of the Romans and Greeks, was the principal ordinary garment worn by men and women (Lk 3:11; 6:29; 9:3; Acts 9:39). It was worn next to the skin and was essentially a long, tight-fitting shirt made of two pieces of cloth sewn together. The material might be wool, linen or leather. The simplest kind was sleeveless. Members of the lower classes often wore nothing more than the tunic in warm weather. At times, they would add a *himation,* a rectangular piece of cloth draped around the body.

Those who could afford it would add a cape fastened at the neck. Soldiers wore a purple version of this, such as the one placed on Jesus before his crucifixion (Mt 27:28). It was worn over the shoulders in pleasant weather and wrapped around the body like a heavy shawl when necessary for warmth (Mt 5:40; 9:20; 24:18; Lk 6:29; 22:36; Jn 19:2; Acts 7:58; 22:20).

Travelers would add a sash or belt to this outfit. It bound a loose tunic, allowing one to walk more freely (Acts 12:8). This was normally a long strip of cloth folded several times and wound around the waist over the tunic. It was often used as a money belt (Mk 6:8). Women wore it about the hips and usually tied it more loosely than did men. The loincloth or waistcloth, a simple piece of cloth or leather, was worn by slaves and laborers about the hips like a kilt or apron. Aprons were worn over outer garments by workers (Acts 19:12).

The typical footgear was leather sandals, much like those of the Romans. Leather soles were common, but felt, cloth and wood soles also existed. A leather thong bound the sole to the foot (Mk 1:7). Upper-class women had sandals elaborately embroidered with silk, silver and gold. In fact, a wealthy woman's sandals might be the richest part of her attire. Palestinians generally removed their footwear during mealtimes (Lk 7:38; Jn 13:5-6).

Jesus and the disciples wore simple clothing. Jesus apparently wore an inner garment since he removed his outer garments (tunic and *himation*) before washing the feet of the disciples (Jn 13:4). His tunic was seamless (Jn 19:23) and therefore had short sleeves and fit closely at the neck. It was apparently a valuable garment, so it may have been given to him by one of the women who helped financially support his ministry (Lk 8:3). According to Josephus, the Jewish high priest also wore a seamless tunic (*Antiquities* 3.161-62). We do not know how such tunics were made. Jesus wore leather sandals on his feet (Mt 3:11). He probably wore the customary white turban on his head, since no Jewish teacher of that day would appear with his head uncovered and Jesus generally observed such morally neutral social mores. This was wrapped around the head, with the ends falling down over the neck, and fastened with a cord under the chin. The disciples probably dressed in similar fashion.

Jews typically wore beards and longish hair, except for those who shaved and cut their hair close in imitation of Roman styles. Paul wore his hair long, except when he took a Nazarite vow (Acts 18:18, cf. 21:24).

Arab men, like many other Near Eastern peoples, wore earrings in pierced ears. Ethiopian women wore a ring through the lip. Dacian and Sarmatian men, and Thracian women, often wore tattoos.[20]

### Burial Practices

*Roman burial.* Death was a constant reality for Roman families, and they took their burial practices very seriously. This was true even in times of peace because of high infant and child mortality and diseases from which they had little protection. For example, about 80 percent of the burial inscriptions discovered in the Roman port city of Ostia are for persons younger than thirty years old.

The dead in the ancient world generally were either buried or cremated. The Romans favored cremation until the second century A.D. when they began switching to burial. The Greeks and Egyptians, like the Jews and later the Christians, usually buried their dead (see the photograph of a Greek woman's burial marker in figure 12.2).

After a person's death, Romans prepared the body for as much as seven days of lying in state. The mourning period among the poor tended to be shorter, usually one night. This was followed by a procession of family and friends through the city gates to the final resting place. Normally a pig was sacrificed and eaten at the grave. The body was burned on a pyre; then the ashes were carried to a tomb along one of the highways leading to the city. Famous persons' bodies might be cremated on a pyre in a public square. The remains of those whose family could afford it were stored in urns and placed in niches in the family's tomb, called a *columbarium*. Burial sites often featured inscriptions calling down curses on anyone who would desecrate the tomb.[21]

Anyone who could afford it was commemorated with a gravestone on which was inscribed one's full name and information about any offices or public rank one held. The gravestones of freedmen often record their professional qualifications and successes. The Romans also honored their dead with sayings in verse and prose. The epitaphs left behind by the poor of Rome show how important they considered the duty to commemorate a relative's death. This tradition seems to have been particularly Roman, but it was readily adopted by people of foreign birth or extraction.[22]

After the burial the family returned home for a rite of purification. Nine days later the family returned to the grave for another ceremonial meal. Sometimes family members visited the grave at regular intervals, such as on the birthday of the deceased.

The freedmen of Roman citizens had the right to be buried in the family tomb of their patron since they were part of his *familia*. They and their descendants were expected to maintain the regular observance of commemorative rites at the tomb. The poorer population used funeral associations, to which they made monthly payments, to assure themselves of a proper burial in one of the great funeral institutions for cremation or, for burial, in the catacombs.[23]

For a long time burial and cremation coexisted, but from the second century A.D. onward, burial began to predominate. It is unlikely that this change was caused by the spread of Christianity. The church was still too small in the second century to exert such an influence on pagan society (see in figures 4.1 and 4.2 photographs of a Christian burial site called the Catacomb of Domitilla).

*Jewish burial.* Palestinian Jews in the New Testament era practiced burial rather than cremation. They buried the dead on the day they died (Acts 5:6-10). They might hire professional musicians and mourners as a public demonstration of their grief (Mt 9:23). The body would be prepared with various spices, wrapped in linen, then placed in a coffin or stone sarcophagus (Jn 11:44; 19:39-40). By custom they visited the body several days later to be sure the person was truly dead and perhaps to finish burial preparations (Mt 28:1-2). Once the body decomposed, they placed its bones in a place of permanent rest in a chest. Archaeologists recently discovered a chest containing the remains of Joseph Caiaphas, the high priest when Jesus was crucified.[24]

*Christian burial.* Christians often used underground communal burial sites called catacombs. In addition to the famous catacombs outside the city of Rome, Christian catacombs have been found in Alexandria, North Africa, Syracuse, Malta and Naples. Several tiers of recesses were excavated along each side of the passages. Stone slabs or bricks sealed the openings of the recesses. Walls and ceilings were often covered in plaster and decorated. Contrary to the assertions of some modern authors, Christians did not bury their dead underground because they were trying to avoid detection by pagan authorities. The Romans respected the rights of all to bury their dead and were too superstitious about cemeteries to bother Christian graves. In fact, the entrances to Christian catacombs were often on main roads, readily visible to passersby. Christians also did not hold worship services in the catacombs. The galleries are far too small for public meetings, and the smell of corpses would have prevented such use.

Remains of Christians can be dated, in a few places, to the second century. The cemetery under Saint Peter's Basilica in Rome, considered by many the burial site of the apostle Peter, dates to the late first century. But scholars differ on whether it was a Christian burial ground at that time. We do not know how Christians disposed of their dead before that date. It seems certain that they practiced burial as opposed to cremation. That we have not discovered their tombs is probably a result of the relatively small number of Christians. It is also possible that they did not mark their tombs with Christian symbols in this early period.

### For Further Reading
*Labor and the Economy*
Hock, Ronald F. *The Social Context of Paul's Ministry: Tentmaking and Apostleship.* Philadelphia: Fortress, 1980.

*Leisure and Games*
Auguet, Roland. *Cruelty and Civilization: The Roman Games.* New York: Routledge, 1994.

*Travel*
Casson, Lionel. *Ships and Seamanship in the Ancient World.* 2nd ed. Baltimore:

Johns Hopkins University Press, 1995.

————. *Travel in the Ancient World.* Baltimore: Johns Hopkins University Press, 1994.

Rapske, Brian M. "Acts, Travel and Shipwreck." In *The Book of Acts in Its Graeco-Roman Setting,* ed. David W. J. Gill and Conrad Gempf, pp. 1-47. Grand Rapids, Mich.: Eerdmans, 1994.

Ramsay, William. *The Cities of St. Paul: Their Influence on His Life and Thought.* Grand Rapids, Mich.: Baker, 1963.

*Dining*

Edwards, John. *Roman Cookery.* Point Roberts, Wash.: Hartley and Marks, 1986.

Paoli, Ugo Enrico. *Rome: Its People, Life and Customs.* Trans. R. D. Macnaghten. New York: David McKay, 1963.

*Burial Practices*

Jones, Rick. "Backwards and Forwards in Roman Burial." *Journal of Roman Archaeology* 6 (1993): 427-32.

Saller, Richard P., and Brent D. Shaw. "Tombstones and Roman Family Relations in the Principate: Civilians, Soldiers and Slaves." *Journal of Roman Studies* 74 (1984): 124-56, 145-51.

Williams, M. H. "The Organisation of Jewish Burials in Ancient Rome in the Light of Evidence from Palestine and the Diaspora." *Zeitschrift für Papyrologie und Epigraphik* 101 (1994): 165-82.

# Chapter 3

# The City in the
# Greco-Roman World

*How much sleep, I ask you, can one get in lodgings here? Unbroken nights—*
*and this is the root of the trouble—are a rich man's privilege.*
*The wagons thundering past through those narrow twisting streets,*
*the oaths of draymen caught in a traffic-jam—*
*these alone would suffice to jolt the doziest sea-cow of an Emperor*
*into permanent wakefulness.*
JUVENAL *THE SIXTEEN SATIRES*1

*And after some days Paul said to Barnabas, "Come, let us return and*
*visit the brethren in every city where we proclaimed the word*
*of the Lord, and see how they are."*
ACTS 15:36

*For here we have no lasting city, but we seek the city which is to come.*
HEBREWS 13:14

NCIENT GREEK AND ROMAN SOCIETIES WERE ORGANIZED AROUND
their cities.[2] All the amenities of culture and all the market facilities
a region offered were located in the city. The city represented all
that *civilization* meant to the upper classes. Farmers and shepherds
from the surrounding countryside came to town to sell their products and buy
manufactured items and specialty goods at the city's daily markets, weekly
fairs and annual holiday bazaars. This is not much different from modern
societies like the United States. Probably most Americans equate *civilization*
with urban life (including what we call suburban life). However, the proportion
of the population that lived in its cities differs dramatically. While over 50
percent of the population in the United States today lives in cities, only 10
percent of the population lived in the thousand or so cities of the Empire in
New Testament times. This is a reflection of the steep pyramidal structure of

this society, the absence of a true middle class.

One of the fascinating aspects of early Christianity is how quickly and completely it made the leap from the countryside to the city. Christianity shifted rapidly from a religion of uneducated, rural folk in Palestine to a faith of more educated people in the cities of the Empire. The change was so dramatic that Christian missionary activity by the second century began to focus on reaching out to the countryside. The term that came to be used for the unconverted, *pagan*, means "country dweller" in Latin *(paganus)*. How and why did this shift take place? The answers lie in an understanding of the tremendous opportunity for ministry the city in the Greco-Roman world represented to Paul and other urban-oriented Christians.

The term *city (polis)*, as used in the New Testament, can mislead the casual reader. This word is used of very different kinds of cities. Some cities were established by or heavily influenced by Hellenistic or Roman culture. These cities were the largest, wealthiest and most powerful, but they were not all alike. As we shall see, cities established by Greeks and by Romans shared some important elements but differed in significant ways as well. Other cities and villages were established by local peoples, such as the Jews of Palestine. Like the Hellenistic kingdoms before her, Rome did not trust the leaders in these cities and so allowed them little influence. These locales had successfully resisted cultural inroads by both Greeks and Romans. They did so in part because the Greeks and Romans virtually ignored towns they considered inconsequential and in part because the local peoples of the eastern Mediterranean saw the Hellenistic and Roman rulers as foreign conquerors very different from themselves.

It is difficult for Americans to relate to a society that has radically different cultures at different levels. The culture of upper-class Americans is distinctly different from that of middle-class and working-class Americans, of course. And we know that a number of so-called subcultures exist among various ethnic groups and in various locales in the United States. But these differences only begin to suggest the kind of distance between the largely rural Near Eastern cultures and the Greco-Roman cities of the New Testament era. The local peoples kept their languages, their religions, their customs, and their values, even while their upper classes by and large were co-opted into the Roman system.

The New Testament is so important to historians because it is one of the few documents that lets us view the inner workings of these cities and villages and their relationships with the cities of their Hellenistic and Roman overlords. For example, we witness the ways in which the Herodian family and the priestly class in Judea were co-opted by the Romans. We also learn about a fascinating

**Figure 3.1. View of a typical forum in a smaller Roman city, Pompeii, Italy. Mount Vesuvius, which erupted in A.D. 79 and buried Pompeii, is in the background.**

*Pharisees*

group of intellectuals, the Pharisees, who possessed the education of an upper class but lacked its privileges and who for the most part refused to be co-opted by the Romans. In fact, one of the reasons Jesus was so critical of them was because he believed they cared about the average Jew and so should have been willing to join his movement. By contrast, Jesus had little to say about the priests or the Herodians, who he may have believed had long before sold their souls to Rome.

## Physical Setting

The cities and larger towns of the Roman Empire were situated on highways, at river crossings and at natural harbors (see map 7). Travelers on the road to a city passed farms, orchards and the homes of farm workers. They might see the arches of an aqueduct bringing water into the city. The first thing they would see of the city was its walls. If the city was located on high ground, as were many cities in Palestine, from a long distance they would see its walls by day and its lights by night. Jesus must have had this image in mind when he talked about the visibility of a city set on a hill (Mt 5:14). The more important cities were enclosed by massive, buttressed walls with watch towers at the corners and on both sides of the city gates. As travelers approached the city, they walked by tombs lining both sides of the road. As they came to the city gate, they saw religious shrines and water wells. They smelled shops that generated too much odor to be located within the city, such as leather tanners. The ancients did in fact have a kind of districting that limited the locations of certain types of businesses.

The city gate (or gates) was large enough to accommodate carts pulled by animals. Travelers who arrived between sunrise and sunset would find the gate open. Otherwise, they would have to seek admittance at a smaller, side door. The doors of great houses were similarly designed. Jesus may be alluding to this arrangement when he urges his followers to enter by the narrow gate rather than the broad one (Lk 13:24).

Inside the walls of a city that predated the Greeks and Romans, travelers found a maze of narrow, winding streets. Ancient Near Eastern cities such as Antioch or Damascus tended to grow bit by bit instead of resulting from a plan. By contrast, a Greek or Roman city was built on a formal grid of streets crossing at right angles. A traveler knew that the street from the city gate bisected the city, extending straight to the agora or forum and typically crossing the city to a gate at the far side. The streets, at least the main boulevards, usually were wider than in ancient Near Eastern cities as well.

The Greeks who took control of the eastern Mediterranean, following the death of Alexander the Great, founded or rebuilt 350 cities. More than 30 of them were in Palestine, including the cities of the Decapolis (Mt 4:25; see map 3). These towns stood out from the native cities. Their principal streets and rectangular blocks, monumental arches, theaters, public baths, gymnasiums, arcades, temples, fountains, colonnade and agoras all marked them as Hellenistic. The main thoroughfares typically were paved, but most of the streets and alleys were dirt. Because of this, continual foot-washing was necessary, even in the city (Lk 7:38-46; Jn 12:3; 13:5-15).

But the Greeks did not do all the Hellenistic construction in Palestine. King Herod the Great of Judea is responsible for a great deal of it, according to Josephus (*Jewish War* 1.422-25). In fact, Herod built much of his reconstructed temple in Jerusalem in the Greek style (*Jewish War* 5.184-227). Predominantly Jewish towns refused to Hellenize, even though prominent Jewish families took on Greco-Roman ways. The average Jewish houses remained small and crowded together, with flat roofs and rooms opening on a courtyard separated from the street by a wall with a gate door (Acts 12:13).[3]

*Dominant landmarks.* Some cities, especially in the East, showed off their wealth by building colonnades along the main streets. This offered a traveler a covered sidewalk into the public square. In a Greek city, the central agora functioned as marketplace and civic center. Shrines and temples stood all around, and colonnades gave shelter to merchants and money changers. The council house provided a small, roofed space for meetings of the council. The town hall housed a central sacred hearth and offered places of honor to statues of gods, heroes and statesmen. Scattered about the city were the precincts of other temples. Each Greek city also had a gymnasium, where young people went to school and exercised and where adults came to watch and to join in the events. Every Greek city of a minimum size also had a theater, where religious festivals were conducted.

In a Roman colony, the central forum usually contained a temple to Jupiter (in honor of his great temple on the Capitoline Hill in Rome) and a *curia* building where the town council met (in imitation of the senate *curia* in the Forum in Rome; see the photograph of the forum in Pompeii in figure 3.1). The typical central forum also had a *basilica* where law cases and business deals could be conducted out of the elements, a smaller temple or two, and statues of distinguished citizens and of the emperor and his family. Other temples were located throughout the city, scattered along the streets or set off in individual precincts. Roman towns typically also had public baths, a modified version of the Greek theater, and often a large amphitheater for gladiatorial games.

Figure 3.2 shows the plan of the city of Pompeii, which was buried by the eruption of Mount Vesuvius in A.D. 79. This city was atypical in some ways, since it was in part a resort town on the coast where a number of wealthy Romans maintained summer homes. But the plan shows the typical elements of a Roman city: a central forum, streets laid out on a grid pattern, a major street running straight through the town, and the public buildings considered essential to civilized life.

In a Near Eastern city, the major monuments were the temple of the guardian

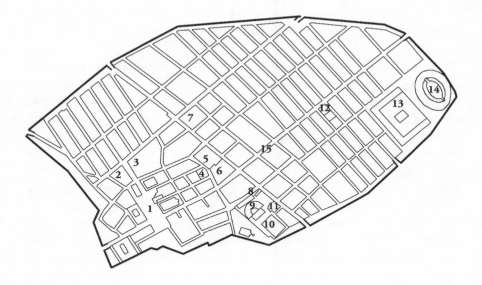

**Figure 3.2. Plan of an ancient city (the Roman city of Pompeii in southern Italy, c. first century A.D.). (1) Forum. (2) Forum baths. (3) Temple of Fortuna Augusta. (4) Inn. (5) Inn of Sittius. (6) Stabian Baths. (7) Central baths. (8) Temple of Isis. (9) Large theater. (10) Gladiators' barracks. (11) Small theater. (12) Bakery. (13) Palestra with swimming pool. (14) Amphitheater. (15) Main street in the city (today called the Via dell'Abbondanza).**

deity and the palace of the ruler, which in the Empire was usually taken over by the chief Roman administrator. First under the Hellenistic kings and then under the Roman emperors, Near Eastern locales such as Palmyra and Jerusalem took on some of the characteristics of Greco-Roman cities (see in figure 8.2 a photograph of the larger theater at Pompeii).

*Subdivisions of the city.* Most streets took their names from prominent buildings or monuments nearby, or from a person honored in the neighborhood. Some were named for the trade plied on that street, for instance, Glass, Incense or Perfume Street. Squares and plazas were also named at times for certain occupations.

Shops selling the basic necessities of life, such as food, could be found throughout the city. However, merchants and artisans usually clustered together with others plying the same trade or craft. Goldsmiths, jewelers, tailors and clothing sellers would be found near the city center. Occupations that involved the transport of large items to the city, such as traders and drovers, understandably congregated near the city gates. In general, the businesses closer to the center of the city were the more respectable ones in Greco-Roman terms: less smelly, less noisy and more oriented to serving the needs of the local elite.

We in the modern Western city are not used to seeing a street lined with many versions of the same business, except perhaps in a downtown garment district or farmer's market, This is a more common occurrence today in other parts of the world. For example, the Akihabara district in Tokyo features block after block of electronics stores. By contrast, in the United States commercial centers often commit in writing not to rent space to a store that sells a product similar to that of a current tenant. Why would similar craftsmen cluster together in the ancient city, instead of spreading out to avoid competition? Although these businesses were in competition, they also benefited a great deal from cooperating with each other. They helped each other get raw materials, shared a water source, helped new arrivals get started and talked together about common interests. In a world without telephone books and automobiles, such a system made it easy for residents to know where to go to find what they wanted. For example, they knew to go to the booksellers' street to find books.

*Housing in the city.* The streets of the city were lined with single-story private homes. In the eastern Mediterranean, plain walls of adobe, often covered with plaster, provided something of a privacy and sound barrier. Instead of looking outward, the homes were oriented around a central garden or courtyard. Though usually single stories, private homes in more populous cities often had multiple stories. The New Testament gives us the example of a house in Troas where a boy fell out of a third-story window (Acts 20:9; for an example of the appearance of an ancient city, see figure 3.3).

The homes of the rich in Hellenistic cities were large and lavishly decorated. The walls were painted with mythological or pastoral scenes, while the floors were covered with images rendered in mosaic tile. Those who could afford to connect to the public aqueduct might install a fountain in the courtyard. Those who could not had to send servants to fetch water from a public well or fountain. A doorkeeper, such as Rhoda in Acts 12, decided whom to admit to the home (Acts 12:13-15). The house of Philemon at Colossae, where Christians and other guests could gather (Philem 22), and that of Gaius at Corinth, which could hold "the whole assembly" of Christians (Rom 16:23), suggest how large such homes could be (see the photograph of the House of Aristides from first-century Herculaneum, Italy, in figure 11.1).

Figure 3.3. Remains of the port city of Herculaneum, Italy. The city was buried by the eruption of Mount Vesuvius in A.D. 79. This is the view of the city one would have had if arriving by sea. The foreground building was a harbor facility.

The old style of a wealthy private home in Italy, still in use in Paul's day, centered on a central atrium that served as an office for the head of the family and a place of honor for the family's ancestors. A hole in the center of the atrium allowed rainwater to fall into a catch basin below and provided light for the room.

In the second century B.C., Rome began erecting multistory apartment buildings *(insulae)*. These apartment buildings probably originated in Rome and the idea spread from there to other cities with dense populations. They were typically built around an inner courtyard that provided light and air to the rooms above. Small shops *(tabernae)* were often built into the outer ring of the first floor of the insulae. Families who operated such small shops often lived in them as well. Sometimes a back room behind or a mezzanine above the main room offered a bit of privacy for the family.

A few "deluxe" apartments might be found on the first floor behind these shops, facing the inner courtyard. By the time Paul came to Italy, rich Romans in the city were more likely to live in these deluxe apartments than in separate homes. These apartments contained a number of rooms, including accommodations for servants. They were suitable for hosting small social gatherings, but they generally lacked kitchens and latrines. In a world without elevators, the most valuable apartments were on the first floor.

Above the ground floor shops and deluxe apartments, one might find two to five floors of apartments. Because the higher stories were built less solidly, the cheapest apartments were always on the highest floors. These most often contained one or two rooms. Interior rooms, probably used for sleeping, received no natural light or fresh air. Most of the apartments had no kitchens. Families either cooked on charcoal braziers located near an outside opening or went out for hot meals. The apartments did not have latrines. Their residents used the small spaces under stairs, chamber pots or the public latrines. Privacy would have been rare.

Within a single apartment, several unrelated families might have separate sleeping rooms but share a common sitting room. These apartments were too small to allow for socializing with friends, let alone for Christian house congregations. Those who lived in such apartments would have to do most of their eating and socializing in public places. Christians living here would need to find a wealthier fellow Christian, or perhaps a sympathetic pagan patron, to host their church.

Slaves typically lived in the homes of their masters. Some residences had slave quarters, but frequently slaves were expected to sleep wherever they could put down a cot. Masters encouraged their slaves to form families, and those who did were more likely to be assigned separate quarters. Trusted and important slaves were allowed to maintain separate residences near the master's home. Slaves who had gained their freedom normally continued to serve their former master and sometimes continued to live in the master's home. Those who moved out of the home almost certainly ended up in the humble homes described above.

It seems clear that the majority of Jews and Christians in the cities would have lived in tiny apartments, in the homes of their masters or former masters, or at the back of their ground-floor shops. Christian house congregations that met in the homes of believers probably met in private homes or first-floor "deluxe" apartments, not in small, upper-story apartments. If Jews were able to congregate in buildings with other Jews, they would have found it easier to practice the dietary and exclusivity demands of their religion. Jews who converted to Christianity would have found their apartment building a natural place to spread their beliefs.

## Urban People

In the Roman world, size was grounds for civic pride. The larger the population of the city and the grander and more numerous its public buildings, the greater the basis for boasting. Residents argued over whose temple or amphitheater was bigger. The loyalty of urban citizens to their city is clear in both Greek and Roman culture. For example, graffiti on a tavern wall in Italy shows the competitiveness: under the boast, "Pergamum, golden city," is written "Rome, golden city."[4]

Rome and Alexandria were the giants of the ancient world, with populations near 1,000,000 and 600,000, respectively. Next were Carthage and Antioch, both near 500,000, then Ephesus, with 400,000. Smyrna and Thessalonica were home to over 200,000 persons. Several more cities had populations over 75,000, but the rest were closer to the 20,000 population of Pompeii.

Official documents give us a number of terms dealing with city citizenship: *citizen, resident* (but not owning real property), *transient* (or *businessman*), and those *outside the walls* (or *rural*). Many local variations of these terms existed. In the second century A.D., the rights of a group in the city of Tarsus came under question:

> a group of no small size, outside the constitution, so to speak, whom some people call "linen-workers" and are irritated by them and consider them a useless rabble and the cause of uproar and disorder.[5]

Though they were mostly native born and admitted to the assembly, they were "reviled and viewed as aliens." This attitude seems to arise from the belief that anyone causing strife in the community must be an alien.

The upper classes gave voluntarily of their wealth to their cities with unparalleled generosity. The sizes of their gifts suggest that many gave well beyond their means, even to the point of mortgaging their estates. Why? They were competing for status with the rich in their community and elsewhere.

The Hellenistic cities of Acts included a significant number of the moderately wealthy. The city councils were large, each with five hundred to six hundred members. The upper stratum of this class included a few families of immense wealth, who would over time join the empire-wide hierarchy as Roman citizens, then equestrians and finally senators.

Life in the warm, dry climate of the Mediterranean was spent largely out of doors. The homes of the commoners were tiny, poorly lit and drafty—mainly places to sleep and perhaps to cook a meal. Shop owners often lived in the corner of their shops. The crowding at home made the spacious public facilities of Hellenistic and Roman cities that much more attractive. Urbanites constantly were reminded of the generosity of the wealthy by the dedication plaques on public buildings. In fact, public areas in Hellenistic and Roman cities typically took up a fourth of the land, counting temples, a forum or two, amphitheaters, streets, market buildings, senate house, basilicas, sports parks, gymnasia and baths.

Residents congregated inside and outside of the city gates, along the streets lined with shops and in small squares featuring wells or fountains. They met in the main square for political meetings, audiences with government authorities (Acts 18:12), and trials and lawsuits. In Eastern cities, the elders of the city gathered to discuss events and make decisions. Crowds, including children, beggars and the crippled, gathered at the entrance to temples (Lk 7:32; Acts 3:2). On festival days, residents came to the theaters, amphitheaters, and circuses. Urgent public meetings, like the one at Ephesus (Acts 19:29-41), might also be held in the theater.

Urban residents often experienced a genuine sense of community. Even in the little alleys, a vibrant sense of community connected the inhabitants. In the daytime, the streets were full of sights, sounds and smells. Neighbors discussed local events. Shopkeepers and vendors took advantage of natural light and warm weather to ply their trades and sell their wares outdoors. A teacher who could not afford to rent a room would teach students on the sidewalk. Restaurant owners often set up chairs alongside the street. The literature of the period is full of complaints by the upper class about the constant noise of city life. In the city, you had to be rich to have any privacy.

In the ancient city, because of the public nature of life, one knew well the moral character of acquaintances and so people would enter into verbal agreements readily. Such a personal promise, though not written down, committed one's community standing to a bargain. This practice seems strange to Americans in a society that encourages written contracts for the simplest agreements. In fact, a Roman might well prefer a man's word to his property or to a deposit. The cement of their daily financial relationships was people, not things. Disputes could be settled by simply swearing under oath, then challenging one's opponent to swear. A reputation for honesty was important to the success, or at least to the status, of a businessman.[6]

The account of Paul's activities in the city of Lystra gives us an example of the degree to which Hellenistic and Roman culture had influenced local peoples in the eastern Mediterranean. Lystra was a Roman colony, established by Caesar Augustus to control the local peoples. As Acts shows, however, many of its residents were locals who spoke neither Latin nor Greek but the local Lycaonian language when they proclaimed Paul and Barnabas gods. Hellenistic culture is apparent as well in their choice of the names of two Greek gods, Zeus and Hermes, for Paul and Barnabas rather than the names of Roman or local Near Eastern gods (Acts 14:8-18).

## Life in Rome

We know a great deal about one city in the Roman Empire: Rome, its capital. In some ways, Rome was unique; it was the largest city, containing a concentration of wealth and power unparalleled for many centuries. In many other ways, life in Rome for the average resident would not have been all that different from life in the other larger cities of the Empire, particularly in the Roman and Hellenistic towns. What I address below applies equally well to many other cities (see in figure 3.4 a photograph of a model of the city of Rome). While based on evidence from the fourth century A.D., most of the city's major elements as seen in this photo were in place in the New Testament era.

The city of Rome in the first century represented an accumulation of wealth unsurpassed in Western society until fairly recent times. Marble façades graced the massive public buildings of its forums. Ever larger temples portrayed the greatness of Rome's gods, who had protected it and given it victory over its enemies. Hundreds of private mansions dotted the hills of the city. Miles of aqueducts brought spring water to public fountains and the homes of wealthy Romans, and sewers removed the city's waste. Rome's population of around one million persons would not be equaled by any Western city until the 1800s.

The majority of people in Rome lived in multistory tenement houses (*insulae*) or in small ground-floor domiciles at the rear of the shops (*tabernae*). The typical apartment had one or two rooms, which opened onto the street or a central courtyard. The same room often served as sleeping chamber, kitchen and socializing area. Sometimes several families shared a set of rooms; each family would have a private bedroom connected to a common room.

Because window glass was expensive, most windows were openings in walls, lacking glass. They were covered with wooden shutters to keep out the cold. The only source of heat was a charcoal brazier located near the window.

The rooms were small, damp, dark and cold, except in the summer, when they were hot and stuffy. Privacy was virtually impossible, and the sounds of the city often made a good night's sleep difficult. The average poor resi-

**Figure 3.4. Model of the city of Rome in the fourth century A.D. The round building at center left is the Colosseum.**

dent of Rome had to get his water at a public fountain and carry it up to his apartment or hoist it up in a bucket. Public toilets were available near the public baths, but chamber pots were often kept under outside stairs. Living behind the shops was no better, except that one had no stairs to climb. It should come as no surprise that the poorer Romans spent most of their waking hours in the streets.

The typical husband and wife of free status left home around sunrise, accompanied by their children, and headed for the small shop in which they worked. Since private mansions and tenement houses often existed side by side, the family members could not help but observe the incredible disparity of wealth in Rome. They might cross paths with the entourage of an aristocrat heading for an appointment. Slaves would precede the group in order to announce the aristocrat's titles and warn people to make way. A great man would be accompanied by as many slaves and free clients as he could muster since the size of the entourage proclaimed his importance.

As they passed through the city, our typical couple might try to distinguish the sound of a conversation from competing voices speaking in Latin, Greek, and other languages, as well as from the sounds of construction. They would probably smell baking bread among the scents of various foods and the stench of sewage, rotting garbage, urine, smoke, unrefrigerated fish and meat in the market, and the sweat of the crowded streets. They would try to stay on the elevated sidewalks where possible in order to avoid the mud and refuse in the streets. At times they would have to walk around piles of waste tossed onto the sidewalk from the apartments above. Many of Rome's streets were narrow and hemmed in by towering apartment blocks. In the heat of the summer, Romans appreciated the shade they provided.

Arriving at the shop, they would open a wooden folding door or grill to announce that they were open for business (see in figure 3.5 a photograph of the remains of wooden shutters from Herculaneum). Roman shops fronted on the street, lining the outside of the ground floor of apartment buildings. They were even built into the outside walls of private homes. They would specialize in one thing, such as baked goods, seafood, book selling or pottery production, but not all vendors had permanent shops. Those who sold food often set up booths in the streets. Itinerant peddlers wandered the streets selling clothing or food. A system of honor and status existed among these shopkeepers outside Rome's official class system. They would have accepted the official system but recognized that they had no real status under it.

Between noon and two o'clock, shopkeepers closed their shops to eat the main meal and escape the heat of the day. A typical shopkeeper might have returned to his *insula* to a meal cooked on the brazier. Unlike the rich, his diet rarely included red meat. His meal could have consisted of fish or chicken along with the basic staples of beans and peas. In addition, he might have bought fresh fruit or vegetables from the local food booths, if he could afford them. Rather than go home, he could also have eaten in a local full-service restaurant (*caupona*) or, more likely, in a simpler restaurant, a *popina*, where wine and some hot food were available. Or he may have gone to a *taberna*, where one usually ate a cold meal while standing at a counter.

Roman businesses typically stayed open until sundown. Shopkeepers tried to get home before dark, since the absence of streetlights gave the ancient city plenty of dark hiding places for robbers. The rich only went out at night in the company of bodyguards. The poor received little help from the token 350 soldiers who patrolled Rome at night. These soldiers were concerned principally with protecting the property of the rich and with preventing riots. If a poor man was beaten or robbed, he had to capture and bring his assailant to the authorities before he could get justice.[7]

We know some things about how and where Jews lived in the city of Rome. The oldest and largest Jewish settlement in Rome was in Transtiberinum (modern Trastevere), across the Tiber River from the center of Rome. Jews continued to live here into the Middle Ages. Its narrow, crowded streets and towering apartment buildings hosted poor, unassimilated immigrants of many nationalities crammed hundreds to a building. It is likely that a number of the free Jews living here worked at the nearby docks on the Tiber. Over time, Jews expanded from Transtiberinum to other areas. Since most of the early Christians were Jews or lower-class Romans, we should expect to find many first-century Christians in Transtiberinum as well.

We can make some educated guesses about the Roman housing of a particular Christian couple, Prisca and Aquila (Rom 16). They were tentmakers who worked in Rome, Corinth and Ephesus, indicating a high degree of mobility. The fact that Aquila and Prisca could afford to own or rent residences capable of seating one or two dozen worshipers shows that they were able to live well above a subsistence level. Their wealth, though modest, exceeded that of most residents of Rome and, therefore, probably that of most other Roman Christians. It seems likely that they were able to rent a deluxe ground-floor apartment in Rome. It also is possible that a house church could have met in the work area of their shop.

Rome was unique among ancient cities in ways beyond its enormous wealth. For example, a majority of the city's residents by the New Testament era were slaves, the descendants of slaves and free resident aliens. Many of the Roman citizens here, who generally despised and resented all foreigners, were the descendants of farmers who had come to Rome to eke out a living after losing their farms. The city's public buildings and private mansions occupied over one half of its sixteen-square-mile area. As a result, density levels in first-century Rome rivaled those of many modern cities. This is all the more amazing when one takes into account the relative inadequacy or absence of public services taken for granted in major cities today.

## Urban Finances

A significant portion of any Hellenistic or Roman city's income was spent constructing and maintaining its public buildings as well as supporting the human resources considered necessary for urban life. Temples, headquarters for administering law and order, meeting houses, archives, gymnasiums, public baths and combatants for the games were all considered essential components of civilized life. Elevated aqueducts were often needed to provide not only fresh water but also water pressure for public and private fountains. Larger cities supported professors and physicians. Smaller Greek cities paid for teachers and trainers in their gymnasiums. The city also paid for a staff of attendants and public slaves to assist city officials. Public slaves attended the public baths and helped maintain the public buildings, aqueducts and roads. Many cities paid watchmen to provide police and fire service.

The most important source of income for cities in the Roman Empire was real estate. Land owned by the city was rented out to farmers. The city would also usually charge merchants for the use of stalls in the public marketplace. Some cities owned and rented housing. The city also might gain additional revenue by lending money at interest. In addition to real-estate-based taxes, cities collected income from tolls and custom duties. Such taxes were usually only 2 or 2.5 percent on imports and exports, but large commercial centers still could generate a great deal of revenue.

In most cities, these sources of revenue fell far short of expenditures. This happened in part because cities apparently did not draw up formal annual budgets. Cities might turn to the provincial governor for help, but if the example of Pliny as governor of Bithynia is typical, this often proved fruitless. For example, the emperor Trajan turned down requests from Pliny to help rebuild a gymnasium and to supply Roman soldiers to protect a small town (*Letters* 10.39-40, 77-78).

Members of the upper classes were expected to make up the difference between expenses and regular income. In Greek cities, the wealthy might be required to pay the expenses of a festival or dramatic performance, to construct or maintain a public building, to maintain a ship owned by the city, or to supply the oil for the local gymnasium. In some Roman cities, laws required a person who had been elected as a magistrate to pay certain fees and to contribute to the expenses of the public games.

Beyond these required contributions, members of the upper classes in search of honor and standing often made lavish, voluntary contributions. Emperors and senators at times funded new temples or established endowments for specific cities. The communities might honor the benefactors in a number of ways: with proclamations of gratitude, statues, grants of honorary citizenship, crowns, seats of honor at the theater, free meals in the town hall or immunity from taxation. Jesus refers to the way "those in authority" expected the honor that belonged to the title of "benefactor" (Lk 22:25). References to the way God supplies spiritual benefits to believers (Gal 3:5; Phil 1:19; 1 Pet 4:11) and bodily needs to the poor (2 Cor 9:9-10) are similar to the descriptions of those who provided choruses at dramatic festivals.[8]

Figure 3.5. **Wooden window shutters on a second-story window, Herculaneum, Italy. This first-century wood survived intact because it was carbonized by the lava mud from Mount Vesuvius that buried the city in A.D. 79.**

## The Cities of the Gospels

In contrast to the large number of moderately wealthy people in Hellenistic cities, the towns of the Galilean narratives in the Gospels seem almost devoid of successful merchants, bankers and artisans. In fact, only one example of a merchant appears in all three Galilean narratives: the pearl buyer who sells everything to secure one very costly pearl (Mt 13:45-46). Rather, we have a world of the very rich and the very poor. For example, in the parable of the rich man with the unfaithful steward, if the steward is dismissed he will have to either do manual labor or beg (Lk 16:1-6). A stark depiction of this world is the parable of the rich man and Lazarus the beggar (Lk 16:19-20).

A number of Gospel stories reflect the rural peasant economy of Palestine. The story of the prodigal son, for example, presents a household with only a few hired servants and a single beast kept for a special feast (Lk 15:11-32). This economy also may be seen in the case of the fisherman Zebedee, who has hired a few servants (Mk 1:20). A vineyard owner goes down to the village square five times to hire harvesters, even though he has a foreman, suggesting a "hands-on" owner of a relatively small vineyard (Mt 20:1-8). The owner of a walled vineyard and barn, with a staff of slaves, appears to be a fairly wealthy man (Mt 21:33-41).

Of course, Jesus was addressing a predominantly peasant, rural audience, so we would expect him to lay stress on the worker, the hired worker, the sower, the homemaker, and those with very little wealth. That we see few persons of moderate wealth is probably a reflection of the focus of Jesus' teaching and of the historical situation.

While we see much of small-time tax collectors in the Gospels, the urban moneylender, a prominent figure in Roman and Hellenistic locales, is a rarity in the Gospels. The moneylender in Luke forgives the debt owed him, and the third man in the parable of the talents is told that he might at least have invested the master's money with a banker (Lk 7:41-42; 19:23; Mt 25:27). The debtors and creditors in the Gospels are different from those in Greco-Roman society, in that there is no mention of charging interest.[9]

*Administration in the cities and villages of the Gospels.* The Hellenistic-Roman cities of Palestine mostly escape mention in the Gospels. Many of them had self-governing councils of several hundred citizens. Most were predominantly Gentile, but in Jamnia, Joppa, Sepphoris and Tiberias, Jews had equal rights and outnumbered Gentiles (see map 3). Only in Jerusalem were Gentiles excluded from civic rights.

By comparison to the Jewish towns and villages in Palestine, the number of genuine Greek cities, with democratic councils, was small. We know of thirty-three such cities in or near Palestine. In Galilee, only Tiberias and perhaps Sepphoris qualify as Greek cities. The democratic council ruled not only the city but also all the villages and towns belonging to its often extensive territory.[10]

Judea and the tetrarchies to the north were administered by the Ptolemaic system of villages grouped into districts known as toparchies. A village clerk administered the village as an official of the central government, and the commandant controlled the toparchy. These villages did not rule their own territory. Unlike self-governing cities elsewhere, those in Palestine usually had no authority over the adjacent territory, which was part of the toparchy. An exception to this was Caesarea Philippi, which controlled its own territory. The Gospels accurately describe this situation when they suggest that a city in Palestine was simply a glorified village; the inhabitants did not govern themselves. When the faithful servant is given rule over five or ten cities, he has been appointed commandant of a toparchy.[11]

The village clerks and commandants focused on the interests of the central government. Unsurprisingly, they are never mentioned in the Gospels. The closest we come to them in the Gospels are the references to those who fronted for them: the tax collectors. What mattered to the average village-dwelling Jew was the authority of the local congregation and the rulers of the synagogue (for example, the story of Jairus in Lk 8:41-42, 49-56; cf. Mt 9:18-26; Mk 5:22-24, 35-43). The reference to those who "love the most important seats in the synagogues and greetings in the marketplaces" assumes a Jewish village context (Lk 11:43; cf. Lk 20:46).

When Christ casts out demons in Gadara, the capital of a toparchy, the local response is quite different from the experiences of Paul in Asia Minor. In Gadara no municipal magistrates or assemblies or officials intervene. Rather, "all the city" comes out to ask him to go away (Mt 8:34; Mk 5:14; Lk 8:37). We also see references to what may be local councils of elders on the model of the Sanhedrin. For example, the angry brother is said to be "liable to the council" (Mt 5:22). This is as far as municipal life extends in the Gospels, and nothing in Josephus contradicts the impression here that the non-Hellenistic villages of Palestine lacked a developed municipal system.

*Village and city in Palestine.* One of the difficulties in studying documents from any culture is understanding how they may use the same terms in the same language in very different ways. The terms village (*komo*) and city (*polis*) had distinct, technical meanings in Greco-Roman culture. A city generally was larger than a village. It had some form of self-rule and buildings dedicated to the public life of the city. But we discover in the Gospels that, in common usage, the distinctions between these terms were not so clear. The Gospels at times use both terms for the same city. Matthew and Luke both refer to Capernaum, Gadara and Bethsaida as "cities" (Mt 8:34; 9:1; 11:20-23; Lk 4:31; 9:10). In contrast with Matthew and Luke, Mark calls Bethsaida a "village" and refers to the "villages" around Caesarea Philippi (6:6, 36). Mark says that Jesus visited the *komopoleis* ("village-cities") of Galilee, which are contrasted with the "city" of Capernaum (Mk 1:38). Mark and Luke use the standard definitions of *city* and *fields* of Gadara/Gerasa more precisely in the story of the swine (Mk 5:14; Lk 8:34).

Josephus, in describing Galilee, clarifies this mixing of terms. He says that Galilee has many cities and that even the very least of its villages contained fifteen thousand inhabitants (*Jewish War* 3.43). Such villages would be rather large by ancient standards, large enough to be called a city under the right circumstances. In fact, the city of Athens in the classical era may have been about this size. Josephus talks elsewhere about four "cities" given by Nero to King Agrippa II. Of the four cities he names, only Tiberias is a city in the Hellenistic sense (*Jewish War* 2.252; *Jewish Antiquities* 20.159). It seems that Josephus used the term *city* to refer to the capitals of toparchies, whether or not they were cities in the technical sense. This may be the approach of the Gospel authors as well. Gadara, for example, was a toparchic capital. Mark's use of *komopolis* for the villages of Galilee is precise. These large Galilean settlements had the population of a city, as Josephus indicates, but the nature of a village. Josephus shows the difference when he says that Philip the tetrarch advanced the village of Bethsaida to the dignity of a city, in both its population and its grandeur.

Peasant farmers congregated in large communities primarily because of the scarcity of farmland and water and the need for defense. In the Greek world, many of these villages were the nucleii of later cities. Cities developed in Greece out of villages that ran their own affairs and administered their own territory. Urban areas developed very differently in Palestine. A land of overlords and princes, its villages remained villages in their lack of self-rule, however large they grew. Places like Tiberias and Samaria, which had Hellenistic governments, did not control the territories outside their walls as did the classic Greek city-state.

Jesus traveled through the small, often anonymous towns of Galilee, seemingly avoiding the major cities of Galilee. Citizens of Sepphoris, Tiberias, the coastal plain and the Decapolis heard none of his sermons. When Jesus did enter the territory of cities in the Decapolis, he remained outside the walls (Mk 5:1; 7:31; 8:27). His parables usually matched his audience, only once picturing an urban merchant (Mt 13:45-46).

*Housing in Palestine.* In Palestine private houses had one or two stories. The rooms of homes in Palestine usually were small, with little ventilation and small windows. As we observed in the cities of the Empire, the wealthy could use window glass, but the poor could only afford wooden shutters, which eliminated natural light when closed. In small towns some families lived in a single room, but most had several. Some extended families slept in one bedroom, but usually each couple and their children had their own room. Larger rooms could be eighteen feet wide. Beds, chairs and benches were common in private homes. The poorest families owned only a few kitchen utensils and their bedding (sometimes only their cloak), and they slept on simple reed mats (Jn 5:8-12) or low cots (Lk 8:16).

Floors in common homes generally were made of beaten clay or basalt blocks, and in homes of those more wealthy, of plaster or stone. The large, uneven pieces of basalt used for flooring were the same material used for the walls in those homes. It would have been easy to lose a coin in the cracks between these blocks (Lk 15:8). The floors of wealthy home owners often were covered in mosaic tile, like those discovered at Pompeii in Italy and at Antioch in Syria. Storage pits were dug down into the floor to hold grain or large clay jars filled with oil or wine. Fire pits also were dug into the floor or surrounded by a low wall to contain the flames. Smoke had to find its way out through door openings and windows since the chimney had not yet been invented. The fire pit served to cook food and to heat the house, supplemented in this function by charcoal braziers. Most cities made some attempt at drainage for rain water and sometimes for sewage. Typically they used stone-lined and stone-covered channels for this purpose, but they also used clay pipe or open half-pipe systems. A visitor to the excavations of ancient Ephesus today can see the clay pipes used in that city. The ancient sewer system of the city of Rome, the Cloaca Maxima, is still at work two thousand years later, helping drain runoff from the water table into the Tiber River.

Because the ventilation was poor in most homes, people cooked out of doors when the weather permitted. Bread ovens have been found both inside and outside of homes. Every home needed an oven, especially since bread was typically baked weekly. Olive oil was stored in special clay jars. Frequently, cisterns were placed inside the open courtyard for water storage. Most people ate with their fingers, while the rich had gold and silver tableware.

Often the homes in Palestine had flat roofs with exterior stairways to the roof. Stairs were usually stone or brick, placed against an outer wall or the wall of the courtyard. Sometimes they were built inside (Mk 13:15). Residents would go up to the roof for privacy and to seek cooler temperatures in warm weather. Roofs were more often framed with wood beams with smaller cross members. They were then covered with small branches or straw, then with clay. Houses in villages of Jesus' boyhood generally were one story, with stairs leading to a flat roof.

In the cities and walled towns of Palestine and elsewhere, houses were built wall to wall. Any open courts lay within the exterior walls and had rooms opening off of them. City walls commonly served as the rear house wall of

homes. One excavated block of houses, surrounded by stree
contained four family units, all facing a common inner courtyard
averaged five persons, as seems likely, the people in that block w
hard-pressed to find any privacy.

With the Hellenistic era, the Middle Eastern city was introduced to more
systematic city planning. Houses became more regular in shape, rectangular,
or even square. Homes of the wealthy added bathrooms with plumbing. Jericho
by New Testament times had become a garden paradise with public baths and
fine homes (Lk 19:1-10). The homes of the wealthy in Roman Palestine were
similar to private homes in Italy, surrounded by a privacy wall, with a covered
atrium or hall and surrounding rooms, behind which was an open courtyard
with surrounding rooms. All this afforded great privacy from urban neighbors
only a few feet away.

## Paul and the City

Paul depended on the city for his livelihood. He reminds the churches several
times that he works with his hands, either to defend himself from charges of
freeloading or as an object lesson. Life as an artisan distinguished him both
from farm workers at the bottom of the social pyramid and from the few at the
top whose wealth depended on their large estates. Even when he constructs a
metaphor of olive trees or gardens, Paul evokes more the schoolroom than the
farm. When Paul lists the places where he has suffered, he divides the world
into city, wilderness and sea (2 Cor 11:26). He does not mention the settled
countryside. Because Paul's world consisted only of cities, he could tell the
Roman Christians that he had "fully preached" the Gospel from Jerusalem to
Illyricum, and others had done the work in Rome (Rom 15:19, 23). Paul had
planted small groups of Christians in some of the strategic cities of the northeast
Mediterranean. The mission of the Pauline circle clearly was conceived from
start to finish as an urban movement.

Even Paul's recollection that after his conversion he abandoned the city for
Arabia fits with this portrayal (Gal 1:15-17). "Arabia" refers not to sandy desert
but to the Nabataean kingdom and its cities. After all, Paul did not stir up the
hostility that led to an attempted arrest in Damascus by roaming the desert
(2 Cor 11:32). He must have been preaching in the flourishing Hellenistic cities
of Arabia, such as Petra, Gerasa, Philadelphia and Bostra. Our sources do not
tell us about the effectiveness of Paul's three years here.

Before Paul's conversion, followers of Jesus had carried their message to
Greco-Roman cities such as Damascus. More important, the movement had
been planted in Syrian Antioch, and there Hellenistic Jews first made converts

among the Gentiles (Acts 11:19-26). After Paul's escape from Damascus (2 Cor 11:32), and a brief consultation with the leaders in Jerusalem (Gal 1:18-21), Antioch became the center of his activities. It continued so for most of the twelve to fourteen years that he spent in "the regions of Syria and Cilicia."[12]

Antioch, the center of political, military and commercial communication between Rome and the Persian frontier and between Palestine and Asia Minor, was one of the three or four most important cities of the Empire and the home of a large Jewish community. In Antioch Paul served his apprenticeship as the fellow worker of Barnabas and others. Also in this city, controversy between Jews and Gentiles first erupted within the church. Thus, within a decade of the crucifixion of Jesus, the village culture of Palestine was left behind, and the Greco-Roman city had become the dominant environment of the movement. In so doing, it had crossed the most fundamental division in the society of the Empire, that between rural folk and city folk.

### For Further Reading

Jones, A. H. M. *The Cities of the Eastern Roman Provinces.* 2nd ed. Oxford: Clarendon, 1971.

Millar, Fergus. *The Roman Near East: 31 B.C.-A.D. 337.* Cambridge, Mass.: Harvard University Press, 1993.

Stambaugh, John E. *The Ancient Roman City.* Baltimore: Johns Hopkins University Press, 1988.

# Chapter 4

# Influences
# on Christian
# Organization

*The sum total of their guilt or error amounted to no more than this:*
*they had met regularly before dawn on a fixed day to*
*chant verses alternately amongst themselves in honor of Christ*
*as if to a god, and also to bind themselves by oath, not for any criminal purpose,*
*but to abstain from theft, robbery, and adultery, to commit no breach of trust*
*and not to deny a deposit when called upon to restore it.*
*After this ceremony it had been their custom to disperse and reassemble*
*later to take food of an ordinary, harmless kind;*
*but they had in fact given up this practice since my edict,*
*issued on your instructions, which banned all political societies.*
LETTER FROM PLINY THE YOUNGER TO TRAJAN1

*If people assemble for a common purpose, whatever name we give them*
*and for whatever reason, they soon turn into a political club.*
LETTER FROM TRAJAN TO PLINY THE YOUNGER2

*Greet Priscilla and Aquila, my fellow workers in Christ Jesus. . . .*
*Greet also the church that meets at their house.*
ROMANS 16:4-5

*Give my greetings to the brothers at Laodicea,*
*and to Nympha and the church in her house.*
COLOSSIANS 4:15

CHRISTIANS TODAY OFTEN TALK ABOUT RETURNING TO THE NEW TES-tament model of an organization. But the New Testament has little to say about the organization of the church. The Gospels record very few comments by Jesus on the subject, beyond acknowledging its existence, the need for leaders and its mission to spread the message. The Epistles give only the outlines of a model for how Christians are to meet, organize and appoint leaders. How then did the churches develop forms of organization? It appears that the churches borrowed from the society models that they considered compatible with their identity as Christians. It makes sense that, in putting together an organization from scratch, the early Christians would use and modify forms with which they were familiar. Using forms of organization from the larger society, at least superficially, had another benefit: it made them less conspicuous in a society that did not recognize their right to meet. But we must consider whether and to what degree the use of these forms affected Christianity itself. This chapter looks at how Christians used and modified two societal structures: the voluntary association and the household.

*Synagogue in Influence* The first Christians were Jewish converts and Gentiles originally attracted to Judaism. So it should not be surprising that some forms from the synagogue show up in the early churches. Like the synagogues, the early churches were overseen by elders. Their meetings included the reading of Scripture, prayer and singing. Visiting teachers were invited to address the group. Like the synagogues, the Christian churches provided a place of belonging and a place for newcomers to a city to make contacts. In cities where multiple congregations existed, the churches, like the synagogues, cooperated with one another in a variety of ways. Of course, the churches added special practices such as Communion and baptism.

The synagogue was not the only model that influenced early Christians. They also saw themselves as a household and met in homes. We should not be surprised if the organization of their churches was influenced by the home setting, as often is the case with modern house churches. Since the household in Roman times differed considerably from ours, it is useful to investigate its nature. The latter part of this chapter will describe how the household model affected the way many early Christians understood the nature of their churches.

But Christianity faced challenges that neither the synagogue nor the household model could address. As long as local authorities saw the earliest churches as part of the Jewish religion, they left them alone since Judaism was a licensed religion of the Empire and its adherents were allowed to organize synagogues. But when, in the late first or early second century, Rome realized that Christianity was a separate religion, the churches had to find a different way to congregate legally. They found it in the Roman voluntary association.

## Voluntary Associations

For three centuries Christians were unable to meet and worship freely because Christianity was not recognized by the Romans as a legal religion. Except in rare cases, the Romans did not attempt to hunt down Christians and prevent them from meeting. But Romans were nervous about unsanctioned organizations, fearing that they could be politically subversive. The second quote at the beginning of this chapter is from an early second-century letter written by the Roman emperor Trajan to his governor in the province of Bythinia, Pliny the Younger. It replies to nothing more sinister than Pliny's request to form a volunteer fire brigade in the town of Nicomedia. Trajan instructs Pliny instead to buy fire-fighting equipment, then to enlist the help of the crowd that forms to watch the fire. The suspicion apparent in this quote that private groups, even when formed legally, tend to become politically subversive, could easily have focused on Christian congregations.

Despite this, the Christians did meet, and did so regularly. Somehow they managed to escape the notice of the authorities most of the time. One way they did this was to register as one of the kinds of associations allowed by Rome. This way they could legally meet, with the knowledge of the authorities and without scurrying around in the dead of night. At the end of this section, we will consider whether such legal "cover" led these groups to adopt the forms and procedures of pagan voluntary associations. Contrary to popular thinking, the Christians in Rome did not escape detection by holding services in the catacombs, their underground cemeteries. These catacombs were public knowledge, they had no large assembly areas, and the odor could not have been tolerated for long.

The Romans used voluntary associations (*collegia*) as a way to exercise some control over gatherings of persons within the Empire. The associations organized for a variety of reasons, but most of the clubs were religious associations organized around the worship of a specific deity. As the name implies, persons voluntarily joined these groups. The Romans neither encouraged nor discouraged membership in an association. They allowed the groups to meet freely, to collect funds and to hold various rituals, but they prohibited the clubs from undertaking any kind of political activity.

Modern Americans often sense these same needs and try to meet them in a variety of organizations. Modern benevolent societies, such as the Elks or the Moose, bear similarities to the ancient voluntary association.

Voluntary associations made it possible for foreigners and members of the lower classes to follow a social life better adapted to their tastes and social conditions. They also gave people an alternative to the social exclusion practiced by the larger society. This kind of society might well recommend itself to Christians. After all, these were people who came from humble origins for the most part, and whose beliefs and practices would make them feel excluded from the larger society. By the New Testament era, the Romans allowed only four types of voluntary associations: professional, religious, burial and household.

Figure 4.1. A Christian burial alcove in the Catacomb of Domitilla, outside Rome, Italy

*Professional associations.* Professional or trade associations were composed of merchants or artisans of a common trade, such as shippers, porters, warehouse workers, bakers, merchants of livestock or carpenters. Some of these clubs had considerable money and influence. While they rarely tried to exert political or economic pressure, they did on occasion use their influence to protect their economic interests. A famous example of this is the protest raised in Ephesus by makers of images of the city's patron deity, Artemis, against the apostle Paul's proclamation of a new God (Acts 19). But we must not confuse trade associations with modern labor unions. They did not conduct strikes, and they did not attempt to control wages or press for better working conditions. Instead, they formed associations simply to pursue honor among their peers.

Professional association members often worked near one another since those with the same trade or profession typically worked on the same street. For example, a trade association in Thessalonica was called the "Purple-Dyers of Eighteenth Street." An association might choose as its patron a government official who could defend the interests of the trade. With the attention that they commanded, the members of a professional association might be given their own seats in the amphitheater, or have their association's festival days put on the official city calendar.

We have no evidence that Christians formed professional associations. However, Christians who pursued the same trade might connect with one another through the synagogue or church, as Paul apparently did with fellow tentmakers Priscilla and Aquila in Corinth (Acts 18:2).

*Religious associations.* Religious associations were organized around the worship of a specific deity. This type of association was quite popular among foreigners since it gave them a chance to worship freely the god or goddess of their homeland. They could follow their ancestral religious practices and provide for their own eventual burial. Freedmen and slaves often joined the religious associations of foreigners, and in this way maintained contact with free fellow expatriates. Modern, quasireligious groups like the Masons are more like some Roman religious associations than are modern churches, in that some associations were more of a social group with religious trappings.

Judaism had been a recognized religion within Rome since the time of Julius Caesar. Because of this, Jews could easily organize synagogues as religious associations. The earliest Christian churches seem to have been regarded as part of Judaism by the Roman authorities, allowing Christians to meet at first without registering as a separate association. In the late first or early second century, it began to be clear to Rome that Christianity was a distinct religion. Nero's persecution of Christians shows that, at least in the city of Rome, the authorities knew this by 64. But this may have been an unusual case. The Edict of Claudius banished Jews from Rome in 49, leaving Gentile Christians without the "cover" of Judaism for some years (Acts 18:2). This may have accelerated the process of differentiation in Rome. It is likely that this process took longer elsewhere.

At times groups with some natural social affinity such as wool workers or veterans, who didn't have their own professional association, would set up a religious one. By adopting a patron deity they took advantage of a loophole in the law and registered themselves as a club whose primary purpose was religious, even though the social pleasures of the monthly meetings were probably more important to most members.[3]

Since only legally recognized religions could form religious associations, Romans would not have allowed Christian congregations to organize in this manner. In some ways American society exhibits a similar attitude toward religion. The American legal system has more than once rejected the claims of a group to be a religion deserving tax-exempt status, ruling that it was not a legitimate religion but a ruse to avoid paying taxes. Of course, the Romans had different criteria for determining legitimacy (see chapter five), with the result that they found Christianity as distasteful as Americans today would find a "religion" featuring ritual sacrifice of dogs or cats.

*Burial associations.* Burial associations were composed of poor people seeking a way to provide themselves with a decent burial. The poor, including freed slaves or slaves without wealthy patrons or owners, were no different from other members of Roman society in their desire for a proper burial. But without help they faced dishonorable burial in a common grave pit. These associations arose in the city of Rome in the first century A.D. At first they were cooperative societies rather than formal *collegia.* They did not need the state's approval to organize, as did other associations, but they had to submit a list of members before the city prefect would allow them to meet.

The photographs in this chapter come from the Catacomb of Domitilla, an underground burial site just outside Rome to the south. It began as a pagan burial site, but in the second or third century it became a Christian burial site and continued in use into the fourth century. Domitilla was an aristocrat of the first century exiled by her relative, the emperor Domitian. She may have been a Christian or at least a sympathizer with Christianity who allowed Christians in her household to use her land for burial.[4]

Members of a burial association paid an initiation fee and a small monthly membership fee. Each member could then count on an honorable funeral, with the surviving members present to provide an appropriate procession outside the walls to a simple grave among tombs owned by the organization. The regular meetings provided significant social contact. Documents of such clubs show that alongside the freeborn members were freedmen and slaves and that the monthly dinners were high-spirited affairs. Some of the restrictions imposed on these meetings are similar to Paul's criticisms of the worship of the Corinthians (1 Cor 11). Under the Flavian emperors, these cooperatives gradually were replaced by associations organized by and for poor residents of Rome.

A passage in Romans suggests that the early Christian congregations, at least those in Rome, acted as burial associations. In Romans 14:7-10, Paul gives us what appears to be a liturgy for use in Christian burial: "whether we live or whether we die, we are the Lord's." Paul could be using this because he knew it was familiar to his Roman Christian addressees.

We know that Christian churches were officially organizing as burial associations by the third century. Christian writers, such as Tertullian, argued that Christians should not be persecuted since they had organized as legal burial associations entitled to assemble. Tertullian says that the Christian groups follow the law for such groups: they require a monthly contribution from each member, and they eat a common meal together (*Apology* 38-39).[5]

*Household associations.* Freedmen and slaves of the same household sometimes formed household associations. Their members might have little in common other than their relationship to a common master or patron. Unlike other associations, they were part of their common master's household and met on his or her property. Greeks and peoples from the Hellenized East predominated in these associations, according to the inscriptions. Household associations were common in the time of Augustus. Our sources do not make clear whether they needed formal approval by the state. The Christian congregations identified with households in the New Testament, for example in Romans 16, may have organized as household associations.

### Characteristics of Associations

Associations admitted members by election or by recommendation of an admissions committee. Officers elected from among the members performed a variety of tasks, including overseeing regular meetings. In all, the associations were microcosms of the community, and through their various offices and events provided members with the opportunity to gain status and recognition. In a similar way, Christians who felt alienated from the larger society looked to the church for a sense of belonging and esteem. The concept of membership also might have appealed to the early Christian congregations, which needed some mechanism for determining who could join the group and who would lead it. Those who advocate church membership today may see the New Testament-era voluntary association as a precedent, but they must remember that such membership was required by the legal stipulations of such societies, not necessarily by the theology of the early church.

Associations also hosted regular banquets. The collection of membership dues let them stage banquets in imitation of the wealthy in a style individual members otherwise could never afford. These banquets were given in honor of the patron deity of the group, but often were not primarily a religious observance. This is similar to the *agape* feast of some early Christians, as described by Paul in 1 Corinthians 11:20-34, including both a common meal and a celebration of Communion. As associations, the churches could legally collect funds from their members, as Paul describes in 1 Corinthians 16:1-2.

Small associations met in an area of a public temple, in a rented hall or in a private house. Corner cafes might serve as informal clubs for the poorer groups. If they could afford it, groups built their own meeting places since Roman law allowed voluntary associations to own property. Such places normally included a small temple dedicated to the group's patron divinity, an open courtyard for meetings, dining rooms for the common meals, a kitchen and service rooms. Based on archaeological evidence, the early Christians met in homes and in buildings provided by a patron or rented by the group. The earliest building that we know to have been renovated specifically to house a church, the so-called meeting house at Dura-Europos, dates to 240.

In fact, many Christian churches owned property by the third century. They

**Figure 4.2. A corridor lined with burial niches in the Christian Catacomb of Domitilla, outside Rome, Italy**

did so either as voluntary associations or in the name of individual Christians. A Christian church in the third century bought or rented a public place for its meetings. When a group of tavern owners tried to claim the space, the emperor Alexander Severus ruled that it was better for the place to be used by a religious group, no matter what god it worshiped.[6]

## Patronage of Associations

Most of these societies depended on donations from one or several wealthy benefactors, or patrons, to supplement their modest dues. Patrons might host a banquet or build a meeting place. The burial associations depended more than other groups on the contributions of a sponsor, since most of their members were poor. But a group's income came from a variety of sources: contributions from members, proceeds from fines levied on members who disobeyed the rules, gifts of patrons and benefactors, and return on the group's investments. Besides the meeting room and banquets, the group spent its resources on funerals for members, sacrifices and gifts to patrons.

Christian congregations also benefited from patrons. Stephanas seems to have been patron of the congregation in Corinth (1 Cor 16:15-18). At Cenchrea, Phoebe is called a *diakonos* (servant or deacon[ess]) and a *prostatis* (Rom 16:1-2). The latter term probably means "patron."[7] Perhaps Lydia served as the patron of the first congregation in Philippi (Acts 16:14-15). The association would reward its patron with inscriptions, honorary titles and a statue and allow him or her to dominate the club. But the Christian congregations often prevented a patron from taking control. In fact, Paul advised the congregation in Corinth to show a little more respect for Stephanas (1 Cor 16:15-18).[8]

## Voluntary Associations and Christian Congregations

Some scholars think that the early Christian congregations not only organized as associations, but also to some degree modeled themselves on them. Like the congregations, membership in associations was a free decision. Associations also had a more or less important place for rituals and cultic activities and engaged in common meals and other fraternal activities. Providing a proper burial and commemoration of the deceased was an important function of many associations. The New Testament does not tell us about the funeral practices of early Christians, but later practice suggests that they placed high importance on honorable burial.[9]

However, Christian congregations differed from voluntary associations in several ways. They demanded far more loyalty from members. Baptism into Jesus Christ meant a total resocialization, in which loyalty to the Christian group was supposed to replace every other loyalty. The only parallel in that era was conversion to Judaism.[10]

The Christian congregations were more inclusive socially than the typical voluntary association. Associations often included men and women. They also may have included freeborn, freedmen and slaves, but they rarely exhibited the equality of roles that we see in the early churches. Christian congregations also had an unusual sense of connectedness. Most voluntary associations, outside of the Jewish synagogues, had little or no contact with similar groups, but the Christian congregations believed they were connected to a worldwide society of like-minded believers.[11]

Despite using the voluntary association as a legal cover, the congregations appear not to have modeled themselves on the associations to any meaningful degree. We find virtually no terminology from associations in the New Testament. For example, Paul does not use the terms for leaders used by associations. The chief officer in an association was called a *magister* (Latin) or *archon* (Greek). Other officials included treasurers, secretaries, legal officers, priests and stewards. The terms that Paul uses for his congregations, such as "ecclesia," "the holy ones," "the elect," and "the beloved of God," do not appear among the titles used by associations. The only term Paul uses that may have been borrowed is *episkopos* ("overseer" or "bishop"; Phil 1:1), a term that appears for officers in voluntary associations.[12] This lack of influence suggests the strength of identity in the early churches.

### Household and Congregation

Present-day Christians often speak of the church as the "family of God." Frequently they use terms based in the family, such as *brother, spiritual father* and *mother church*. How much influence did ancient concepts of the family have on the early churches?

The life of the church as depicted in the New Testament occurs in homes. After Jesus' ascension, the disciples assemble in an "upper room" (Acts 1:13), in the same "house" (Acts 2:2) where Matthias is chosen to replace Judas and where Pentecost occurs. When Peter is released from prison, he goes to the house of Mary, the mother of John Mark, which was a congregational meeting place (Acts 12:12). This may have been a household of Hellenized Jews (as opposed to Palestinian Jews) since the apostle James is not there (Acts 12:17).

The Christians in Jerusalem met in various houses (Acts 2:46) where they heard the apostles teach (Acts 2:42). Some sold their homes and gave the money to the apostles, who gave it in turn to those in need (Acts 4:34-35). Before his conversion, Saul entered "house after house" and dragged Christians to prison

(Acts 8:3). Both as convert and as missionary, Paul accepted hospitality in the house of Judas in Damascus (Acts 9:10-12, 17), from Jason's household in Thessalonica (Acts 17:5), from various houses in Ephesus (Acts 20:17-20) and another in Troas (Acts 20:5-8), from Philip in Caesarea (Acts 21:8), and from Mnason's household in Jerusalem (Acts 21:15-17). Paul lived in his own rented house at Rome (Acts 28:30).

Clearly the household was a major setting of the life of the early church. But its importance was greater than simply that of a convenient place to meet. The groups meeting in households were the basic cells of the early Christian movement. A congregation might form around the nucleus of a familial house-hold. In fact, some New Testament texts mention the conversion of entire households (Acts 11:14; 16:15, 31-34; 18:8). This would include all relatives within the household, as well as other persons connected to it such as slaves and freedmen. Other believers would join that church because they shared something in common (such as occupation or ethnicity) with the original household's members. They also might join because they were converted by members of the household.

A church might form around a household whose members had not all converted. For example, the slave Onesimus converted only after he ran away from his Christian master, Philemon (Philem 10). In some cases, the head of the household seems not to have been a believer (1 Pet 2:18; 3:1). For example, when Paul greets those "who belong to the household of Aristobulus," but not Aristobulus himself, he seems to be talking to slaves or freedmen belonging to Aristobulus who had formed a church within his household, but without his participation (Rom 16:10). Writing from Ephesus, Paul sends greetings from Aquila and Prisca "together with the church in their house" to the church in Corinth (1 Cor 16:19). Three other passages use a similar formula (Rom 16:3; Philem 2; Col 4:15). Paul has baptized the "house of Stephanas" in Corinth (1 Cor 1:16; cf. 16:15-16). The Christians mentioned in Romans 16:14-15 may well be members of three household congregations.[13]

Placing the church within the household structure was more significant than it might seem. The house gave Christian meetings a sense of privacy and intimacy. It provided a place to cook and eat the common meal as well. Its space was limited, of course; even the homes of wealthy benefactors probably would not have accommodated comfortably more than fifty persons. Congregations in smaller homes likely were closer to ten or twenty members. Thus, as Christianity grew, it would have to expand to numerous house churches. This resulted at times in the development of factions within the larger church of a city. It is likely that the factions addressed by Paul in 1 Corinthians 1—4 were based in different households.

The early Christian congregations met in homes, but to what degree were they influenced by the model of the Greco-Roman household? The nature of Greek and Roman families is presented at length in chapter eleven. For purposes of answering this question, it will suffice to summarize several key points about families in the New Testament period.

The first-century household among the Greeks and Romans was defined in terms of the head of the family. The oldest male in the blood line of the family, was called the *paterfamilias* by the Romans. Every living thing over which he held authority was part of the household: relatives by blood, women who married blood relatives, slaves, former slaves, even livestock. A number of laws protected and maintained the position of the father and husband.[14]

The size of the family varied considerably. In terms of children, high infant and childhood mortality rates meant that a woman had to give birth to five children in order to see two grow to adulthood. Evidence from the era suggests that the average family would have consisted of two to three children at a given time. Not all families could afford slaves, and those who could typically owned only one or two.

The head of the family in all ancient Mediterranean societies, to our knowledge, exercised very strong control over his wife and children. The Roman family head *(paterfamilias)* controlled all the finances of the home. His wife might give him advice, but all family decisions were his to make. He decided whether he would rear a child born to his wife, how his children would be educated and who they would marry.

Any slaves attached to the family were owned by him alone. Thus he had the legal right to make any decisions involving them. A slave freed by him still owed him certain duties. The new freedman became the client of his former master, who now was regarded as his patron. A client owed certain debts of duty and honor to a patron, as I explain elsewhere. Thus, the head of the family united the members of the family in his roles as husband, father, master and patron.

Women in Greco-Roman families generally ran the domestic area of the household, subject to the approval of their husbands. They oversaw the domestic slaves and other workers, as well as the nurture and education of their children. Both Greeks and Romans believed in the inherent superiority of men. They both believed that women lacked men's capacity to resist sexual temptation and thus needed to be protected. The Greek ideal was to seclude women within the home, allowing them out in public only at certain times and under the watchful eyes of male family members. At the center of the traditional Greek home were the women's quarters, which were off limits to male visitors and even to some male members of the family. By contrast, the Romans allowed women to join them in public events, such as dinner parties, but they kept a close eye in particular on the unmarried young women.

Families were extended in terms of authority but often nuclear in terms of living arrangements. That is, frequently adult sons lived in homes separate from (but often near) their parents. Nevertheless, the father maintained power over his adult sons until his death. In Roman families, he legally owned everything possessed by any member of his family, even his adult sons. But these extended families typically did not span many generations. Evidence from burial inscriptions indicates that families with three generations of living members were rare; most Romans apparently did not live to see their grandchildren grow up.

## Authority and the Congregations

One would expect a Christian congregation that modeled itself on the Roman household to have authority structures. It should be controlled by an individual male patron. Like a nuclear family under the control of a *paterfamilias* elsewhere,  it should submit itself to the authority of someone else at a higher level. It should have no place for participation by the members of the congregation in decisions. A Christian congregation following this model should also exhibit certain attitudes about the various members of the group. It should make clear distinctions between men and women, and between slave and free. Slaves in particular should be second-class citizens within the congregation. Let us see how closely the early churches fulfilled these expectations.

In terms of authority, the early Christian churches accepted strong lines of authority both within each congregation and from the outside. It appears that frequently a household congregation's patron was also among its spiritual leaders. We should not be surprised if persons who formed a house church from those they had converted became the recognized spiritual leaders of the new church. In addition, the head of a household understandably would exercise some authority over the Christian group in his home and would have some legal responsibility for it. In some cases, the host of a house church was its financial patron. It was natural for wealthier Christians, who possessed larger homes and greater resources, to host house churches. Examples of Christians as both patrons and leaders include Lydia in Philippi (Acts 16:14-15) and Prisca and Aquila in Rome, Corinth and Ephesus (Rom 16; Acts 18).

However, in contrast to the Greco-Roman patronage model, the New Testament establishes no connection between financial patronage and congregational authority. Those who contributed to the group's financial support were

*They spll dol.*

not thereby entitled to a place of leadership in the group. Undoubtedly, churches at times experienced conflict when a patron felt entitled to lead even if he or she was not a recognized spiritual leader of the church, but the New Testament never endorses such a feeling.

In terms of authority outside of the congregation, the churches see themselves as part of a larger household, the "household of God." The New Testament presents Jesus Christ as the "head" of the church (Eph 1:22; Col 1:18), and the "cornerstone" of the household of God (Eph 2:19-20). This establishes the principle that every Christian household congregation is under the authority of a single spiritual *paterfamilias*, Jesus Christ. Did this transfer to human leaders? The cities mentioned in the New Testament contained multiple assemblies meeting in different households, which appear to have cooperated with one another from the beginning. We see in Corinth, for example, the household of Stephanus, the temporary household of Aquila and Prisca, that of Titius Justus, and of Crispus, whose whole household converted (1 Cor 1:16; Acts 18:2, 7, 8). Gaius probably also hosted a congregation in addition to being, or before he became, "host . . . to the whole church" (Rom 16:23).[15] Romans 16 refers to at least three congregations in Rome.

Paul and others in the New Testament gave numerous instructions to the churches, which they appear not to have challenged (although they clearly did not always follow them precisely). By the late second century, the congregations throughout the Empire came to accept the authority of one bishop over all of the churches in a given city. Unlike the Greco-Roman family, the members of Christian congregations participated to some degree in decisions made by their leaders. For example, Paul tells an entire congregation to expel an unrepentant sinner (1 Cor 5:5) and to keep away from backsliders (2 Thess 3:6, 14-15). In addition, the Epistles are nearly all addressed to the general members of congregations, not to its leaders. The instructions within them are, with few exceptions, addressed to the average Christian.

### Member Relations in the Congregations

Some New Testament congregations did make distinctions along class lines, as we can see from the New Testament passages that decry this practice. For example, James condemns those Christians who give more honor to the wealthy visitor than the poor one: "But you have insulted the poor. Is it not the rich who are exploiting you?" (Jas 2:6). Paul criticizes the Corinthian Christians for allowing inequities in their agape feasts: some eat very well, while others go hungry. He asks, "Or do you despise the church of God and humiliate those who have nothing?" (1 Cor 11:22). Such practices continued over time. The

Christian writer Hermas, in the early second century, rebukes the wealthy members of the Roman church for preferring the company of rich pagans to that of poor Christians. Hermas says that they feared the Christians would ask them for a loan. We do not know how common such practices were, but clearly some churches struggled with class discrimination.

The early congregations also made gender distinctions, despite a belief that *gender* men and women have equal position in Christ. Paul's statement in Galatians 3:28 establishes a standard unique for the time: "There is neither Jew nor Greek, slave nor free, male nor female, for you are all one in Christ Jesus." The sense is that all have the same standing before God; all have the same relationship with Christ. This flatly contradicts assumptions in Greco-Roman society that some persons were by nature superior to others. The New Testament clearly makes distinctions between men and women, as noted in the last chapter, whether these were meant to be universal or limited to a certain circumstance.

Such distinctions permeated all ancient institutions. The synagogues clearly made distinctions on the basis of gender. So while we cannot conclude that the Greco-Roman family model brought such discrimination into the church, it probably encouraged the temptation to fall back into patterns of behavior that people in that day had accepted from childhood, long before they became Christians.

A study of the Christian congregations in the city of Rome indicates that at least some churches organized along ethnic lines. Does this mean that the churches made the kind of distinctions we see in Greco-Roman households?

Romans 16 mentions at least three house churches. The first is "the church in [the] house" of Prisca and Aquila (Rom 16:3-5). Since its leaders were Jewish (Acts 18), it likely was a house church of Jewish Christians. The second is the house congregation that included "Asyncritus, Phlegon, Hermes, Patrobas, Hermas, and the brothren who are with them" (Rom 16:14). All of these names are Greek; none of them is Jewish. Three were common to the Hellenized East, and three were common slave names in Rome. The third house congregation is that of "Philologos, Julia, Nereus and his sister, and Olympas, and all the saints who are with them" (Rom 16:15). Julia is a Latin name; the rest are Greek. Julia most likely was a Greek slave who took a Latin name upon manumission. Philologos and Nereus were common slave names in Rome. That Nereus knew who his sister was suggests that he and his sister were descendants of freed slaves; they probably would have been separated if they had been born into slavery. Thus, the first of these three congregations was predominately Jewish, while the other two were composed largely of Greek-speaking Gentiles who were slaves or former slaves. Two other house churches may be addressed in verses 10 and 11, which refer to "those who belong to the [household of] Aristobulus" and "those in the Lord who belong to the [household] of Narcissus." These slaves or freedmen may have formed their own household congregations.

We do not know how common this was, but organization along ethnic lines is not surprising when one considers that ethnic groups in the cities tended to live in certain quarters of the town. For example, the Jews tended to settle in certain areas of Rome, particularly along the Tiber river just across from the heart of Rome. Christians would naturally join congregations geographically close to them.

### Member Relations and Christian Household Rules

Codes of household behavior, or household rules, appear in many places in the literature of the ancient world. These codes tell us a lot about how ancient authors thought the family should function (see the more complete discussion in chapter eleven). Like the pagan codes, the early Christian household codes usually defined relationships between members of individual households, not relationships between members of a house church, but these rules for governing a household likely would have been adapted to become moral instruction for the church (Col 3:18—4:1; Eph 5:21—6:9; 1 Pet 2:13-21; 3:1-7; 1 Tim 2:1—6:2; Tit 2:1-10). Thus, we need to examine them to see if and how the early Christians might have used Greco-Roman household models to define authority and relationships within the church.

Codes of behavior written by Romans usually were addressed to the head of the household only. Women, children, and slaves normally were addressed in the third person. By contrast, the New Testament passages listed above address wives, husbands, children, fathers, slaves and masters in the second person.[16] This suggests a recognition of the basic equality of various classes of humans before God, even as it lays out specific roles for them. By analogy, it suggests equality among the members of the Christian congregation, regardless of position, race, gender or status. Such a belief is in harmony with Paul's emphasis on the basic equality of members of the body of Christ although they may perform different functions (1 Cor 12).

The Greek philosopher Aristotle described the household as consisting of three lines of authority, all controlled by the same man: husband to wife, father to children and master to slave (*Politics* 1.3).The Romans had a similar view. They disputed the ability of any but a free man to make decisions, as Arius Didymus wrote in describing the emperor Augustus's position that "a man has the rule of this household by nature, for the deliberative faculty in a woman is inferior, in children it does not yet exist, and in the case of slaves, it is completely absent."[17] The household codes in the New Testament passages above seem to follow the same three areas of submission and obligation: wives to husbands, children to parents and slaves to masters.[18] But on closer examination, we see important differences.

Aristotle says that the husband's rule over the wife is like an aristocracy, because he is more capable to rule and thus superior to her. But the husband still gives her areas to control within her ability (*Nicomachaean Ethics* 8.10). He also says that "the male is by nature fitter for command than the female" (*Politics* 1.12). By contrast, the New Testament passages above do not assert that the husband is in any way superior to his wife or more capable of making decisions; rather they say that God has put him in this position.[19]

Aristotle says that the father's rule over his child is like a monarchy, because he is concerned for the welfare of the child, not about how the child can benefit him (*Nicomachaean Ethics* 8.10). The New Testament tells children to obey their parents, in the spirit of Old Testament injunctions to obedience (e.g., Ex 20:12, quoted in Eph 6:2-3) rather than in keeping with the philosophy of Aristotle.

Aristotle believes that the master's rule over a slave is like a tyranny, since the purpose of the relationship is strictly the benefit of the master (*Nicomachaean Ethics* 8.10). He also says that "a slave is a living possession" (*Politics* 1.4). The New Testament household passages say that Christian masters should treat their slaves humanely, acknowledging that they share the same ultimate Master. They never suggest or imply that a slave may be seen as a possession. While Aristotle seeks to justify slavery (*Politics* 1.5), the New Testament does not. The New Testament does not suggest that the master should be obeyed because he is more capable (either by nature or experience); rather a master should be obeyed because God commands it.

What do we learn from this chapter? The early Christian congregations found value in borrowing from both voluntary associations and Greco-Roman households, but the nature of the churches was not fundamentally changed as a result. The early congregations were more complex than the analogy of the household can reveal. For example, their religious practices borrowed little if any from the traditional domestic cults of Greek and Roman households. Concepts of authority that differed from the household model must have come from some other source, such as the synagogue. Although the models of the association and the household did not change the nature of the church, the former model helped the early Christians organize without interference from the authorities, and the latter helped them begin to work out how Christians would think of and relate to one another in the church.

## For Further Reading

Jeffers, James S. *Conflict at Rome: Social Order and Hierarchy in Early Christianity.* Minneapolis: Fortress, 1991.

Keener, Craig S. *Paul, Women and Wives: Marriage and Women's Ministry in the Letters of Paul.* Peabody, Mass.: Hendrickson, 1992.

Kloppenborg, John, and Stephen G. Wilson, eds. *Voluntary Associations.* London: Routledge, 1996.

Osiek, Carolyn, and David L. Balch. *Families in the New Testament World: Households and House Churches.* Louisville, Ky.: Westminster John Knox, 1997.

# Chapter 5

## Religion in the
## Greco-Roman World

*[The Jews] think it as great a crime to eat pork,*
*from which their parents abstained, as human flesh.*
*They get themselves circumcised, and look down on Roman law,*
*preferring instead to learn and honor and fear*
*the Jewish commandments, whatever was handed down by Moses*
*in that arcane tome of his. . . . But their fathers were the culprits;*
*they made every seventh day taboo*
*for all life's business, dedicated to idleness.*
JUVENAL *SATIRE* 14.98-106

*So Paul, standing in the middle of the Areopagus, said:*
*"Men of Athens, I perceive that in every way you are very religious.*
*For as I passed along, and observed the objects of your worship,*
*I found also an altar with this inscription,*
*'To an unknown god.' What therefore you worship as unknown,*
*this I proclaim to you."*
ACTS 17:22-23

**M**OST RESIDENTS OF THE ROMAN EMPIRE LOOKED AT RELIGION differently from the way most religious Americans do today. While Americans for the most part prefer to keep religion separate from the state, the ancients saw the state as inseparable from religion. Throughout their history, Americans have seen religion as a very private act between the individual and his or her God. By contrast, most ancients saw religion more as an expression of identification with an ethnic or geographic community. However, we should not make the mistake of concluding that, because their religion was more an external identification with a group than an individualized commitment, it was somehow less serious. The Romans on the whole took religion very seriously.

Because they accepted the existence of many gods, Romans usually were tolerant of other religions, even when they considered them distasteful. But they became intolerant, even repressive, when they feared that a religion threatened their way of life. Jews and Christians, as we shall see, generally benefited from this tolerance although they also suffered Roman repression.

### The Nature of Ancient Religion

Ancient religion began as a religion of farmers. It grew out of sacrifices and ceremonies invented to bless the fields. The ancients believed that they were surrounded and protected, or threatened, by many invisible powers. Their ceremonies either called upon the gods for help or kept them at bay.

The religions of the Greeks and Romans were contract religions based on mutual trust between gods and humankind. The original purpose of their religions apparently was to gain the cooperation of the gods. Thus, there arose a body of rules telling what had to be done or avoided in order to influence the gods for good. These rules were not a code of behavior, but governed the proper performance of rituals, such as how to say a blessing or sacrifice an animal. Greeks or Romans could believe whatever they liked, so long as they performed the rituals properly.

In essence prayer was an attempt to coerce the forces of nature. The prayer began with an invocation, a reminder of past benefits or a reference to the god's power to confer benefits. It then stated the request, almost always accompanied by a promise to do something for the god in return. Such promises ranged from a simple sacrifice or commemorative plaque to the building of a temple. Ritual dances and animal sacrifices often accompanied the traditional prayers. For example, the Roman who sought the gods' favor would for a time avoid taboo things such as strangers, corpses, newborns and places previously struck by lightning. In fact, the Romans were obsessed with performing the rituals in a certain, precise way. One wrong syllable or gesture could invalidate the prayer:

> The text for invoking a happy omen is different from that for averting an ill or that for making a request. The highest officials pray in fixed forms of words, and to make sure that not a word is omitted or spoken in the wrong place, a prompter reads the text before them, another person is appointed to watch over it, yet another to command silence, and the flute-player plays to mask all other sounds. (Pliny the Elder *Natural History* 23.10)

The contrast with early Christian worship, in which the leaders improvised prayers, avoided Roman repetition and focused more on instruction, would have been very clear to both Christians and pagans. However, we must be careful not to read modern forms of Christian worship back into the first century. The average early Christian certainly put more emphasis on identifying with the group, and less on individual preferences, than does the average American Christian.

**Figure 5.1. The Temple of Apollo, Corinth, Greece. Behind the temple but not visible is the Corinthian forum.**

The characteristic form of worship, public and private, was the sacrifice. Depending on the god and the occasion, it might be a bull or cow, a pig, a sheep, a bird, a special cake, or incense. An animal sacrifice was first stunned with a hammer; then its throat was slit. After its entrails were examined to make sure it was an acceptable offering, certain inedible parts were burned on the altar. The edible parts were usually cooked and eaten by the priests in a meal honoring the god. Leftovers were sent to local meat shops for sale. Since this was a major source of meat for these shops, the question of eating meat sacrificed to idols was an important one for Christians in a city with strong pagan religious activity, such as Corinth (1 Cor 10:25-31).

The Greek and Roman gods were worshiped mainly as defenders of empire, nation or city (see table 5.1 for a summary of the major Greek and Roman state gods and their functions). But individuals also at times expressed personal devotion to the gods and took seriously their obligations to them. This is not to say that all ancients sought to communicate directly with the gods of Rome. For example, among the Romans only the head of the family, the *paterfamilias*, performed the religious rituals of his family. *Pietas*, from which the English word piety comes, refers to the Romans' unqualified acceptance of their obligations to the gods, to the state and to their elders. Later authors celebrated Octavian's revenge on the murderers of Julius Caesar, his adoptive father, as an act of *pietas* to the glorified Caesar. Among the Greeks, the male head of the household similarly led the family's religious rituals.

By the time of Jesus and Paul, philosophers had long questioned the existence of the official gods. Political leaders, even the priests of these gods, were often motivated more by social and political goals than by personal religious belief. The common people of the Empire often were more interested in the local or minor deities of their areas than in the gods of the official state religion.

Before any important affair of state, whether a meeting of the popular assembly or an army's march to war, the Romans sought the will of the gods. Typically, they analyzed the flight of birds or examined animal entrails. An appearance of vultures was considered especially good luck. The official calendar was full of festivals to the gods. Instead of vacations or weekends, a Roman's work routine was broken up by periodic days or even weeks of religious observances. The Saturnalia festival, occurring in late December, celebrated the god Saturn, who represented the good times of the past that the celebrants hoped would return again. The Christian holiday of Christmas was instituted in later centuries, in part to take the place of this pagan festival.

**The Greek Gods**
As one would expect from the foregoing discussion, many of the Greek gods were agricultural in origin. For example, Zeus was a sky god who sent the rain; Demeter brought forth the grain from the earth; Dionysus caused the grapes to grow and the sap to flow in trees; Aphrodite was concerned with reproduction and fertility; Artemis was associated with the monthly cycle of the moon; local demigods were thought to inhabit rivers, trees and woods and to protect those who lived nearby. Other gods presided over more urban activities: Athena was connected with politics, war and industry; Hephaestus was god of the blacksmith and artisan; Hermes was the patron god of the merchant and messenger; and Ares was the sponsor of war. The stories about these gods depict them as very powerful, but subject to the failings of human nature. The early Christians saw these gods as spirits of the antichrist rather than as creatures of the true God (1 Cor 10:20-21; Rev 16:14; 18:2). Early Christian writers point out the

weakness in any theology based on the traditional myths and constantly
fun of the behavior of the gods in the old stories.

A popular Greek god in the time of Paul was Apollo, supposed son of Zeus,
whose cult centered in Delphi. Here, a priestess acting as oracle or mouthpiece
of the god had long made prophecies. Many temples had been and were being
built to Apollo in the time of Paul. People saw in Apollo a source of guidance
(see in figure 5.1 a photograph of the Temple of Apollo in Corinth).

| Roman | Greek | God/Goddess of |
|---|---|---|
| Jupiter | Zeus | sky (father of gods) |
| Juno | Hera | women |
| Minerva | Athena | crafts, war |
| Apollo | Apollo | youth, music, prophecy |
| Aesculapius | Asklepios | healing |
| Mars | Ares | war |
| Vesta | Hestia | hearth, household activities |
| Mercury | Hermes | shopkeepers, thieves, eloquence (messenger of the gods) |
| Ceres | Demeter | fertility, grain |
| Vulcan | Hephaestus | fire, smiths |
| Neptune | Poseidon | sea |
| Venus | Aphrodite | love |
| Diana | Artemis | woods (Roman), moon, women and slaves |
| Fortuna | Tyche | farming (Roman), good luck |
| Bacchus | Dionysus | wine, debauchery |
| Castor/Pollux | Castor/Pollux | sailors (twin gods) |

Table 5.1. The traditional gods and goddesses of the Greeks and the Romans

Asklepios, the god of healing, was also popular in the New Testament era.
Popular belief in miraculous healing helped spread this cult. The cult was
strongest in Epidavros, southeast of Corinth (see in figure 5.2 a photograph of
the amphitheater at Epidavros). Patients would sleep in the temple there in the
hope of receiving a vision that would tell them how to be cured. Many people
felt they were healed or greatly helped. Christians typically responded to such
claims by suggesting that any legitimate cures were performed by demons. The
amphitheater at Epidavros is one of the best-preserved examples of an ancient
Greek theater.

In classical Greek mythology, Artemis was the sister of Apollo, equated by
the Romans with Diana, the moon goddess, huntress and protector of woman-
hood. But the Artemis mentioned in Acts 19:23-40 has little in common with her
Greek namesake. She was really a Lydian mother-goddess, worshiped at the
mouth of the Cayster River long before the Greeks came to Ephesus. At Ephesus,

Artemis may have been a goddess of fertility. Her temple attendants included eunuch priests. Her image (Acts 19:35) probably was a meteorite. The silver shrines (Acts 19:24), as well as models of clay and marble, may have been replicas of her sanctuary. The temple of Artemis in Paul's day was one of the seven wonders of the world. Worship of the Ephesian Artemis extended into Greece, Gaul, Rome and Syria.

Hermes was the son of Zeus, half brother of Apollo. He was seen as the god of eloquence and the divine herald. This is why Paul was identified with him in Acts 14:12. As a master thief and trickster, and god of good luck, he was also the patron saint of traders and thieves. He is identified with the Roman god Mercury.

Zeus was the head of the Greek Olympian pantheon (Acts 14:12). His statue at Olympia was one of the seven wonders of the ancient world, and his temple at Athens was the largest in Greece. His worship was still widespread in New Testament times, with representations in art found at Tarsus and temples at Gerasa, Tannur and Salamis. Jupiter was the sky-god of the Latins, identified later with Zeus. He is mentioned in Acts 14:12-13 and 2 Maccabees 6:2.

Peoples in New Testament times could have very different conceptions of gods of the same name, and a missionary like Paul had to be sensitive to this. For example, in Athens Paul suggests a connection between the Christian God and Zeus when he applies to God a comment made about Zeus in Acts 17:28 (NRSV): "For we too are his offspring."[1] But he did not dare compare the Christian God to Zeus in the city of Lystra, perhaps because its residents looked too anthropomorphically at Zeus to make him a good point of connection with the Christian God. We see this in Acts, when the Lystrans proclaimed Barnabus as Zeus (Acts 14). These Lystrans may have been thinking of the story of the humans Baucis and Philemon, who reputedly entertained the gods Zeus and Hermes without knowing who they were and were richly rewarded (Ovid Metamorphoses 8.626-724).

**The Gods of Rome**
At first the Romans did not think of their gods as persons with histories and human passions, but Etruscan and Greek influence changed this. Once Rome came into contact with the Greek colonies of southern Italy, the Romans began fusing much of Greek religion with their own. But they never placed as much emphasis on the human aspects of the gods as the Greeks did. The Romans believed, as did most polytheists of the day, that there was always room for one more god. They were never sure that they had discovered all the gods that existed.

In Rome's early days, its principal deity was Numa. Gods specific to the household were popular in early Rome: the Genius, representing the life-blood of the family (and much later incorporated into the cult of the emperor); the Penates, or embodiment of the storehouse; Vesta, the spirit of the hearth; and Lar, the luck of the family. The *lares* were good spirits associated with certain localities and worshiped at crossroads. Caesar Augustus would later try to find legitimacy for his cult of emperor worship by linking it with the *lares*. Reverence for ancestors was a powerful force in Roman life. This involved the subordination of the individual to the family and to the society.

The most powerful deity among the peasants, and the first official Roman state god, was Jupiter, who threw thunderbolts from heaven. He later was identified with the Greek Zeus. A triad of gods was formed when Jupiter was joined by Juno, the protectress of women, and Minerva, the goddess of craftsmen. Later came Mars, the god of war and of hard labor, who eventually was identified with Ares, the Greek god of war. Saturn was a god of agriculture.

Vesta was goddess of the hearth, the combination fireplace/cooking area that formed the emotional center of an early Roman home. A vestige of this notion of the hearth as a home's center remains today in the saying, "keep the home fires burning." Vesta's temples (like those visible today in the Roman Forum) always were circular, probably in imitation of the round huts of the earliest Romans. Her cult was attended by the "Vestal virgins" and remained very important to Rome throughout its history.

Janus was the god of the door. As part of the state religion, the gates of the temple of Janus were formally closed when the state was at peace, open when Rome was at war. Ceres was the goddess of fertility, Mercury the protector of shopkeepers, and Vulcan the god of fire and smiths. The seas were ruled by Neptune.

Diana, originally an Italian goddess of the woods, came to be identified with the Greek Artemis, and became a special goddess of women and slaves. Fortuna, originally a goddess of farming, became the goddess of good luck once she was identified with the Greek goddess Tyche. The goddess of love, Aphrodite, was renamed Venus by the Romans after they borrowed her cult from the Greeks. Julius Caesar claimed her as an ancestor. Dozens of other minor deities were patrons of various occupations, regions, or families.

The twin brothers Castor and Pollux were the patron gods of sailors. The ship on which Paul sailed from Malta to Puteoli bore their insignia (Acts 28:11). Poseidon reputedly gave them power over winds and waves (see figure 5.3). Their temple at Rome stood next to the Basilica Julia in the Roman Forum.

**Mystery Religions**

The state religions of the Greeks and Romans proved unsatisfying for some. Those who longed for a sense of salvation, and for a more personal connection with a deity, often looked for them in the mystery religions. The mystery religions in Greece in fact attained the status of a public cult or state religion over time. These religions were just starting to become popular in the New Testament era. During the first century A.D., they were still relatively small, localized cults in various parts of the Empire (see below). By the third century, new cults merged many of the old mystery religions together, toned down some of their elements, and created cults with broader appeal and much larger followings.

Nearly every region of the Mediterranean world had its own mystery religion.[2] Although they had certain beliefs and practices in common, they were distinct religions. Central to them was how they used the annual plant cycle of sowing and reaping to symbolize a cycle of life, death and rebirth among humans. The concept of an afterlife, which was never very important for traditional Greek and Roman religions, was a significant element in mystery religions. In addition, secret ceremonies were central to mystery religions (hence the "mystery" element). Those who were initiated into the cult's secret rites were thereby bound to their fellow adherents. The initiates also learned the central secret of the group, typically involving how to achieve union with the cult's deity. Another common element of mystery religions was a myth telling how the deity had either defeated his or her enemies or returned to life after death. As the cult member shared in the god's triumph, he or she was redeemed from the earthly and temporal. The mystery religions had little use for doctrine or argumentation. Instead, and in addition to their desire for redemption, they emphasized the pursuit of a sense of oneness with their god and ultimately the attainment of immortality.

The religion of the Olympian gods had little impact on the average Greek peasant farmer. These gods, when they took an interest in human affairs, were depicted as being interested only in the affairs of great men or of nations. They had no interest in the common people. The mystery religions of Greece, which go back at least to 1500 B.C., appealed to such people.

The cult of Demeter was perhaps the oldest Greek mystery religion. In the myth, the god of the underworld kidnappped Persephone, daughter of Demeter, goddess of the soil. Demeter's absence in pursuit of them caused vegetation to stop growing. To prevent all humans from dying, Zeus allowed Demeter and Persephone to be reunited each year for a short time, thus allowing annual cycles of plant growth. The rites connected with this cult, the Eleusinian

Mysteries, were held each year in Eleusis near Athens.

The Orphic mystery religion of Greece began in Thrace as the orgiastic cult of Dionysus. It toned down the more savage elements of the earlier religion and added a sacred literature that offered salvation through personal purification and secret ceremonies. This religion was strongly dualist, teaching that the soul is imprisoned by the body and must be released from the body's corrupting influences. It espoused the belief that the soul can become purer through repeated reincarnations.

The cult of Isis originated in Egypt, but spread throughout the Empire as it changed nature. It started as a typical Near Eastern religion, in which Isis was the goddess of heaven, earth, sea and underworld and was assisted by her husband, Osiris. In some versions of the myth, Isis brings Osiris back to life after he is killed by his brother. When Alexander the Great's general Ptolemy took power in Egypt, c. 300 B.C., he changed the religion in order to bring together Egyptian and Greek beliefs and practices. He replaced Osiris with a new god, Serapis. The religion's elaborate rituals and emphasis on human immortality made it popular, and by the mid-first century A.D. it could claim an impressive temple in the center of the city of Rome.

The cult of Cybele, the Great Mother or Corn Mother, was very popular around the Mediterranean in the New Testament era. Starting as a nature goddess in Phrygia, she came to be seen as the mother goddess of all gods. The cult's central myth taught that Cybele drives insane her human lover, Attis, when he is unfaithful to her. When Attis castrates himself and later dies, Cybele goes into mourning and so introduces death into the world. But then she preserves Attis's body from decay (or turns him into a tree), and life is restored to nature. Its most well-known ritual was the *taurobolium,* in which initiates lay underneath boards on which a bull was sacrificed, catching its blood on their faces and sometimes drinking the blood. Its priests typically were eunuchs, having duplicated Attis's action as part of the annual rites.

The cult of Mithra originated in Persia, but it had undergone significant changes in Syria before it achieved its popular form. Roman soldiers apparently first brought it into the Empire and would eventually help carry it as far north as Britannia. Its core myth described the god Mithra springing to life from a rock, battling the sun and then slaying a bull, an act that represented the first act of creation. This slaying gave rise to the human race. Heavy with dualism, Mithraism saw humans as trapped in the struggle between good and evil. The souls of humans on earth were seven levels removed from their original home in heaven and contaminated by contact with the body. The soul that passed the tests of this life would eventually reunite with the good god. Mithra was seen as a mediator to help humans fight evil and as a judge of humans. The cult made extensive use of astrology and astrological symbols. It was the only mystery religion that called on its followers to live an ethical life. It did not share other mystery cults' notions of a life-death cycle. Mithraism would become the most important of all mystery religions in the Empire, even rivaling the popularity of Christianity for a time, but in the New Testament era it was relatively unknown.

### Rome and New Religions

In general, the Romans readily accepted foreign deities. From the third century B.C. on, many Romans began adopting new religions. This was in part because things had not been going well for Rome in its wars against the Carthaginians, and many felt the need to seek additional divine help.

The first mystery religion to become popular among Romans was that of Cybele. It was brought from the East in 204 B.C., along with its ecstatic services and cultic orgies. Because this goddess was served by castrated priests, the Roman Republic did not allow its citizens to be initiated. Yet Rome allowed the Temple of Cybele to be erected at a prominent location and made her annual festival an official holiday. The worship of Bacchus (god of wine and debauchery, Dionysus to the Greeks) became popular in Rome about the same time. The worship of Isis and Serapis came a bit later, but also became very popular among the Romans.

The expectations of the mystery religions were quite a change from the Roman state religion, whose gods made no demands on the individual and promised him or her no personal rewards. The new cults promised Romans an afterlife, a sense of belonging and an emotional excitement absent from the state religion. However, formal initiation into the cult was usually too expensive for most to afford. Numerous religious groups in American history have featured elements of mystery religions and offered similar promises of special knowledge, a sense of purpose and special access to the divine. They often feature ecstatic experiences, even orgiastic rituals. More extreme forms have included Jim Jones's cult in Jonestown, Guyana, the Heaven's Gate cult in San Diego, California, and David Koresh's Branch Davidian cult in Waco, Texas.

Mystery religions differed from Christianity in important ways. They dramatized the annual decay of vegetation and the revival of life in the spring. The annually repeated nature of this death-life motif is quite different from the once-for-all depiction of the death and resurrection of the God of Christianity. The presence of a concept of resurrection from death to life in these cults has been exaggerated, as has the presence of a notion of redemption.[3] In addition,

Figure 5.2. The amphitheater at the Asklepios cult complex, Epidavros, Greece. The staging in the foreground was for an Aristophanes play performed during the author's visit.

the figures at the center of these cults were mythological, not historical persons. Unlike Christianity, the mystery religions asserted that the initiate would be absorbed into the divine.[4]

Romans and Greeks usually felt that their way of life was not threatened by mystery religions. They wanted to stay in the good graces of all the gods after all. But some Romans suspected that behind the secret meetings and cultic vows lurked political conspiracy, threats to public order and traditional morality, and even treason. In the late Republic and early Empire, they sought with mixed success to limit the influence of some of these cults. When Roman authorities did ban or restrict the practice of certain foreign cults (such as the cult of Dionysius in the second century B.C. or that of the Druids in Gaul), it was on the grounds that they posed some threat to public order. We see modern parallels to this in the prosecution by American federal and state authorities of groups such as the Church of Jesus Christ of Latter-Day Saints (Mormons), for condoning polygamy, and of the Santería church in Florida, for practicing ritual animal sacrifice. Both were considered out of step with American values and a threat to the social order on some level.

## Roman Religion at the Onset of the New Testament Era

The late Republic brought a change of attitude toward the Roman state religion. While Romans continued to build massive temples to the traditional gods, the educated and wealthy classes began to doubt the existence of the gods. The ruling elite did not give up the state religion; that would have been impossible since it was so intertwined with the politics of Rome. But offices such as that of the high priest of the state religion became purely political offices, sought after by political climbers like Julius Caesar and Caesar Augustus. Many of the elite turned privately to astrology for guidance, even while they maintained public worship of the Roman gods.

Some Romans attributed the civil wars at the end of the Republic to this loss of commitment to the traditional gods. The first emperor, Caesar Augustus, sought to validate his rule by presenting himself as leading Rome back to its long-lost roots. He stressed the ancient Roman belief that prosperity and peace depended on fulfilling one's duties to the gods. He began a systematic religious restoration. In Rome alone he restored eighty-two temples, reinstituted many forgotten rites and festivals, and filled vacant priestly offices. He attempted to limit the intrusion of new cults into the city of Rome.

For Augustus this was not about restoring religious faith and practices; it was about using Roman tradition to mask his assumption of powers that no one person had held before. Because of this, he made a number of changes to Roman religion designed to weaken or eliminate the independent power of religious leaders. For example, he (and his successors) assumed the post of high priest *(pontifex maximus)*. He deprived the priestly colleges of their influence over political decisions. Instead, the colleges were reoriented to serve the emperor. Public divination, a religious practice common in the Republic, fell into disuse. The taking of the auspices, especially by generals, came to be treated as a privilege of the emperor. This is because both of these rituals could be used, for example, to assert that the gods were opposed to an emperor's actions.[5]

Roman religion, as practiced by many, if not most, during the Empire, was characterized by formal observance of the rituals with little conviction. Proper performance of the rites of Roman religion became a symbol of one's respect for the state and appreciation for tradition, not necessarily a sign of personal belief.

## Emperor Worship

While Augustus was primarily concerned with reestablishing traditional religious practices, he did contribute one important religious innovation: the cult of the emperor. Emperor worship was a way for Roman leaders to establish their power in the eastern Mediterranean. It also served to focus the loyalty of provincials on the person of the emperor. This cult was readily accepted by those peoples of the eastern Mediterranean who for centuries had been taught to venerate their rulers as gods. For example, the Egyptians considered their pharaoh the incarnation of the god Horus. Long before Augustus, Alexander the Great and his successors recognized that they could use these beliefs to cement their control over the Near East. The Greeks and Macedonians found this ruler cult hard to accept at first, even though they had myths about humans like Heracles who joined the gods of Mount Olympus.

The initial impetus for emperor worship came from communities in the East that were anxious to erase the memory of their support for Augustus's enemies. Cults to Augustus sprang up spontaneously in the East, at first over the mild public objections of Augustus. But Roman governors and officials did a great deal to encourage and support the new cult. As a result, the imperial cult was accepted fairly quickly throughout the East.[6]

It took longer to establish the cult of the emperor in the West. This is because the Romans were not used to the concept of a deified ruler. To make it work there, Roman officials had to take a more active role in setting up local cults, and Augustus had to make some compromises (see the photograph of the temple of the emperor cult in Herculaneum, Italy, in figure 11.2). He decreed that Romans should worship not himself but only his *genius,* the divine spirit that presided over his life and from which his power emanated. This was simply an extension of the traditional Roman concept that the members of a Roman household were to offer incense to the *genius* of the head of the household. He also connected the new cult with an old one, that of the personification of Rome herself, Roma. Thus, in the West his cult was named the cult of Roma and Augustus.

During the first century A.D., the cult of the living emperor became an accepted feature of public life. Oaths were sworn by the genius of the emperor. The Greek term *kyrios* ("lord") was used to refer to the emperor Nero, as we see in the language of the governor of Judea, Festus (Acts 25:26). The emperor Vespasian and his son Titus were called "savior." His other son, Domitian, expanded the concept of the divinity of the emperor and scandalized his fellow Romans by demanding that they address him as "lord and god" *(dominus et deus).* He was assassinated not long thereafter. After his death, the cult of the emperor reverted to a low-key pledge of allegiance to the emperor.

The Romans did not require anyone to worship only the emperor; they allowed people to retain their own religious beliefs. This caused no problem for the vast majority of subjects, who believed in many gods. Though they would have a favorite god, they thought it no lack of devotion to him or her to offer sacrifices to other gods. Only the Jews and Christians had serious religious problems with emperor worship. The Jews could not worship the emperor without violating the exclusivist requirements of their religion (which the Greeks and Romans did not understand, but usually tolerated). Fortunately, they had been granted a special exemption from emperor worship. Despite this exemption, Herod the Great of Judea built several shrines dedicated to Augustus and emperor worship in Caesarea, Samaria and Panias (Josephus *Jewish War* 1.407). The Jews did offer sacrifices at the temple in Jerusalem on behalf of, not to, the emperor.

Christianity benefited from the Jewish exemption as long as it appeared to be a sect of Judaism, but it was never granted its own exemption from emperor worship. For the most part the act of emperor worship was voluntary and could be avoided by Christians. It only became a problem for the average Christian on those occasions when emperor worship was used as a loyalty test. For example, Pliny the Younger, while governor of Bithynia in the early second century A.D., required those accused of being Christians to perform the ritual as a way to affirm their allegiance to the emperor and to deny their Christian faith (*Letters* 10.96).

Devotion to the emperor could be demonstrated by sacrificing a bull or offering incense to the emperor's image. This was usually a public ritual performed by priests or magistrates. The ministers of the cult often were imperial or municipal officials appointed as magistrates or priests. In the time of Jesus and Paul, special associations were established to tend the cult. These were the Augustales, composed of prominent freedmen in each town. A board of six was chosen each year to preside over their activities. As former slaves, they were barred from being elected to the senate in Rome or the local councils, but many had money and influence nonetheless. As Augustales, they could also gain dignity and recognition because they were performing an important duty in the public life of the community.[7] Military officers or public officials who were Christians would have found it extremely difficult to avoid taking part in the imperial cult.

A number of New Testament commentators have seen a connection between Rome and its cult of emperor worship and the book of the Revelation. The reference in Revelation 17:9 to seven heads of the "beast," which are "seven hills on which the woman [the great harlot] sits," has been taken as a reference to the famed seven hills on which Rome was founded. The woman is identified later as "the great city that rules over the kings of the earth" (Rev 17:18). The connection to emperor worship is seen in Revelation 13, where this same beast is worshiped by all the people of the earth (Rev 13:4, 8). As the emperor of Rome (e.g., Nero and Domitian) had persecuted Christians, Revelation predicts that this beast will war on the people of God. In this interpretation, Revelation 14:9-10 is warning Christians not to engage in emperor worship. Over the centuries, identifications of Rome as the home of the beast have diverged, some suggesting that the imagery in Revelation refers strictly to events in the first century, centering on Rome as the new Babylon, while others have focused on Rome as the cultural mother of a future, revived Roman Empire.

The emperors' use of this cult bears some resemblance to modern politicians' identification with American symbols, such as the flag, the church, or even apple pie, as a way to gain the trust and respect of the citizens. For much of its existence, the United States has had an informal mixture of Protestant Christianity and patriotism, a so-called civil religion, that has had some of the feel and impact of the emperor cult. For example, this informal union gave political and economic notions such as individual liberty, democracy and free enterprise a sacred or sacrosanct status, concepts that one may oppose at the cost of harsh criticism. The phrase "America, love it or leave it" gives something of this flavor. In addition, American civil religion meant that those who were not members of a Protestant Christian church, such as Jews and Roman Catholics, were at times seen as un-American.

### Roman Attitudes Toward Other Religions

Whether in Italy or in the farthest province, the Empire's cities hosted a variety of religions. This reality forced the Romans to deal with a variety of religious beliefs and practices. The relative peace of the early Empire allowed merchants, artisans, colonists, religious leaders and others to move freely from place to place. When people settled in a new region, they brought their native religion. Foreign settlers in a city often found people from the same country and joined together in worship. Depending on their beliefs, they might set up a shrine or a meeting place. As their numbers grew, they might demand some civic recognition. Over time, their religion became part of their city's religious establishment.[8]

Once the transplanted religious group established itself, its members sometimes began trying to convert locals. Usually this took the form of inviting people to observe the rituals and learn about the beliefs. Converts usually were not expected to renounce their belief in or even devotion to all other gods. Some religious groups held meetings at regular intervals. They worshiped their god

Figure 5.3. Bronze statue of Poseidon, the Greek god of the sea (National Museum, Athens, Greece). Originally he would have held a trident in his right hand.

with various rituals, usually including a banquet. These groups often registered with the Roman state as religious associations (see chapter four). When they could afford it, or when they found a wealthy benefactor, they built a temple or meeting place that reminded them of their native culture. Over time, as the religious group became assimilated to the local society, it modified its places of worship to look more and more like the local Greek or Roman temples.

*Acceptance.* The Roman state normally had no trouble incorporating a new religion into its system. Once conquered, the vanquished were allowed to retain their own religion, though in the period of the Empire, Rome also required them to adopt worship of the emperor. The Romans reasoned that, when foreign gods allowed their peoples to be conquered, they were submitting themselves to the gods of Rome and to Roman sovereignty. In like manner, the gods of allied nations were thought to have friendly relations with the Roman gods. So long as the supremacy of Roman religion was maintained, the state did not feel threatened and so tolerated other religions. The transplanted religions of immigrants from conquered or allied lands found the Romans likewise accommodating, so long as they did not try to pull Romans away from the state religion. Mystery religions, though often not the religion of specific peoples, had partially fused with city religions of the East during the late Republic. Because of this, in general they received the same official recognition.

The Roman attitude toward Judaism exemplifies this policy of toleration. In 161 B.C. the Jewish leader, Judas Maccabee, requested Roman protection from the ravages of the Seleucid monarch, Antiochus IV. Wanting to weaken the Seleucids, Rome agreed to a declaration of friendship with Judea. In the following century, the Jews gave both Julius Caesar and Octavian valuable military assistance. This led to a series of official edicts and letters to Greek cities in the East, instructing them to permit resident Jews to observe their traditional religion. Jews were allowed to pay the Jewish temple tax rather than the normal Roman taxes and to worship and organize freely. Even more important, they would not be required to participate in emperor worship. These privileges were not altered until after the destruction of the temple in Jerusalem in A.D. 70.

*Distaste.* Many Romans found other religions personally distasteful, even potentially threatening. In fact, the emperor Claudius (41-54) came to see the Eastern mystery religions then popular in Rome as too powerful to be ignored. He tried, with some success, to exert control over them. Juvenal, a first-century A.D. Roman aristocrat whose wealth had been confiscated by Emperor Domitian, believed that the flood of Eastern immigrants into Rome, with their outlandish languages and religions, was bringing the city to ruin (Juvenal *Satire* 3.62-64).

As time went on, Roman culture exerted a strong influence on the many religions of the eastern Empire, changing them and sometimes destroying them. Aspects of Roman religion often fused with local cults. For example, a local deity might be seen as a manifestation of some Roman god or goddess. This began in the Roman colonies and strategic cities of the East, where Roman presence was strong. But the peoples of the eastern Mediterranean rarely adopted Roman religion wholesale. Some did not see it as much different from Greek religion. Others held little regard for Roman culture in general, so they did not find its religion particularly attractive. Besides this, the Romans for the most part had no desire to uproot local religions, except for those associated with political independence.

Rome was not always comfortable with the privileges and exemptions it had granted to the Jews. As time went on, the memory of Jewish support for Rome dimmed and was replaced in many Romans' minds by a perception that the Jews both in Judea and abroad were more trouble than they were worth. Many Roman leaders long before the Jewish revolt in A.D. 66 concluded that the Jews were unwilling to cooperate with provincial authorities in Judea or to coexist peacefully with Gentiles in the cities of the Empire.[9] Cicero called Judaism a "barbarous superstition" (*Against Flaccus* 67).

Juvenal's writings are very critical of Jews and Judaism. He wrote, "Jews will sell you whatever dreams you like for a few small coppers" (*Satire* 6.547-548). Juvenal criticizes Romans whose parents had adopted Jewish beliefs, as the initial quote of this chapter makes clear. This passage shows a clear lack of appreciation for Judaism, but Juvenal's real problem is not with Jewish religion. Rather, he is concerned that Romans have forsaken their traditional religion and turned to Judaism. Many Romans shared his concern that Rome would suffer the disapproval of the gods if enough Romans turned their backs on them. While Judaism gained numerous casual followers among the Romans, it apparently made few full converts. The strict dietary regulations and the required circumcision for men, not to mention the need to avoid contact with Gentiles, made full conversion a major sacrifice. Many of these partial converts would find it much easier to convert fully to Christianity once it came on the scene.

A number of Romans apparently experienced a similar distaste for Christianity. The Roman historian Tacitus called first-century Christianity a "deadly superstition" and "mischief" and asserted that Christians were "notoriously depraved." He believed that their guilt as Christians deserved "ruthless punishment" and that their presence in Rome proved that all "degraded and shameful practices collect and flourish in the capital" (*Annals* 15.44). In the early second century, Pliny the Younger called Christianity a "wretched cult" and "degenerate sort of cult carried to extravagant lengths." Pliny was concerned that Christianity was stealing people away from the state religion. He referred to the Roman "temples which had been entirely deserted for a long time" and the "sacred rites which had been allowed to lapse" before his persecutions scared people away from Christianity (*Letters* 10.96).

Nevertheless, the Romans usually left Christians alone. This is why P[ so frequently able to escape the clutches of his opponents, despite the fact that the Romans were aware of his religious activities. Paul's status as a Roman citizen was more important to the Romans than his religion. Since his activities occurred largely among Jews and other non-Romans, and since the churches in his day were few and small, the authorities sensed no threat to public order from first-century Christianity.

*Repression of religion.* Why were the early Christians persecuted at times? Only in light of the nature of Roman religion and its evolution, as outlined above, can we understand the complex reasons. Roman repression of religions was selective, sporadic and short-lived. Emperors typically moved against a cult when they believed it threatened law and order. Religions considered morally repugnant by the Romans, such as that of the Celtic Druids in western Europe, were systematically eliminated. Tiberius treated Egyptian cults harshly, but his successors saw no reason to continue the repression. No cult was as actively persecuted as were astrology and magic. Nevertheless, they became very popular at all levels of society, so much so that Roman emperors became concerned that astrological forecasts might lead to political revolt.

Overall, Rome was not very successful at controlling religious innovation. As it turned out, Christianity was the main beneficiary of this lack of control. The Christians' denial of the gods of Rome earned them the label of atheist. Their refusal to take an oath by the emperor's guardian spirit led to the suspicion that they did not support his earthly supremacy. Despite these concerns, the emperors rarely tried to hunt down and eliminate Christians before the mid-third century.

The Romans at first considered Christianity a sect of Judaism, and so ignored it. But by the 60s A.D., Rome began to recognize the difference. A fire in 64 ravaged most of the center of Rome. Ten of the city's fourteen regions suffered damage. Although Nero began an aggressive rebuilding program, and at great expense provided for the immediate needs of the victims, Tacitus says that his efforts could not "banish the sinister rumor and belief" that the fire was intentional. Although Tacitus seems to believe the rumors that Nero ordered the fire, we have no evidence for this beyond the fact that Nero was able, as a result of the fire, to build his palace, the "Golden House," on a far grander scale (Tacitus *Annals* 15.44) Either way, Nero needed to remove blame from himself in the minds of the angry Roman public.

Nero found appropriate scapegoats, according to Tacitus, in the Christians. The Christians made good victims because, unlike most religious groups, they totally rejected the gods of Rome. Of course, the Jews too rejected other gods, but the Jews were a known commodity; the Christians were a mysterious combination of Jews, Greeks and Romans. They acted like a single people, even though they represented many nations. To the Romans this clearly was unnatural. Even members of the mystery religions, who also came from various nations, did not claim this kind of unity. In addition, many Christians anticipated the imminent destruction of the world by fire. Tacitus adds:

> Despite their guilt as Christians, and the ruthless punishment it deserved, the victims were pitied. For it was felt that they were being sacrificed to one man's brutality rather than to the national interest (*Annals* 15.44).

Hundreds of Roman Christians, perhaps several thousand, lost their lives in this persecution. Tacitus says that "an immense multitude" was convicted (*Annals* 15.44). Clement uses a similar phrase when he says that "a great multitude" was put to death at this time (*1 Clement* 6:1). This may be hyperbole since most scholars place the size of the Roman church at this time at somewhere between a few hundred and two thousand persons. The unanimous testimony of later Christian tradition is that Peter and Paul were both put to death under Nero. It should be noted that none of these persecutions took place in the Colosseum (Flavian Amphitheater). It would not be built for another fifteen years, long after Nero's death. Even after its construction, we have no evidence that Christians were ever persecuted in this famous arena.

The Roman Christians also made an easy target because most of them had low status and power in the society. Tacitus's description of the persecution indicates that the members of this religion were for the most part noncitizens. A citizen could not have been executed in the ways Tacitus describes: dismemberment by wild dogs, crucifixion and death by fire.

We get further insight into the Roman attitude toward Christians in an exchange of letters at the beginning of the second century A.D. between the emperor Trajan and the governor of the province of Bithynia, Pliny the Younger. Pliny tells Trajan that when an informant accuses people of being Christians, he questions the accused. He gives them three chances to deny their faith. If they still profess Christianity, Pliny says he has them executed, for "whatever the nature of their admission, I am convinced that their stubbornness and unshakable obstinacy ought not to go unpunished" (*Letters* 10.96). Those who denied Christianity were released after they reviled the name of Christ, repeated a ritual to invoke the presence of the gods and burned incense to the emperor's image. On investigation, Pliny found Christianity harmless enough, just "a degenerate sort of cult carried to extravagant lengths." Trajan basically approved of Pliny's practice, but he told Pliny not to go hunting for Christians or to accept the word of anonymous informants.

Thus, early Roman persecution of Christianity did not represent opposition to the theological beliefs of the church, or even overt opposition to Christianity itself. As far as we can tell, no edict was passed against Christianity in the first one and a half centuries of its existence. Rather, it was a religion that simply did not fit any of Rome's categories: its monotheism prevented Roman religion from absorbing it, and its followers were not from a single conquered or allied people. As a result, it could not be a legally recognized religion. In addition, its adherents stubbornly refused to respect the simple rituals of Roman religion, such as burning incense to the emperor's genius. Such people were considered likely to support political insurrection and even outright revolt.

Ironically, the Roman leaders in the first century never in their wildest dreams could have imagined how Christians would one day close up the temples of the gods and make Christianity the new state religion. Once that happened, the church would inherit some of the trappings of the earlier religion. For example, the Pope is called *pontifex maximus,* or high priest of the Christian religion, borrowing the term from Roman state religion. In addition, the term "Queen of Heaven," which later would be applied to Mary the mother of Jesus, originated with Eastern mystery religions.

**For Further Reading**

Burkert, Walter. *Greek Religion.* Trans. John Raffan. Cambridge, Mass.: Harvard University Press, 1985.

Ferguson, John. *The Religions of the Roman Empire.* New York: Cornell University Press, 1970.

MacMullen, Ramsay. *Paganism in the Roman Empire.* New Haven, Conn.: Yale University Press, 1981.

Nash, Ronald H. *Christianity and the Hellenistic World.* Grand Rapids, Mich.: Zondervan, 1984.

Rose, H. J. *Religion in Greece and Rome.* New York: Harper & Brothers, 1959.

Ste. Croix, G. E. M. de. "Why Were the Early Christians Persecuted?" *Past and Present* 26 (1963): 6-38.

# Chapter 6

# Governing of the Provinces & Palestine

*[Julius Caesar] thought priority must be given
to organizing the provinces and districts into which he had just come
so that they would be free from internal disturbances, would adopt
laws and judicial procedures, and would cease to fear external enemies.*
THE ALEXANDRIAN WAR 65

*And when the governor had motioned to him to speak,
Paul replied: "Realizing that for many years
you have been judge over this nation, I cheerfully make my defense."*
ACTS 24:10

W E CAN LEARN A NUMBER OF LESSONS FROM A STUDY OF HOW
Rome governed its empire. A principal one is that the Romans
did not govern primarily for the welfare of the people of the
provinces. Their system was not designed, even had it worked
ideally, to promote justice among the provincials. It was designed to support
the interests of the leaders back in Rome, whether that meant collecting the
maximum amount of taxes possible or protecting the Empire from threats to its
stability from within or without. In this context, it is not hard to understand the
resentment that developed toward Rome in Judea and elsewhere.

## Organization of the Provinces
The province was the basic unit of administration in the Roman Empire. Sicily
became the first Roman province in 227 B.C. From the time of Sulla (first century
B.C.), proconsuls (those who had attained the office of consul) were sent to
govern more important provinces (see map 7 for the names and locations of the
Roman provinces in the New Testament era). Propraetors (those who had
attained the office of praetor) were sent to less important ones.

*Under the Republic.* Rome's administration of overseas provinces began in the second century B.C. with its conquests in Spain, northern Africa, Macedonia, Asia Minor and southern Gaul (present-day France). Rome had little experience administering foreign lands and did not believe in the use of professional civil servants. Instead, it modeled the administration of these provinces on its military organization. Provincial governors were sent out for one-year terms with the kind of autonomous power (called *imperium*) that military commanders were granted in conducting war. Governors of provinces had the freedom to govern as they saw fit, as long as the taxes were collected and any insurrection was put down.

A proconsul was a senator appointed as provincial governor. His staff was quite small by modern standards. His chief assistant, a young senator elected as a quaestor for that year, usually had responsibility for the finances. The governor could also take with him as aides several legates, senators who might be of high rank. The legates served as military commanders when necessary. The governor also usually brought some relatives and clients (see appendix A) to assist him. All of these persons served as volunteers. The governor's professional staff consisted of a private secretary, several scribes, an honor guard (the lictors) and a few others.

Clearly, Rome was a far cry from a modern government bureaucracy. This was nowhere more true than in the absense of the backbone of government in our world, permanent civil servants. This meant that every change in the governor brought provincial governing to a grinding halt while the new leader replaced the existing bureaucracy with his own. Those waiting for a judgment by the outgoing governor would probably have to wait months for the new governor to pick up their cases. During the Republic, this typically happened once a year in every province.

Provincial governors were deeply involved in the politics back in Rome. The welfare of people in their provinces rarely ranked at the top of their priorities. They also were often tempted by easy opportunities to enrich themselves and the politically influential Roman businessmen in their province. The provincial charter, written by Rome when the province was established, provided the only written guidelines for governing. Under such circumstances, Rome often did not provide either predictable or just governance.

Since the governor and his staff had to pay their own expenses, an honest governor could find provincial government very costly. Unfortunately for the provincials, many of the governors came to the provinces to make a fortune, not to spend one. Roman literature records a number of trials against governors for extorting money from their provincial subjects. The governor Verres, prosecuted for corruption, said that a governor needs to make three fortunes in the provinces: one to pay off the debts he incurred in getting elected to the office in the first place, one to bribe the jurors in case he is indicted and another to live on for the rest of his life.

The fact that such corruption trials took place indicates that the Romans did not officially approve of governors getting rich off the provincials. But for the charges to be effective, they had to be brought by persons of high social standing. Then a senator had to be convinced to introduce the case. Roman aristocrats with interests in the province, such as land holdings, sometimes brought the charges on behalf of the province. It also helped if the governor had enemies in the senate who wanted to use the charges to help put him out of power. The court which heard these charges was manned by both ranks of the Roman ruling class, the senators and the equestrians, both of whom were hesitant to convict one of their own unless they had personal interests at stake. Probably most instances of extortion and corruption by governors went unproven and unpunished.[1]

*Under the Empire.* In 27 B.C. Augustus put forth the Act of Settlement to consolidate his power and to improve the administration of the provinces. He divided them into senatorial and imperial provinces. The senatorial province was governed as during the Republic: by a proconsul or propraetor on a one-year term. Proconsuls are mentioned three times in the New Testament: Acts 13:7-8, 12 (Sergius Paulus of Cyprus); Acts 18:12 (Gallio of Achaia); and Acts 19:38. The governors of the senatorial provinces were men who had worked closely enough with the emperor for him to feel assured of their loyalty. In these provinces, the locals had accepted Roman rule and represented little threat of revolt. As a result, military forces could be kept to a minimum. The senatorial provinces formed an inner ring around Italy.

Though the emperor had great influence on the selection of proconsuls and propraetors for the senatorial provinces, they did not come under his direct control until the latter part of the second century A.D. However, a provincial community could go over the head of the governor and appeal to the emperor, who might send the governor a letter of advice. This is similar to the right of a Roman citizen to appeal a legal decision to the emperor, as did the apostle Paul (Acts 25:11). The proconsul or propraetor was under no obligation to consult with the senate or the emperor before making decisions. Since he possessed *imperium*, the proconsul had supreme power in his province. He could take any action short of "extreme cruelty" toward provincials who were not Roman citizens so long as he did not take their money or property. (See in figure 6.1 a photograph of the judgment seat of the governor of the Roman Province of Achaea. It was located in his provincial capital, the city of Corinth.)

Figure 6.1. The *bema* (judgment seat) of the governor in the Corinthian Forum, Greece. The apostle Paul would have stood approximately where the camera is located, watching the proconsul Gallio render judgment from the top of the *bema*. Behind Paul were the local meat markets. Behind the *bema* was the Upper Forum, surrounded by government offices.

By contrast, the imperial provinces lay toward the frontiers of the Empire. Most of the legions, also under the emperor's control, guarded the frontiers from these provinces (see map 6 for the location of the legions in the New Testament era). The emperor used two types of governors to oversee the imperial provinces: legates and prefects/procurators. Both possessed *imperium;* unless and until the emperor intervened they were free to act as they saw fit. Legates governed those provinces in which Roman soldiers were stationed. Normally they had attained the office of praetor. Legates in the more important provinces, such as Syria, usually also had attained the office of consul. The legate or procurator commanded the most important legion in his province. Syria was governed by a legate named Quirinius in A.D. 6 (Luke 2:2). Judea was always under imperial control, whether under a client king or a Roman governor.

The governors of Judea came from a group of imperial administrators, named procurators or prefects, used to govern relatively small areas that required special treatment. For the most part this meant quasimilitary governing of newly acquired areas, or of peoples considered potentially rebellious. Mauritania, the island of Sardinia, Egypt and several districts in the Alps were governed by procurators. Procurators were taken from the order just below the senatorial, the equestrian. Before A.D. 44 these governors, like Pontius Pilate, were called prefects. An inscription discovered in 1961 calls Pilate *Praefectus Iudaeae,* "Prefect of Judea." Normally the troops under the command of procurators were not from the regular legions but were noncitizen auxiliary troops. They were usually recruited locally. The commanders of the troops, and often their centurions, were usually Roman citizens. An example of this is the military tribune stationed in Jerusalem, Claudius Lysias (Acts 22:27-28; 23:26). Procurators probably had the same powers as proconsuls and legates.[2]

At first, only a few important provinces were held by the emperor: Lusitania, Tarraconensis, Gaul, Syria, Cilicia, Cyprus and Egypt. The senate controlled the rest: Asia and Africa, governed by former consuls, and Sicily, Sardinia, Baetica, Macedonia, Achaia, Dalmatia, Crete and Cyrene, Bithynia and Pontus, governed by former praetors.

A number of territories, especially in the eastern part of the Empire, were governed by client kings. These were native dynasties approved by Rome, who ruled with one eye on their people and the other on Rome. Judea was ruled by the dynasty of Herod from 40 B.C. to A.D. 6, and again from A.D. 41 to 44. Cappadocia was a client monarchy until the death of its king in A.D. 17. Between Cappadocia and Syria lay Commagene, which was ruled by client kings for all but twenty years of the New Testament period.

### Administration of the Provinces

*Authority of the governor.* The governor, whether proconsul, propraetor, legate or prefect, wielded the power of Rome in his province. He was bound by the provincial charter to honor specific arrangements for tax exemption and other prerogatives, and the provincials could complain about his administration to the senate or emperor. Otherwise, his exercise of *imperium* was very nearly absolute. He made deals with the local authorities in the cities or tribes. He exercised police powers through his command of the legions, if any were stationed in the province, or more often through a smaller military unit made up of auxiliary troops composed of non-Roman citizens. He heard law cases and pronounced capital sentences. Tax collection was normally delegated to the cities.

The permanent staff of an imperial province consisted of imperial slaves, freedmen and soldiers. They stayed in the province even when it changed governors. To judge by the best-documented example, Bithynia-Pontus, the senatorial provinces were still ruled as under the Republic. Most in the first century A.D. had no regular archives or permanent personnel. The clerical assistants of the proconsuls and provincial quaestors were still the scribes of the old Republic system, who came out with the new governor and went home with him, taking all of their records with them.

The small staff of a provincial governor could not hope to and never intended to directly govern the province. Rome did not care how local cities and regions in the provinces were governed, so long as the taxes were collected and allegiance to Rome remained firm. In this sense the Empire was an association of over a thousand cities ruled indirectly by Rome. Direct government normally was left to provincials whom Rome had co-opted into its system, and thus could be trusted to do Rome's bidding. Some of these were Roman aristocrats in Roman colony cities, but most were members of the local aristocracies in the towns of the provinces. Rome had a right to expect their support since they had benefited by allegiance to Rome in a number of ways. As members of local governments in Roman provinces, they were granted Roman citizenship. In addition, they could expect Roman support in conflicts with political opponents unfriendly to Rome. However, governors looking to gain wealth and status through burdensome taxation or a war could cause a lot of problems for these local aristocrats, who had to explain Roman actions to their citizens. First-century revolutionaries in the province of Judea believed that the priestly class had sold out to the Romans, and in the Jewish revolt of A.D. 66-73 the revolutionaries put to death many priests as traitors.

As one can see from this section, even the more efficient governments of the senatorial provinces did not make providing justice to the people their first priority. Their purpose was to maintain the imperial system. The very limited interest of governors in local affairs, which did not threaten the stability of the society, is illustrated in the account of Gallio and Paul in the book of Acts. At Corinth, Paul is accused by Jews before Gallio, the proconsul of the province of Achaia, of teaching beliefs "contrary to the law." Gallio simply refuses to render judgment because he believes that the charge comes under the jurisdiction of Jewish laws (Acts 18:12-16).

*Administration through the cities.* As indicated above, the Romans governed through the cities of the Empire (see map 7 for the major cities of the Empire). In some respects it is best to think of the Empire as a collection of cities of varying sizes that controlled the farmlands around them. Most of the cities of the Empire had ten thousand to fifteen thousand inhabitants, but many had only a few thousand. At the other extreme were the great cities with hundreds of thousands, such as Alexandria, Antioch and Carthage. Major cities were concentrated along the Mediterranean coast or along the great rivers of Greece. These facts are critical to understanding how and why Paul and his missionary team focused on the major and strategic cities of the Empire. They were making use of the systems of disseminating information and spreading influence established by the Romans and the Hellenistic kingdoms before them.

Throughout the Empire there were four main types of cities: the Roman colony, the municipality, the temple city and the traditional Hellenistic city. The Roman colonies and municipalities were especially privileged under Roman law. Around six hundred cities in the Empire, most in Spain and North Africa, fell into one of these two, very similar, categories. In all the eastern provinces there were strikingly few Roman colonies and municipalities. This is probably because the network of existing Hellenistic cities was so dense that it was not possible to insert many new colonies.

In the early Empire era, the most important type of city was the Roman colony. Its original settlers were Roman citizens sent out from Italy or from Roman legions. Non-Romans who lived in or around them were often granted Roman citizenship as well. Colony citizens, because of their Roman citizenship, were exempt from tribute and most forms of taxation, and their government was based on a Roman model. Philippi was such a colony (Acts 16:12), as was Corinth, where Roman colonists lived together with noncitizen Jews and Greeks (Acts 18:4-8). The ancient Greek city of Corinth had been destroyed a century earlier by the Romans. It was refounded as a Roman colony by Julius Caesar in 46 B.C. Caesar moved a number of poorer Romans from Rome to Corinth to populate the new colony.

The division between Romans and non-Romans is visible in the account of Paul's arrest in Philippi recorded in the book of Acts. It shows how readily Romans in a Roman colony could turn on people identified as Jews trying to disrupt their traditions (Acts 16:19-23). Originally, Roman colonies were settled by Roman citizens with a standard Roman city constitution. Beginning with Claudius, Rome began to confer the title of Roman colony on existing cities. This practice became widespread in the second century.[3] The highest officials in a Roman colony were the two *duumviri*, corresponding to the consuls in Rome and referred to in Acts by the Greek term *archontes* or *strategoi* (Acts 16:19-39). Their official attendants were the *lictors* ("rod bearers," Acts 16:35, 38), who carried bundles of rods (the *fasces*) as a sign of their office. The lictors were responsible for arresting and scourging criminals.[4] These rods were probably the ones used to beat Paul and Silas (Acts 16:22).

Other cities were known as municipalities or *municipia*. This title originally referred to free or federate cities that enjoyed some degree of autonomy. During the Empire, Roman municipalities usually came into existence when a previously existing city, which had a large number of Roman citizen residents, was designated a city with full Roman citizenship rights. The city was allowed to govern itself and in return promised to render military service and active political support to Rome. A city that received this benefit would enjoy immunity from all state taxes and freedom from oversight by the provincial governor.

A number of Greek city-states had voluntarily allied with Rome at one time or another and thus enjoyed a special status as free or federate cities. Unlike those in Roman colonies, its citizens did not become Roman citizens. A federate city like Athens paid no tribute to Rome and was independent of the provincial government of its province (Achaia). Ephesus was a free city in the province of Asia. It had its own senate and assembly and considered itself the principal site for the worship of the goddess Artemis. But a free city's independence lasted only as long as Rome trusted the city's leaders. This helps explain why the clerk of the assembly in Acts 19 was so anxious to avoid a public disturbance over the activities of Paul. He realized that the Romans might look on unauthorized meetings, which could not readily be explained, as seditious and consequently revoke their free status.

Temple cities, where state and religion were fused together, enjoyed a special status. These included cities like Jerusalem, dedicated to the worship of Jehovah, and Hierapolis, in Syria, dedicated to the worship of Atargatis. Judea had been recognized as a temple state by the Persians, the Ptolemies and the Seleucids. Even when the Romans replaced the line of Herod with a Roman prefect, the Jewish high priesthood had charge of most of Judea's internal affairs. Under Augustus, Jerusalem's sacred status was respected. For example, Roman military standards, which bore the image of the emperor, were not brought into the city out of deference to Judaism's opposition to graven images.[5] Judeans were allowed to use capital punishment only to protect the sacred temple from Gentile violaters.

Still other cities simply continued their old constitutions, especially in the Greek East. In some of these cities a democratic form of government survived: a citizen assembly, a smaller council and an elected board of magistrates who often retained the titles from the old days of Greek freedom. Certainly Roman influence made itself felt, even in these cities. During the Empire, many of them added a magistrate to serve as priest of the cult of emperor worship. Because the Romans were suspicious of democracy, however, they made sure that the power of policy-making was held by a few at the top who could be expected to support Roman interests. These local aristocracies were satisfied with and proud of their membership in the Roman Empire and remained loyal to Rome. The revolts in Judea were an exception, but even then the revolts came from below, not from above; the priests and Sadducees seemed content to collaborate with the Roman authorities.

*Governing in the eastern provinces.* Rome faced some language and culture barriers in its rule of the eastern provinces. Although Greek was the common language of the eastern provinces, Latin was the official language of the Roman colonies in the East. Over time, as Romans intermarried with locals, Greek came to overtake Latin as the language of the inhabitants of the colonies. Latin was also the language of the army in the East. During the early Empire, Latin was probably understood by all serving soldiers, including auxiliaries who may have known little Latin before enlisting. All official military documents were in Latin. Despite all this, it is likely that a great many Roman citizens in the East could not speak Latin.[6] This clearly would have complicated the governing process.

Rome had to deal with conflicts at times between peoples of different classes and ethnic groups. Old ethnic rivalries, like that between the Greeks and Jews of Alexandria, were ongoing problems for Roman rule. In A.D. 17 the emperor Tiberius sent Germanicus to address problems in the provinces and kingdoms of the Near East. Germanicus met with the legate (governor) of Syria, the king of Nabataea and ambassadors from the king of Parthia, whose kingdom lay to the east of Palestine.[7]

Rome appears to have used its military forces to deal with disputes and problems only when other methods were unsuccessful or inappropriate. An example of this is the dispute in 12 B.C. between the kingdom of Nabataea and the kingdom of Judea, both under Roman dominance (see map 3). After the king of Nabataea helped residents of Trachonitis, a part of Herod's kingdom, rebel, Herod repressed the rebellion and wanted to attack Nabataea. He requested from the Roman officials in Syria permission to do so. When Nabataea ignored the legate of Syria's ruling that it pay a fine to Herod and that refugees on both sides be restored, the legate gave Herod permission to invade Nabataea. Herod later reported on his actions to the legate. When the king of Nabataea later died and was replaced without Roman consent by Aretas IV, Augustus became directly involved (cf. 2 Cor 11:32). At a personal hearing of the issues, he at first considered giving Nabataea to Herod but decided to confirm Aretas as king. No Roman forces were involved. This shows how important personal and written communications were in places where Roman influence was rather limited.[8]

But the Romans were willing to commit forces when needed. When the death of Herod the Great in 4 B.C. was followed by revolts within his kingdom, the legate of Syria sent one legion of soldiers (around six thousand men) to assist the Herodian royal army in putting down the revolts. When he discovered that the legion was in grave danger, the legate led his remaining two legions and a number of auxiliary troops into Judea. This means that the three Roman legions stationed in Syria were at one point all operating in Judea. This was a massive commitment of forces to a relatively small place; it shows how nervous the Romans could get about potential uprisings.

The relationship between emperor and provincial governors was in some ways like the relationship between the federal government and state government in the United States. The states have autonomy in most areas, in theory, but frequently are forced by decisions on the federal level to change their practices in those areas. An example of this is education, which is supposed to be the responsibility of the states. But federal money has been withheld from states in order to coerce them to implement federal educational mandates. The ability of Roman citizens in the provinces to appeal to Caesar (see chapter seven) reflects a value similar to that in the United States: that the citizen of each state is also a citizen of the United States and because of this may seek justice in federal courts denied him at the state level. Of course, the emperor was able to exercise more personal power than is the president of the United States.

In other respects, Rome's relationship to its empire bears similarities to the Russian Empire under both the Tsars and the Soviets. Both Rome and Russia had to deal with peoples of different languages, ethnicities and cultures. Both sought to do so by training an elite from the conquered peoples in their language and culture. Both realized that many of their subjects did not truly support their regimes. Both employed a secret service to discover disloyalty before it became public (though Rome's version was quite primitive by modern standards). Both used force, sometimes massive force, to put down revolt before it spread to other peoples. The most significant difference is that the Soviets, unlike the Romans and Tsars, tried to convince the common people of the rightness of their rule.

## Governing of Palestine

The Hellenistic monarchs, like the later Romans, attempted to control Palestine by assimilating it into their culture. They only partially succeeded, and that fact explains much about Judean events and attitudes in the New Testament era. It also is the basis for understanding why the Judeans would attempt to win independence from Rome in A.D. 66 and again in the 130s.

In considering the governing of Palestine prior to and during the New

Testament era, we must look at two issues: the attempts to assimilate Palestine to Hellenistic culture and the direct governing of the area by Hellenistic powers. The Jews, like many Near Eastern peoples, adopted a veneer of Hellenistic culture. It permeated the upper classes and most major cities but did not replace the local cultures in the villages of the lower classes (the vast majority of the population). The Jews for the most part also preserved the traditional nature of their chief city, Jerusalem.

Hellenization in Palestine involved two phases. Following the death of Alexander the Great and the division of his empire among his generals, the Jews came first under the control of Egypt, which itself was controlled by Alexander's general Ptolemy (see map 2). Residents of Palestine faced little pressure to adopt Greek culture under the Ptolemies. Then Palestine came under the sway of Syria, which was part of the descendants of Seleucus, another of Alexander's generals. Palestine's lack of Hellenization irritated its new rulers, especially Antiochus IV Epiphanes. He was used to forcing peoples to give up their traditional ways and assimilate into his empire. The Jews, however, proved unwilling to make these accommodations and ultimately, under the Maccabees, threw off Seleucid control in 142 B.C. (see chapter thirteen). But even as an independent state, Judea could not easily rid itself of the Hellenizing influences that had taken root. Greek cities abounded on its fringes.

*Roman conquest of Palestine.* After it successfully threw off the Seleucids, the Jewish Hasmonaean dynasty ruled an independent Judea. The descendants of Simon gradually conquered the surrounding peoples, until Alexander Jannaeus (103-76 B.C.), the first Hasmonaean to call himself "king," ruled a monarchy nearly as large as the kingdom of David and Solomon. Alexander's wife, Salome Alexandra, ruled a peaceful kingdom for nine years after his death. But peace was broken when their sons, Aristobulus and Hyrcanus, contested for the throne. In 63 B.C. each appealed to the Roman general Pompey to support his cause. Pompey, who at the time was turning the remnants of the Seleucid Empire into the Roman province of Syria, used this request as a pretext to intervene and conquer Judea. This conquest led to the deaths of a number of Jews and the enslavement of several thousand more. Pompey even committed the sacrilege of entering the holy of holies, the inner sanctum of the temple, which only the high priest was allowed to enter. Despite having conquered Judea, Rome did not consider it a threat or worth the expense of turning into a province. Instead, it recognized Judea as a semi-independent client state. Pompey made Hyrcanus high priest and titular leader of Judea, but not king.

The Roman conquest of Syria allowed Rome to organize the surrounding area according to a well-defined defensive strategy. The borders of Rome were protected with small client kingdoms that represented no threat to Rome and that served as buffer states to protect Rome from more powerful countries beyond the Roman orbit, especially the Parthian Empire to the east of Judea. The Roman general Pompey gave independence back to the Greek cities along the Mediterranean coast and in the Decapolis region between Judea and Galilee (which had been captured by the Hasmonaeans and forced to convert to Judaism years before). The city of Strato's Tower (later renamed Caesarea by Herod), as well as Sepphoris and Scythopolis, were given autonomy. These cities helped form a barrier between the remaining Jewish holdings: Galilee to the north and Judea and Idumaea to the south. The Romans saw these actions as returning territory to its rightful inhabitants, from whom the Romans could now expect great loyalty, but many Jews saw this as an unjust encroachment on their legitimate holdings.[9]

*The rise of Antipater.* In 55 B.C., the Romans appointed a new ruler, called a *procurator,* for their client state of Judea. They chose Antipater, the Idumaean prince who had been the power behind the Hasmonaean dynasty for years. The Idumaeans were a tribe whom the Hasmonaeans had forced to convert to the Jewish religion. Antipater was willing to be useful to the Romans whenever the opportunity presented itself.

Such an opportunity came in the winter of 48-47 B.C., and it brought significant privileges to the Jewish people. Julius Caesar was camped in Alexandria, having pursued the remnants of Pompey's army there. After Pompey's death at the hands of the Egyptians, Caesar intervened in a succession battle between Cleopatra VII and her brother. In the process, his troops became trapped in the palace quarter of Alexandria by Egyptian troops. Antipater helped to extricate Caesar, earning great appreciation for himself and for Judea. Caesar confirmed his position as procurator of Judea and gave him Roman citizenship. Caesar allowed him to rebuild Jerusalem's walls, which Pompey had torn down. Caesar also reduced Judea's tribute payments. In this way, the leadership of Judea passed from the Jewish dynasty of the Hasmonaeans to an Idumaean family. Hyrcanus II was allowed by Antipater to continue as high priest. Although Judea received welcome benefits, it came even further into Rome's orbit.[10] Of course, the latter was probably inevitable.

Caesar repeated and enlarged upon the Jews' right to religious liberty as granted to Simon in the previous century. He granted to Jews the right to observe the sabbath, freedom from military service (since this would inevitably conflict with observance of the sabbath), the right to maintain the temple and observe the Jewish festivals, and protection against attempts to destroy the Jewish Scriptures. Jews would be exempted from the obligation to worship the emperor but would be expected to revere him. They were also excused from participation in pagan religious rituals.

*Herod the Great of Judea.*[11] Antipater's sons, Herod and Phasael, continued his policies. When the eastern Empire came under Marc Antony's control in 42 B.C., they were appointed joint tetrarchs of Judea (including Galilee, Peraea and Samaria). In 40 B.C. the Parthian Empire to the East overran Syria and Judea. It deposed the high priest Hyrcanus II and installed his nephew Antigonus as high priest-king. Parthia was trying to win legitimacy with the Jews by returning rulership to the Hasmonaean line. Phasael was executed by the Parthians, but Herod escaped to Rome where he was declared king of the Jews.

| Form | Title | Leader | Dates |
|------|-------|--------|-------|
| Client kingdom | King | Herod the Great | 37-4 B.C. |
| | Ethnarch | Archelaus | 4 B.C.-A.D. 6 |
| Roman province | Prefect | Coponius | A.D. 6-9 |
| | Prefect | Marcus Ambivius | A.D. 9-12 |
| | Prefect | Annius Rufus | A.D. 12-15 |
| | Prefect | Valerius Gratus | A.D. 15-26 |
| | Prefect | Pontius Pilate | A.D. 26-36 |
| | Prefect | Marullus | A.D. 37-41 |
| Client kingdom | King | Herod Agrippa | A.D. 41-44 |
| Roman province | Procurator | Cuspius Fadus | A.D. 44-46 |
| | Procurator | Cumanus | A.D. 48-52 |
| | Procurator | M. Antonius Felix | A.D. 52-59? |
| | Procurator | Porcius Festus | A.D. 59-62? |
| | Procurator | Albinus | A.D. 62-64 |
| | Procurator | Gessius Florus | A.D. 64-66 |

Table 6.1. The rulers of Judea in the New Testament era

The reconquest of Judea by Herod and the Romans was completed in 37 B.C. Herod convinced Antony to execute Antigonus. Herod's choice for high priest was the next Hasmonaean in line, only seventeen years old, Aristobulus III. When Aristobulus drowned a few months later, many suspected Herod of arranging it in order to keep the Hasmonaeans out of power. Herod attempted to legitimate his position with the Jews by divorcing his wife, Doris, and marrying Mariamne, the granddaughter of Hyrcanus II.

While the battle of Actium raged (31 B.C.; see appendix A), the forces of Herod of Judea were on campaign, on Mark Antony's orders, against the king of Nabataea for the latter's nonpayment of tribute. Soon after his victory over Antony that same year, Octavian met with Herod. Herod pledged Octavian his loyalty and was confirmed as king of Judea. Octavian placed under his rule the regions of Judea that Cleopatra had recently occupied, along with a number of Greek cities along the Mediterranean and on both sides of the Jordan.

During his thirty-three-year reign, Herod proved both able and ruthless. He never became popular with the Jewish people, who considered him a foreign upstart who had deposed the rightful ruler and whose power rested on the might of Rome. Caesar Augustus believed in his loyalty to Rome, and in 27 B.C. he gave Herod many of the Greek cities on the Mediterranean coast and in the interior, as well as a large territory east and north of Galilee. When Augustus sent a force against the Sabaeans in 25 B.C., Herod supplied five hundred auxiliaries. A few years later, after defeating a revolt in the area east of Galilee, Augustus added several regions (Trachonitis, Batanaea, Auranitis and Ituraea) to Herod's territory. This made Herod's kingdom approximately the size of the ancient united kingdom of Israel under David and Solomon and further secured his loyalty to the Empire.

Herod founded many new towns for Jews. On the site of Samaria he founded Sebaste, and on the site of Strato's Tower he founded Caesarea, a city and artificial harbor. He used a new kind of concrete recently invented by the Romans, which could set up underwater, to construct the harbor. Caesarea became the principal port of Judea and later the residence of the Roman governor. Herod named Sebaste and Caesarea for members of the Roman imperial family in an attempt to prove his loyalty.

Herod began a massive Jewish temple rebuilding program in 19 B.C. Herod's temple was completed long after his death, in A.D. 63, only to be destroyed by the Romans in 70. He also built and rebuilt fortresses throughout Judea, including the famous fortress at Masada.

As further indications of his identification with Greco-Roman civilization, Herod built a Greek theater and a hippodrome (horse track) in Jerusalem. He made Greek, instead of Aramaic, the official language of government. He earned Jewish ill will by building numerous temples to pagan deities in the Hellenistic cities of Judea and throughout the eastern Mediterranean. The Jewish historian Josephus describes Herod as having an "irreligious spirit" and as "cruel to all alike and one who easily gave in to anger and was contemptuous of justice" (*Jewish Antiquities* 17.191).

Herod was seen by many Judeans as an outsider who treated the Jews contemptuously. Many lived in great fear, according to Josephus. Although Josephus does not mention a slaughter of male infants like the one described in Matthew 2:16, the story is consistent with Josephus's portrayal of Herod as ruthless and suspicious of any perceived rival.

After Herod's death in 4 B.C., a number of bands of guerrillas rose up in revolt. The Roman governor of Syria, Quinctilius Varus, had to send troops on two occasions to put down the disturbances. As mentioned above, at one point

Varus brought into Judea three legions (about fifteen thousand men), an unknown number of auxiliary troops and troops from allied kingdoms. His campaign ended with the crucifixion of two thousand Jewish prisoners. Varus temporarily left one legion behind in Judea. It probably returned to Syria after Augustus confirmed the division of the Judean kingdom based on Herod's will.

After the death of Herod, Sabinus, a procurator of equestrian rank who oversaw taxation and payment of the troops, took charge of the royal treasuries in Jerusalem. He did so apparently because Herod's will left a great deal of money to Augustus and to Varus, and Rome wanted to be sure they received this money.

### The Division of Palestine

This brings us to the New Testament era. It is important to see how Rome superintended the division of Palestine among Herod's sons if we would understand the political dynamics behind New Testament events (see map 3 for these divisions). One lesson is that these rulers on the whole, even though they were not Roman governors, seemed more concerned with pleasing Rome than with serving the interests of the Jewish people. Of course, they would seek to justify their compromises with Rome as accommodation to a difficult situation. After all, Rome held all of the cards. There is some truth to this, but the energy with which they went about proving their loyalty to Rome seems more than was necessary just to keep the lion at bay.

Herod's will divided his kingdom among three of his sons. These sons all had been raised in the city of Rome and so were immersed in Roman culture and ways of thinking. They, along with dissatisfied relatives of Herod and a Jewish embassy seeking dissolution of Herod's dynasty, brought their claims to Augustus in Rome. Augustus for the most part ratified the will of Herod, although he did grant semi-independence to several Greek cities that had been under Herod's rule (including at least Gadara, Hippos and Gaza). Antipas was made tetrarch of Galilee and Peraea. His half brother Philip was designated tetrarch of the territory east of Galilee, which Augustus had given to Herod. Archelaus, the full brother of Antipas, was given about half of Herod's kingdom. He was named ethnarch of Judea, Samaria and Idumaea.

*Philip.* Philip ruled from 4 B.C. to A.D. 34. Luke 3:1 describes his territory as "the region of Ituraea and Trachonitis." It also included Aurantis, Gaulantis, Batanaea and the area around Paneas. This area is east of Galilee, north of Decapolis, and south of the tetrarchy of Abilene. His rule was relatively tranquil. His capital was the town of Paneas, rebuilt as a Hellenistic city and renamed Caesarea in honor of Caesar. It was commonly called Philip's Caesarea or Caesarea Philippi to distinguish it from the Caesarea built by his father on the coast (Mt 16:13). Philip rebuilt the fishing village of Bethsaida at the northeast corner of the Sea of Galilee (Mk 6:45; Lk 9:10) as a Hellenistic city named Bethsaida Julias, in honor of Augustus's daughter Julia. Most of Philip's subjects were non-Jews, so he did not have to be too concerned about Jewish religious sensibilities. In fact, he ordered the printing of coinage bearing the images of the emperors Augustus and Tiberius, a sacrilege to devout Jews. Josephus considered Philip tolerant and moderate. When Philip died in A.D. 34, his tetrarchy was put under the legate of Syria.

*Herod Antipas.* Herod Antipas served Roman interests well as tetrarch ("ruler of a quarter") of Galilee and Peraea from 4 B.C. to A.D. 39. The references in Mark and Matthew to Antipas as "King Herod" (Mk 6:14, 22, 25-27; Mt 14:9) follow the habit of the local people, who referred to him as king even though he never rose above the level of tetrarch. Antipas is called "Herod the tetrarch" elsewhere in the New Testament (Mt 14:1; Lk 3:19; 9:7; Acts 13:1).

He executed John the Baptist (Mt 14:1; Lk 3:19), who had publicly criticized Antipas's marriage. Some time before A.D. 30 Antipas had discarded his current wife, the daughter of the Nabataean king, and married Herodias. Herodias was the granddaughter of Herod the Great's sister Salome and sister of Herod Agrippa (see below). In order to marry him, Herodias had to divorce her current husband, one of Antipas's stepbrothers (Philip according to Mark; Herod II, the son of Herod the Great by Mariamne II, according to Josephus). Such a divorce was acceptable in the Greco-Roman world and legal for Roman citizens like the Herods, but it was a violation of the Jewish law, which forbade marrying the wife of one's living brother (Mt 14:1-11; Lk 3:19-20). Josephus says that John the Baptist was imprisoned because he had a large following and therefore was suspected of revolutionary motives. Perhaps Jesus was thinking of this particular divorce and remarriage when he declared, according to Mark 10:11-12, that whoever divorces his wife and marries another commits adultery.

Later, the father of Antipas's first wife, the king of Nabataea, used this divorce as a pretext to attack and defeat the forces of Antipas. Josephus says that many Jews believed this defeat was God's punishment on Antipas for his execution of the "good and righteous" John (*Jewish Antiquities* 18.109-24). The current legate of Syria, Vitellius, was ordered by the emperor to bring forces to the defense of Antipas after Antipas wrote for help. However, before Vitellius took his troops into battle, he learned of the death of the emperor. He promptly marched back to Syria, allowing Antipas to be defeated.

Mark's brief sketch of the Galilean court of Herod Antipas is a classic portrait of a petty king of this era: "Herod on his birthday gave a banquet for his lords and military commanders and the leading men of Galilee" (Mk 6:21 NASB). His term for "lords" occurs also in the Roman historian Tacitus's description of the barons of Armenia, and the Septuagint uses it to refer to the "lords" of Belshazzar (Tacitus *Annals* 15.27; Dan 5:23). They appear to be not just upper-class men (Mark's "leading men" probably refers to the upper class) but the inner circle of the king's government. The term for "military commanders" *(chiliarchoi)*, despite its Roman overtones, refers here to the kind of commanders of the forces that the king in the parable sent against his rebellious subjects (Mt 22:7). The fact that they are only "commanders of a thousand" is in keeping with the small size of Antipas's tetrarchy. Antipas would not have had more than a few thousand soldiers. That a Latin term, *speculator,* is used for the "executioner" sent to order John's beheading suggests the strong Roman influence over a petty Jewish prince (Mk 6:27).[12]

Sepphoris in Galilee was a center of rebellion following Herod the Great's death, perhaps because of its ties to the priestly Hasmonaean dynasty. It was burned and its residents sold into slavery. Later, Herod Antipas rebuilt it as an "ornament of all Galilee" (Josephus *Jewish Antiquities* 18.27). Although most of its citizens were Jewish, Sepphoris supported Rome in the revolt of A.D. 66.

Antipas respected Jewish sensibilities when it suited him to do so. For instance, he built the city of Tiberias and named it for his friend and master, the emperor Tiberius. Herod Antipas had become friends with Tiberius when he was growing up in Rome. Tiberias was intended to be primarily a Jewish city. According to Josephus, Antipas ignored the discovery of an old cemetery within the city limits, which made the city unfit for Jewish habitation according to the Torah (Num 19:11-16). Antipas finished the city, but he had to bribe and force poor Jews to live there. While the majority of the population was Jewish, the city constitution followed Greek customs. Tiberias had a democratic council of six hundred members, elected officials and a mint to make its own coins. By the end of the first century, the Sea of Galilee would be renamed the Lake of Tiberias under the influence of this city.

Events in Antipas's career provide chronological anchors for Luke's narrative. The Gospel of Luke refers to four interventions by Antipas: his arrest of John at the beginning of Jesus' mission (Lk 3:19-20); the conversion of Joanna, the wife of his procurator Chuza in the first phase of Jesus' mission (Lk 8:3); his alarm at the new preaching of Jesus at the time of the mission of the twelve (Lk 9:7-9); and the warning that Antipas wanted to kill Jesus, along with Jesus' response, toward the end of the mission in Galilee (Lk 13:31-32).

The Gospel of Luke alone gives Antipas an important role in the execution of Jesus (Lk 13:31; 23:6-12). Here as elsewhere Luke seems to argue that the

Romans were not ultimately to blame for Jesus' death. Luke does not mention the mocking of Jesus by Roman soldiers referred to in the other Gospels, and Luke is the only Gospel to have Pilate declare Jesus' innocence three times (Lk 23:4, 13-16, 22). This does not mean that Luke invented the incident with Antipas, but it indicates that he may have played down sources critical of the Romans and emphasized those showing Jewish antipathy to Jesus. Pilate referred Jesus' case to Antipas because Jesus' home region, Galilee, was under Antipas's rule. Antipas may have felt gratitude for the deference Pilate showed him by doing so. Luke 23:12 says that Antipas and Pilate became friends from that day.

Antipas's actions in mocking Jesus were politically savvy. He neither legally condemned Jesus, which would have been unpopular with his people, nor exonerated him, which could have made trouble for him with Rome. His actions demonstrated his unwillingness to protect a subject accused of fomenting rebellion against Rome and his support for whatever decision Pilate would render. Such an action was likely to impress Pilate and help smooth over the strife between them. It should be noted that Luke's statement that Antipas and Herod became friends at that time suggests that Antipas's treatment of Jesus showed loyalty to Rome and its influence in Palestine. Luke can hardly be seen as somehow excusing Rome from responsibility for Jesus' death.

The desire to revolt, so prevalent among the Jews of Judea in the Gospel accounts, seems to have been absent in Antipas's territories. Antipas ruled Galilee as tetrarch until he was deposed by the emperor Gaius Caligula in A.D. 39. According to Josephus, Antipas was persuaded by his wife, Herodias, to petition Gaius for the status of king. Agrippa likely convinced Herodias to make this suggestion as a way to discredit Antipas as power-hungry. Her brother, Herod Agrippa, then told Gaius that Antipas was in league with Rome's great enemy in the region, Parthia. He added that Antipas had stockpiled enough weapons to arm seventy thousand men. Antipas was unable to disprove the charge and was exiled. His tetrarchy was added to Agrippa's kingdom in 41 (Josephus *Jewish Antiquities* 18.240-56).

*Archelaus.* Archelaus ruled as ethnarch ("national ruler") over Judea, Samaria and Idumaea (Mt 2:22). His rule seems to have been quite brutal. In fact, in A.D. 6 an embassy of leading Jews and Samaritans convinced Emperor Augustus to depose Archelaus. Augustus exiled him to the Rhone Valley in Germany, and turned his territory into an imperial province under the control of a prefect of equestrian rank. This action shows that Rome was at times responsive to claims of unjust administration by the upper classes in Rome's conquered lands. It also shows that Rome was becoming concerned about the ability of local rulers to maintain control, and beginning to feel the need to intervene directly. With Philip's death in 34 and Antipas's deposition in 39, Rome little by little took direct control of the entire region. It would govern Palestine directly from this point on, except during the four-year rule of Herod Agrippa (see below).

### The Roman Province of Judea

In A.D. 6, Rome established in Judea a new kind of province. Judea became a second-rank imperial province whose governor was a prefect of equestrian rank rather than a legate of the higher, senatorial rank. This action shows that, while Judea was not of the strategic importance of a Syria or an Egypt, Rome considered it troublesome enough to require direct control.

The prefect of Judea commanded a small number of non-Roman auxiliary troops trained by Romans. Some of these auxiliaries may have been once among the troops Herod recruited in Sebaste and Caesarea. The administrative center of the province was Caesarea, but troops were stationed in Jerusalem's fortress of Antonia next to the temple. Romans probably also occupied the palace of Herod in the upper city. As far as we know, placement of a garrison in a provincial city was rare in the early Empire. Clearly the importance of the temple as a rallying point for national sentiments made Jerusalem an unusual place.[13]

The Jewish Sanhedrin in Jerusalem functioned as a kind of senate of the province. Its members were drawn from leading families in the usual provincial

pattern. The presiding officer was the high priest Annas from A.D. 6 to 15. The high priest was the most important political person in Judea after the governor (Mt 26:3; Lk 3:2; Jn 18:24; Acts 4:5-6). Because of this, the Roman governor controlled the appointment of the high priest, as had Herod and Archelaus.

The Romans also kept custody of the high priestly garments, releasing them to the Jews for religious festivals only four times a year. We know of no other local religious cult over which the Romans exercised this degree of official control. The Romans did, however, allow the Jews control over most other religious matters. For example, they permitted Jews throughout the Empire to send to Jerusalem the annual temple tax of half a shekel. Jews also were exempted from participating in emperor worship. Instead, they offered sacrifices every day in the temple on behalf of the emperor.

*Syrian oversight of Judea.* The prefect of Judea was under the supervision of the legate of Syria, who was a senator and who commanded Roman soldiers. On several occasions, the legate of Syria had to address problems in Judea. In A.D. 6 the legate of Syria was Publius Sulpicius Quirinius. He oversaw the liquidation of Archelaus's estate and, in accordance with Roman practice under Augustus when setting up a new province, ordered a census to determine how much tribute Rome should expect from Judea.[14]

Quirinius was engaged at the same time in a census of the province of Syria. In 27 B.C. the imposition of a similar census in Gaul led to local disturbances and resistance. The census in Judea provoked an uprising, led by Judas of Galilee. Judas and a Pharisee named Saddok argued that submission to Rome was a form of slavery and that God would assist the fight for freedom (Josephus *Jewish Antiquities* 18.1). In fact, this census gave impetus to the creation of the zealot movement. Despite the disturbances, the census was completed and tribute began to be paid. The question of whether to pay this census was difficult to answer directly, as the Gospels make clear. A religious leader who said yes risked losing all support of the people, whereas one who said no risked the charge of inciting revolt. The Gospels indicate that some Pharisees and Herodians tried to trap Jesus with this issue (Mt 22:16-22; Mk 12:13-17; Lk 20:20-26).

From A.D. 6 on each Jew in Judea had to pay both tribute to Rome in the form of a property tax and a tax for the Jewish temple. The tribute imposed on Judea apparently was severe. Only a few years later, in A.D. 17, the provinces of Syria and Judea petitioned Rome for a reduction of the tax (Tacitus *Annals* 2.42.7). Matthew and Mark refer to this tax with a Greek transliteration of the Latin word *census* (Mt 22:15-22; Mk 12:14-17), while Luke uses the Greek word for tribute (Lk 20:21-26).

*The Roman governors of Judea.* The New Testament mentions by name only three of the fourteen Roman governors who served between A.D. 6 and 66. The most famous is Pontius Pilatus (Pilate), who executed Jesus. The other two are Marcus Antonius Felix and Porcius Festus, who appear in the Acts account of Paul's arrest and imprisonment in Caesarea (Acts 23—27). None of these fourteen governors excelled in tact and sensitivity toward Jewish sensibilities (see the chronology in appendix A for a list of the governors of Judea).

The first prefect of Judea, a Roman of equestrian status named Coponius, ruled from Caesarea but kept a Roman garrison in Jerusalem under a military tribune. He resided in Jerusalem during the great festivals when rioting was most apt to occur. This custom was followed by later prefects, including Pilate.

Josephus tells us that Coponius came with the power to order capital punishment (*Jewish War* 2.117). Coponius was succeeded in A.D. 9 by Marcus Ambivius, who was succeeded in 12 by Annius Rufus. In 15, Valerius Gratus replaced Rufus. In three years, Gratus deposed and appointed four high priests, probably to enrich himself from the bribes offered for this important post. The last high priest Gratus appointed was Joseph Caiaphas, son-in-law of Annas,

ᴡas high priest when Gratus first became prefect (Jn 18:23-38). Caiaphas
:d from A.D. 18 to 36.

*Pontius Pilate.* Pontius Pilate succeeded Gratus as prefect of Judea in 26 and
served until 36. Both the New Testament and the Jewish historian Josephus tell
us that Pilate's relationship with Jewish leaders in Judea was often rocky. Early
in his administration, Pilate brought into Jerusalem by night military standards
that bore medallion busts of the emperor. This was contrary to the custom of
his predecessors and highly offensive to many Jews. When the Jews of Jerusalem saw them the next day, they besieged Pilate with complaints. They even
followed him back to Caesarea, ignoring his threats of military response. When
Pilate saw that a mass uprising was brewing, he gave in and removed the
images (Josephus *Jewish War* 2.169-74; *Jewish Antiquities* 18.55-59).

On another occasion, Pilate attempted to set up golden shields inscribed with
his and the emperor Tiberius's names on the walls of Herod's palace in
Jerusalem. Although the shields bore no image, the Jews apparently considered
this a violation of the religious sanctity of Jerusalem. The practice of emperor
worship, which by then had become well established in the East, and which the
Jews violently opposed, may have made the Jews suspect that Pilate intended
to institute this practice in Jerusalem. When Tiberius received a letter of complaint from the leading Jewish citizens (including Herod Antipas and three of
his brothers), he ordered Pilate to move the shields to the temple of Augustus
in Caesarea. This relocation of the shields to a site of emperor worship suggests
that the shields indeed were religious symbols.

One of Pilate's building projects brought yet another clash with the Jewish
leaders in Judea. Pilate built an aqueduct to bring water to Jerusalem from the
southern hills (Josephus *Jewish War* 2.175-77; *Jewish Antiquities* 18.62). This led
to an uproar when the Jews in Jerusalem found out that Pilate had taken money
from the temple treasury to pay for the project. Pilate used troops to break up
the demonstrations, killing a number of Jews in the process. This is the closest
account in Josephus to an incident mentioned in Luke 13:1, where Pilate is said
to have mingled the blood of Galileans with their sacrifices. Since Pilate had no
jurisdiction in Galilee, and since Galilean Jews came to Jerusalem to sacrifice,
such an incident most likely would have occurred during a major religious
festival. If Galileans were in Jerusalem for a festival when Pilate used troops to
put down the demonstrations, Galilean Jews might well have been killed. Of
course, Luke may have been referring to a different incident.

Pilate had to consider how his actions in Judea would be interpreted by not
only the emperor Tiberias but also by Sejanus, Tiberius's chief adviser. Sejanus
seems to have encouraged anti-Semitic actions throughout the Empire. After

Sejanus was condemned for treason in 31, Tiberius apparently was more sympathetic to the wishes of the local Jewish authorities in the Sanhedrin. But prior to Sejanus's downfall, Pilate would have needed to consider carefully how Sejanus might interpret his actions with regard to the Jews. This may explain his conduct at the trial of Jesus (no later than 30), and the role of Barabbas, who may well have been a zealot (if so, his terrorist activities may have led to his arrest (Mk 15:7).

Pilate demonstrated his ruthlessness once again in A.D. 36. A group of Samaritans had followed a Samaritan prophet to Mount Gerazim in Samaria. This prophet's claims of a messiahlike identity apparently worried Pilate enough that he sent soldiers to break up the group. A number of people died in this incident. Samaritan leaders complained to the legate of Syria, who ordered Pilate to return to Rome to explain his actions to the emperor Tiberius. By the time Pilate arrived in Rome, Tiberius was dead (A.D. 37), but Pilate was not allowed to return to Judea.

A letter written in 40 by Herod Agrippa to his friend, the emperor Gaius Caligula, describes Pilate as "naturally inflexible, a blend of self-will and relentlessness" (Philo *Legatio* 301). Philo of Alexandria, a contemporary of Pilate, describes in a letter to the emperor Gaius the crimes of Pilate, which included "the briberies, the insults, the robberies, the outrages and wanton injuries, the executions without trial constantly repeated, the ceaseless and supremely grievous cruelty."[15]

In the absence of a prefect of Judea, the governor of Syria, Vitellius, acted as governor of Judea as well. He replaced the high priest Caiaphas with Jonathan, son of Annas. Vitellius tried to pacify the Jews by returning the high priest's vestments to the high priest's keeping. Josephus says that he wrote to Tiberius for permission before doing so (*Jewish Antiquities* 15.11.4). In keeping with Roman custom, the new emperor Gaius appointed a new prefect, Marullus. Marullus continued to administer Roman government in Judea until the death of Gaius in A.D. 41 (Josephus *Jewish Antiquities* 18.89).

The Gospel accounts of Jesus' trial before Pilate differ somewhat in details. In general, Luke and John are the most positive toward Pilate. For example, Luke has Pilate say three times that he finds no guilt in Jesus (Lk 23:4, 14, 22), while John has him say it twice (Jn 18:38; 19:4) and has him try to release Jesus three times (Jn 18:39; 19:11, 15). In addition, only Luke includes the incident with Antipas (Lk 23:7) and only John has Pilate defend the inscription above Jesus (Jn 19:19-22). Finally, both downplay the scourging and mocking of Jesus by the Romans. Luke mentions only the mocking soldiers at the cross (Lk 23:36), and John mentions only in passing that Jesus is scourged (Jn 19:1).

132 The Greco-Roman World of the New Testament Era

By contrast, Matthew and Mark have extended passages on the scourging, which put Pilate and the Romans in a more negative light (Mt 27:27-31; Mk 15:16-20). They do not portray Pilate as emphatic in his declaration of Jesus' innocence or in his attempts to release him. On the other hand, all four accounts agree that Pilate found no legal reason to execute Jesus and did so reluctantly, at the behest of the leaders in Jerusalem. Matthew's unique contribution is to mention the dream of Pilate's wife and Pilate's apparent attempt to follow her warning, which has the effect of softening the portrayal of Pilate.

It would not be correct to conclude that Luke and John give dramatically more positive portrayals of Pilate and the Romans. If all we knew about Pilate came from these accounts, we might conclude that he was disinterested in Jewish religious affairs, generally willing to perform justice but sophisticated enough to realize that doing the right thing could have grave consequences for his political survival. The Gospel portraits do not conflict with the descriptions of Josephus and others, but the latter suggest that he was more insensitive to Jewish religious concerns and less capable of political compromise than we might have suspected based on the Gospels.

*Herod Agrippa.* The Romans made Herod Agrippa king of Judea in 41. He ruled until 44. It may seem strange that the Romans, after governing Judea as a province for thirty-five years, returned it to a Jewish monarch. But Agrippa was a Jewish monarch who had assimilated Roman values more thoroughly than any of his predecessors, and he had friends in high places.

Born in 10 B.C., Agrippa was spirited away to Rome by his mother Berenice (niece of Herod) shortly after his grandfather Herod killed his father Aristobulus in 7 B.C. In Rome, Berenice became close to Antonia, the mother of Claudius and grandmother of Gaius Caligula. Berenice's mother, Salome, would later develop a strong friendship with Livia, wife of Caesar Augustus. Agrippa thus mixed with the children of the imperial family at an early age and established relationships that served him well in later years.

While Jesus Christ was approaching his crucifixion, Agrippa was a young man in Rome pursuing a lifestyle far beyond his means. The death of his good friend Drusus, son of the emperor Tiberius, left Agrippa outside the imperial circle and with huge debts. To escape his creditors, Agrippa left Rome for Idumaea, the homeland of his grandfather. He contemplated suicide before his brother-in-law (and half uncle), Herod Antipas, tetrarch of Galilee and Peraea, put him in charge of the financial affairs of his new capital, Tiberias. After a short time he tired of the life of a civil servant, and by 32 or 33 he moved to Syria where an old friend from his Roman days, Lucius Pomponius Flaccus, was now governor. In 36 Agrippa was caught peddling influence with the governor.

To flee this charge and his mounting debts in Syria, Agrippa returned to Rome. Tiberius received him warmly, and Antonia, apparently out of affection for Agrippa's mother and in regard for his friendship with her son Claudius, lent him the money to pay his debts. Sensing that Gaius's star was rising, Agrippa cultivated his friendship. Agrippa's influence on the young man apparently was strong and lasting. Some months after arriving in Italy, Agrippa was imprisoned because he had wished for the emperor Tiberius's death in a conversation with Gaius. Antonia made sure he was comfortable in prison.

Agrippa used his influence with the emperor Gaius to protect the Jewish people on at least one occasion. In the city of Jamnia sometime in the late 30s, the local Jews attacked and desecrated a new altar to the cult of emperor worship. In revenge, Gaius ordered the abolition of the Jewish cult at Jerusalem and sent the Roman Petronius at the head of three legions to enact his order. The pleas of Herod Agrippa helped convince Petronius to delay the action. Soon thereafter, while the order was still pending, Gaius was assassinated and the order expired. After the death of Gaius, Agrippa played intermediary between the next emperor, Claudius, and the senate, when that body initially resisted accepting him as emperor (Josephus *Jewish War* 2.184-213).

In 41 Claudius appointed Agrippa king in an effort to calm the rising tensions in Judea. Until his death in 44, Agrippa ruled a united Galilee, Peraea and Judea. In many ways Agrippa was the perfect political choice. The Romans knew him and trusted him to rule with their best interests at heart. He could also claim to be the most legitimate ruler of the Jews based on his grandmother's connection to the Hasmonaean dynasty. And he was perhaps the least disliked by the Jews of all the Herodians. Agrippa persuaded the emperor Claudius to speak in favor of Jewish rights in Alexandria and around the Empire (Josephus *Jewish Antiquities* 19.279, 288), but Agrippa was always Rome's man, regardless of his bloodline.

Acts reports a meeting between Agrippa and embassies from Tyre and Sidon (Acts 12:20). They had angered him and were seeking to regain his favor. They needed his support because much of the lands around them were part of his kingdom, and their economies depended on commerce with his kingdom. The apparent absence of the legate of Syria is another indication that he did not intervene in Judea unless forced to by circumstances.[16]

Agrippa's royal army was at least partly composed of the provincial auxiliary troops that had served the last prefect of Judea. They passed back into Roman service on the king's death in 44. That the Romans would allow a client king to control Roman-trained troops is another measure of Claudius's faith in Agrippa.

Agrippa observed the Jewish festivals, offered daily sacrifices and defended the dominance of Pharisaic Judaism by imprisoning and executing members of rival groups, such as the early Christian community. Acts says that when Agrippa saw that his arrest of James, the brother of John, "pleased the Jews," he also arrested Peter.[17] This depiction harmonizes with Josephus's description of Agrippa as someone who devoted himself to Jewish rights and causes.

But Agrippa was thoroughly pro-Roman and Hellenistic in his tastes. He preferred to live in Caesarea rather than Jerusalem. His coins were stamped with his image, in Greco-Roman fashion. According to Josephus, he was celebrating a festival of the cult of emperor worship when he suddenly collapsed in great pain. Some at the time attributed it to divine retribution for his behavior. Josephus says that as he stood in the stands at the games, the sunlight reflecting off his clothing made him appear superhuman. Some of the nobility there hailed him as divine, and, since he did not correct them, he was immediately felled with a heart attack, which led to his death five days later (*Jewish Antiquities* 19.343-52). Acts 12 places him in his palace addressing a delegation from Tyre and Sidon when he is hailed as a god and "an angel of the Lord struck him" and he died. Despite differences over location and other details, Josephus and Acts agree that Agrippa was struck down by God for accepting praise as a deity.

### Judea Reverts to a Province

Following the death of Agrippa in 44, Judea reverted to a Roman province. The emperor Claudius had intended to give the kingdom to Agrippa's son, Agrippa II, who had been raised at Claudius's court. But the boy was only sixteen when Agrippa died, and Claudius decided he was too young for the position.

Judea province once again was governed by a Roman of equestrian rank, now called a procurator, but no different in function or authority from the earlier prefects. The first of these, Cuspius Fadus (44-46), allowed the Gentiles from Caesarea and Sebaste who composed his auxiliary troops to stay in Judea against Claudius's orders. Fadus demanded custody of the high-priestly robes that Roman prefects had held from A.D. 6 to 36. The Jewish authorities appealed to the new legate in Syria, Cassius Longinus, for the right to retain them. Longinus brought a large force to Jerusalem to support Fadus in this demand, in case the Jews resisted. The Jewish leaders then sent an embassy to the emperor Claudius in Rome, who, influenced by Agrippa II (then in Rome) and others, granted the Jews' request. This is another clear example of how Roman policy could be influenced by personal contact.

**Figure 6.2. The Arch of Titus, Rome, Italy. Built in the late first century A.D., this arch commemorates Rome's victory in the Jewish Revolt, A.D. 68-74.**

Soon after this, King Herod, brother of Agrippa I and ruler of Chalcis, asked for and was granted by the Romans authority over the temple and its funds and the right to select the high priest (Josephus *Jewish Antiquities* 20.15-16). Why did the Romans do this? They probably saw it as a way to pacify the Jews. This meant that Judeans were subject to the Roman governor in some areas, but in other areas they answered to a Jewish king who ruled a separate kingdom.

Fadus put to death a Jewish rebel named Theudas. Acts 5:36 mentions Theudas but does not say how he died.

Under the next governor, Cumanus (A.D. 48-52), the Romans once again injured Jewish sensibilities and had to deal with protests and uprisings. One or more Galilean Jews were killed by some Samaritans while they passed through Samaria on their way to Passover in Jerusalem. Cumanus's failure to prevent a reprisal by Jews led to the deaths of a number of Samaritans and Jews. The Samaritans appealed to the current legate of Syria, one Ummidius Quadratus. After several hearings, Quadratus executed several people and sent the Samaritan and Jewish leaders (including the high priest Ananias), along with Cumanus, to the emperor. Here Agrippa II once again showed his ability, though barely twenty years old, to influence the emperor. Based on Agrippa's counsel, the Samaritan leaders were executed and Cumanus was exiled (Josephus *Jewish War* 2.245-46). An incident in Luke, some twenty years earlier, reflects this hostility between Jews and Samaritans when Jesus and his disciples were refused permission to travel through Samaria on their way to Passover (Lk 9:51-56).

The next procurator, Marcus Antonius Felix (52-59?), once had been the slave of Antonia, daughter of Mark Antony and mother of the emperor Claudius. Felix's brother, Pallas, also a freedman, became chief accountant of Rome's public treasury under Claudius. Pallas may have helped his brother get this post in Judea. As an indication of the power and status Felix had achieved, all three of his wives were of royal birth despite his slave origin. His wife when he met the Apostle Paul was Drusilla, youngest daughter of Herod Agrippa I and sister of Agrippa II. Contrary to traditional Jewish religious law, Felix married Drusilla without converting to Judaism. In addition, Drusilla divorced her previous husband to marry him. This may not have been unusual among the upper classes of Jews who had largely assimilated to Roman standards, but it would have grated on the sensibilities of many lower-class Jews. Felix used troops to put down a self-proclaimed Jewish prophet from Egypt who planned to liberate Jerusalem. About this time, the apostle Paul was apparently mistaken for this Egyptian (Acts 21:38).[18]

Josephus says that Felix tended to side with the Greek-speaking residents of Caesarea in their disagreements with the Jewish residents, even when the former killed a number of Jews (*Jewish War* 2.270). The Roman historian Tacitus found it obscene that a former slave like Felix could hold the authority of a governor. Upper-class opposition to upward mobility of any kind may be reflected in his appraisal of Felix: he "practiced every kind of cruelty and lust, wielding the power of a king with all the instincts of a slave" (*Histories* 5.9).

By contrast, the author of Acts seems to consider Felix an enlightened ruler. For example, a Jewish spokesman shows gratitude to Felix for the "long period of peace" he has brought to Judea, and Paul expresses confidence that Felix will give his case a fair hearing (Acts 24:2-3, 10). Paul's expression of confidence in him was misplaced, however. Felix let Paul's trial drag on for two years (Acts 24:27). But even a Roman citizen in the provinces, such as Paul, had every reason to avoid antagonizing a Roman governor. Local leaders had even more reason not to mention past atrocities.

The narrative in Acts tells us that Felix's wife is Jewish. It does not mention that their union violated Jewish law, but it does say that after Paul talked to them about "righteousness, self-control and the judgment to come," Felix became afraid and sent Paul away (Acts 24:24-25). The reason for presenting these themes, rather than talking about the resurrection of Christ, would have been clear to the reader who knew about the impropriety of the marriage of Felix and Drusilla. Acts also tells us that Felix engaged in the (not uncommon) practice of accepting bribes from prisoners (Acts 24:26).

Felix's successor, Porcius Festus (59-62?), reportedly sent troops to put down the rebellious followers of a self-proclaimed Jewish savior. He heard Paul's case quickly and consulted Agrippa II, by this time a local king (see below). Festus agreed to Paul's request to be sent to Rome for trial (Acts 24:27—26:32). Festus seems to have been a man of higher caliber than Felix, but the damage to Roman-Judean relations had already been done. The Jews were disgusted and permanently alienated. Festus died while in office. Judea had no governor for several months following his death. During this interim a number of Christians, including James, the brother of Jesus, were stoned to death.

The next governor, Albinus (62-64), stole private property and extorted additional taxes from the people of Judea, according to Josephus. He allowed imprisoned rebels to bribe their way out of jail (*Jewish War* 2.277-343).

His successor, Gessius Florus (64-66), was even worse than Albinus, according to Josephus. He sided with Greeks against the Jews, stole money from the temple treasury, allowed his soldiers to kill and plunder, and violated Roman law by crucifying upper-class Jews with Roman citizenship (see chapter nine).[19]

*Herod Agrippa II.* Agrippa II was the son of Agrippa I and the great-grandson of Herod the Great. When King Herod of Chalcis, uncle of Agrippa II, died around A.D. 50, Agrippa II was fourteen years older than when his father died. Now Claudius decided it was time to allow him to rule. So Claudius gave him Chalcis as well as the care of the Jewish temple and the right to appoint the Jewish high priests. Agrippa II would appoint six high priests during his rule. Although Judea was a Roman province, Agrippa's close connections with Rome and its emperor allowed him to call into session the Sanhedrin. He was also able to maintain a palace in Jerusalem. He built an addition to this palace, in violation of Jewish custom, to allow him to see the temple sacrifices (Josephus *Jewish Antiquities* 20.191). In A.D. 53, the emperor Claudius took back Chalcis and gave Agrippa a kingdom that included the former tetrarchy of Philip in northeastern Palestine. The new kingdom also incorporated two nearby territories, including the region of the Decapolis mentioned in the New Testament. This marked the first time in 40 years that the Decapolis had passed out of direct Roman rule. Agrippa ruled this area from 53 to 93.[20]

The book of Acts illustrates the complexity of government in Judea in the 50s and 60s (Acts 21:17—27:1). The riot when Paul was accused of taking a Gentile into the temple probably resulted from the resentment many Jews felt toward occupation by Gentiles and the reverence they felt for the temple. If this accusation was calculated by Paul's Jewish opponents, it was a shrewd move. Since the care of the temple was not under direct Roman control, violations of its sanctity might be punished without Roman involvement. But the handling of Paul indicates an uncertainty about jurisdiction between Jewish and Roman authorities that probably was not uncommon, especially where the temple was concerned. Paul was first allowed to address the crowd directly, then the next day brought before the Sanhedrin at the request of the Roman tribune in Jerusalem, then taken by a guard of 470 soldiers to the Roman governor in Caesarea.

The speeches at Paul's hearing in Caesarea reflect the politics of jurisdiction in a Roman province (Acts 24). Tertullus, a representative of the high priest Ananias, commends the governor for his reforms. He accuses Paul of stirring up dissension, something that always concerned the ruling Romans, and of desecrating the temple, knowing that the Romans understood the sensitivity of this issue. He accuses the Roman procurator of violence in taking Paul from them. He ends by expressing confidence in the governor's ability to rule properly. Thus Tertullus pursued a careful course of acknowledging Roman sovereignty while maintaining certain traditional rights of the Jews under Roman rule. The other speech, by Paul, also expresses respect for the governor's rule. He denies the charges of stirring up unrest and of desecrating the temple.

Paul remained in prison in Caesarea for two years before Agrippa II and his sister Berenice made an expected diplomatic visit to Festus, the new governor in Caesarea. They, along with Festus, heard Paul's case. Agrippa found Paul innocent of any serious charge (Acts 25:13—26:32).

Acts does not comment upon the relationship of Berenice and Agrippa. Josephus tells us that Agrippa II was widely rumored to be having an incestuous affair with her, his recently widowed sister (*Jewish Antiquities* 20.145). In light of Josephus's information, the account in Acts becomes clearer. If Agrippa was indeed having an affair with his sister, Paul's claim that Agrippa is "expert in Jewish customs and issues" paints a portrait of a supreme hypocrite (Acts 26:2-3, 26-27). Perhaps Paul's appeal to Agrippa's knowledge is really a subtle attack on his current lifestyle. This would have been pretty cheeky of a man in jail, but it would not have been the first time Paul showed such moral courage.

At the beginning of the great Jewish rebellion in 66, Agrippa made a long speech, arguing that God was now with the Romans and condemning what he considered to be the non-Jewish behavior of the rebels (Josephus *Jewish War* 2.345-404).

*The Jewish revolts.* Revolts occurred by the Jews in the 60s and again in the 130s. They seem to have been inspired by a belief that, while humanly the odds against success were great, God could and would help bring about a miraculous liberation as he had in the second century B.C. Under the procurator Gessius Florus in A.D. 66, a dispute between Greeks and Jews in Caesarea led to an unsympathetic show of force by the Romans. Zealots responded by seizing the fortress at Masada and massacring its Roman garrison. The priestly establishment joined the revolt when it suspended sacrifices on behalf of the emperor. This amounted to a declaration of war against the Empire. In response, Jews were massacred in many cities (Josephus *Jewish War* 2.456-58, 477-80, 559-61).

The emperor Nero named the Roman general Vespasian as legate in charge of the war in Judea. Vespasian's forces consisted of three regular Roman legions, accompanied by around fourteen thousand auxiliary troops and cavalry and some eighteen thousand soldiers supplied by neighboring dependent kingdoms. By the middle of 68, Rome had regained control of the whole area except for Jerusalem. The war was interrupted for a year when Nero died and his generals fought for the succession. Vespasian was one of the claimants, and he used Caesarea and Antioch as his main bases of operations. While Vespasian sought support from other Roman leaders for his bid to become emperor, his son Titus continued the war in Judea. Following a year-long siege, Titus captured Jerusalem in 70, destroyed the temple, and tore down the city walls. The last fortress to fall, in 73, was Masada (see in figure 6.2 a photograph of the Arch of Titus, erected next to the Roman Forum to commemorate the Roman victory).

After 70, the Romans took steps to improve the administration of Judea province. The post of governor was upgraded to the rank of imperial legate and given to men with experience in provincial government. A full legion of professional soldiers was stationed in Jerusalem. The Romans required Jews to continue paying the temple tax, but now the tax was paid to the Romans for the maintenance of the temple of Jupiter erected in Jerusalem.

### Roman Governance and the Gospels

While Acts provides a lot of information about Roman governance, the Gospels have little to say about it. In the Gospels, Rome appears as an oppressing overlord, hovering behind the scenes. It is never forgotten, but it is simply not an issue in the daily life of the average Galilean and Judean.

The government above the level of the village in the Gospels, for the most part, is a world of kings and princes, not of emperors, legates and procurators. This world only existed for a brief time, just before and during the New Testament era. It was a complicated pattern of minor principalities, extending from the kingdom of Petra and the Nabataean Arabs in the south to the princedom of Commagene in the north. Beyond King Herod and the tetrarchs of Palestine were petty kingdoms such as those of Samsiceramus of Emesa, Tarcondimotus of the Cilician mountains and Ptolemy of the Ituraean kingdom in Lebanon and Anti-Lebanon. Even smaller units existed, including the principality of Theodore around Philadelphia, which included three other cities, and the dominion of Lysanias, who ruled in Abilene between Anti-Lebanon and Damascus (Lk 3:1; Josephus *Jewish Antiquities* 20.137-40; *Jewish War* 2.247-49).

This world of petty kings arose in the void created by the decline of the Seleucid and Maccabean powers (around 100 B.C.). These kings were at their peak in the time of Claudius (mid-first century A.D.). By A.D. 105 all these kingdoms had been incorporated into Roman provinces.[21]

In the parable of the king and his debtors, for example, the king's servants or ministers are slaves. But these slaves own property on a big scale, like the ministers of the Great King of Persia in the Greek historian Herodotus (Mt 18:23-24). A similar image is present in the story of the wedding feast for the king's son. Here one village defies the king's authority, and the king sends armed men to destroy it (Mt 22:2-14).

The same view of the small kingdom appears in Luke's version of the parable of the talents (Lk 19:12-27). A "man of noble birth," who has inherited his kingdom (unlike the Roman approach to governing) leaves his slaves to manage his affairs while he goes off to be installed as king. He later rewards the faithful slaves with the governing of toparchies in this new kingdom. His subjects rebel by sending an embassy after him to request a new king and are punished. The underlying notion seems to be that of a client king and his overlord. Some see here a parallel with the embassy to Caesar Augustus that objected to the appointment of Herod the Great as king of Judea (Josephus *Jewish Antiquities* 17.299-303). But it could just as well be inspired by memories of the Hellenistic monarchy of the Seleucids.

Luke touches on the late Hellenistic monarchy when Christ talks about the "kings of the Gentiles" who "lord it over them; and those who exercise authority over them call themselves Benefactors" (Lk 22:25; see also Mt 20:25). This clearly refers to Hellenistic kings, who regularly used *Benefactor* as one of their titles.

The pattern of life in the Gospels, social, economic, civil and religious, is exactly what one would expect in the isolated district of Galilee based on other historical records. The virtual absence of Greco-Roman influences is a testimony to the authenticity of the Gospel accounts. As one would expect, only when the scene changes to Jerusalem does the Roman administrative machine show up, with the procurator or prefect and his troops and tribunal.

**For Further Reading**

Jones, A. H. M. *The Cities of the Eastern Roman Provinces.* 2nd ed. Oxford: Clarendon, 1971.

Millar, Fergus. *The Roman Near East: 31 B.C.-A.D 337.* Cambridge, Mass.: Harvard University Press, 1993.

Richardson, Peter. *Herod: King of the Jews and Friend of the Romans.* Columbia: University of South Carolina Press, 1996.

# Chapter 7

# Tools of Governance:
## *Finances, Law & the Military*

*In those days a decree went out from Caesar Augustus*
*that all the world should be enrolled. This was the first enrollment,*
*when Quirinius was governor of Syria.*
*And all went to be enrolled, each to his own city.*
LUKE 2:1-3

*If therefore Demetrius and the craftsmen with him*
*have a complaint against any one, the courts are open,*
*and there are proconsuls; let them bring charges against one another.*
*But if you seek anything further,*
*it shall be settled in the regular assembly. For we are in danger*
*of being charged with rioting today,*
*there being no cause that we can give to justify this commotion.*
ACTS 19:38-40

*And when it was decided that we should sail for Italy,*
*they delivered Paul and some other prisoners*
*to a centurion of the Augustan Cohort, named Julius.*
ACTS 27:1

OVERSEEING AN EMPIRE OF 50 MILLION PERSONS WAS NO SMALL TASK, especially in the absence of modern technology and bureaucratic methods. Of course, we must realize that the Romans never thought to attempt the level of oversight typical of a modern state. As long as the taxes or tribute were on time, and no attempt was made to rebel from Rome, the Romans allowed local leaders to do most of the governing. Nevertheless, Rome used a variety of tools to govern and control its far-flung empire. Chief among these were its system of finances and taxation, its legal code and its military.

### Finances and Taxation
An empire the size of Rome required large and continuous streams of revenue

to function. Rome's total annual revenue in the New Testament era was some-where between 100 and 200 million denarii, about 10 percent of the overall product of the Empire. Although Rome had gained great wealth through its wars of conquest before the time of Christ, by the first century A.D. taxes had become its principal source of income. Its limited military conquests during this era brought in far less booty than in the preceding century.

The public treasury of Rome paid for the public services of the city of Rome and the administrative expenses of the senatorial provinces, the provinces run by the Roman senate. But the expenses of the imperial provinces, those run by the Roman emperor directly (such as Syria, Egypt and Judea), were paid out of the *fiscus,* the personal treasury of the emperor. Imperial provinces were more expensive to govern than senatorial provinces, primarily because the armies were typically stationed in them (see map 7 for locations of the provinces and chapter thirteen for information about each province).

The emperor, from Augustus on, functioned as the single patron of the Empire. The emperor paid the expenses of the governors in the imperial provinces. He paid the salaries of soldiers throughout the Empire. A special fund provided separation pay when a soldier was honorably discharged. The emperor maintained an immense household of slaves and freedmen, not only in Rome but throughout the provinces. The imperial freedmen managed the local cults of emperor worship and looked out for the emperor's interests in each locale. The imperial treasury paid for special projects like harbor works, roads and military camps. Frequently the emperors put on elaborate games and spectacles or gave special gifts to all the citizens. But the emperor did not see himself as a philanthropist. He used the revenues from taxation in the imperial provinces and from other sources to fund these expenditures as well as to pay for his building projects and personal needs back in Rome.

*Types of tax.* Taxes were levied not on Roman citizens but on noncitizen provincials. During the early Empire, two types of direct taxes existed: *tributum soli* and *tributum capitis.* The former was a fixed-rate property tax assessed on land, houses, slaves and ships within each province. The annual rate in the province of Syria in this era was 1 percent.

The latter type of tax was a poll or head tax, levied on men ages fourteen to sixty-five, and on women twelve to sixty-five. The Synoptic Gospels identify this tax as one denarius per person per year (Mt 22:15-22; Mk 12:14-17; Lk 20:21-26). A census was taken at the formation of a province to determine who should pay this tax (see below). Such a flat tax favored the wealthy, who could pay it far more readily than could the mass of peasants. In some provinces the head tax applied only to males, but in Syria and other places it applied to everyone.

In addition to the property and poll taxes, Rome imposed a number of indirect taxes on its provinces. These were customs or tolls on imports and exports and on goods passing through a province, road money, bridge tolls, and harbor dues (Mt 9:9; Mk 2:14; Lk 5:29). Caesar Augustus introduced several new taxes during his rule: a 1-percent sales tax, a 4-percent tax on the sale of slaves and a 5-percent tax on inheritances (except those from close relatives) over 100,000 sesterces (about $4 million in modern terms; see below).

Greek and Roman cities sometimes imposed taxes. Any direct taxes they collected, for example on real estate, went directly to the imperial coffers in Rome, but they could keep the revenue from customs duties and toll taxes they imposed. Although low by our standards, usually around 2 percent, these taxes could supply significant income to a city that handled a lot of trade. The average city, however, might well find it hard to fund all its basic services on such income (Pliny the Younger *Letters* 10.98-99).

Jews also had to pay religious taxes. They paid a half-shekel temple tax to finance the construction and maintenance of Herod's temple. They also paid tithes on produce to support the priests in Jerusalem. All Jews outside of Palestine were required to send their temple tax to Jerusalem (Josephus *Jewish Antiquities* 14.110). After the A.D. 70 destruction of the temple in Jerusalem, all Jews in the Empire were required to pay Rome an extra poll tax of two denarii each year, equivalent to the half-shekel temple tax. This was used to maintain the temple of Jupiter built on the former site of Herod's temple.

In Capernaum, Peter is asked, "Does not your teacher pay the tax?" (Mt 17:24-27). After Peter catches the fish with a coin in its mouth, Jesus asks, "From whom do kings of the earth take toll or tribute *[censum]*?" This passage often is taken to refer to the two-drachma temple tax. More likely the tax they have in mind is a governmental one. The term *censum* and the reference to "kings" indicate that they are talking about the Roman tax system brought to Judea in A.D. 6.

The story of Christ and the tribute of Caesar is appropriate in its location at Jerusalem within the Roman province. Christ asks not just for a coin but for "the money for the tax" (Mt 22:19). The implication that the Roman tax could only be paid in Roman coin fits with our understanding of that time.[1]

*Collection of taxes.* During the late Republic, when most of its provinces were added, Rome used private enterprise to handle tasks such as tax collection. Companies formed by the second rank of Rome's aristocracy, the equestrian order (senators were forbidden to engage in this kind of enterprise), would bid for the right to collect taxes in a certain province. The highest bidder would then send out his agents, called publicans *(publicani)* or tax farmers (so called

Figure 7.1. The amphitheater of Ephesus, in which the Christians were confronted (Acts 19)

because they raised tax revenue for Rome like a farmer raises crops), to make the collections. They were named for the Roman public treasury *(publicum)*. They had to collect enough money to cover their bid before they could begin to make a profit, and Rome did not limit the amount they could collect over their bid. The Roman general Pompey, after his conquest of Palestine in 63 B.C., used tax farmers to collect tribute. The Roman publicans used local officials as their tax collection agents.

This system allowed an enormous amount of graft and corruption since tax farmers could use the power of the Roman army to collect as much money as they thought possible. The directors of these companies frequently became rich and powerful back in Rome. Thus, a provincial governor who sought to combat abusive practices in his province could find himself in a lot of trouble back home. For example, the Roman consul Rutilius Rufus took on the tax farmers of the province of Asia during his administration of that province. Upon his return to Rome the next year, he was forced into exile. As a result, most governors did not try to tangle with the tax farmers.[2]

When Julius Caesar came to power, he eliminated the Roman tax-farming system in the Near East. In Judea, he gave the ethnarch and high priest Hyrcanus responsibility for tax collection. Not long before his death in 44 B.C., Caesar authorized the rebuilding of Jerusalem's walls and lowered Judea's taxes. Herod the Great (37-4 B.C.) was allowed to use his own officials to collect taxes for Rome.

Caesar Augustus abolished tax farming throughout Rome. Roman officials in the cities of the Empire took up the responsibility of collecting taxes on behalf of the imperial government. In the semiautonomous state of Galilee, taxes were collected by officials under the supervision of Herod Antipas (4 B.C. to A.D. 39).

 *Publicans.* While direct taxes were collected by imperial officers, in Palestine indirect taxes (customs and poll taxes) were still collected by the highest bidders among the tax farmers. They used the same kind of local tax collectors that the publicans had used: small, sometimes quite prosperous merchants whose low social status is well illustrated in the Gospels (Mt 9:9-13; Mk 2:14-17; Lk 3:12-13; 19:1-10).

Zacchaeus, called a "chief tax collector," may have been the contractor for the revenues of Jericho and may have supervised a number of collectors. At the least he supervised a collecting district. Most of the New Testament publicans, like Levi/Matthew (Mt 9:9; Mk 2:14; Lk 5:27), were lesser officials. Levi, for example, may have been a local customs official, collecting taxes for a local treasury rather than for Rome. They might have their "place of toll" located where the residents could not easily avoid them: by city gates, on public roads or on bridges. Levi's post at Capernaum probably was near the sea on the important trade route entering Galilee from Damascus.

Publicans were despised by the scribes and the people. This hostility is evident in expressions like "tax collectors and sinners" (Mt 9:10-11; 11:19; Mk 2:15-16; Lk 5:30; 7:34; 15:1) and "the tax collectors and the harlots" (Mt 21:31) and their equation with Gentiles (Mt 18:17). Why were they despised? Besides being victims of the universal dislike for paying taxes, their work offered opportunities for extortion, which clearly many took (Lk 3:12-13). Since paying taxes to a foreign power was hateful and commonly seen as unlawful (Mt 22:17), the publicans were regarded as traitors to their nation and willing tools of their oppressors. In addition, because their work required constant contact with Gentiles, they would have been considered ceremonially unclean.

Some Jews complained bitterly about Jesus' association with publicans (Lk 7:34; 15:1-2), but Jesus found the tax collectors willing to hear his message and refreshingly free from hypocrisy (Lk 18:9-14). Publicans were attracted to Jesus because he showed himself "a friend of tax collectors" (Lk 7:34; 15:1-2).

*Census.* A census was necessary to count the heads and enforce the tax.

During the reign of Augustus, surveys were held in all the provinces. The censors would query each family head regarding name, age, and the financial and legal status of each member of his or her household. The standard practice was to take a census when a new province came into existence, but censuses were taken at other times as well.

Luke refers to a census as the occasion for Mary and Joseph's trip to Bethlehem (Lk 2:1-3, quoted above). The Luke 2 passage presents two difficulties: the timing of the census and the description of it as universal. In A.D. 6 the governor of Syria was Publius Sulpicius Quirinius, a Roman senator and later consul (Josephus *Jewish Antiquities* 18.1). He ordered a census to determine how much tribute Rome should expect from the new province of Judea. Luke 2:2 appears to refer to this census since it refers to Quirinius as governor of Syria. But the timing is wrong if we take the verse to say that this census occurred at the time of the birth of Jesus, probably ten years earlier.

It is unlikely that the author would make this mistake since he shows a solid knowledge of history. F. F. Bruce has suggested that this verse might better be translated, "This census was before that made when Quirinius was governor of Syria," on the basis that Luke is warning his readers not to confuse this earlier census with the well-known one in A.D. 6.[3]

Several sources speak of earlier censuses that might have included one at the time Jesus was born. Papyri indicate that, at least in some places, Rome apparently took a census every fourteen years during this era.[4] The earliest certain date for a papyrus census document is A.D. 34 (so earlier censuses at fourteen-year intervals would have occurred in A.D. 20, A.D. 6 and 8 B.C.). An edict in Egypt in A.D. 104 orders all persons "to return to their domestic hearths" to be enrolled. Tacitus and Suetonius mention three censuses taken during the rule of Augustus (Suetonius *Augustus* 27; Tacitus *Annals* 1.11). The second of these is generally believed to have occurred sometime between 8 and 4 B.C. This coincides chronologically with the probable time of Joseph and Mary's journey to Bethlehem and with the census mentioned in Luke 2.

But between 8 and 4 B.C., Palestine was technically independent of Rome. Rome did not take censuses in the lands of its independent allies. Since it did not collect taxes directly in such lands, it had no reason to take a census. So we do not know why Rome would have or how it could have ordered such a census. Perhaps Herod the Great agreed to allow the census at Rome's urging for some unusual reason. For example, perhaps there was a dispute between Herod and Rome about how much tribute should be sent to Rome, and Rome conducted a census to determine this for itself.

Another problem is that there is no precedent for Rome to impose a census in Galilee where Mary and Joseph lived, either in A.D. 6 or earlier, since that land was not part of the provinces of Judea or Syria. Roman tribute was never raised in Galilee during Jesus' lifetime (it was part of the independent tetrarchy of Herod Antipas). Perhaps Joseph for some reason was considered a resident of Judea for tax purposes.

The reference to a worldwide census in Luke may reflect the fact that all the lands directly controlled by Rome in that part of the world, Syria and Judea, were undergoing a census in A.D. 6. Clearly, we do not have a fully satisfactory resolution to this conflicting evidence. The author of Luke seems too careful a historian to make such a mistake, yet his statement cannot be reconciled easily with what we know about Roman census taking.

*Taxation and expenses in the Near East.* Did the income from taxation in provinces like Syria and Judea exceed the amount spent on them by Rome? Rome clearly received a surplus of tribute from provinces such as Asia and Cappadocia (north of Syria), where only a few auxiliary troops were stationed. But did the heavy military presence in provinces like Syria and Judea mean that Rome took in less than it spent on these provinces? The province of Judea probably contributed between 2 and 5 percent of Rome's total income. However, it appears that the cost of governing Judea exceeded this amount, so that Roman involvement here represented a net fiscal loss. When Cappadocia was converted from a dependent kingdom into a Roman province, the emperor Tiberius announced that the increased income from this province now allowed him to cut the 1-percent sales tax levied elsewhere to 0.5 percent. The relatively small auxiliary garrison there clearly made Cappadocia a money-making province for Rome. By contrast, the historian Appian implies that the governing of Britain cost more than the tribute it provided (*Roman History* 7). However, based on what we know about the income of Roman soldiers, officers and government officials, the whole Syrian region (including Palestine) probably took in enough revenue to offset expenses.[5]

### Weights, Measures and Coins

*Weights and measures.* A variety of terms is used for measurements in the New Testament (see figure 7.2). The word for *measure* in Luke 16:7 denotes a large measure of around eleven to seventeen bushels. The *measure* in Matthew 13:33 and Luke 13:21 was equivalent to 1.5 *modii* or twelve quarts. The "bushel" in Jesus' illustration was a small measure of grain equaling about eight dry quarts or a peck (Mt 5:15; Mk 4:21; Lk 11:33). The "measure" in Rev 6:6 held about a quart, considered a man's daily ration of grain in classical Greece. The *metretes* in John 2:6 equaled around nine gallons, so each jar held around eighteen to twenty-seven gallons. The "measure" of oil in Luke 16:6 equaled about ten gallons, for a total of 1,000 gallons of oil. A small "pot" (as in Mk 7:4) held about one pint.

A sabbath day's journey in New Testament times was five or six *stadia,* or 3,000 to 3,600 feet. The Mount of Olives was said to be a sabbath day's journey from Jerusalem (Acts 1:12). The "mile" in Matthew 5:41 was the Roman mile. Literally 1,000 paces, it was fixed at 4,854 feet, just short of a modern mile. The "furlong" *(stadion)* was 607 feet, or 1/8 of a Roman mile. The "fathom" *(orguia)* in Acts 27:28 is the distance of a man's arms stretched out, about six feet. The fathom was used by sailors to measure water depth. The *cubit* (lit. "forearm") was eighteen inches (Jn 21:8; Rev 21:17). Jesus used the term metaphorically to speak of adding time to one's life (Mt 6:27; Lk 12:25).

The weight of a "talent" varied greatly, ranging from fifty-eight to eighty pounds. The name was later applied to a unit of coinage with differing but high values. The term occurs only in Matthew 18:25, Matthew 25:15-28 (both of money) and Rev 16:21 (of weight). The "pound" was a Roman pound of twelve ounces. It is used in John 12:3 in reference to the ointment poured on Jesus' feet and in John 19:39 in describing the spices used for Jesus' burial.

*Coinage.* The economy of the Roman Empire depended thoroughly on the use of coinage (see figure 7.4 for the relative values of some coins in the Empire). Once the imperial government used coins to pay its troops and its suppliers and contractors, those coins circulated throughout the society. The Roman imperial mints produced large-denomination silver and gold coins. Coins also could be issued by Roman governors, local kings and free cities. In some provinces, local coins bore the names of the proconsul as well as the image and superscription of Caesar, but not in the Greek province of Achaea. The local coinage in its capital, Corinth, was municipal; it bore the names and titles of the municipal magistrates. In Cyprus the names of proconsuls appear on coins of the Julio-Claudian period. Governors of Judea did not put their names on coins issued in Judea. They generally issued coins with neutral symbols such as palm trees and olive branches instead of pagan symbols, but Pilate was an exception to this rule. For example, his *lepton* coin bears the name Tiberius Caesar and an augur's wand (to Jews a symbol of unlawful divination; cf. Deut 18:10; see in figure 7.3 a photograph of coins from the New Testament era).

Among the local kings who minted coins was Herod the Great. He was the first Jewish ruler to use the Greek language on his coins, instead of Hebrew, and the first to put a date on his coins. For the most part, Herod avoided using hated Roman symbols. Two of his sons, the rulers Archelaus in Judea and Herod Antipas in Galilee and Peraea, used neutral symbols on their coins. But his son

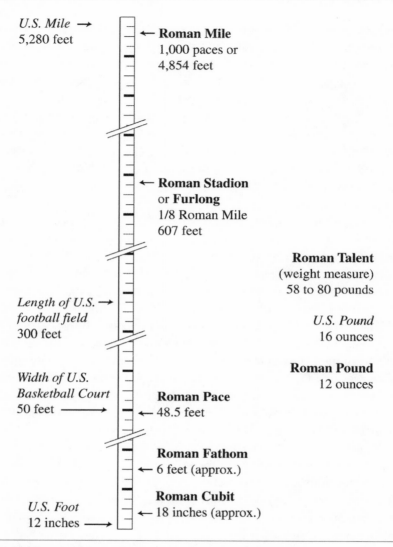

**Figure 7.2. Some weights and measures in the New Testament**

Herod Philip, ruling the largely Gentile area of Ituraea and Trachonitis, put on his coins the image of the emperor on one side and the Jewish temple on the other. Herod Agrippa I (A.D. 37-44) went further. He put the emperor on one side of his coins and goddesses and pagan temples on the other. The coins of Herod Agrippa II (A.D. 50-100) bore his own image and that of a goddess.

Independent cities in the region that minted coins included Ascalon, Antioch, Tyre, Damascus, Sidon, Byblos, Gadara, Seleucia, Beirut, Gaza and Caesarea.

The standard silver denomination was the *denarius,* known in the East by its Greek equivalent, the *drachma* (translated "silver coin" in Lk 15:8-9). In the first century A.D. the denarius was minted mainly at Rome under imperial direction. The parable of the vineyard suggests that a denarius was a generous day's wage for farm workers (Mt 20:1-16). In the fifth century B.C., one drachma per day was the standard wage for skilled workers who helped construct the buildings on the Acropolis in Athens. One drachma would buy a sheep, and five would buy an ox (Lk 15:8-9). A two-drachma coin equaled the Jewish half shekel and was enough to pay one person's annual temple tax (Mt 17:24). The *stater,* such as the one Peter was instructed to find in the mouth of a fish (Mt 17:27), was worth four drachmas. The *mina* (Lk 19:13-25) equaled 100 drachmas, and the *talent* (Mt 18:24) was worth 6,000 drachmas.

When Jesus was asked about paying taxes, he asked for and was shown a denarius (Mt 22:17-19), the legal coin used to pay the poll tax. He asked them whose image and inscription it bore. The denarius of that time read on one side (in abbreviated Latin): "Tiberius Caesar, August Son of the Divine Augustus." The other side read "Pontifex Maximus" (high priest of the Roman religion) and showed Tiberius's mother, Livia, holding a branch and scepter. Consequently, the coin represented to Jews the power of the hated Roman government and its blasphemous cult of emperor worship. Jesus avoided condemning the tax by telling the Jewish leaders to give to Caesar the things that were Caesar's (Mt 22:21).

Smaller denominations in bronze were used for day-to-day transactions. In the western part of the Empire, these were produced in central mints. In the East they were produced by individual cities and territories. The standard small denomination was the *as,* often known in Greek as the *assarion.* The official rate of exchange was one denarius for sixteen *asses,* but at times it took eighteen, twenty, or even twenty-four *asses* to obtain one denarius. This is probably because moneychangers were adding their fees to the rate of exchange.

Moneychangers provided a useful service: the bronze coins from one town often were not accepted by another town in normal commerce, in the same way that merchants in one nation today usually will not accept currency from another nation. Denarii were accepted everywhere, but at some point the average person would receive change from a transaction in smaller, local bronze coins. People who traveled a lot would have to constantly exchange the coins of one locale for those of another or for denarii.

From the Gospels, we know that in Palestine two *asses* would buy four or five small sparrows (Mt 10:29; Lk 12:6). The cost of bread to feed the five thou-

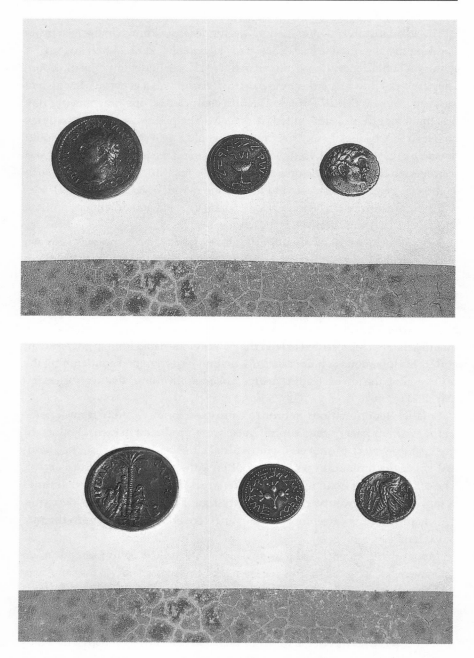

Figure 7.3. Reproductions of coins from first-century A.D. Palestine, with the obverse side above and the reverse below, *left to right:* Judea Capta, minted A.D. 77 to commemorate the conquest of Judea; shekel, A.D. 69; and shekel from Tyre, A.D. 54/55.

sand would have been about two hundred denarii (Mk 6:37). Based on this calculation, one denarius would buy enough bread for twenty-five lunches, and one lunch would cost less than one *as*. The good Samaritan assumes that two denarii will cover most of the costs of several days' food and lodging at a country inn (Lk 10:35). In first-century Italy, two *asses* would buy enough flour to make a pound of bread, and one to four *asses* would buy a liter of wine, depending on quality.

An itemized bill for a night at an inn in central Italy shows the value of an *as* in Italy. Wine cost one-sixth *as*, bread one *as*, and the main dinner two *asses*. Hay for the customer's mule cost two *asses*. An inscription from Pompeii lists expenses for nine days for what appears to be a group of three, averaging 1.5 denarii per day per person (Pliny, *Natural History* 18.88-90; *Corpus inscriptionum latinarum*, 4:1679, 5380).

For the everyday needs of the common person, a variety of smaller denomination coins was in circulation. The *semis* was equal to one-half *as*; the *quadrans* to one-fourth *as*. The *lepton*, the "widow's mite" (Mk 12:42; Lk 21:2), consisted of two *lepta*, which Mark explains is equivalent to one *quadrans*. The gap between the *as* and the denarius was filled by several brass coins: the *dupondii*, worth two *asses*, and the *sestertii*, worth four *asses*, or one-fourth denarius. The Romans usually referred to prices in terms of sestertii rather than denarii. All of these coins could have been found in the markets of Syria, for example, from the time of Pompey. In the first century, there was a wide variety of Roman coins and Roman provincial units. By the second century, Roman coins had replaced most of the others.

We cannot accurately translate ancient monetary terms into modern American dollars since the modern economy is so different from that of the first  century and the value of the dollar is so fluid. But to comprehend the relative value of the different denominations, let us assume that forty dollars is a minimum daily wage. That would make an *as* roughly equal to two dollars. A sparrow would then cost one dollar, a loaf of bread four dollars and a liter of wine about two or four dollars; a widow's mite or *lepton* would be worth about fifty cents. The *minas* that the nobleman apportions to each of ten servants (Lk 19:12-20) would be worth over $2,000. When Judas suggests selling the woman's ointment and giving it to the poor, he imagines that it would bring 300 denarii, around $5,000 (Mk 14:5). A Roman soldier in the regular army received 225 denarii per year, or $9,000. Auxiliary soldiers, such as those stationed in Palestine, received 200 denarii per year, or $8,000. At the other end of the spectrum, a Roman citizen was required to possess wealth greater than 250,000 denarii, or $10 million, to become a senator.

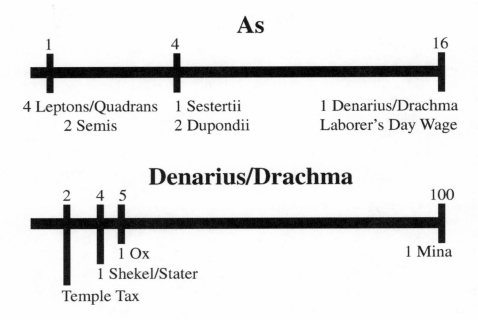

Figure 7.4. Some coins in the New Testament era

Clearly, these numbers do not relate well to income and prices in the modern world. For example, the current poverty level in the United States is far above the wage of Roman soldiers translated into modern dollars. It would be wrong to conclude from this that Roman soldiers were forced to live in conditions of poverty in the first century A.D. We must also realize that the average wage earner in the New Testament era had much less left over for luxuries than does his modern counterpart.[6]

### Law

*Roman law and local law.* By the New Testament era, Roman law had come to supersede Hellenistic law throughout the eastern Mediterranean. The only exception to this was the internal governing of the few free cities of the East (see chapter three). But these free cities had to be careful not to offend Rome in the exercise of their laws and had to treat Roman citizens according to Roman law (see below).

Roman law defined in legal statutes major offenses against persons, society and the government. This system dealt for the most part with offenses by the upper class and government officials. It did not cover many crimes, including those of common persons. These crimes, called *cognitio extra ordinaria*, were judged case by case by a magistrate. With the advice of a council, this magistrate could determine what was legal and illegal, and what punishment was appropriate. In the city of Rome, the city prefect performed this function. At the beginning of his appointment, he would issue a list of the principles by which he would decide such cases.[7]

In the provinces, the governor performed this function. He had a great deal of freedom when dealing with *cognitio extra ordinaria*. First, he would decide whether to consider the charge and determine whether the alleged conduct was a crime. When Paul was brought before Annius Gallio, the proconsul of the province of Achaia (Acts 18:12-17), Gallio decided that it was a dispute internal to the Jewish community and refused to hear the case (see below).

Pliny the Younger, governor of Bithynia (north of Asia province) at the beginning of the second century, expressed confusion about this type of case in letters to the emperor Trajan (*Letters* 10.96). He asked Trajan which constituted a crime: simply confessing belief in Christ, refusing to offer incense to the emperor's image, or the various immoral actions alleged against Christians. This uncertainty shows that there was no specific legislation forbidding Christianity. Thus, judges around the Empire had to deal with Christians on a largely individual basis. This helps to explain why Christians in the first two centuries were persecuted only sporadically, at specific times and places. Trajan, followed by Hadrian, said that Christians must not be hunted out, but persons who are accused publicly by two witnesses, and convicted of being Christian, should be punished.

Within a province the governor normally became involved only in cases involving public order. Smaller legal matters were left in the hands of local officials, who continued to follow the traditional systems of the individual cities or kingdoms. In Judea, the Sanhedrin and the high priest continued to observe and enforce the laws of Moses and could expect the Roman authorities to recognize their right to do so. The authority of the Greek cities was limited to their own territory. Paul and Barnabas and their hosts took advantage of this by keeping on the move: they appeared before the magistrates in one town like Thessalonica, paid a security deposit and moved on to another town. Their accusers then had to start over with a new set of magistrates and laws (Acts 17:5-10).

On some occasions, matters of jurisdiction are not clear to us and may not have been clear to the people involved. Scholars disagree about whether Jewish authorities in Jerusalem had the power to execute condemned criminals. But evidence from around the Empire indicates that local courts did not have the jurisdiction to execute criminals, so it is reasonable to conclude that Jewish authorities did not have broad powers to execute (see the one exception below). Thus, the killings of the disciples James and Stephen, and the attempted stoning of the woman taken in adultery (Jn 8:1-11), are more in the nature of lynchings. Pilate's execution of Jesus shows that the trial was a Roman proceeding, with conviction based on the charge of sedition, as will be seen below.

Judges and governors would announce their legal decisions from the *bema*, a raised platform used by public speakers. This term appears twelve times in the New Testament, usually translated as "judgment seat" and referring to the place of judgment of a Roman governor (Mt 27:19; Jn 19:13; Acts 18:12, 16-17; 25:6, 10, 17; Rom 14:10; 2 Cor 5:10). *Bema* in Acts 12:21 refers to the thronelike speaker's platform of Herod Agrippa in Caesarea.

The "judge" in the Gospels is an un-Roman and un-Hellenistic figure. The Gospels speak of judges where Acts speaks of city magistrates, the annually elected leaders of Hellenistic and Roman cities. The depiction of the judge who will throw you into prison until the last cent is paid if you do not agree with your enemy before trial is neither Roman nor Greek in tone (Mt 5:25; Lk 12:58). In this and in the story of the judge and the widow (Lk 18:2), the judge seems to be a permanent fixture whom no one can control. No term in Roman usage corresponds to the Greek term for *judge* used here. Certain Roman officials had as one of their many functions that of judging cases, but the Gospels seem to depict a man whose main function is judging.

Interestingly, Josephus uses this term for *judge* as the Gospels do when he says that the Roman legate of Syria, Quirinius, was sent by Caesar to be the judge of that nation (*Jewish Antiquities* 18.1). This use of *judge* is just one of many indications in the Gospels that Greco-Roman civilization had not deeply penetrated the world of the rural peasant in the Near East. While the cities were Hellenized and becoming Romanized, the rural population in Jesus' day probably still resisted these influences to one degree or another.

*Crime and punishment.* The cities of the Empire generally exercised police power through a board of locally recruited and supervised watchmen. The  watchmen apparently were rather ineffective, except in the Roman colonies of Philippi and Antioch of Pisidia. In Jerusalem the high priest had his own police force, the temple guard, under the command of the captain of the temple. This unit arrested Jesus (Jn 18:3, 12) and the apostles (Acts 5:24-26) and guarded Jesus' tomb (Mt 27:65).

The Roman governor also enforced public order through the troops under his command. In the imperial provinces, these troops generally amounted to one or more legions. In the small province of Judea, the governor only had six cohorts (including the "Italian cohort" of Acts 10:1). Each cohort contained six hundred men and was commanded by a military tribune from the second tier of the Roman elite, the equestrian class (Jn 18:12; Acts 21:31-40; 25:23). Special assignments were sometimes entrusted, in the early Empire, to a military police corps of *speculatores,* one of whom executed John the Baptist (Mk 6:27). Police duties such as the escort of prisoners might also be assigned to soldiers. Julius, a centurion of the "Augustan cohort," oversaw a small group of prisoners (Acts 27:1).

Judicial magistrates used a wide variety of punishments. Even before the trial, noncitizen suspects were imprisoned and beaten with whips or cudgels as part of the preliminary examination *(coercitio).* The English word *coerce* comes from this Latin word. Penalties varied with the mood or judgment of the magistrate, the nature of the crime and extenuating circumstances.

Romans, like most ancients, did not punish people with imprisonment. Prisons were used simply as places of detention while awaiting trial or punishment. The Roman equivalent of long incarceration was exile, in which the convicted person was exiled to an island or remote city for an indefinite period (often for life). This punishment usually was reserved for the upper classes. A relatively lenient penalty in that day was a fine.

In recounting his sufferings for Christ, Paul says that he was beaten with rods three times (2 Cor 11:25). The magistrates of a Roman colony like Philippi possessed special powers. Each magistrate was allowed two *lictors.* The lictors carried bundles of rods that symbolized the magistrate's authority but were also used to administer beatings. These magistrates had authority equal to that of a military tribune in the Roman army but could only use that authority in time of war. The records of a similar Roman colony in Spain show that these magistrates possessed the right to issue monetary fines to citizens and could even seize their property. It is very unlikely that even in a Roman colony a municipal court could hand out severe punishments. We know for certain that they were not allowed to put slaves to death.

If the convicted person was of lower status, he might be sold into slavery or condemned to lifelong toil in the mines or the gladiatorial arena. Before being sent off, such a convicted prisoner was beaten severely with a *flagellum,* a vicious flail tipped with pieces of bone or metal. Such a beating also preceded most forms of capital punishment, including crucifixion.

Romans used the death penalty for a variety of crimes. Some death penalties  were specific to certain crimes. In Rome a vestal virgin (see chapter five) who violated her oath of chastity was buried alive. Distinguished Romans and prisoners of war might be strangled in prison or ordered to commit suicide. A condemned prisoner might be tied to a stake naked, whipped with rods, then blindfolded, made to kneel, and beheaded with a sword. Burning at the stake was originally a Roman punishment for arson. This is one reason that Nero burned many of the Christians he accused of setting fire to Rome in A.D. 64. However, this was such an unusual punishment that it led to widespread revulsion in the city. At the same time, Romans did not object to the condemnation of criminals "to the beasts" at the gladiatorial shows. The condemned were tied to stakes, and lions or other wild animals were released into the arena to kill them. Christians would suffer such executions in later centuries.

Crucifixion was usually reserved for slaves and vicious prisoners of war, although it was inflicted on citizens from time to time. This form of punishment existed for centuries before the Romans came along. For example, Alexander the Great practiced it. The Romans probably learned it from the Carthaginians of North Africa. This form of execution was designed to be slow and painful. The condemned person's weight was supported for the most part by his arms. Muscle spasms, cramps and insects added to the pain, and death usually came through gradual suffocation. Romans sometimes broke the legs to increase the weight and bring death more quickly. Christians did not use the cross as a symbol in their artwork for the first two centuries, perhaps because of the shame people associated with death by crucifixion.[8]

The Sanhedrin in Jerusalem evidently had the authority to administer the thirty-nine lashes to offenders. Jewish law specified that a flogging be a maximum of forty lashes, but in order to avoid violating that law, it became customary to give "forty lashes save one." Paul says that he had been given this punishment, though probably by local synagogues (2 Cor 11:24). The traditional Jewish form of capital punishment was stoning, prescribed for idolatry, sorcery and adultery. We know with certainty of only one condition under which the Jews could administer capital punishment: an inscription on the temple warned any Gentile, including a Roman citizen, that violation of the sacred area (the inner Court of the Jews) was punishable by immediate death by stoning. The Romans apparently gave the Jews this concession because they realized how inflammatory a desecration of the sacred areas of the temple would be. In general, the Jewish leaders were not supposed to concern themselves with crimes such as murder, sacrilege or adultery (Philostratus, *Lives of the Sophists* 1.25.2).

### Christians and Roman Law

According to the New Testament, Christian forgiveness is to play a role in the courts. While a Christian is to abide by the decisions of the courts (Rom 13:1-3), he is not to seek satisfaction from them. Jesus counsels his followers that if one of them is the offender he is to make amends and avoid court (Mt 5:23-24). Paul expresses concern at the Corinthian Christians' frequent use of courts to settle disputes between themselves, disputes that probably involved financial transactions (1 Cor 6:1-11).[9]

*Jesus and Roman law.* Jesus and Paul had different social statuses and so were dealt with very differently by Roman law. Paul had a good Hellenistic education and was evidently a respected citizen of the important Gentile city of Tarsus. Jesus, so far as we know, had no formal education and came from a humble Jewish village. Most important, Paul was a Roman citizen, while Jesus was not.

The Gospels tell us that Jesus was found guilty of blasphemy by the Jewish Sanhedrin before he was turned over to the Romans. The Jews did so because they could not carry out capital punishment on their own. The Romans carefully guarded the power to execute. Only free cities within the Empire, such as Ephesus, had the right to execute outside of Roman courts. Jerusalem was by no means a free city, and considering Judea province's disruptive history (see appendix A and chapter six), Rome would never have allowed it the unrestricted practice of capital punishment.

Matthew and Mark give a more specific account of the trial, but Luke fills in a number of additional details. All three accounts correctly reflect Roman law of the era. Matthew and Mark indicate that Jesus was brought before Pilate early in the morning, after a nightime session of the Sanhedrin (Mt 27:1; Mk 15:1). This agrees with Jewish concerns and Roman practices. Although a nocturnal meeting of the Sanhedrin was unusual, it makes sense that the leaders were concerned to hurry things along because of the upcoming festival. In addition, they would have known that a Roman aristocrat typically conducted most of his business early in the morning, beginning at dawn or shortly thereafter. If the Sanhedrin had met in the morning, its leaders could not have approached Pilate until the afternoon, and he might have refused to deal with them.

The trials of Jesus fit well with what we know about Roman law and governance. Jesus was not accused of breaking a specific Roman law. Thus, he was tried by Pilate under *extra ordinem,* the procedure for charges against provincials not covered by the law. Matthew tells us that the trial was a formal one, since Pilate sits on his judgment seat to hear it (Mt 27:19). The official charge is not stated in the Gospels, but Pilate's question, "Are you the King of the Jews?" indicates that Jesus was being charged with sedition against Rome (Mt 27:11). Josephus tells us that the leaders of sedition following the death of Herod were proclaimed kings by their followers (*Jewish Antiquities* 17.10) Luke adds the charge that Jesus told Jews not to pay tribute to Rome (Lk 23:2).

Pilate could not ignore a charge of insurrection against Rome. He asked Jesus to defend himself, and when Jesus refused to do so Pilate once again requested a defense (Mk 15:2-4). Pilate demonstrates the Roman distaste for convicting defendants who would not defend themselves. Pliny the Younger, writing in the early second century, tells us that he gave Christians three chances to deny their faith and thus defend themselves against execution (*Letters* 10.96).

Even so, the Gospels say that Pilate tried to release him with just a light beating or a stern warning (the term in Lk 23:16 could be taken either way). Provincial governors often used this form of punishment when dealing with unruly juveniles. John says that when Pilate refused to convict Jesus on political grounds, the Jewish leaders told him to convict him of a capital offense on their original, religious grounds (Jn 19:7). As a Roman governor, Pilate had the power to ratify a capital conviction made according to local laws, even if they differed from Roman laws. But John says that Pilate still resisted, until the Jewish leaders suggested that he would be branded not a "friend of Caesar." This term had nothing to do with personal friendship. It was a technical, political term in Pilate's day, used at times to indicate a person who was an official representative of Rome. It appears that they were threatening to cause him to lose his position. In fact, only a few years later, Samaritan leaders would complain to the governor of Syria about Pilate and have him sent back to Rome (see chapter six).

Once Pilate agreed to execute Jesus, he had him beaten more severely (Mt 27:26; Mk 15:15). This severe beating is what one would expect in such a case. Such a severe scourging was never a punishment in itself but a preliminary to other punishments such as execution.

Why did Pilate send Jesus to Herod before finally convicting him? Herod ruled over Galilee, the location of Jesus' home and much of his activity. Roman governors in this period had the discretion to refer defendants to their province of origin, even if they were accused of committing a crime elsewhere. Pilate might have reasoned that, if Jesus had practiced sedition in Judea, he had done so in Galilee as well. Pilate did not have to send Jesus to Herod, however. He may have done so simply to be rid of a distasteful trial or out of courtesy to Herod.

*Paul and the local authorities.* An understanding of Roman law sheds light on the failed efforts to prosecute the apostle Paul in various cities of the Empire. For example, at Philippi, a Roman colony, a conflict first occurred between the apostles and Gentile interests (Acts 16:19-20). Because of this, the apostles were brought before the municipal magistrates and charged with causing riots and

Figure 7.5. **Reproduction of a Roman legionary's armor, first century** A.D. **This is the** *lorica segmentata,* **or segmented armor, that was replacing the breastplate as the armor of choice in the New Testament era.**

introducing an alien religion. The latter charge rested on the fact that a Roman citizen was not allowed to take part in a religion not sanctioned by Rome. In practice he might do so, as long as his cult was not involved in political or social crimes. Paul's accusers at Philippi charge that he was "advocating customs that are not lawful for us as Romans to adopt or observe" (Acts 16:21 NRSV). Livy, writing during the time of Caesar Augustus, cites a similar principle as one reason for the prosecution of the Bacchanalian cult in Rome in the second century B.C. However, he believed that the main motive for prosecution was the crimes committed by the cult's adherents, not their religious beliefs (Livy 39.16.8-9). In addition, Augustus and Tiberius did not allow Roman citizens to adopt the Druid religion of the Celts of western Europe because of its depraved practices (such as human sacrifice).

The situation in Philippi differs in that its focus is on Christianity's un-Roman nature, not on allegations of depravity (so far as we know). Although this charge of advocating an un-Roman religion was unusual for that day, it was not unparalleled, and perhaps reflects the desire of Romans in a colony so far from Italy to preserve their Roman culture. Perhaps because of their fear, and perhaps because of the physical appearance of Paul and Silas, the magistrates did not give them a chance to declare their Roman citizenship or to defend themselves in any way. They imprisoned Paul and Silas. Acts reports that an earthquake that evening caused the doors of the prison to open. The jailer awoke and was about to kill himself when Paul stopped him. Romans considered suicide the only honorable action in some cases where one's actions have seriously disgraced oneself. The jailer may also have anticipated being executed when his superiors discovered his negligence. Acts tells us that the jailer saw in all this the action of Paul's God, converted and was baptized (Acts 16:34).

When the magistrates' guards, the lictors, came the next day to escort Paul and Silas out of town, the disciples refused to go without an apology. Paul said, "They have beaten us in public, uncondemned, men who are Roman citizens, and have thrown us into prison" (Acts 16:37 NRSV). The centurion in Philippi was alarmed because he had bound a man against whom there was no formal charge, and the magistrates were upset because they had chastised a Roman citizen without trial. This agrees with a Roman law, the *lex Iulia*, that forbids a Roman citizen from being beaten or bound by a magistrate without provocation or by any other person in any circumstance. Paul complains about being beaten "without trial." This confirms what we know about Roman law, that a citizen could be flogged after a legitimate trial and sentencing. The magistrates apologized in person, and asked them to leave town.

The legal procedure followed at Philippi is consistent with Roman practice. Private accusers made the charge, and the magistrates arrested the accused. If the case had not been abandoned, the next step would have been to arraign the prisoner before the proconsul.

*Ephesus.* The actions taken against Paul and his associates at Ephesus were similar to those taken at Philippi (Acts 19:24-40). The hostile group again was

Gentile. Here the master silversmith Demetrius organized what looks like an unofficial meeting of the local assembly in the town's large amphitheater, apparently to pressure the civic authorities to take action (see figure 7.1). The town clerk (*grammateus*, literally the "clerk of the people") was the elected head of the city officials. He tried to calm the crowd and offered the accusers two options: they could appear before the proconsul's courts if they had a private judicial dispute, or they could go before the regular, lawful assembly of the city if their charges involved public interests. The allegation that Paul and his friends were interfering with the sale of silver models of the temple of Artemis would have constituted a private dispute. The allegation that they were attacking the prestige of the city of Ephesus, even though it involved no specific impiety toward the goddess, could be considered a broader public charge and so have gone to the municipal assembly. The town clerk in Ephesus warned the crowd that if a riot occurred, they would not be able to explain it satisfactorily to the Roman authorities (Acts 19:40).

This scene could not have taken place two centuries later, by which time the local assemblies had nearly ceased to exist. Even in Paul's day, the Romans wanted to eliminate the local democratic assemblies. Local assemblies were afraid of doing anything that might cause the Romans to disband them.

The prominence of the town clerk as portrayed in Acts fits with the evidence we have from the cities of Asia Minor. In general this person was the chief administrative officer, annually elected, of the city magistrates. He had a staff of permanent clerks, responsible for the paperwork of the city. Documents from Ephesus show that the town clerk was superior to the city council members. He appeared on the coinage of the city as chief magistrate from the time of Augustus. Ephesus also had a second, less prominent clerk, called the "clerk of the council." Thus it was natural for the silversmiths to first approach the town clerk with their complaint.

The clerk referred to the meeting as unlawful or irregular. City assemblies appear to have had monthly regular meetings and generally two or three extra meetings per month. Although the meeting is not a regular one, the statement in Acts 19:41 that the clerk "dismissed the assembly" has a technical sound. It appears that the town clerk convened the meeting as an irregular assembly but wished to dismiss it quickly since he found no legitimate reason for it.

Paul was advised by a group called the "Asiarchs" not to attend this ad hoc meeting (Acts 19:31). This term may refer to the annually elected leaders, and perhaps the ex-leaders, of the council of the province of Asia. It also may refer to the administrators of the various temples of the imperial cult under the charge of high priests. Or it may refer to the city deputies of the provincial council.[10] In any case, apparently Paul had wealthy and powerful friends at Ephesus.

*Thessalonica.* Paul and Silas's Jewish accusers at Thessalonica at first tried to bring them "out to the crowd." That is, they tried to bring them before the local assembly (Acts 17:5-9). When this failed, they took Jason before the magistrates. The court of a free city was one place where severe punishment could be inflicted, at least on non-Romans, without invoking the governor. The accusation against the apostles included the charge of acting contrary to the decrees of Caesar (Acts 17:7). We don't know what this meant, unless it referred to the crime of advocating a religion not sanctioned by Rome. Whatever it meant, it was not strictly relevant in the court of a free city outside Roman jurisdiction. Thus, the city magistrates had no reason to take serious action. The magistrates asked for and received from Jason a pledge or security of the good behavior of his guests. This was an accepted Roman and Greek civic practice. After giving this pledge, Jason sent them off to Berea, beyond the jurisdiction of the magistrates of Thessalonica.

In several towns Paul took advantage of the fact that there was no intercity authority except that of the Roman governor. If the proconsul or legate did not take an active interest in him, a troublemaker could continue his career indefinitely by moving from city to city. We have no evidence that different cities ever acted in concert in such cases. Once he left their city, the magistrates lost interest in him.

The last resort for cities trying to control their populations was the confiscation of property. Travelers with no local assets to protect, like Paul and Silas, were more difficult to handle. This helps explain why Paul's enemies in Thessalonica went after Paul's host. Jason, who had assets in the city, was seen as Paul's guarantor. Uneasy at the political charges against Paul and Silas but lacking a legal basis for prosecution, the city magistrates were only too ready to dodge responsibility and get the preacher to move on. Paul's accusers, when they discovered that he had gone to Berea, went to Berea and had to start their accusations all over again.

*Corinth.* Sometime between July and October of A.D. 51, Rome sent a new proconsul, Lucius Junius Gallio, to govern the province of Achaea from its capital in Corinth. Gallio was born to a well-known Roman family. His father was Marcus Annaeus Seneca, a professor of rhetoric. Gallio was the younger brother of the renowned Seneca, Stoic philosopher and tutor to the future emperor Nero. The latter Seneca's works are still read today. The change of name came when he was adopted by his father's friend, Lucius Junius Gallio, who needed an heir. When he came as proconsul to Corinth, Gallio was one rung away from the top level of the *cursus honorum,* the ladder of office and honor for senators. He had held the office of praetor before becoming a provincial governor, but he had not yet served as a consul in Rome. That would come later. Unfortunately we know little about his tenure as proconsul in Corinth.[11]

Corinthian Jews brought Paul before Gallio, charging, "this man is persuading men to worship God contrary to the law" (Acts 18:12-17). The account here is consistent with the workings of the *cognitio extra ordinem,* in which the judge has the right to decide whether to accept a novel charge. In mid-second century, some judges rejected even the generally recognized charges against Christians and dismissed the cases outright (Tertullian *Letter to Scapula* 3-5).

The Jewish residents at Corinth, presumably not citizens of Corinth (since the passage in Acts distinguishes the Jews from Corinthian citizens), seem to be asking the proconsul to enforce their religious laws. They had no right to expect this, especially within the territory of a Roman colony like Corinth. According to Josephus, the Jewish communities of the Roman world were protected against local government interference in their religious and social customs (Josephus *Jewish Antiquities* 14.10; 19.278-91). An edict of Claudius regarding the Jews throughout the Empire reads in part, "It is proper that the Jews through the world under Roman rule should keep their native customs without let or hindrance." The purpose of this edict was to confirm the time-honored Jewish privilege of toleration. City governments at Pergamum, Sardis and Ephesus, for example, had been interfering with Jewish assemblies. We have no evidence that local Jewish leaders had the legal right to force obedience on their members, let alone enlist the state in that effort.

In any case, this may not have been the actual charge against Paul. Acts 18:13 says that Paul persuaded "men," not "Jews," to a different form of worship. The Jews may have been accusing Paul of preaching to Romans a religion in conflict with Roman law, as was the charge at Philippi and perhaps at Thessalonica. Such a charge would be more likely to succeed before a Roman governor in a Roman colony. Some of the new Christians, former full or partial converts to Judaism, were indeed Roman citizens (Titius Justus, Paul's host, for example), and many had been baptized (Acts 18:7-8). But Gallio thought the Jewish accusers were referring to the Jewish religion and Jewish law. He ended the hearing with the precise words a Roman magistrate used when refusing to exercise his right to judge an *extra ordinem* case: "I refuse to be a judge of these things" (Acts 18:15).

Once Gallio dismissed their case, Acts says that "they all" began beating Sosthenes, identified as the leader of the Jewish synagogue in Corinth. It is not clear whether his attackers were Jews or Gentile Corinthians, or both. Based on

Paul's reference to a brother named Sosthenes in 1 Corinthians 1:1, it may be that this Sosthenes at the time at least sympathized with Paul, and that the Jews were punishing him for it. Gallio takes no notice, because he does not want to interfere with the Jewish authorities as they punish one of their own (who presumably is not a Roman citizen or a citizen of Corinth). On the other hand, perhaps some Gentile observers, needing little excuse to attack the Jewish community in their town, beat Sosthenes as leader of the Jewish accusers for bringing an invalid case. Gallio would have had no motivation to interfere here either, so long as a riot did not ensue, since the Jews for the most part were not citizens, and thus Gallio would have little interest in protecting them.[12]

*Paul before Felix.* The appearances of Paul before the procurators Felix and Festus are classic examples of the *extra ordinem* procedure in the provinces. The basic elements of this procedure are all present: issues of jurisdiction, the important role of private accusers assisted by an attorney, charges based on the *extra ordinem* system, and the governor's power to delay a decision.

When Paul was first brought before Felix, Felix asked him from what province he came. When Paul tells him he is from Cilicia, Felix says that he will judge him (Acts 23:34-35). At that time a governor had the right (which would later become the standard procedure) to send a defendant back to his home province for judgment. But like Judea, Cilicia was a dependency of the legate of Syria. We know that the legate of Syria exercised military authority in Cilicia as late as A.D. 52, some five years prior to the trial before Felix. Years later, it would become a completely separate province with its own legate. If at the time of Paul's trial Cilicia was still under Syria, Felix could not send Paul to Cilicia and would hesitate to send a minor trial between Jews to the busy governor of Syria. In addition, because Paul's home town, Tarsus, was a free city *(civitas libera)*, its citizens were exempt from normal provincial jurisdiction.

The establishment of this trial before Felix fits the norm of that day and place. Five days after Felix's preliminary inquiry, the attorney ("orator") Tertullus presented the charges against Paul. Legal representation in this kind of trial was common, though not required. In the trials before the emperor Trajan, described by Pliny the Younger, the parties appear with or without attornies as they please *(Letters* 4.22.2; 6.31.9-11). Paul's accusers were at first Jews from Asia province, then some leaders from Jerusalem. The prosecution of Paul here was a formal one, as is clear both from the letter of the military tribune Claudius Lysias to Felix (Acts 23:30) and from Felix's preliminary inquiry: "I will give you a hearing when your accusers arrive" (Acts 23:35 NRSV).

Based on our knowledge of the *extra ordinem* system, Paul must have been charged with stirring up strife. His accusers tried to convince the governor, apparently unsuccessfully, that Paul was not simply contesting Jewish beliefs but was disrupting Jewish communities throughout the Empire. This was intended to give the charge a political twist since no Roman governor officially would convict a person of violating religious beliefs or customs. The letter of the tribune Lysias to Governor Felix shows that Lysias did not accept this connection. Acts reports that Lysias found Paul to be "accused concerning questions of their law, but . . . charged with nothing deserving death or imprisonment" (Acts 23:29 NRSV). Festus later agreed with this assessment, saying that the charges against Paul were not what he "was expecting" (probably meaning no charge of which he was prepared to take notice judicially), but were points of disagreement about the Jewish religion—nothing worthy of death (Acts 25:18-19, 25).

The charge of stirring up strife was normal under the *extra ordinem* procedure. The facts were alleged, and the governor was expected to make of them what he would. Because the charge was political, the governor was reluctant to dismiss it immediately. But because the evidence was theological, he could not truly understand it or properly convict someone based on it. In addition, Tertullus presented no witnesses to the alleged actions of Paul.

A similar charge had been brought against the Jews of Alexandria a few years earlier. The emperor Claudius described the actions of the Jews as "stirring up a universal plague throughout the world" *(Letter of Claudius to the Alexandrines)*. This is almost identical to the charge against Paul, "a real pest [literally 'plague'] and a fellow who stirs up dissension among all the Jews throughout the world" (Acts 24:5). The Jews may well have phrased the charge this way to mimic the words of Claudius written around fifteen years earlier and undoubtedly known to Jewish leaders in Jerusalem.

The original charge was made by Jews from Asia province, who did not show up to support their charge. Paul exhibits knowledge of Roman law when he objects that they ought to be present to make their charges (Acts 24:18-19). Roman law looked very unfavorably on accusers who did not press their charges in person. In fact, the former emperor Claudius advocated penalties for this offense. A few decades later, Pliny the Younger wrote of a husband who accused his wife of adultery, then hesitated taking her to court. He was summoned to court and ordered to accuse her before the trial could progress (*Letters* 6.31). The disappearance of the Asian Jewish accusers probably meant dropping at least one of the charges: that Paul took a Greek named Trophimus into the temple (Acts 21:29; cf. 25:19).

It is not surprising that Felix postponed the trial to await the arrival of the military tribune Lysias, the only independent witness who could speak to the charge of civil disturbance. Probably a further hearing was held, in which Lysias was unable to shed any light on the specific charges. At this point, Felix should have dismissed the case against Paul. Acts says that he kept Paul in prison in the hope of obtaining a bribe from him. Perhaps Felix had heard of the money recently brought by Paul to the Jerusalem church. The laws against a governor receiving bribes carried severe penalties, but bribe-taking still occurred (although less frequently than under the Republic), and Felix, as a freedman, had no inherited wealth upon which to rely.

Acts says that before Lysias brought Paul to Felix in Caesarea, he summoned the Sanhedrin to discuss the charges against Paul (Acts 22:29-30). Some argue that Lysias could not have done this since neither the Sanhedrin nor any municipal council in the Empire needed the permission of a Roman official to meet. But Lysias had every right to request that the Sanhedrin hold a special meeting to help him understand the charges against Paul. This meeting was not a trial, but it became necessary when Paul told the tribune that he was a Roman citizen and thus under the jurisdiction of Roman law. Lysias acted properly, according to what we know of Roman law, when he collected evidence, told Paul's accusers to make their charges before the governor, sent a report to the governor and later reported in person to Felix.

Felix left Paul in prison for two years, awaiting a judgment that never came. This imprisonment did not violate Paul's right to appeal or prevent him from appealing. A more cautious governor might have shipped Paul off to Rome before an appeal. It was not unusual for a provincial governor to leave a case undecided when he ended office. In fact, Josephus considered it unusual when a later governor of Judea, Albinus, actually dealt with all the pending charges and executions once he heard that he was about to be replaced (*Jewish Antiquities* 20.215).

A Roman governor had little to lose by holding a man with no political influence, like Paul, if it meant not angering his upper-class opponents. Felix's capital, Caesarea, was largely Gentile in population, but with a large and vocal Jewish minority. Strife between the two communities was common. Caesarean Jews believed they were entitled to equal civic rights with the Gentiles in the city. At one point a dispute over this even led to riots, which Felix had to quell by force. Years later, anger at Rome's denial of equal rights for Caesarean Jews will contribute to the revolt against Rome in A.D. 66. It is not surprising that Felix would have tried to toss the Jews a bone by keeping Paul in prison. Felix knew that the Jews were capable of bringing formal charges against him since they had done so against the last two governors of Judea, Pilate and Cumanus (Josephus *Jewish Antiquities* 18.88-

89; 20.134-36; *Jewish War* 2.241-46). If this was his strategy, it worked. Provincial leaders never filed charges against him, despite various troubles in his administration (Josephus *Jewish War* 2.13).[13]

*Paul before Festus.* Felix was succeeded as governor of Judea by Porcius Festus, a man with no experience in Jewish affairs and, unlike Felix, with no Jewish wife to advise him. Perhaps motivated by a desire to establish good relations with the Jewish leaders in Jerusalem, Festus agreed to reopen the case against Paul.

Like the trial before Felix, the new trial was a formal prosecution. We see this in Festus's use of his tribunal (Acts 25:6, 10) and his consultation with his council (Acts 25:6). In addition, Paul's accusers returned, but this time without an attorney (Acts 25:6-7). Festus's explanation to Agrippa II, that it is "not the custom of the Romans" to condemn a man before he meets his accusers face to face and can make a defense (Acts 25:16), is in harmony with what we know about Roman law.

Festus's decision to hear the case against Paul in Jerusalem (Acts 25:9) understandably concerned Paul. It showed that Festus either was in a frame of mind to make concessions to the Sanhedrin or did not understand what he was doing. The governor would have been foolish to issue a potentially inflammatory ruling in a city that bore such animosity toward Rome. Festus might even have gone as far as to use the Sanhedrin as his advisory council in this matter. Although there was no substance to the charges against him, Paul likely did not want to risk putting his fate in the hands of his accusers. Therefore, Paul chose to appeal to Caesar (Acts 25:11). Festus seems relieved at Paul's appeal and readily grants his request.

One of the original charges against Paul was a capital crime that might lay within the jurisdiction of the Sanhedrin: that of a Gentile violating the Temple precincts. Josephus reports a speech by the Roman Titus that recognizes the Sanhedrin's right to execute those who violate the temple (*Jewish War* 6.124). The actions of Festus after Paul's appeal to Caesar were driven as much by the relationship of governors to the emperor as by the technicalities of the law. Agrippa comments that Paul could have been set free if he had not appealed to Caesar. But nothing in Roman law prevented Festus from acquitting Paul after he appealed. However, no governor would want to be accused of circumventing the authority of the emperor by ruling once the appeal was made, especially if he had hopes of future advancement. In addition, such an acquittal would have been very unpopular with Jewish leaders in his province. When Paul says that he "was compelled to appeal to Caesar" when the Jews objected to his imminent acquittal, he probably means not that someone coerced him to appeal but that he saw it as a last resort (Acts 28:18-19). Why had Paul not appealed to Caesar under Felix? Perhaps he believed that Felix understood he was innocent and was willing to wait until Felix decided to release him. But he had little reason to feel such assurance with Festus.

Festus was required to send an explanatory statement to Rome along with Paul. He sought the help of the Jewish King Herod Agrippa II in preparing this statement (Acts 26:24-27).

*Paul at Rome.* Before what tribunal would Paul be tried in Rome? What happened to him? Most scholars agree that the praetorian guard in Rome took charge of prisoners sent from the provinces to the jurisdiction of the emperor. For example, the emperor Trajan in the early second century ordered a certain offender from the provinces to be sent in chains "to the prefects of my Praetorium" (Pliny *Letters* 10.57). We also know of a distinguished prisoner in Paul's day who was in the hands of the praetorian prefect (Tacitus *Annals* 11.1).

This position is supported by the letter to the Philippians, probably written from Rome, which refers to those in the "whole praetorian guard" who have heard about Paul (Phil 1:13). In addition, a variant reading in a number of manuscripts of Acts 28:16 inserts after "And when we came into Rome" the phrase "the centurion handed over the prisoners to the commandant of the camp." If this variant is historical, it would confirm that Paul was held by the praetorian guard. The term "commandant of the camp" probably refers to the *princeps castrorum,* the head administrator of the *officium* of the praetorian guard. This was in fact the most likely official to have executive control of prisoners awaiting trial at Rome in this period.

Did Paul appear before Nero? Until the time of Nero, the emperors themselves heard such appeals. But according to the Roman historian Tacitus, Nero announced at the beginning of his reign that he would not judge cases in person as had Claudius before him (*Annals* 13.4.2). At least until the year 62, Nero apparently avoided hearing cases unless he had a personal interest in them. Nero probably would have delegated a case like Paul's to someone else and would have involved himself in it afterwards only to confirm the verdict. Nero may well have sat on the cases against Christians involving the fire in Rome in 64. But if Paul was tried before this time, not long after the two-year period of stay mentioned in Acts 28:30, he probably did not appear before Nero. Very early traditions make Paul one of the victims of Nero's persecution in 64, but Paul's appeal probably would have been heard before this, say in 62 or 63. If, however, he stayed in Rome or returned to Rome, his high visibility would have assured his arrest in 64.

Why was Paul not brought to trial in Rome for at least two years? This may be because of the failure of his accusers to appear in Rome. It also may be because of the congestion of the court list. Even Claudius, who took an active interest in the court, used unorthodox methods to cut down the number of cases. With an emperor like Nero, who had little interest in the court and spent a lot of time out of town, delays likely increased. If Paul had as much freedom to preach as Acts indicates, he might not have wanted to expedite his case, even if he could.

Paul's case may never have come to trial. He could have been released without trial, although no law existed that required his release after a certain length of time if his accusers did not appear. Nero, like other emperors, might have simply released certain prisoners in order to strengthen his popularity or to shorten the overload of pending court cases. A case such as Paul's, with a defendant who had waited over two years and accusers who perhaps had failed to come to Rome, would be a likely candidate for dismissal.[14]

## The Roman Military

*Development.* Most people today would be surprised to learn that Rome's early

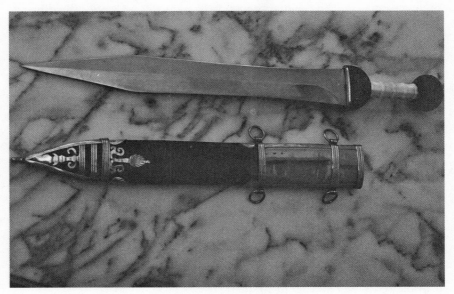

Figure 7.6. The *gladius* or short sword of the Roman legionary. This dual-edged sword usually had a wooden or bone handle.

conquests (up to the second century B.C.) were achieved with the use of a nonprofessional army of unpaid volunteers. Its soldiers were peasant farmer draftees from among its citizens. They were expected to supply their own weapons, food and clothing for the year they would serve.

But by the second century B.C., the number of self-sufficient farmer citizens had declined dramatically as they died in warfare or lost their lands to wealthy neighbors using slaves to do the farming (see appendix A). This circumstance forced Rome to begin to using poor citizens. Since they could not support themselves, someone had to pay them small salaries and provide their equipment. The Roman senate did not want to bear this cost, so it made the fateful decision to have Roman generals provide for the needs of their soldiers. The soldiers naturally looked upon their generals as their patrons and felt obliged to support them as would any good client. The senate did not realize that, in time, the soldiers would come to identify more with generals, such as Marius, Sulla, Pompey and Julius Caesar, than with the Roman state. This in turn helped bring about the civil wars of the late Republic, as soldiers showed their willingness even to march on the senate in the city of Rome in support of their general.

The first emperor, Caesar Augustus, recognized that he had to weaken this relationship in order to improve stability in the state, as well as to protect his own position. He made soldiers dependent on the Roman state, rather than on their general, for their pay and retirement. Soldiers during the Empire enlisted for a fixed twenty-year period and received either land or money when they retired.

After his defeat of Marc Antony and Cleopatra, Augustus moved to cut expenses by reducing the size of the military. In A.D. 6 Augustus set up a military treasury to pay the retirement bonuses of the approximately nine thousand men who were discharged each year.

In the first century, Rome maintained no fixed borders or clear lines of defense. The legions served as mobile infantry forces able quickly to attack in enemy territory, to suppress revolts in the provinces and to prevent foreign invasions. As a result, Roman soldiers did not live in permanent quarters. They slept in tents, or at best in winter quarters constructed of wood, in defensive camps that could be raised or broken down in a day or two. Status distinctions were very clear even here. In one excavated legionary fortress, the legate in command had a richly decorated 75,000-square-foot residence, while the lowest-ranking soldier had about 50 square feet of personal space.

Even a highly mobile force could not be everywhere at once. Rome had to rely in part on the reputation of its army to keep provincials or external foes in line. It might take several weeks or even months to mount a response to a revolt or invasion, but most provincials knew that Rome would win in the end. Rebels not killed in battle or executed thereafter, whether men, women or children, would be sold into slavery.

Service in the army always remained a great privilege of the free full citizen. A citizen fortunate enough to be appointed to the praetorian guard (which was concentrated in Rome from A.D. 23 on) had to serve only sixteen years instead of twenty and was paid triple the salary of a regular legionary. The power of the praetorian guard grew over the years until it became the central support base of the emperor and virtually controlled selection of the emperor. Emperors expended a great deal of money and influence to secure and keep the support of the guard. The phrase *en holo to praitorio* in Philippians 1:13 most likely refers to "the whole praetorian guard" in Rome. When Paul singles out the praetorian guard among those who have heard why he is in prison, he demonstrates an understanding of the importance of this group.

*Structure.* The Roman army in the New Testament era consisted of regular

## Thirty Regular Legions plus Auxiliary Legions

### Officer Title

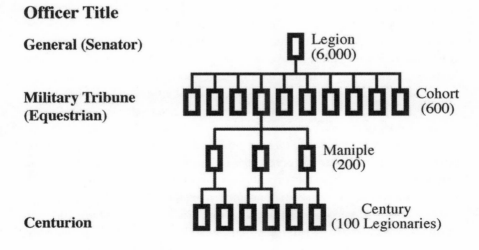

**General (Senator)** — Legion (6,000)

**Military Tribune (Equestrian)** — Cohort (600)

— Maniple (200)

**Centurion** — Century (100 Legionaries)

Figure 7.7. **Structure of the Roman army. The Roman army consisted of thirty legions plus auxiliary legions.**

Roman soldiers and auxiliary soldiers. The former were free Roman citizens, some 150,000 strong, who served in approximately thirty Roman legions (see map 6 for the location of the legions in the first century A.D.). Probably about half of all Roman soldiers died in service. Those who survived could hope, as veterans, to join the ruling class of a town.

The Roman legion included six thousand soldiers under the command of a general (see figure 7.7). The general, who might also be governor of a province, was assisted by military tribunes and chief captains. Legions were composed of ten cohorts of six hundred men each. Cohorts were each divided into three maniples. Each maniple contained two centuries, each under the command of a centurion. The New Testament uses "legion" only to refer to demons (Mk 5:9, 15; Lk 8:30) or to angels (Mt 26:53). The New Testament makes general reference to cohorts three times (Mt 27:27; Mk 15:16; Acts 21:31). It also refers to two independent, volunteer cohorts by name: the Augustan and the Italian (Acts 10:1; 27:1). A cohort composed of auxiliaries was stationed in Jerusalem in the tower of Antonia next to the temple (Josephus *Jewish War* 5.238-44). It was not common practice to station troops inside a major city, but Jerusalem had been the focal point for Jewish unrest for many years. Centurions are mentioned twenty-three times in the New Testament (e.g., Mt 8:5; 27:54; Mk 15:39; Lk 7:2; 23:47; Acts 10:1; 23:17; 27:1).

The officers in the Roman military came from the upper classes. Aristocrats were expected to spend some time in the army as part of the *cursus honorum*, the career path to high office. Some were more capable than others, but none had more than theoretical training in warfare before taking up their first commission. Because of this, the career centurion was the pivotal figure in the Roman military. The situation is analogous to the modern military, where the career noncommissioned officers are often described as the backbone of the service. But modern officers serve under experienced officers longer before gaining the right to command.

The army, with its abundance of private soldier and noncommissioned officer ranks, offered many opportunities for promotion. The highest rank open to lower-class citizens was that of centurion. The origin and career of a centurion was similar to that of a modern noncommissioned officer, but the centurion's responsibilities were closer to that of a modern company commander. He normally served twenty years. The highest rank of centurion was the commander of the first century of a legion, the *primus pilus*. This put him at the top of the sixty centurions in a legion. After one year's service at that rank, he could retire with a bonus of 150,000 denarii (more than enough to enter the equestrian class, and about $6 million in today's money).[15]

*The Roman auxiliary.* As time went on, Augustus realized that his thirty legions were not sufficient to meet the defense and security needs of the Empire. Romans in the past had used "auxiliary" soldiers, non-Roman citizens, in limited capacities as cavalry or for a specific campaign. Augustus initiated a more systematic use of auxiliaries. He began augmenting the regular Roman legions with auxiliary legions composed of free non-Roman citizen provincials. The "cohorts" and cavalry "wings" were usually named for the tribe from which they were recruited.

Auxiliary soldiers who completed twenty years of service won full Roman citizenship for themselves, their children and their descendants. Their marriages were recognized under Roman law as well (Roman law gave no legal standing to the marriages of noncitizens). The total number of soldiers thus recruited became as high as the number of Roman legionaries. We have evidence of grants of citizenship to auxiliary soldiers and sailors from the time of Claudius onward. However, not all auxiliaries were this fortunate. The tribune who commanded the auxiliary cohort stationed in Jerusalem, Claudius Lysias, says that he had to buy his citizenship (Acts 22:28).

*Armor and weapons.* The Roman helmet was designed to protect the head, face and neck without blocking vision or hearing (see figure 7.5). It might be decorated with enameled studs. Helmets worn by officers (centurion and above) were topped by crests so that their men could follow them in battle. In the first century A.D., the breastplate was replaced with a jacket made of metal strips held together on the inside by leather straps. It was very flexible but heavy, and soldiers had to help each other put it on. Under his armor the soldier wore a coarse woolen tunic that reached to midthigh. They eventually added breeches under the tunic, especially necessary as Rome pushed its conquests into colder, northern climes. The belt or apron was a soldier's badge of office, so he always wore it over his tunic. Decorated leather strips hung from the front of the belt, giving some protection to the groin area. A heavy pendant weighed down the end of each strip. Military sandals were made of leather. Patterns of iron hobnails on the soles were designed to distribute weight and stand up to long marches. A soldier's shield usually was rectangular and wooden, with a metal cover over the center handle. It could be used both defensively and offensively.

The first-century Roman soldier was equipped with a double-edged dagger and a short sword. Both were Roman copies of Spanish weapons. The sword hilt was often made of wood, but it was also sometimes made of bone or ivory. The sword was a stabbing weapon, rather than a hacking weapon like the long swords of the Gauls. Because of its small size, it was a very effective weapon in close quarters. Foot soldiers also carried spears. Through most of the Republic this was a thrusting spear. By the late Republic it was replaced by the *pilum*, a heavy javelin with a long, narrow steel point. It was designed to pierce both shield and armor and then break so that it could not be thrown back. While at a distance, the Romans would let these fly at the enemy. The shower of javelins often broke an enemy's charge. The Roman soldiers would then pull out their short swords and move in for close combat.

Soldiers carried cloaks that could cover themselves and their packs, providing warmth and some rain protection. The pack contained personal items and food for three days. A soldier's armor, pack, tool kit, dish and pan weighed ninety pounds or more.

It is not certain whether Paul in Ephesians 6:10-17 has in mind the Roman or traditional Greek soldier. The former would have been more recognizable to his readers, even in Ephesus, since by his day the Romans had controlled that area for some time. His term for the whole armor of God (*panoplia tou theou*, Eph 6:11, 13) refers to the full combat equipment of a soldier. Any soldier worth his salt knew that he had to have every part of his equipment in order to be ready for battle.

*Military pay.* Soldiers then as now were paid according to rank. In the first century the top centurion, the *primus pilus*, received 15,000 denarii per year, the next nine centurions each received 7,500, and the remaining fifty centurions were each paid 3,750. The common Roman soldier in the regular legions received only 225 denarii per year, about $9,000 in today's money. In the second century the soldier's pay rose to 300 denarii. Out of this they were expected to buy their food, clothing and weapons. When he retired, the common soldier could expect to receive a 4,000 denarii bonus. Pay for auxiliary troops was much lower: 200 denarii for elite troops, 150 for cavalry, 100 for infantry.[16]

When his legion defeated the enemy, a soldier could expect to share in the spoils of war. The value of persons sold into slavery was the sole booty of the general, but other spoils were divided among the soldiers according to rank. The division of spoils at the Roman general Pompey's triumph (first century B.C.) shows how this worked. Pompey had conquered a good deal of the Near East and amassed a tremendous amount of booty. The staff officers received 800,000 denarii each, the military tribunes 180,000 each, the centurions 30,000 each, and the privates 1,500 each.

When one realizes that auxiliary soldiers were only paid the equivalent of one hundred days of a day laborer's wage for an entire year's service, it isn't surprising that many soldiers supplemented their salaries. They often did so through unofficial activities including outright extortion. In part because of this, Roman soldiers were not well liked by provincials, especially in a province like Judea.

*Military families.* Some soldiers were married before entering the military, but many were not. As a way of maintaining a soldier's single-minded loyalty to the state, Augustus prohibited soldiers beneath a certain rank from marrying during their time of service (Dio, *Letters* 60.24.3). However, many ignored this. Even though they could not marry legally, many took wives and raised families. Typically their "wives" were non-Romans, whom they often took with them while in service. Since Roman citizens could form a legal marriage only with other citizens, even after retirement neither their marriage nor their children would be recognized legally.

No social stigma was attached to illegitimacy or to what we would call common-law marriages, but the legal downside could be significant. For example, if a soldier died in service, his illegitimate wife had no claim to the return of her dowry, and the soldier could not name her as an heir in his will. At times emperors addressed this by recognizing the marriage of a retired Roman soldier and recognizing as citizens children born to this union after his retirement. Children born before his retirement probably were never granted citizen status.[17]

*The Near East.* The position of governor of Syria was a powerful one in the New Testament era, not least because it came with control of four regular Roman legions. In fact, until the late 60s, this was the entire Roman military presence in the Near East. Traianus, commander of one of the legions in Judea during the Jewish War (A.D. 66-73), became governor of Syria a few years later. His son Trajan went on to become emperor.

Rome concentrated these forces in Syria to counter the threat posed by the kingdoms of Armenia and Parthia to the east. This threat probably explains why the governor of Syria delayed in sending forces to deal with the increasing violence and unrest in Judea during the early 60s.

No legion was stationed in Judea on a regular basis until after the Jewish War. Instead, the local auxiliary forces were deployed essentially as a police force, as Acts makes clear. They acted to prevent rioting, to guard prisoners and to execute criminals. For this reason Rome stationed extra troops in Jerusalem during Passover. These auxiliary troops were drawn mainly from the local Gentile populations of Caesarea and Sebaste.

The normal route taken by Roman forces, when they had to intervene in the territories of dependent kingdoms or in the minor province of Judea, was south along the coast through Berytus (modern Beirut), Tyre, Ptolemais and Caesarea. Because of their strategic importance to Rome, by the late 70s A.D. all of these cities, except Tyre, had become Roman colonies. They functioned as outposts of staunch Roman support in a region that had not fully accepted Roman rule.[18]

*Military terms in the New Testament.* The term *praetorium* occurs several times in the New Testament. It is a Latin term, transliterated into Greek, meaning "leader" or "chief." At first, it signified the tent of the praetor (general) in the Roman army. Later, it denoted the general's officers who assembled in his tent as a council. Still later it referred to the official provincial residence of a governor (Jn 18:28). This was technically the part of the residence where justice was administered, or the court at the entrance of the residence. It also designated imperial troops who acted as bodyguards.

The Greek term appears in Matthew 27:27; Mark 15:16; John 18:28; 33; 19:9; and Acts 23:35 translated as "common hall" or "judgment hall." Scholars differ over the location of Pilate's praetorium in Jerusalem, where Jesus was judged. Some locate it in the Fortress Antonia, but most place it in Herod's old palace. In Caesarea, Herod's great palace was used as the procurator's praetorium by Felix; it was Paul's place of imprisonment (Acts 23:35).

The centurion from Capernaum in the heart of Galilee, mentioned in the New Testament, was not a Roman soldier but probably part of the army of Herod Antipas. Antipas ruled the independent tetrarchy of Galilee at this time. He applied Roman terminology to his military, perhaps because he was raised in Rome (Mt 8:5-13; Lk 7:1-10). At the execution of John the Baptist, Antipas's officers included *chiliarchoi* (Mk 6:21, 27). The term *chiliarchos* is the Greek equivalent of a Roman military tribune. This term clearly reflects Roman influence, but it does not refer to Romans.

John the Baptist's execution was carried out by a *speculator*, as indicated in Mark 6:27. The speculatores were a kind of secret police, a special body of imperial guards of centurion rank. They tended to appear in moments of military intrigue. Their duties were taken over in the second century by the *frumentarii*, the secret police. Mark correctly used the term for the Herodian soldier who executed John.[19]

## For Further Reading

### Taxation

Brunt, P. A., ed. *The Roman Economy.* London: Blackwell, 1974.

Finley, Moses I. *The Ancient Economy.* Berkeley: University of California Press, 1973.

Frank, Tenney, ed. *An Economic Survey of Ancient Rome.* 6 vols. Baltimore: Johns Hopkins Press, 1933-1940.

### Law

Crook, J. A. *Law and Life of Rome.* Ithaca, N.Y.: Cornell University Press, 1967.

Jones, A. H. M. *The Criminal Courts of the Roman Republic and Principate.* Totowa, N.J.: Rowman and Littlefield, 1972.

Watson, Alan. *Roman Law and Comparative Law.* Athens: University of Georgia Press, 1991.

### *Military*

Campbell, J. B. *The Emperor and the Roman Army, 31 B.C.-A.D 235.* New York: Oxford University Press, 1984.

Isaac, Benjamin. *The Limits of Empire: The Roman Army in the East.* Oxford: Clarendon, 1993.

Webster, Graham. *The Roman Imperial Army of the First and Second Centuries A.D.* 3rd ed. London: A & C Black, 1985.

# Chapter 8

## Social Class & Status in the Empire

*Petty trade is sordid, but if it is large and extensive,*
*importing many goods from all over and offering them for sale without deception,*
*it is not too shameful; rather, if in satiety or, better,*
*in contentment it retreats from the harbor to country estates,*
*it seems most rightfully deserving of praise.*
CICERO1

*He said also to the man who had invited him,*
*"When you give a dinner or a banquet, do not invite your friends*
*or your brothers or your kinsmen or rich neighbors,*
*lest they also invite you in return, and you be repaid.*
*But when you give a feast, invite the poor, the maimed, the lame,*
*the blind, and you will be blessed, because they cannot repay you.*
*You will be repaid at the resurrection of the just."*
LUKE 14:12-14

*For if a man with gold rings and in fine clothing comes into your assembly,*
*and a poor man in shabby clothing also comes in,*
*and you pay attention to the one who wears the fine clothing and say,*
*"Have a seat here, please," while you say to the poor man, "Stand there,"*
*or, "Sit at my feet," have you not made distinctions*
*among yourselves, and become judges with evil thoughts?*
*Listen, my beloved brethren. Has not God chosen those who are poor*
*in the world to be rich in faith and heirs of the kingdom*
*which he has promised to those who love him?*
*But you have dishonored the poor man. Is it not the rich who oppress you,*
*is it not they who drag you into court? Is it not they who blaspheme*
*that honorable name by which you are called?*
JAMES 2:2-7

THE PEOPLE OF THE ROMAN EMPIRE WERE DIVIDED BY VERY DEFINITE social classes and indicators of social status (see figure 8.1). Everyone knew his or her place in the social order. When we talk about social classes in American society, we usually mean income levels such as upper, middle and lower. But our concepts of social class and status bear little resemblance to those in ancient societies. Imagine a society in which the gulf between the upper class and all others was so wide that their members had virtually nothing in common. Imagine that you were forbidden by law to marry someone of another class, and upward mobility was frowned upon. Imagine a legal system that always favored the upper class. Imagine a society in which, with very few exceptions, your status at birth determined the course of your future life. While we may be able to think of examples of this kind of separation in American society, it is nothing like the chasm between those at the top and those at the bottom in Roman society that existed at all times in every place. Thus, we have to understand the nature and importance of class and status in order to appreciate fully the relationships between persons in the New Testament.

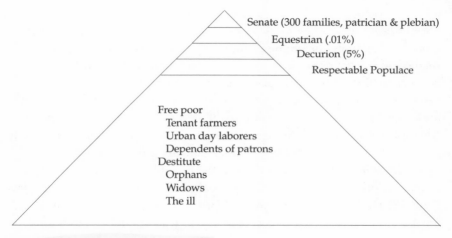

Senate (300 families, patrician & plebian)

Equestrian (.01%)

Decurion (5%)

Respectable Populace

Free poor
   Tenant farmers
   Urban day laborers
   Dependents of patrons
Destitute
   Orphans
   Widows
   The ill

**Figure 8.1. Social class in the Roman Empire**

*Class* indicates the group of persons into which one is born and, with few exceptions, that to which one will belong until death. Romans used the term *order (ordo)* to describe the classes in their society, but they used the term somewhat differently from the way we use the term *class* today. Membership in a given order gave one greater honor and privileges than those possessed by members of a lower order.

*Status* is a more fluid term, in that the various markers of status could change over time and might conflict with one another. Take the example of a former slave with great wealth, several of whom we find in the New Testament era. Wealth could help lessen the negative connotations of having once been a slave, but could not overcome them—at least not in the perception of members of the upper classes. A set of categories based on the concept of honor marked one's status in Roman society. One achieved honor and *dignitas* (more complicated than the English term *dignity,* which comes from it) by activities that increased one's esteem in the community.

As one might expect, wealth was an important indicator of status in the Greco-Roman world, but it was by no means the only indicator. Education also was valued, but it did not in itself convey status. The Romans evaluated a person's status based on whether the person was a citizen or a foreigner, patron or client, free or slave, ethnic Roman/Latin or not, voluntary ally or conquered enemy, male or female, and married or unmarried. These categories each had a specific value for Romans. For example, a well-educated, wealthy, noncitizen, former slave would have been thought lower in status than a poor, uneducated, freeborn citizen.[2]

## Social Class

It is useful to know something about the various classes in Roman society. A small group at the pinnacle of the Roman social hierarchy held the power in the society: the senatorial, equestrian and decurion orders. These orders together made up only about 1 percent of the population, but they constituted the leadership of almost all elements of public life—far more so than in modern America. For example, a Roman aristocrat might have held simultaneously positions as business leader, priest, judge, military officer and politician.

*Senatorial order.* In the early days of the Republic, the Roman senate was composed of the heads of the traditional aristocratic families. By the late Republic, it had become an assembly of former senior magistrates (consuls and praetors). For most of its history, the senate was limited to three hundred members.

The *cursus honorum* was the regulated career of offices open to new senators. A young man from a senatorial family could join the senate once he could claim ownership of property worth one million sesterces (250,000 denarii). Beginning in his late teens, the young man would serve first with one of the commissions overseeing the mint, road management or legal affairs. Then he would spend two or three years as a military tribune (officer) in a legion. Around age twenty-five he would become a quaestor and officially enter the senate. A few years later, he would attempt to win election either as a tribune of the plebs or as an aedile. At age thirty, he would be eligible for election to the praetorship. During the Empire era, the senator would usually hold three or more offices after his service as praetor. Such offices included command of a legion, govern-ance of a minor province such as Judea or Cilicia, supervision of the treasuries, oversight of the Italian public roads, or administration of justice, grain distribution or public works.

After this he might be elected consul, the highest office he could hold. More than half of all senators never attained the consulship. A former consul could become governor, usually for three years, of one of the major provinces. There he might also command up to four Roman legions, as did the governor of Syria province. Former consuls also served in the major offices of the city of Rome, such as city prefect. At virtually every turn, a senator's career could be advanced or halted by the emperor. If he wished to advance, the senator continually had to prove his loyalty to the emperor.

One's status within the senate was determined primarily by the offices one held or had held, by one's achievements in war, at court or in legislating, the number of one's clients (see below), and one's wealth. New members of the senate came from the sons of senators and from the equestrian order (see below). A person with equestrian status who had served in or been available to serve in ten military campaigns was eligible to run for election as a quaestor. By the first century B.C., promotion to the senate came with election to this administrative office.

The emperors gradually allowed non-Romans, then non-Italians, to join the senate. By mid-second century A.D., only 57 percent of the new senators were coming from Italy. Almost half of the non-Italians in the senate were from the eastern provinces. In this way, the Romans consciously incorporated the ruling classes of conquered peoples into their system. These local rulers came to realize that they had much to lose if they allowed their people to revolt, and so they actively supported Roman rule.

Some senators were incredibly wealthy. The two largest fortunes of the time about which we know each amounted to 400 million sesterces (or 100 million denarii). This equals about one year's income for the entire Roman Empire in this era. It is similar in value to about one and a half million tons of wheat, or over thirty-seven times the value of the greatest private fortune in England in 1700. If we value one denarius (one day's wage for a common laborer) at $50, their fortunes each would be worth $20 billion.

We know the most about the wealth of a senator named Pliny the Younger. His 20 million sesterces placed him twenty-first on the list of known rich men of the period and would make him a billionaire in modern terms. Pliny was governor of the province of Bithynia at the end of the first century A.D. Like other senators, the foundation of his fortune was land—farmland and pasture land. In fact, 17 million of his 20 million sesterces were invested in land. Just one of his farms, in Tuscany, produced an annual income of 400,000 sesterces.

Other income came from the interest on loans he had given out. He owned a number of houses and farms and about four hundred slaves. Pliny was not stingy with his money. He made very generous donations. For example, he gave 1,800,000 sesterces to his freedmen, 500,000 for a private foundation to support children in his hometown, 200,000 to establish a library, and various amounts for temples and gifts.[3]

Why was so much senatorial wealth tied up in land? The Romans believed that the only socially acceptable business for a senator was agriculture. In fact, a law in 218 B.C. virtually prohibited senators from engaging in overseas trade. Roman aristocrats considered trade to be basically dishonest since it involved buying products at one price and selling them for a higher price without doing anything to increase their value. This was a time-honored tradition, as reflected in the Gospels. The rich mentioned there generally owe their wealth to agriculture (Mt 13:3-4; 21:28; 25:14-30; Lk 19:11-27). By the New Testament era, however, this was more show than reality. Seeing the great fortunes to be made in various areas of commerce, some senators hired others to pursue unacceptable but profitable business interests on their behalf. They also found in government service a chance to enhance the family fortune. A provincial governor could gain great personal wealth through business contacts, special perquisites and the extortion of provincials. In addition, army commanders and officers received the lion's share of any booty gained in battle.

While senators exerted great influence on events in the New Testament era, they were generally out of sight of those who wrote the New Testament. We meet in its pages two senators in their capacities as provincial governors: Sergius Paulus of Cyprus (Acts 13:7-8, 12) and Annaeus Gallio of Achaia (Acts 18:12-17). Acts 19:38 refers to proconsuls, who are of senatorial status.

*Equestrian order.* This order originated in the early Roman Republic. At that time, any citizen serving in the Roman army on horseback was called an *equite*, "equestrian." Such a person needed a certain level of wealth in order to provide his own horse as well as his weapons and other supplies. The term later expanded to refer to a second order of Roman society below the senatorial level.

Members of the senatorial order constituted about 0.002 percent of the Mediterranean world. The equestrian class added perhaps less than another 0.1 percent. Even in Italy, at its richest, the equestrians made up no more than 1 percent of the population. In poorer regions, and everywhere in the countryside, equestrians were much rarer. Estimates of the number of equestrians empirewide, in the time of Caesar Augustus, vary from 10,000 to 20,000.[4]

The sons of senators were automatically enrolled in the equestrian order. Censors appointed by the people under the Republic, later by the emperor, decided who else to admit. A son petitioned for admission based on moral excellence, net worth equal to 400,000 sesterces (100,000 denarii) and proof of free birth for two generations. In modern terms, this makes them all million-aires. The censors looked for men who had proven themselves dependable on the battlefield, in court and as patrons to their clients. The wealth requirement reflects a basic Roman assumption: wealthy men are more likely to be honest and honorable because financial need has never forced them to be otherwise.

Equestrian careers usually began with service as a military tribune in an auxiliary legion (see chapter seven). Senators filled the military tribune post in regular legions. Since the military tribune who examined Paul in Jerusalem, Claudius Lysias, belonged to an auxiliary legion, he was of equestrian rank. Following this, the equestrian might be appointed a procurator. Pontius Pilate, like many of the governors of Judea, was an equestrian. An equestrian also might oversee the inheritance taxation of several provinces or become an imperial treasury official. Second century A.D. inscriptions indicate that some 650 government posts were open to equestrians.

In fact, equestrians could hold offices exceeding those of senators in power. This was because the emperors felt they could put greater trust in equestrians, who owed their positions to them, than in senators. For example, offices always filled by equestrians included: commander of the fleet of Rome, commander of the security police in Rome, oversight of the entire procurement and supply of food for the capital, the governer of Egypt, and the commander of the praetorian guard.

The equestrian Burrus had an astonishing career. He rose from military tribune to procurator, then to praetorian prefect. In this last post his influence over the young emperor Nero made him one of the most powerful men in the Empire, despite his equestrian status. Finally, Burrus was made an honorary member of the order of consuls, even though he had never belonged to the senate, let alone been elected consul.[5]

Equestrians typically provided the financial resources for commercial ven-tures since senators were prohibited formally from doing so. Many made enormous fortunes in overseas trade, large-scale money transactions, tax col-lection and many other types of business. They supplied many of the basic needs of a state that shunned a professional bureaucracy, such as military supply, transport and major construction projects.

From the time of Augustus on, a number of former slaves were raised by the emperor to the equestrian rank. For example, the procurator of Judea who first heard Paul's defense in Caesarea, Marcus Antonius Felix (A.D. 52-59?), was once the slave of the mother of Emperor Claudius. This shows that the rule requiring two generations of free birth before being admitted to the equestrian order was being relaxed. A Roman centurion who had served long and well had a good chance to become an equestrian. Quite a few equestrians eventually were made senators during the Empire era.

The New Testament refers to a few more equestrians than senators. Besides Marcus Antonius Felix, mentioned above, all of the Roman governors of Judea, such as Pontius Pilate and Porcius Festus (Acts 24), were equestrians.

*Decurion order.* The aristocrats of the cities around the Empire formed the lowest rung of the upper classes. They made up the decurion order, the *ordo decurionum.* Also called municipal senators, they ruled the cities of Italy, the Roman colonies and other cities that followed the Roman model. Eastern municipal senates varied in size from thirty to five hundred members. They were the local wealthy landowners, merchants and traders. However, we should not think of them as forming a unified class since their wealth, status and influence varied greatly.

A freeborn citizen meeting the local property qualification, twenty-five to thirty years of age and not involved in dishonorable trade, could become a decurion. If selected, he would find service as a decurion costly. For example, decurions were expected to serve one year without pay in a city office and to make monetary contributions to the community. They oversaw local commerce, collected taxes and presided over civic events. In return, they received increased social status and perquisites such as good seats at the games, preferential water supply, meals at public expense and legal privileges.

Wealth qualifications for this order were set locally and varied depending on the wealth of the region. In the prosperous Italian city of Comum, decurions needed property worth 100,000 sesterces, one-tenth of that needed to be a senator. Less prosperous towns had to lower their qualifications in order to have enough decurions. In the smaller cities of North Africa, the membership quali-fication was 20,000 sesterces. Clearly, a great gulf separated the senate in a large Italian city from that in a small provincial town.

In the eastern Mediterranean, most decurions were Greeks and Hellenized Near Easterners. In fact, with the exception of a few individuals who made it into the equestrian and senatorial orders, the Hellenistic upper classes were to be found among the decurions of the Roman era. One might have expected that the Romans, when they took control of the eastern Mediterranean, would have confiscated all of its wealth and replaced its wealthy upper classes with imported Romans, but this did not happen. Yes, the Romans did appropriate a great deal of wealth in this part of the world as elsewhere. Local upper classes who resisted being conquered did lose everything, but this was extremely rare. Instead, the pattern is a symbiotic relationship between the Romans and the local upper classes. The Romans, having no desire to get bogged down in direct rule of their provinces, realized that they needed to maintain local upper classes favorable to their rule. They allowed the Hellenistic upper classes to retain their wealth, and the Romans gave them additional benefits if they would only help keep their people pacified and make sure that the taxes were paid on time. For their part, the local aristocracies soon learned that giving up independence and self-determination in exchange for political peace and economic prosperity was a good deal for them. That the lower classes did not always appreciate this deal is clear in Judea, where the Herodians and the priestly caste, the lower aristocracy in alliance with the Romans, were unpopular with many Judeans and suffered much from fellow Jews during the Jewish revolt of A.D. 68-74.

The New Testament names two men who are clearly decurions (and also Christians): Dionysius, a member of the Areopagus in Athens (Acts 17:34), and Erastus, the city treasurer of Corinth (Rom 16:23).

Figure 8.2. The Grand Theater in Pompeii, Italy. The theater was used to stage plays that were attended by Romans of all social classes. Off camera to the right is the gladiatorial practice arena.

*Respectable populace.* Below the ruling classes there existed a large group of persons of middling wealth and status, whom the Roman historian Tacitus called the *populus integer*, the "respectable populace." This group was composed of small landowners, craftsmen and shopkeepers, including those who worked alongside their slave or wage laborers. It also included the middle and lower ranks of Roman citizens in the army, from centurions to ordinary legionary soldiers and veterans. These were people of some moderate substance, though with various social backgrounds. Included were former slaves who had gained Roman citizenship. They had attained moderate wealth and status virtually equal to that of "respectable" Romans. Also in this category were freeborn Greeks, perhaps with Roman citizenship. Their level of respectability in the eyes of the upper classes was in direct proportion to the amount of work they did through the agency of others, rather than with their own hands.

Provincial cities were peopled by a group with similar occupations, wealth and local status, although most of them lacked Roman citizenship and so would have had less status in the eyes of Romans like Cicero. We should avoid the temptation to call this a middle class since such a modern term would be misleading. But these people did have income and status that located them somewhere between the elite at the top of the social pyramid and the mass of subsistence farmers at the bottom. Unlike the modern middle class, they constituted only a few percent of the population. Probably most of the urban-dwelling Christians named in the New Testament belong to this group.

The respectable populace highly valued honesty in business dealings, preferring a person's promise to collateral. In imitation of the aristocracy, they feasted as lavishly as they could. The less wealthy among them joined street or craft associations (see chapter four) where they could find comradeship and share the cost of great banquets and funeral expenses. In this group, as among the equestrians, we find people who had some degree of upward social mobility.

*The poor.* At the bottom of the social pyramid were the free poor. Tacitus calls them the "shabby people" *(plebs sordida)*, who frequented the circus and theaters *(Histories* 1.4). He reveals a prevalent attitude among the elite when he places them alongside low-status slaves (those not owned by one of the great Roman houses) and "spendthrifts and bankrupts." The poor spent most of the day working to meet immediate needs or trying to find work. Many of the poor in Italy were tenant farmers or city dwellers whose ancestors had lost their farms through indebtedness. A few were able to rise above this state, but others who had fallen into overwhelming debt were continually joining it. The poor tended to congregate in the cities, where they had a better chance of finding day work or other means of support. Often the larger the city, the larger the proportion of poor. In the city of Rome, they made up something like a third of the population. Their situation was not helped by the fact that the state did not provide for the needs of the aged, widows, orphans, the disabled or the sick. The only exception to this was a modest subsidy of the price of grain, provided to Roman citizens in the city of Rome. Some other cities also made special provisions to feed the poor (Strabo, *Geography* 14.2.5), but it was never enough.

The poor in the cities supported themselves by piecework at the docks, in construction or on farms. The poor might survive by attaching themselves as clients to well-to-do patrons (see Roman patronage, below). Or they might steal or beg. Among the beggars were those who appear frequently in the Gospels: the sick, the blind, the lame and the lepers.

## Social Status

Considerations of social class can only take us so far in our understanding of Roman social relations. We must also use the category of status in understanding the social places of peoples in the cities of the Empire.

*Wealth and status.* The vast majority of the Roman world's wealth was in the hands of a very small number of persons (see table 8.1). Even more than today, not all wealthy persons in that day enjoyed high social status, but virtually everyone with high status in the Roman world was wealthy. The upper classes regularly practiced "conspicuous consumption" as a way to demonstrate their social and political status. For example, when a donor to a public work was publicly acknowledged, the amount of the gift was also indicated. This practice continues today whenever a wealthy donor's name is attached to a building he or she helps fund and the amount donated is reported in the news. A senator's wife could be spotted in the streets of Rome from a distance by her fancy litter as well as her expensive clothing and jewelry. The senator was easily identified by the broad crimson stripe on his toga and by the large retinue that attended him.[6] Conspicuous consumption in the form of showy material possessions continues today, of course.

Romans considered wealth an essential requirement of the virtuous life. In contrast with the popular American idea that the wealthy are less honest because power corrupts, the Roman elite believed that only the rich could afford to be honest. They reasoned that the poor must do whatever is necessary to survive and so are more likely to lie, cheat and steal. The poor who had to work the land with their own hands or, worse yet, hire themselves out to others are despised in the surviving writings of the upper class. The concept of the poor as "blessed" (Mt 5:3; Lk 6:20) would have been incomprehensible to Greek and Roman aristocrats.

**Citizenship and Freedom**
Wealthy freeborn citizen
Imperial freed (citizen) slave
Imperial slave
Wealthy freed citizen slave
Poor freeborn citizen
Poor freed citizen slave
Wealthy freeborn noncitizen
Poor freeborn noncitizen
Freed noncitizen slave
Urban domestic slave
Farm slave
Mining slave

**Patrons and Clients**
Patrician patron
Upper-class plebian patron
Client of powerful patron
Client of weak patron

**Age and Sex**
Adult male with no living father
Adult male with living father
Widowed adult female with inde-
  pendent resources
Widowed adult female
Married adult female
Child—male then female

Table 8.1. Social status in the Greco-Roman world. Markers of social status by category from high to low, showing relative status in each category.

The wealthy typically delegated the work of maintaining and increasing their fortunes to slave and freed managers. The attitude of the rich man, described in Luke 12:16-21 as obsessed with increasing his wealth and holdings, was not at all uncommon among the elite of the Empire.[7]

Wealth was an important component of social status, but it was not a sufficient indicator for those in the highest social strata. Advanced education and the ability to speak well were also important. But to be honored among the elite, one needed above all things the right family of origin. The phrase used as the mark of distinction for a Roman sums this up: "by family and wealth." A Roman's name generally announced his heritage and thus his class. As a result, stealing a family's name was considered a crime.

Cicero gives us a spectrum of honor and wealth among the upper classes. At one end is inherited wealth, since active pursuit of wealth aroused misgivings. Just below this in honor is wealth gained during one's life but now enjoyed in retirement. Lower in honor and approaching the unrespectable is wealth still being accumulated.

For the upper class in the cities of the provinces, however, wealth was by far the most important component of status. For example, a decurion of the city of Tymandus, an army veteran, reportedly was not respected for his military service, his lineage or his education. He was respected for his money.[8] An army private's retirement bonus could help him assume the leadership of a village. An officer's bonus could get him into the council of a large provincial center. If decurions had enough money, and spent it on the proper offices and public works, they were accepted. However, the decurion needed wealth and time to gain true honor. In fact, his family might not be accepted as truly part of the ruling class until his grandson reached adulthood, and only if his family had conducted itself honorably during that time.

Roman society was very static by our standards. We are used to a society in which upward mobility is a general expectation of life (even if not always realized). Roman society did provide some opportunities for social mobility, and some persons were able to see their status rise in their lifetimes. This upward social mobility came usually through the accumulation of wealth. In fact, a few rose from poverty to great wealth. In rare cases they gained enough social prominence to challenge the positions of persons at the very top of the Roman hierarchy. The talent and aggressiveness of an individual certainly contributed to his or her upward mobility, but the sponsorship of someone in authority also was a major factor. For example, the emperors promoted prosperous or promising provincials to the equestrian or even senatorial order.

Slaves who gained freedom generally saw a rise in their social status during their lifetimes (see chapter eleven). Social mobility occurred more in Italy than elsewhere because of the much higher numbers of freed slaves there. As one moved eastward, society became more and more immobile. Leadership in the cities was monopolized, generation after generation, by the same small, ruling classes.

The very existence of upwardly mobile persons challenged the established order of a static society dedicated to keeping the upper classes on top. In the surviving sources, the upper classes shudder at how consuls chosen from the newly rich demean the very office they hold. They are indignant at wealthy ex-slaves who claim precedence over Romans of good family. Greeks and Romans in the ruling classes saw it as the duty of every citizen to preserve the boundaries of class. Cicero said, "Rank must be preserved."[9]

*Benefits of high status.* Ancient society provided a number of special benefits to those of high class and status. Those with the highest status in a locale could claim the front seats at shows, they had the right to wear and display certain symbols of their status, and when the state distributed money, food or wine, they were entitled to a bigger portion than were the poor. The concept "To him who has will more be given, and he will have abundance" (Mt 13:12; Mk 4:25; Lk 8:18) was a principle of Roman society, if in a very different sense from Jesus' meaning. Separate courts tried the upper and lower classes and levied separate punishments. The upper classes could not be sued by their social inferiors, and they received more lenient penalties if convicted of a crime.

A person's place at table and the quality of food served depended on the person's status. This was true both of private dinner parties to which a rich patron invited some clients and of public banquets given by an aristocrat for fellow citizens. The dispute at Corinth that Paul takes up may reflect this practice: the host at a Christian agape feast is acting like a patron at a banquet, making distinctions between the guests with higher status and those with lower status (1 Cor 11:17-34).[10] The Epistle of James depicts a similar situation, in which a stranger with a gold ring and fine clothes is given a seat of honor while a poor stranger is given a place of dishonor (Jas 2:1-6). Equestrians wore a special gold ring and a tunic with a narrow crimson stripe, and they sat in seats of honor in the theater. It is likely that James does not have in mind an equestrian (because they were so few); he probably is describing simply a wealthy businessman with a ring.

*Patronage and status.* Personal relationships were far more important to the functioning of ancient society than they are to the modern Western world. Roman aristocrats traditionally developed reciprocal ties of friendship. Friends of similar social station could be counted on to provide hospitality when one was traveling, or a loan when one was in need of cash. Dealings with the lower classes were guided by the tradition of the patron-client relationship.

The patron was seen as the protector of the client. The patron owed the client legal help and protection from powerful enemies. The client in turn owed the patron respect and deference. Seneca observed that this reciprocal exchange, which he called *beneficia,* was a custom "which more than any other binds together human society."[11]

A patron's social status was measured in part by the number and status of his clients. During the Republic, a client was expected to support his patron's political campaign for public office. Even after the Empire brought an end to political campaigning, patronage remained an important social basis of the aristocracy. Public attendance on one's patron was required and often consumed the better part of a client's morning hours if not the entire day. Clients provided an aristocrat with a retinue that accompanied him around the city or ornamented his receiving room, thereby announcing the aristocrat's social importance. For his day's attendance, the client was rewarded with a small basket (the *sportula*). It generally contained food and small presents. Trajan restricted its value to six and one-quarter sesterces per day: a small remuneration if one had to attend errands of his patron for the better part of the day.[12]

A client might be invited to a patron's banquet table simply to witness the latter's wealth and power, not out of genuine friendship. In such cases the client could expect to be the butt of jokes and to receive food and wine far inferior to that of honored guests, as Juvenal laments (*Satires* 5).

Freed slaves normally became the clients of their former masters. In the first century, the free citizen owed only moral obligations to his patron, but the freedman owed him legal obligations as well. Augustus used this relationship in establishing the imperial bureaucracy. As a result, members of the *familia*

*Caesaris,* imperial slaves and freedmen, were recognized as special representatives of imperial authority. They came to exert at times greater influence than many of those born into the ruling elite.[13]

Something like the patron-client relationship existed in the world of the Gospels. Wealthy landowners were like patrons of their tenant farmers (Mt 21:33-41; Mk 12:1-9; Lk 20:9-16). The rich in Palestine took a position of superiority over the poor at meals (Lk 12:35-38; 14:12-24; 17:7-10).

*Attitudes toward the lower classes.* An important factor in understanding the part played by social status in Roman society is to see how those with high status viewed those with low status. The "honorable ones" looked down upon the "humble" across the social distance between them much as the rich man looks at Lazarus in Jesus' parable (Lk 16:19-31). Classical literature is filled with upper-class sneers at the laziness, poverty and servility of the poor.

Cicero speaks with disgust about virtually half the population of eastern Mediterranean towns when he talks of "craftsmen, petty shopkeepers, and all that filth of the cities" (*Pro Flacco* 18). Cicero shared with others in his class the notion that physical labor coarsened body, soul and manners. Most ancient authors write that the better part of humanity is mental and spiritual. No person of refined taste could bear to be a smith, tanner or butcher.

The Roman upper classes regarded the creation of art as beneath them since so much art in their era was produced by Greek slaves. Seneca refused to include painting, sculpting and working in marble in the liberal arts, considering them sordid pursuits. Cicero says that the work of the artisan is vulgar and that nothing is noble about a workshop. But medicine, architecture and teaching at the advanced level are honorable occupations "for those to whose social position they are appropriate." (*Brutus* 73).

Ultimately, Roman aristocrats believed that the poor should be held in contempt because they had no money. The aristocrats saw poverty itself as ugly and dishonorable. They apparently felt little sympathy for the plight of the poor. "To certain people I shall not give, even though there is need, because there will still be need even if I give."[14] One Pompeiian wrote on a wall, "I hate poor people. If anyone wants something for nothing, he's a fool. Let him pay up and he'll get it."[15] The Epistle of James appears to have this kind of attitude in mind when it cautions Christians against playing favorites with the rich: "Is it not the rich who oppress you, is it not they who drag you into court? Is it not they who blaspheme that honorable name which you are called?" (Jas 2:6-7).

### Class, Status and the New Testament
The New Testament refers to groups of non-Christians in the cities in ways that

suggest their social status and class. The wealthy and privileged non-Romans in the cities of the Empire are represented in Acts by the "leading men of the city," the "ladies of good estate" as at Antioch and Berea, and perhaps by the Asiarchs as at Ephesus. The ladies of good estate, clearly members of a proper-tied class, reappear at Thessalonica (Acts 13:50; 17:4, 12; 19:31).

The social statuses of Christians place them for the most part in the middle and lower range of class and status. Overall, the typical Pauline Christians were free artisans or merchants with a small income. Their congregations brought together people from several social levels. Most of these probably could do little more financially than to provide a living for their families. But others were wealthy enough to travel and to act as patrons for Paul and the young Christian communities. The extreme top and bottom of society are absent from the churches of the New Testament, however. Based on the New Testament, the churches included no senators or equestrians and at most two decurions (Dionysius in Athens and Erastus in Corinth). The New Testament depicts no Christians at the bottom of the status ladder: agricultural day workers, peas-ants, or dependent handworkers. Certainly some Christians came from this level, but perhaps not a majority at first. However, the New Testament makes clear that a number of Christians were slaves or former slaves. Few Christians were Roman citizens, and fewer still enjoyed much status in the larger society.

Within each social level we see several levels of status. A number of Chris-tians mentioned in the New Testament had high status in one area (such as wealth) but low status in another (such as Roman citizenship). Often such people had this "status inconsistency" because they were upwardly mobile, seeing a change in their status during their lifetimes. We find slaves (including imperial slaves) and former slaves who had become successful and wealthy in business. We find artisans and traders who appear high in wealth but would have been low in occupational status. We find wealthy, independent women whose gender lowered their overall status despite their wealth, and wealthy Jews whose ethnicity did the same for them.[16]

We can identify nearly eighty names in the New Testament associated with Paul. We have clues about the social status of thirty of them. Luke was a physician with a Latin name (Col 4:14; Philem 24). Doctors were often slaves; perhaps Luke was a doctor for some Roman *familia*, receiving the name of his master (Lucius) when he was freed. Tertius (Latin name), one of the Corinthian Christians (Rom 16:22), apparently was a scribe or at least trained as a scribe. This could make him either a slave or a freedman, or perhaps a free member of the local government. Ampliatus (Rom 16:8) probably was a slave since his was a common slave name. He may have lived in Rome but met Paul in the East while traveling on his master's business.

Gaius had a Roman name and a house large enough to board Paul and to accommodate all the Christian groups in Corinth (1 Cor 1:14; Rom 16:23). He must have been wealthy. Crispus, head of the synagogues in Corinth, was a man of high prestige and also probably well to do. Paul singles out these two men of high status, Gaius and Crispus, as men whom he personally baptized in the early days of the Corinthian congregation (1 Cor 1:14).

Erastus, the city treasurer of Corinth, is mentioned in connection with Paul (Rom 16:23). Just this century archaeologists discovered an inscription from the New Testament era naming an Erastus as donor of the paving east of the theater in Corinth. He made this donation in return for being named to the office of *aedile*. This was a major magistracy, one of whose tasks was to manage the public games. The office of *aedile* is not normally translated as "city treasurer," the office associated with Erastus in Romans 16:23, but city treasurer was an office often held in Corinth before one moved up to *aedile*. So the donation inscription could refer to the same Erastus as in Romans, just in the next step of his career.

Aquila and Prisca met Paul in Corinth (Acts 18:2f). Aquila, and perhaps Prisca, originally came from Pontus. They seem to have been relatively wealthy since they moved around a lot, maintained sizable households in three different cities and apparently acted as patrons for Christian congregations. Their occupation, tentmaking, was low in status but not at the bottom. As Eastern provincials and Jews, but assimilated to Greco-Roman civilization, their extraction places them somewhere between middle and low in status. The fact that Prisca is named before her husband once by Paul and two of three times in Acts suggests that she had a higher level of status than he.

Phoebe was an instrumental member of the church at Cenchrea (Rom 16:1-2). The terms Paul uses for her have led to much debate. The term *diakonos* could refer to an office, as it seems to in Philippians 1:1, or it may mean "missionary" or even "helper." Paul also calls her "a helper (*prostatis*) of many and of myself as well" (Rom 16:2). *Prostatis* was used in this era in two ways: to refer to an official function in some Hellenistic cities, a kind of executive officer, or more generally to refer to a leader, for example, of a club. It also is used of protectors or patrons in the Roman sense. The first meaning does not fit the context since it is unlikely that Phoebe was Paul's leader in some way. But she might well have acted as a patron, like Lydia, Philemon and others, providing Paul and his associates with monetary support and lodging. Chloe, who likely was on business of her own to Rome when she carried Paul's letter, was probably rather wealthy and a leader of some sort in the Cenchrean congregation.

Mark, cousin of Barnabas and at times a fellow worker of Paul, may have had some wealth since his mother in Jerusalem had a home large enough to host a meeting of Christians (Acts 12:12; Col 4:10; Philem 24).

Lydia, the Thyatiran dealer in purple fabrics, was a Gentile worshiper of the Jewish God who, when she encountered Paul in Philippi, converted to Christianity along with her household (Acts 16:14-15). She persuaded Paul, Silas and their companions to stay in her house (Acts 16:15, 40). She probably had some wealth since purple cloth was a luxury item and her home was large enough to accommodate several guests. Her name, occupation and place of origin all place her among the Greek-speaking merchants who had settled in Philippi alongside the Italian colonists. It was unusual for a woman to head a household and business unless she had inherited them. She probably took over her father's or husband's fortune and business at his death.

Titius Justus, a Gentile convert to Jewish ways, had a house next to the synagogue in Corinth. He housed Paul, Silas and Timothy here and so must have had some wealth. His name suggests he possessed Roman citizenship.

The instruction to "aspire to live quietly, to mind your own affairs, and to work with your own hands . . . so that you may . . . be dependent on nobody" suggests that the majority of Thessalonian Christians were skilled or unskilled manual workers (1 Thess 4:11-12). They had no store of wealth and so had to work in order to eat. This instruction applied not to slaves, who did not work in order to make money and buy food, but the congregation still may have included some slaves. Paul tells the Corinthians that on the first day of the week each of them should "put something aside and store it up, as he may prosper" in order to contribute to the care of the poor in Jerusalem (1 Cor 16:1-4). Clearly he was speaking to people who were able to save money but had little if any accumulated capital at the time. By contrast, Paul mentions the "extreme poverty" of the Christians in Macedonia (2 Cor 8:2). Paul apparently did not mean by this complete destitution since Macedonian Christians also were able to contribute to the Jerusalem collection.[17]

**For Further Reading**

Friedländer, Ludwig. *Roman Life and Manners Under the Early Empire*. Trans. L. A. Magnus. 4 vols. New York: Dutton, 1908-1913.

MacMullen, Ramsay. *Roman Social Relations*. New Haven, Conn.: Yale University Press, 1974.

Saller, Richard P. *Personal Patronage Under the Early Empire*. London: Cambridge, 1982.

Theissen, Gerd. *The Social Setting of Pauline Christianity: Essays on Corinth*. Philadelphia: Fortress, 1982.

# Chapter 9

# Citizenship

*By similar bounty [Emperor] Otho sought to win the affections
of the cities and provinces. He bestowed on the colonies of Hispalis
and Emerita some additional families, on the entire people
of the Lingones the privileges of Roman citizenship.*
TACITUS HISTORIES 1.1

*But when they had tied him up with the thongs,
Paul said to the centurion who was standing by, "Is it lawful for you
to scourge a man who is a Roman citizen, and uncondemned?" . . .
So those who were about to examine him withdrew from him instantly;
and the tribune also was afraid, for he realized that Paul
was a Roman citizen and that he had bound him.*
ACTS 22:25, 29

*But our citizenship is in heaven, and from it we await
a Savior, the Lord Jesus Christ.*
PHILIPPIANS 3:20 NRSV

THE APOSTLE PAUL WAS A ROMAN CITIZEN, BUT JESUS CHRIST WAS NOT. While most people in the eastern part of the Roman Empire were not Roman citizens, a number of citizens do make an appearance in the accounts of the New Testament. How important was Roman citizenship? What was its significance for the spread of Christianity? What do Roman citizen names in the New Testament tell us? In order to understand these and other questions about New Testament references to citizenship, we must appreciate the nature and importance of citizenship in that day.

Roman citizenship in the time of Christ was a valuable commodity. Only about five million of the over fifty million inhabitants of the Empire at that time were free and full Roman citizens. Sources from Cicero to Acts give the Roman citizen overseas a kind of sacrosanct quality. In time, as more and more provincials gained citizenship, this sense of significance would dissipate. In fact, by the end of the first century, Pliny the Younger, in talking about mistreatment of Romans in the provinces, would focus more on their social class than on their standing as citizens (*Letters* 2.11.8). But the New Testament reflects a time when Roman citizenship still meant something, before a large number of enfranchisements in the mid- to late first century diluted the value of citizenship.[1]

Of course, Roman citizenship did not begin to bring the kind of privileges attached to citizenship in a modern democracy. It did not mean one could have an active part in the political process since the emperors had eliminated election to offices. For most it did not mean entitlement to social services. This is because about the only such service was a grain price subsidy, and that only applied to the city of Rome. But like a modern democracy, it did allow one to serve in the regular military (noncitizens could only enlist in Rome's auxiliary legions).

### Privileges and Obligations of Roman Citizens

Roman citizenship was highly esteemed in the first century. Those who possessed it were entitled to special protection by the Roman government from the accusations of noncitizens and from the more extreme forms of punishment. Citizens were held in higher honor than noncitizens, even if they were of slave origin. Roman citizens could vote in public elections in Rome, though by the first century B.C. this right lacked any real meaning. They could attend the games and public performances in the theaters and amphitheaters of the city (see figure 9.1). Jesus probably would have been treated differently by Pontius Pilate had he been a Roman citizen. In any case, his lack of citizenship made it easier for Pilate to give in to Jesus' opponents.

Roman citizenship also exempted one from many taxes. Roman citizens in the provinces typically did not pay the standard taxes sent as tribute to Rome. The most important tax in the Empire was the land tax, levied on "non-Italic" land. This included all land outside of Italy, except for the Roman colonies in the provinces; they were considered Italic land. Thus, the land of citizen residents in such colonies were exempt. Provincials who received Roman citizenship did not automatically escape the duty to pay local city taxes, but they might be granted this immunity as an extra privilege. However, this did not mean that they escaped all taxes. Taxation on market sales, on the sale and freeing of slaves, and on custom dues affected everyone engaged in those affairs, regardless of citizenship.

Only Roman citizens had the full protection offered by Roman law, for example, when buying or inheriting property, making legal contracts, adopting children or getting married. Marriage among noncitizens was not recognized by Roman law.[2] The Roman state would investigate the murder of a citizen but not that of a noncitizen. A citizen could not be beaten without the benefit of a trial, and a citizen was not subject to the more torturous forms of execution such as crucifixion.

By the time of Christ, a Roman citizen could not be interrogated using torture, could not be executed without a trial, and could even resist trial by magistrates outside Italy. A person who invoked this right would then be tried at Rome for the offense. However, the citizen could not then appeal the authority of the jury courts in Rome. The Roman citizen was thus protected, throughout the Empire, from a provincial governor's jurisdiction over capital crimes and the use of torture.

By the early second century, rather than attempting to try the cases themselves, provincial governors automatically sent to Rome for trial Roman citizens charged with certain offenses. For example, in the year 64 the proconsul of Asia sent a Roman citizen in chains to Nero for trial (Tacitus *Annals* 16.10.2). In the early second century A.D., a Roman citizen and member of the local aristocracy of Ephesus, Claudius Aristion, was charged with treason in the province of Asia and sent to the emperor Trajan for trial (Pliny *Letters* 6.31).

It appears that provincial governors could, by Paul's day, hold trials and carry out sentences against Roman citizens for crimes such as murder, adultery and forgery without allowing an appeal to Rome. As the number of citizens in the provinces grew, the courts of Rome would have been deluged with such cases. However, in cases of treason (as in the case of Claudius Aristion above) or in unique cases outside the normal statutes (as in Paul's case, see chapter seven), appeal to Rome was allowed. Felix, the governor of Judea, granted the apostle Paul's appeal to Caesar. Felix may have done so more to get rid of Paul than because he felt he had to do so (Acts 25:12).[3]

Each class had its unique duties and privileges, connected to level of wealth and position in the local community. The principal duties of Roman citizens under the Empire were military service and taxation. In the first century A.D., all free inhabitants of the Empire could be drafted into service in either the regular legions (for citizens) or the auxiliary legions (for noncitizens). A 5-percent inheritance tax was charged to Roman citizens only.

The experiences abroad of some modern citizens of major powers may bear similarity to what Roman citizens experienced in the eastern Empire. Both at times are shown deference, even respect, as citizens of a powerful people. But at other times they are jeered or mistreated by locals who resent the great power and wish to take out their resentment on its citizens. The apostle Paul certainly seems to have been wary about proclaiming his citizenship.

**Paths to Citizenship**
The simplest way to become a citizen was to be born to a citizen father (Rome

determined citizen status based on the father's status). The apostle Paul says he was born a citizen (Acts 22:28).[4] Citizenship could also be acquired by legal grant. Under the Roman Republic, only individuals with ties to Latin civilization (for the most part, residents of Italy) were granted citizenship. But from the time of Augustus on, foreigners were awarded citizenship more and more frequently following some active display of loyalty to Rome.

**Figure 9.1. Exterior of a Roman amphitheater, Pompeii, Italy. Its capacity was about fifteen thousand persons. Only Roman citizens were allowed to attend events in such arenas.**

The Roman senate and the great generals of the late Republic had the power to grant Roman citizen status to men of free birth. The emperors regularly granted citizenship to individuals and even to entire communities. Collective awards of citizenship were at first very infrequent. Julius Caesar used them in part to widen the pool of military recruits, but collective awards were also given to territories that had thoroughly adopted Roman values. Less scrupulous governors made money in the provinces by selling citizenship to locals.

We have no evidence of how Paul's family acquired citizen status. Some have speculated that his father or grandfather was granted citizenship along with other members of the ruling class in Tarsus. If his father had served in the Roman auxiliary army, he could have been granted citizenship when he retired, but it would have been nearly impossible for an observant Jew to be in the military because of sabbath, dietary, and association restrictions. It is improbable that Paul was more than a third-generation citizen, since very few Eastern provincials had citizen status earlier than the first century B.C.

Non-Roman soldiers were given citizenship upon discharge from the army (usually after twenty-five years of service). This citizenship would be passed on to their children. One can see clearly in Acts 22:26-29 the respect that Roman citizenship could elicit.

The steady increase in the number of Roman citizens in the early Empire was caused in large part by the continual freeing of slaves by Roman citizens. Year after year, thousands of freed slaves received limited rights of citizenship, even while many upper-class Greeks in the East considered citizenship beyond their grasp.

During the Republic, Rome did not allow its citizens to hold any other citizenship. The provincial who became a Roman had to relinquish his city citizenship. This rule exempted Roman citizens from local taxes and civic obligations since only citizens of a city had these responsibilities. Under Augustus a series of edicts eliminated this immunity. As a result, by the time of Paul one could hold multiple citizenships. In practice, this meant Roman citizenship and citizenship in one's city of origin. Paul identifies himself as both a citizen of Tarsus, "no mean city" (Acts 21:39), and a citizen of Rome (Acts 22:25-28).

## Proof of Citizenship

In a society where status determined all of one's rights, it was very important to be able to prove that one was a Roman citizen, a freeborn person or a legally freed former slave. A system of birth registration was established in A.D. 4 for those born as Roman citizens. Boys were registered typically on the ninth day after birth, girls on the eighth day. Those who received citizenship by grant had their names recorded on a different register. Yet another register recorded the grants of citizenship to soldiers in the Roman auxiliary legions.[5]

When auxiliary soldiers were granted citizenship, a "certificate of Roman citizenship" *(diploma civitatis Romane)* was issued and could be used as an identity card.[6] Apparently such documents were not issued to private persons granted citizenship. It is likely, however, that the emperor sent the new citizen a letter recording the grant. A grant of citizenship also had to be recorded in the tribal list at Rome, when the new citizen was enrolled in one of thirty-five tribes. The grant also would have been recorded in his city of residence. A municipal census every five years checked the lists of Roman citizens throughout Italy and in the provincial cities that were composed of Roman citizens (such as the Roman colonies at Philippi, Corinth and Iconium).

A Roman citizen not living in a Roman colony was registered in his city's taxation tables, which were drawn up as part of the periodic provincial censuses. By the time of Paul, Roman citizens were liable for local taxes, unless they had obtained a grant of immunity. The Greek cities, like Rome, typically used a tribal system to classify their citizens. These local records could be consulted to determine the validity of a person's claim to Roman citizenship.

If a citizen's name did not appear in the archives, he or she could produce a copy of the grant of citizenship or, if the person was born a Roman citizen, the birth registration. The grant of citizenship, like the military certificate of citizenship, was signed by seven witnesses. If the document's authenticity was challenged, the person could try to produce those witnesses. Of course, this would prove quite difficult outside of one's city of origin. Such a document might be forged, but the laws against this kind of forgery were stiff. The certificate of citizenship was a wooden diptych, small enough for citizens to carry when they went out of town. However, we do not know if people did so. Most citizens, other than merchants and soldiers, did not travel much; Paul's extensive travels were quite unusual. The difficulty in proving one's Roman citizen status away from home may help explain why Paul only rarely asserted his rights as a Roman.

The Roman military tribune in Jerusalem who questioned Paul, Claudius Lysias, expressed surprise that Paul was a Roman citizen. This is probably because Lysias knew Paul was a Jew. Few Jews possessed Roman citizenship, and fewer still were citizens from birth. Of course, a number in the Jewish upper class, most notably the descendants of Herod the Great, were Roman citizens, but Lysias knew from the circumstances that Paul was not in that class. The only physical sign of citizenship was the Roman toga, and Romans in the Eastern provinces apparently wore the toga only on special occasions. A large and heavy wrap that virtually immobilized one arm, the toga was unpopular even in Rome by Paul's day. Paul would have avoided wearing a toga in Palestine, where he wished to identify with his fellow Jews and was not inclined to reveal his Roman status.

### The Citizen Name

The traditional name for a male Roman citizen had three parts: the *praenomen*, *nomen*, and *cognomen* (see table 9.1). The *nomen* was the name of his clan. The *praenomen* at first distinguished individual members of the clan from one another. A father gave this name to his son at nine days of age. The first son usually was given the same *praenomen* as his father. By the late Republic, only about half of the thirty-odd *praenomina* that ever existed were still in use. By the end of the Republic, the *cognomen* replaced the *praenomen* as what we call the first or given name. Its use among the ordinary citizens began in the time of Augustus. Regular use of the *cognomen* in the army probably dates to the reign of Claudius. The *cognomen* was at first a nickname (e.g., *Maximus*, "lofty," *Glabrio*, "bald", or *Rufus*, "red"; see Rom 16:13). In larger clans, the *cognomen* helped distinguish between different branches of the clan. In these and in some other cases, the *cognomen* would be handed down from father to son. At times, further descriptive names might be added. The majority of *cognomina* in the Republic were unflattering, but flattering *cognomina* became popular in the Empire. A general was at times given the name of the people he conquered, such as *Africanus, Germanicus* or *Britannicus.* Sometimes this name was passed on to his descendants.[7]

| | | | |
|---|---|---|---|
| **Praenomen:** | Early use—personal name | | |
| | Later use—more formal name | | |
| **Nomen:** | Clan or family name | | |
| **Cognomen:** | Becomes the personal name | | |
| | At first an unflattering nickname | | |

| Praenomen | Nomen | Cognomen |
|---|---|---|
| *Females:* | | |
| (none) | Julia | Prima |
| (none) | Caecilia | Metella |
| | | |
| *Males:* | | |
| Gaius | Julius | Caesar |
| Titus | Flavius | Vespasianus |
| Gaius | Marius | (none) |
| | | |
| **In New Testament:** | | |
| | Titius | Justus |
| | Sergius | Paulus |
| | Claudius | Lysias |

**Table 9.1. Names of Roman citizens**

People in the eastern part of the Empire usually went by one name. They might add to this the name of their father to distinguish themselves from others with the same name. They also took or were given nicknames at times, but these nicknames generally were not used in formal contexts. A new recruit to the Roman auxiliary army was sometimes given a Roman name at the moment of enlistment. This happened even though he would not be granted Roman citizenship until he retired many years later. When an auxiliary soldier retired and received citizenship, he typically adopted the *praenomen* and *nomen* of the current emperor and added his personal name as a *cognomen*. In the Greek-speaking East, a new Roman citizen would take a Roman *praenomen* and *nomen* but would continue to be known by his third name. He would normally pass on to his son the first two names but give him a new third name.

Slaves had only one name, either the name they had before enslavement or a name assigned to them by their master. With the consent of the master, a slave could name his or her child. Upon receiving their freedom and Roman citizenship, male slaves of Romans normally took the *praenomen* and *nomen* of their master. Rather than take the *cognomen* of his master, a former slave usually kept as *cognomen* the name he had been called as a slave. Some changed their personal name to a Roman name or made their name more Latin sounding, probably seeking greater respectability.

The naming of Roman women went through several changes over the centuries. In the early days of Rome, Roman women had two names: a personal name *(praenomen)* and a family name *(nomen)*. By the late Republic, they were given only one name, the feminine form of the family name. By the early Empire, they once again had two names, the feminine form of the family name followed by a *cognomen*. The *cognomen* usually was the feminine form of the family *cognomen*. For example, the daughter of L. Caecilius Metellus was called Caecilia Metella. The *cognomen* also could derive from her mother's family. Multiple daughters were usually identified by the family name, the *nomen*, plus terms like *Prima, Secunda* and *Tertia* ("First," "Second" and "Third"), or *Major* and *Minor* ("Greater" and "Lesser"), identifying their order of birth. Roman women did not take the family name of their husbands since after marriage they usually remained, in legal terms, a part of their birth family (see chapter twelve).[8]

### Citizen Names and the New Testament

Acts and the Epistles use three ways of naming people,[9] all of which correspond to the way those classes of persons typically were named in the first century. A single name is used of private persons not Latin by birth. If they are Latin names, they are either *praenomena* (Lucius, Titius) or *cognomena* (Paulus, Secundus, Pudens). Upper administrative officers are named in the contemporary informal style, either by *cognomen* or by *nomen* with *cognomen*. Roman citizens of lower degree are indicated in a way appropriate to each class—the *nomen* for auxiliary centurions and the double name for a private citizen (Titius Justus). The Epistles, which are more private in nature, not surprisingly follow the Eastern style of using the single name for private citizens.

That Paul has both Aramaic and Latin names ("Saul, who is also known as Paul," Acts 13:9) could indicate that he was a second-generation citizen who was not yet using his Latin name (Paulus) exclusively. But this was more likely a matter of local custom. Greek-speaking Jewish citizens of Doura frequently had both Aramaic and Greek names. Acts twice gives two names for persons who are not Roman citizens: "Simon who was called Peter" and "Simeon who was called Niger" (Acts 10:18; 13:1). In addition, the author of Acts may be trying to distinguish Paulus the apostle from Sergius Paulus, the proconsul of Salamis, whom he mentions twice in the preceding two verses. This may also help explain why Acts suddenly switches at this point from using *Saul* to using *Paul* for the apostle.

*Paulus* would have been the *cognomen* of Paul's citizen name, but we have no idea what were his *praenomen* and *nomen*. *Paul* was probably chosen by his parents as the closest Latin equivalent to the Hebrew Saul. While Greeks typically used their Greek name as the *cognomen* of their citizen name, non-Greeks usually chose a Latin name of similar sound or meaning. For example, those named for the Near Eastern deity Baal often took the Roman citizen name Saturninus (after the Roman god Saturn). An ancestor of Paul could have been named for his Roman patron named *Paulus*, but few Roman aristocrats bore this name in this era.

Claudius Lysias, the military tribune in Jerusalem, tells Paul that he paid a large sum of money for his citizenship (Acts 22:28). Since this incident took place a few years after the death of the emperor Claudius and he bears the Claudian *nomen*, Lysias most likely acquired his citizenship from that emperor. Lysias's rank indicates that he held an equestrian commission in the Roman auxiliary army. Lysias may have been a common soldier who was promoted to military tribune. Before Claudius, officers such as tribunes typically came from the equestrian class. By the time of Lysias, it was possible for a common soldier to be promoted to centurion, then through a bribe to gain Roman citizenship and a military tribunate. The fact that Lysias treats Paul as a social equal suggests that he had been promoted up through the ranks and lacked equestrian status. As an equestrian he would have treated Paul as an inferior. Lysias did not buy citizenship but most likely bribed imperial bureaucrats to insert his name on the list of candidates for citizenship. Claudius appears to have taken no action against such abuses of the system, as Nero later would (for example, Tacitus *Annals* 14.50.1).

It is very difficult to determine whether persons named in Acts are Roman citizens. We need two names, *nomen* and *cognomen*, to be certain that a person is a Roman citizen. But, like the rest of the New Testament, Acts follows the general custom of non-Romans and identifies a person by one name and, if necessary, by the name of his father as well (for example, "Sopater, . . . the son of Pyrrhus," Acts 20:4). Even a Latin name, if a single name, is no sure indication of Roman status. Nevertheless, the number of Latin names among the associates of Paul seems quite high. Some of them may have been Roman freed slaves, since we cannot tell by the name whether a person is freeborn or freed. Slaves freed by Roman citizens frequently became half citizens or quarter citizens, depending on the nature of their manumission. Such persons had some of all of the civil rights, but none of the political rights, of full Romans. Depending on their status, their citizenship may not have been transferable to their children and may not have extended legal protection to their estate after their deaths.

Only one person in Acts, beside Roman officials, has the names of a Roman: Titius Justus, a Gentile sympathizer with Judaism in Corinth, whom Paul visited (Acts 18:7). Only one person in the Epistles bears the proper double name of a Roman: Pontius Pilatus (see 1 Tim 6:13). Priscilla and Aquila may have been citizens, but we cannot be certain. Priscilla's name is Latin, and she may have been from Rome. But Aquila is from the Greek East, from Pontus. Gaius could be the name of a citizen descended from a Roman family with the *nomen* of Gaius, a few of which existed (Acts 19:29; 20:4). However, Gaius was also a common *cognomen* in the provinces.

When referring to Roman citizens, Acts sometimes uses only the *cognomen*, as with Felix, Gallio and Festus (Acts 23:27; 24:22, 27; 25:1, 4). But at times it uses both *nomen* and *cognomen*, as with Sergius Paulus, Claudius Lysias and Porcius Festus (Acts 13:7; 23:27; 24:27). Pilate is Pilatus in Acts and Pontius Pilatus in 1 Timothy (Acts 13:28; 1 Tim 6:13). We find similar naming practices in Roman writings of the time (for example, Pliny *Letters* 2.11; Seneca *Letters* 30.1; 24.1, 4).

The two centurions named in Acts, Cornelius and Julius, are called by their *nomena*, not their *cognomena* (Acts 10:1; 27:1). Since no legionary forces were stationed in Judea, we know that they served in the auxiliary forces. Cornelius belongs to one of the Italian cohorts, a special group recruited in Italy (with replacement soldiers recruited locally; see Josephus *Jewish War* 2.268). Well into the first century A.D., Roman citizen soldiers maintained the old tradition of referring to one another by *praenomen* and *nomen*, not by *cognomen*. Because of the small number of *praenomena*, in practice this meant using primarily the *nomen*. Such a practice would also make clear his Roman citizen status since it identified the Roman family through which he was enfranchised, such as the Cornelii or Julii.

## Roman Citizenship and Roman Law

A provincial noncitizen, like Jesus, had no claim to be tried by the rules of formal and informal Roman law. By contrast, a provincial Roman citizen like the apostle Paul enjoyed special protections. For example, he could not be executed by the governor's court. In the case of most personal crimes, a formal act of accusation was required, and a lawyer brought charges and recommended penalties against the accused. The case was heard by the governor, assisted by a council of advisers. Since no written law was involved, the accuser had to let the governor decide if the accused action was indeed punishable. The point here is that a provincial governor, whether a proconsul, legate or procurator/prefect, dealt with accusations involving provincial noncitizens as he saw fit, whereas formal procedures must be followed with Roman citizens.

By the time of Paul, the Roman citizen could claim the right of appeal, *provocatio*, to avoid interrogation using torture, execution without trial, private or public arrest, and even trial itself by magistrates outside Italy. A person who claimed this right would then be tried at Rome for the offense but could not appeal the authority of the jury courts in Rome. The Roman citizen was thus protected, throughout the Empire, from a provincial governor's jurisdiction over many capital crimes and the use of torture. The exceptions were capital crimes such as murder, adultery and forgery. As the number of citizens in the provinces grew, the courts of Rome would have been deluged with such cases. But in cases of treason, or in unique cases outside the normal statutes of the *ordo* (as in Paul's case), appeal to Rome was allowed. In A.D. 64 the proconsul of Asia sent a Roman citizen in chains to Nero for an unknown offense (Tacitus *Annals* 16.10.2). By the early second century, provincial governors automatically sent Roman citizens charged with certain offenses to Rome for trial rather than attempting to try the cases themselves.

## Citizenship and the Cities of the East

Nearly everyone within the Empire was under the jurisdiction of Roman authorities. The only exceptions were residents of cities with special treaties giving them local jurisdiction (see chapter three). Depending on the treaty, resident Roman citizens might or might not be subject to the local authorities; usually they were not. Natives who had acquired Roman citizenship enjoyed the same status as did other Roman citizens. Depending on the legal charge, both Roman citizens and citizens of free cities were able to choose whether to be tried by local courts or Roman courts, those of the governor or of the emperor. Inhabitants of the Greek East who were not Roman citizens were normally subject to the local laws.

Romans in the Eastern provinces lived in a different legal and social atmosphere from citizens in the western provinces. In the West, particularly in Italy, Roman civilization predominated and Roman citizenship was regularly granted to whole communities. Over time, the provinces in the West were becoming extensions of Italy in many ways. But in the Eastern provinces during Paul's day, the culture was still predominantly Hellenistic and the language was Greek. Rome had not yet granted citizenship to all the citizens of any existing city in the East. Apart from the Roman colonies established by generals and emperors in the century or so before Paul, no city in the eastern Empire was made up predominately of Roman citizens. An indication of the importance of Roman colonies is the fact that Paul's travels often took him through them. He visited Antioch and Lystra in Asia Minor, Corinth in Achaea, Philippi in Macedonia, and Alexandria Troas in Asia. All of these were Roman colonies settled by retired Roman soldiers.

Even in Roman colonies, a majority of the population may not have been Roman citizens. Acts suggests that the Roman colonies of Antioch, Lystra and Corinth had as many Greeks and Jews as they had Romans (Acts 13:14; 16:2; 18:4). Elsewhere, in the hundreds of Greek and half-Greek cities of the East, Roman citizens were rare. Lists of inhabitants, and even lists of city magistrates from the Greek cities of this period, often include no recognizable Roman citizens.

Frankly, Roman citizenship was not that valuable to the average inhabitant of a Greek city. If he was poor, the only thing it allowed him to do was enter the regular army. If he was rich, he could spend his way into the equestrian order and thus into public service, but this required both a lot of money and the right contacts in Rome. We have certain knowledge of only a dozen Roman citizens from the East during the New Testament era who were able to build careers as equestrians. They served as high military officers or procurators. A Roman citizen of non-Roman extraction may well have regarded his citizenship as we regard an honorary degree: of little practical use under most circumstances.

A man like Paul, neither rich nor destitute, could at most have used his Roman citizenship to become a city magistrate in his home town. This may explain why Paul seems to think of himself first, and with pride, as a citizen of Tarsus and only refers to his Roman citizenship when he needs its privileges.

Paul first identifies himself to Lysias as "a Jew, from Tarsus in Cilicia, a citizen of no mean city" (Acts 21:39). Tarsus was, after all, the greatest city in Cilicia (southwest Asia Minor), both in prosperity and in intellectual achievement. He also identifies himself as a citizen of Tarsus when he addresses the Jews in Acts 22. Only when he is about to be scourged does he say that he is also a Roman citizen (Acts 22:25).

### Roman Citizenship and Christians

In Philippians, Paul says that his listeners are not like those whose minds are "set on earthly things," but their citizenship (or community) is in heaven (Phil 3:20). The word for citizenship here, *politeuma*, originally had the meanings "to be or live as a citizen," "to act as a citizen (by taking part in political life)," or "to share in state government, to rule the state."[10] It may be that neither Paul nor his readers had Roman citizenship in mind, but it is noteworthy that Paul is addressing residents of a Roman colony, and one of the three cities in Acts where he appeals to his Roman citizenship. Since most of his readers would not have been Roman citizens, they would have understood what it was like to live as foreigners in an earthly city. Paul may have been telling them that the citizenship, the identification, that should truly matter to them is citizenship in the kingdom of heaven.

But the great lesson of Paul's exercise of his rights as a citizen may not be the metaphor of the Christian as a citizen of heaven. Rather he may be illustrating how a Christian who is also a citizen of an earthly realm can use the advantages of that citizenship. Paul resorts to claiming the privileges of Roman citizenship three times in Acts: in Philippi (16:37), in Jerusalem (22:25) and in Caesarea when he appeals to Caesar (25:11).

Although freedom from interrogation by torture was one of the more practical advantages of Roman citizen status, Paul did not claim Roman citizenship simply to escape bodily harm. For example, in Philippi Paul does not profess Roman citizenship until the day after he is beaten and imprisoned. Then he does so in order to extract an apology for the beating before leaving the city. Paul derived no obvious benefit from this since he was about to be released from prison and sent out of the city anyway (Acts 16:22-40). Perhaps he felt that his honor and that of his God had been wounded.

In Jerusalem, Paul announced his citizen status just as he is about to be scourged (Acts 22:25). Paul clearly was seeking to avoid bodily harm, but he also was appealing to the Roman tribune as a protector and wanted to give Claudius Lysias another reason to provide that protection instead of lumping Paul in with the other Jews of Jerusalem. Later, in Caesarea, Paul used his citizen status to appeal to Caesar (Acts 25:11). This was probably because he determined that he was not going to get justice from the governor's court and would rather face his opponents in a Roman court. He may well have reasoned that his opponents would not follow him to Rome, and his case would have to be dismissed (see chapter seven for more on Paul's trials).

**For Further Reading**

Balsdon, J. P. V. D. *Romans and Aliens.* London: Duckworth, 1979.

Sherwin-White, A. N. *Roman Law and Roman Society in the New Testament.* Oxford: Oxford University Press, 1963.

————. *The Roman Citizenship.* 2nd ed. Oxford: Clarendon, 1973.

# Chapter 10

## The Jews in the Cities

*You know how large a group they are, how unanimously they stick*
*together, how influential they are in politics.*
CICERO ON JEWS IN ROME, PRO FLACCO 28

*This people has already made its way into every city,*
*and it is not easy to find any place in the habitable world*
*which had not received this nation and in which it has not made its power felt.*
STRABO, QUOTED IN JOSEPHUS JEWISH ANTIQUITIES 14.115

*And when they heard it, they glorified God. And they said to him,*
*"You see, brother, how many thousands there are among the Jews*
*of those who have believed; they are all zealous for the law,*
*and they have been told about you that you teach all the Jews*
*who are among the Gentiles to forsake Moses,*
*telling them not to circumcise their children or observe the customs."*
ACTS 21:20-21

THE PRESENCE OF JEWS THROUGHOUT THE ROMAN EMPIRE HAD A SIG-
nificant impact on the spread of Christianity. We see Jewish communities nearly everywhere Paul and the other early Christian disciples
travel. But the Jews were by no means the only ethnic and national
minority in the cities of the Empire. Resident foreigners made up a significant
part of many major cities of Rome. Some were brought to the city as slaves,
while others came willingly, seeking to take part in the general prosperity of
the cities.[1]

In general, resident foreigners had to abide by the laws and customs of the
host city. But if they formed a large enough contingent, they might occupy a
sector of the city and exercise some level of self-rule so long as they stayed out
of trouble.

Those who voluntarily left one city for another were often small business
owners: traders and crafts workers. The New Testament portrays this movement in persons such as the tentmakers Priscilla and Aquila. Aquila, a Jew from
Pontus in northern Asia Minor, was in Rome with his wife Priscilla by the time

Figure 10.1. The famous main road in Ephesus, paved in marble. Paul began his missionary work here in the synagogues of the city. The Jewish population of Ephesus probably was fairly large, as it was in the two largest cities of the Empire (Rome and Alexandria).

Claudius expelled Jews from the city (49). They moved to Corinth and played host to fellow tentmaker Paul. When Paul left Corinth, Priscilla and Aquila went with him as far as Ephesus (see figure 10.1). Here they soon became leaders of the Christian community and probably continued to practice their trade (Acts 18:1-3, 18-28; Rom 16:3; 1 Cor 16:19). When Paul wrote to the community in Rome in the late 50s, they were there again and hosting a house church (Rom 16:5).

## The Jewish Dispersion

The dispersion of Jews from Palestine occurred in several stages. The first great dispersions took place in 722 B.C. in the north, under the Assyrians, and in 586 B.C. in the south, under the Babylonians. Ptolemy I of Egypt (322-285 B.C.) took many Jews in captivity to Alexandria during his invasion of Palestine. Alexandria's importance as a Jewish center dates to this time. Antiochus of Syria (223-187 B.C.) forced about two thousand Jewish families to move from Babylon to Phrygia and Lydia in western Asia Minor (cf. 1 Pet 1:1). The Roman general Pompey, after capturing Jerusalem in 63 B.C., sent many Jews to Rome as slaves. The forcible suppression of Jewish revolts in A.D. 70 and 135 led to further dispersions. The descendants of many of these Jews never returned to Palestine.

By the time of Christ, Jews were widely dispersed throughout the cities and countryside of the Empire and beyond. From the time of the Babylonian captivity, Jews outside Palestine greatly outnumbered those in the land. In New Testament times, only about 2.5 million Jews lived in Palestine, while 4 to 6 million lived outside of Palestine (Philo *Legatio Ad Caium* 36). The regions of Mesopotamia, Syria/Asia Minor and Egypt each had more than 1 million Jewish residents, while Italy and North Africa each had around 100,000 Jews. The Jews in Egypt for the most part lived in and around Alexandria and made up about 10 to 15 percent of the population.

There was a substantial Jewish population in virtually every town of any decent size in the Mediterranean region. The largest urban populations in the Empire were the 200,000 Jews in Alexandria and the 50,000 in Rome. Most Jews in the dispersion lived in cities, where they could pursue a variety of trades and could often find fellow Jews with whom to associate. Jews in much of Europe would continue to be city dwellers for many centuries.

Jews were represented in nearly every social class. Jewish soldiers served in the armies of the Hellenistic kings, and some of them rose to the highest ranks. Hellenistic rulers found it to their advantage to have communities of Jews in their realms since they usually represented a stabilizing influence. The Jews also frequently made themselves an invaluable part of the business community. The customs of the Jews were widely known if poorly understood.[2]

The history of Jewish presence in two cities, Sardis in the east and Rome in the west, illustrates the circumstances of Jews in the cities of the Empire. Sardis, in western Asia Minor, was host to a permanent Jewish community by the late third century B.C. In the first century B.C., according to Josephus, the Roman governor of Asia Minor confirmed the right of "the Jewish citizens in our city" to come together and have a communal life and adjudicate suits among themselves, and that a place be given them in which they may gather together with their wives and children and offer their ancestral prayers and sacrifices to God. . . . (*Jewish Antiquities* 14.259-61)

The council further instructed the magistrates to set aside a place for the Jews "to build and inhabit" and the market officials to provide "suitable food" for the Jews.[3]

The Jewish community in Rome dates to at least the second century B.C. It grew considerably when the Roman general Pompey's conquest of Judea in 63 B.C. resulted in the transportation of thousands of Jewish captives to Rome. Many eventually gained their freedom and took up residence in the city, most on the left bank of the Tiber River. Many Jews live in this area even today. Organizationally, the Jews in Rome were a diverse community of congregations. No single organization controlled the synagogues; no single head of the Jewish community existed in Rome. This loose structure allowed Christianity to penetrate Rome and the Jewish congregations of Rome more easily. Jewish Christians could preach from synagogue to synagogue without fear of a central leader limiting their movements.

In 49 the emperor Claudius expelled Jews from Rome (Acts 18:2). The Roman biographer Suetonius tells us this was because of disorders instigated by someone named Chrestus. Chrestus was a common variant spelling of Christus, and Suetonius may have misunderstood his sources to be saying that this Chrestus was present in Rome. If so, we may have here an indication that Christian missionary activity in Rome was causing turmoil in the synagogues. Probably a number of Jews determined to be connected to the trouble were expelled. Although Acts 18:2 says that Claudius ordered "all Jews" to leave Rome, this does not mean that such an intent was carried out. It is highly unlikely, perhaps impossible for legal reasons, that Claudius could have expelled every one of the fifty thousand Jews in Rome. For example, some would have been slaves, and thus the property of Roman citizens. The Jews were allowed to return a few years later, after the death of Claudius in 54 if not before, but it appears that they were prevented from assembling for some time thereafter, presumably to prevent further disorder.[4] More Jewish slaves were brought to Rome after the destruction of Jerusalem in 70. The Roman Jewish community represented a broad range of economic wealth and social status.

We find Jews among the local government officials, especially in Egypt. The sources tell of Jewish police, magistrates, clerks, tax collectors and granary clerks. There were Jewish landowners, peasants, agricultural workers (both free and slave), craftsmen, merchants, shippers and moneylenders. A decree by the emperor Claudius in 41 reconfirmed the ancestral rights of Alexandrian Jews to practice their customs but denied them the right to be called citizens of Alexandria. This legal situation was probably similar in other cities. Often Jews only could become citizens of the city in which they lived by taking part in its pagan religious practices, which observant Jews would have refused to do.

### The Jews and Their Neighbors

Most Jews in the dispersion kept a lower profile than did their independence-seeking brothers in Judea. At times, their ethical teachings and community cohesiveness attracted their Gentile neighbors to Judaism, but the ritual requirements of their religion, such as living apart from Gentiles and following a strict dietary regimen, could make them seem aloof. These customs also made them stand out from other foreign groups and prevented them from fully socializing into the larger society.

This was a kind of anti-Semitism, but for the most part it reflected the distaste and envy that any distinctly different group generated. Of course, the Jews' tendency to keep to themselves enhanced their otherness. European anti-Semitism, colored by the accusation that the Jews should be held responsible for the crucifixion of Jesus, was a much later development.

The cities of the Roman world expected certain behavior from their members. All were to contribute services according to their means (e.g., military service, payment of taxes) and to participate in the society's common religious cults. But Jews often could not fulfill these expectations. They would have found it difficult if not impossible to serve in the army since it would have required violations of sabbath laws and dietary regulations and participation in pagan religion. Jews could not worship the image of the emperor, as was expected of every politically loyal person within the Empire. They could not take part in public festivals that involved eating meat previously offered to pagan gods. In order to avoid trouble, they at times asked the authorities for specific exemptions. These exemptions were often granted by Roman authorities, as they had been by Persian and Hellenistic authorities before them. Among these privileges were the right to observe the sabbath and to send each year a half-shekel tax to Jerusalem for the maintenance of the temple, exemptions from contributing money to and participating in the celebrations of civic cults, and the freedom to exercise legal jurisdiction within their own communities.

During the later first century B.C. and the first century A.D., several Greek cities moved to limit such Jewish privileges. This probably reflects in part the hostility felt by some Greeks and Greek cities toward the early and continued alliance of Judea with Rome in the latter's conquest of the Greek East.

The Jews (like most foreigners) were not respected by most of the Roman elite. Cicero called Judaism "a barbarous superstition" and its followers a "mob." Juvenal depicts Jews as beggars and fortune tellers who had no permanent residence. He writes that the sabbath rest demonstrates their laziness.[5]

## Hellenization of the Jews

The Jews realized that their very identity depended upon maintaining separation from the community at large, but they faced pressure to adopt the values and practices of their neighbors. The Jews of the diaspora had already left behind Aramaic for the language of the Greeks. That the Hebrew Scriptures were translated into Greek (the Septuagint) indicates that by the second century B.C. many Jews could not read Hebrew. Jews were often educated in the Greek gymnasium, including its training in athletics and in rhetoric.

Jews in the cities adapted their lives to the larger Gentile society to greater or lesser degrees. Some gave up their religious beliefs and practices entirely. We have examples of people with Jewish names making dedications to pagan gods. Tiberius Julius Alexander, the nephew of the Jewish philosopher Philo of Alexandria, apparently abandoned his faith in pursuit of success. His career included stints as procurator of Judea and prefect of Egypt. He could not have held these high posts as a practicing Jew.[6]

Jews in the modern world continue to deal with the pressure to assimilate. Some, such as Hasidic Jews in America, have chosen to isolate themselves from the larger society. Others have taken a more accommodating path, even giving up many traditional beliefs and practices.

## The Synagogues

Meetings of smaller groups of Jews often were held in private homes. Once the group grew and could afford to do so, it would move to a dedicated building. The size and grandeur of the building generally reflected the size and wealth of the local Jewish community. A group of ten or more adult male Jews could call itself a synagogue. A small synagogue discovered on the island of Delos, in use in the New Testament era, consists of a simple room with benches, entered from a courtyard through three doors facing eastward toward Jerusalem. The size of such a congregation in antiquity may have been limited by practical considerations, such as how far observant Jews would have to walk to attend the sabbath service. Larger cities hosted a number of synagogues. (The city of Rome had at least eleven.)

Jews gathered in synagogues for worship on the sabbath and on holy days, and for education in the Torah at other times. The larger buildings included separate rooms for other purposes, such as collection and distribution of food or the baking of unleavened bread. Synagogues also helped Jews connect with one another. This was especially useful to new arrivals, who would have been able to meet fellow Jews in the same occupation. The main synagogue in Alexandria even had areas dedicated to different trades. This would have been useful to Joseph and Mary when, according to the Gospels, they fled with the infant Jesus to Egypt. They most likely would have stayed in Alexandria. Among its huge Jewish population, they may even have been able to find a relative. Paul, entering a city for the first time, would also have found it useful to make contact with fellow tentmakers through the synagogue. In fact, Paul may well have met fellow tentmakers Priscilla and Aquila in this way (Acts 18:2).

The synagogues governed the administrative, educational and juridical needs of their congregations. They distributed a large portion of donated funds to their poorer members. In cities like Rome, they were autonomous bodies that associated with each other only loosely. In cities like Alexandria, by contrast, the various synagogues were organized under a single leader and composed a formidable political entity. Each synagogue had its own head over religious activities (*archisynagogos*, Acts 13:15; 18:17). A council governed its secular affairs. The members of the council were called "elders" or, like the chief magistrates of a Greek city, "archons."[7]

## Gentile Converts

Gentiles showed various degrees of allegiance to Judaism, attracted by its monotheism, high moral standards, the sincerity of the Jews and their well-defined identity. Jewish traveling merchants, who Josephus implies were all over the world, were the missionary agents. Josephus mentions several conversions of royalty to Judaism.

Since Judaism around the Empire was influenced in differing degrees by Hellenism and Roman culture, Gentiles would have faced varying degrees of difficulty in converting. Those outposts of Judaism that had not as fully assimilated to the culture around them would require Gentile converts to make more personal sacrifices and behavioral changes, in addition to adopting new beliefs. Our sources do not tell us whether this resulted in fewer converts. The comments below apply in general to Gentile conversions, with the understanding that some specifics of conversion would have differed from place to place.

A Gentile who entered the community as a full member was called a "proselyte." She had to adhere to the dietary laws and the commands of Torah. New proselytes often received a formal cleansing baptism, and males were circumcised. Given the severity of these requirements, it is not surprising that full conversions were apparently few and that more women than men fully converted. One of the few recorded conversions from among the upper classes is Fulvia, a Roman aristocrat in the reign of Tiberius (Josephus *Jewish Antiquities* 18.81-84).

Others accepted Jewish teachings and ways of doing things but did not fully convert. They were attracted to the moral teachings of traditional Judaism and kept the sabbath. They were taught from the Greek translation of the Hebrew Scriptures. Although they expected to share with ethnic Jews in God's blessings, they were not an integral part of the synagogue's organization and were looked down upon at times by ethnic Jews. Such persons could sympathize with Judaism without renouncing public duties such as sacrificing to the official gods. They could show their devotion by contributing money or a building.

A number of the earliest converts to Christianity in the cities, according to the Acts of the Apostles and the letters of Paul, were partial converts to Judaism. Partial converts apparently found attractive a religion like Christianity, which offered the advantages of Judaism without the disadvantages of joining the religion of a specific people that placed so many restrictions on them.

### The Synagogue and the Pauline Congregation

The spread of the Christian gospel to the cities of the Empire was aided considerably by the widespread existence of Jewish synagogues. Acts indicates that missionaries like Paul made a number of early converts in them. In addition, the early churches often were taken by the authorities to be part of the synagogue, and thus left alone. The early congregations also learned a lot from the synagogues. For example, their early worship was similar to that of the synagogues, including Scripture reading and interpretation, prayers and common meals. Their Scriptures at first were the Jewish Scriptures, and only later did they include the letters and Gospels of the apostles. They provided similar support and care for the less fortunate in their congregations. Like the Jewish community, Christians were expected to settle internal disputes without resort to civic authorities (1 Cor 6:1-7).

Differences also existed between the Christian congregations as represented in the New Testament and the synagogues. For example, the terminology of functions and honors was different. Paul did not call the assembly of Christians a synagogue, and he did not use the terms for synagogue leaders in his letters. Second, women in Paul's groups had a much greater role. Finally, Paul did not require membership in an ethnic community and maintenance of the related rituals and observances, such as circumcision. While some Christian groups, the so-called Jewish Christian communities, retained a number of these rituals, they became a steadily smaller minority as time passed.[8]

**For Further Reading**

Cohen, Shaye J. D. *From the Macabbees to the Mishnah*. Philadelphia: Westminster Press, 1987.

Donfried, Karl P., ed. *The Romans Debate*. Rev. ed. Peabody, Mass.: Hendrickson, 1991.

La Piana, George. "Foreign Groups in Rome During the First Centuries of the Empire." *Harvard Theological Review* 20 (1927): 183-403.

Leon, Harry J. *The Jews of Ancient Rome*. Rev. ed. Peabody, Mass.: Hendrickson, 1995.

Safrai, Schmuel, and Moses Stern, eds. *The Jewish People in the First Century*. 2 vols. Philadelphia: Fortress, 1974.

# Chapter 11

# Slavery

*Where then there is such a difference as that between soul and body,*
*or between men and animals (as in the case of those whose business*
*is to use their body, and who can do nothing better),*
*the lower sort are by nature slaves, and it is better for them as for all inferiors*
*that they should be under the rule of a master. . . .*
*It is clear, then, that some men are by nature free, and others slaves,*
*and that for these latter slavery is both expedient and right.*
ARISTOTLE *POLITICS* 5

*Every one should remain in the state in which he was called.*
*Were you a slave when called? Never mind. But if you can gain your freedom,*
*avail yourself of the opportunity. For he who was called in the Lord as a slave*
*is a freedman of the Lord. Likewise he who was free when called is a slave*
*of Christ. You were bought with a price; do not become slaves of men.*
1 CORINTHIANS 7:20-23

*Perhaps this is why he was parted from you for a while,*
*that you might have him back for ever, no longer as a slave but more than a slave,*
*as a beloved brother, especially to me but how much more to you,*
*both in the flesh and in the Lord. So if you consider me your partner,*
*receive him as you would receive me.*
PHILEMON 15-17

SLAVERY HAD BEEN A PART OF LIFE FOR THE PEOPLES OF THE MEDITER-
ranean for many centuries prior to the New Testament era. Nearly
every culture had its own form of slavery. For the most part, slaves in
this era were persons captured in war or their descendents, those sold
into slavery to pay debts, those abandoned as infants and raised as slaves, and
those captured by slavers. Some Near Eastern peoples killed outright all their
enemies instead of enslaving them. Others, such as the Assyrians, transplanted
conquered peoples to new locations (as they did with the Jewish northern
kingdom in 721 B.C.). In the classical era, the Greeks enslaved their enemies in
great numbers. The Romans at first killed enemy soldiers who surrendered, but
at some point they began enslaving enemies instead. Any free person, Roman,
Greek or Near Eastern, had the legal right to own a slave. Virtually no one

questioned the justness of slavery.

Italy during the early Roman Republic (c. 500-200 B.C.) was home to relatively few slaves. Most of the farm labor was performed by peasant farmers and members of their households. Larger landowners sublet their land to landless peasant farmers. But in the later Republic, especially after the Second Punic War (c. 200 B.C.), three circumstances helped transform Rome into a "slave society": the great increase in the landholdings of rich Romans, the depletion of the native workforce as its members were conscripted to fight its continual wars and the introduction of massive numbers of captured enemies into the slave market. As an example of the last point, in 146 B.C. alone, fifty thousand persons captured at the destruction of Carthage were brought to Italy as slaves.

## Importance of Slavery to the Empire

A slave society is defined as one in which slaves make up at least 30 percent of the population. Once the slave population reaches this size, it becomes large enough to transform the society's entire economy and even its culture. The other example of a slave society in antiquity is the Athenian Empire of the classical era (more than three centuries prior to New Testament times). When the empire of the Athenians fell in the fourth century B.C., the lack of prisoners of war meant a decline in numbers of slaves. As a result, slaves in Greece probably would have been born into slavery for the most part. Modern-era slave societies include certain Caribbean islands, Brazil and the southern United States. In fact, by the eighteenth century, one of every three residents of the slave states in the southern United States was a slave.[1]

By the time of Augustus and Jesus, Italy had become such a society: Slaves accounted for something like 2 to 3 million of the 7.5 million inhabitants of Italy. Over time, Rome became dependent on slaves to supply a significant portion of its workforce. Most of these slaves worked in agriculture. This allowed Rome to send into the military more of its citizen farmers, traditionally the backbone of Rome's army. It also helped drive many poor farmers off their land and into the growing cities of Italy.[2]

Many Romans who owned slaves had just one or two, but wealthier slave-owning Romans in the New Testament era owned many more. Writing just before this period, Pliny the Elder reports that one Roman owned 4,116 slaves. A number of wealthy Romans owned hundreds of slaves. However, we must not generalize about the Empire based on slavery in Italy. Slaves were probably closer to 10 percent of the population elsewhere in the Empire.

In some ways slaves were more efficient than free hired labor because they were always available for their owners' personal use or for hiring out to others.

The Romans could work slaves harder than they could work free farmers. Agricultural slaves typically worked two hundred days per year, while free farmers generally worked only one hundred. In other ways slaves were more troublesome because they had to be housed and fed even when there was no need for their labor. Slaves thus represented competition to the free labor market, but they did not replace the hired hand.

### Source of Slaves

Slaves came from a number of sources. Many were prisoners of war. Some were captured on land or sea by professional slavers. The 1 Timothy list of sinful persons includes a reference to these slavers as "kidnappers" (*andrapodistes*, 1 Tim 1:10). Others entered slavery as infants because their mothers were slaves or because their parents abandoned them and those who found them raised them as slaves.

Many sold themselves or were sold by others into slavery. In the latter case, parents at times sought to pay off debt by selling a child. The New Testament does not address this practice. In the former case, people might sell themselves to pay off debt, to secure a more stable life or to climb socially. Life in slavery, at least with a decent master, could be more predictable and less demanding than the life of a poor free person. Since Romans often freed their slaves, and since the freed slaves of Roman citizens typically received Roman citizenship (see below), one could improve his social status through enslavement. Paul may be warning against this practice when he tells the Corinthians, "You were bought with a price; do not become slaves of men" (1 Cor 7:23).[3] It is likely that Erastus, the Christian and city treasurer of Corinth (Rom 16:23), had to sell himself temporarily into slavery to the city in order to hold this important position. He would have gained his freedom again within a short time.

The practice of enslaving those who could not pay their debts was common in Palestine. Jesus refers to this in the parable of the unmerciful slave (Mt 18:23-34), which refers to imprisonment for debt and sale into slavery to pay one's debt. Although Jesus never calls for an end to slavery, several elements in this parable suggest that he opposed it, at least to pay debts. First, the king initially shows mercy and decides not to sell his servant into slavery to pay off the great debt owed him. Second, the king is angered at the servant's lack of similar mercy toward a debtor. In the same vein, Jesus' prayer to "forgive us our debts, / As we also have forgiven our debtors" may well have in mind material as well as moral debts, coming as it does after the reference to "daily bread" (Mt 6:11-12).[4]

Some Christians in first-century Rome sold themselves into slavery to provide food for others and to buy others out of slavery (who presumably had worse masters; *1 Clement* 55:2). We do not know how widespread this practice was, but it tells us a great deal about the level of commitment to others that some Christians felt.

Slave markets ensured a steady supply of slaves to a society that had become dependent on them. Life in slavery began when a person was captured and turned over to a slave wholesaler. The wholesaler then took him to a slave distribution site. Major slave markets in the East were located in Ephesus, Byzantium, Alexandria, the Greek island of Delos and Side in Pamphylia. A number of cities in Italy also hosted such sites. Roman law required the nationality of slaves to be revealed since certain groups were believed to make better slaves. For example, Syrians were thought to be excellent, submissive slaves. Syrians and Bithynians were considered good litter bearers because they were taller than average and thus provided the occupant with better visibility and a better view. According to the Roman writer Varro, Gauls were much better animal herders than were Spaniards (Varro *Res rusticae* 2.10.4).

The wholesaler sold slaves at the slave emporium to a retailer, who in turn sold the slaves at auction. The slaves were put on a platform, bare feet coated with chalk, where they endured the poking and prodding of the auctioneer. The auctioneer was required to reveal not only the slaves' nationalities but also if they had been troublesome to their former owners. This information affected a slave's value.

Prices for slaves varied widely, depending on ability, experience and appearance. Price also fluctuated dramatically based on supply and demand. We know of slaves who sold for as little as 1,200 sesterces, and others who sold for as much as 200,000 sesterces. Prices were usually higher in Rome than in the provinces.[5]

In general, the slave trade was less active in the peaceful years of the Empire. By the first century A.D., the majority of new slaves were born to slave parents. So slaves referred to in the New Testament for the most part were born as slaves.

Slavery in the modern Western world differed from slavery among the Romans in part because of the racial and cultural origins of the slaves. Slaves brought from Africa to the Americas, for example, were a different race than their masters. By contrast, most slaves in the Roman Empire were of the same race as their masters. Thus, most could not be identified as slaves on sight. In addition, African slaves in the West spoke a different language, worshiped different gods and held some very different values from those of their new masters. Not so in the ancient world. Many slaves in Roman times spoke Greek and came from Hellenized societies, and so shared a common bond of culture, a common frame of reference, with their owners. Even when their religions differed from those of their Roman owners, the differences were not so great, and the Roman belief in multiple gods made them more accepting of new religions than were the Christian masters in the modern New World.

## Occupations of Slaves

Slaves had a wide variety of functions. The largest percentage of slaves worked the farms of Rome. Organized in slave gangs, they worked the massive farms of wealthy farmers in Italy and North Africa. State-owned slaves who worked in mines and quarries had the hardest life of all. Few could expect to gain their freedom, and many were worked into an early grave.

Many slaves worked as domestic servants in wealthy households, experiencing the certainty of food, shelter and the chance to save money and buy their freedom by the time they had passed middle age (see in figure 11.1 a photograph of the House of Aristides). They worked as spinners, weavers, clothesmakers, menders, wetnurses, child nurses, kitchen help and general domestics. Roman slaves rarely had to carry water and usually did not make all the household's clothes, unlike Greek slaves.

Slaves in wealthy homes were often given special training. They worked as clerks, secretaries, ladies' maids, clothes folders, hairdressers, haircutters, mirror holders, masseuses, readers, entertainers, midwives and infirmary attendants. Male and female slaves were always employable for sexual purposes. Attractive girls and young women were at the mercy of their male masters, and attractive young boys might be kept for sexual purposes by homosexual men.[6]

However, slaves in the city were not all domestics. Many if not most of imperial Rome's artisans, its potters, sculptors and painters, were slaves. Many of the most respected doctors in Rome were slaves of Greek origin. Slaves were also teachers, cooks and managers. They maintained the public facilities of the cities. The gladiators who entertained residents of any self-respecting Roman city were for the most part slaves. Municipal slaves were owned by local cities to assist in the maintenance of public property and as jailers.

Jobs held by female slaves were more limited than those held by men. Men were more likely to bring a valuable skill with them into slavery. A captured woman who was not employed as a domestic servant might become a midwife, an actress or a prostitute.

Some slaves held positions of great responsibility. This is in part because the Romans were willing to train promising slaves and also because persons taken in the conquest of a city or kidnapped might be highly skilled and capable. Slaves at times were used to run the farms of absent landowners and to manage the owner's shipping or trading business. For example, Onesimus, a slave of a

Christian named Philemon, apparently was traveling on some assignment of his master's when he decided to run away (Philemon).

Slaves belonging to the households of the wealthy or moderately wealthy in some ways lived a better life than the free poor of the city. Unlike the free poor, such slaves normally were assured three meals a day, lodging, clothing and health care. Urban slaves who were being prepared for posts in the government received a superior education. Many slaves, though not in the imperial bureaucracy, were better educated than the freeborn poor.

Figure 11.1. The *peristyle* or courtyard of the House of Aristides, a New Testament-era Roman home, Herculaneum, Italy. Many domestic slaves would have been employed to maintain such a home and its owners.

The most fortunate slaves of all, those who belonged to the emperor, probably lived longer lives than did the free poor. Imperial slaves (see below) sometimes owned their own slaves, traveled in pomp and luxury on the emperor's business, and commanded deference from all but the highest aristocrats. When acting on behalf of the emperor, they had authority even over freeborn Romans. After gaining their freedom they could rise to prominence among the freeborn. Former imperial slaves more than once rose to wealth and prominence and joined the class of respectable free Roman citizens.[7]

The New Testament shows slaves in a variety of settings. Jesus' parables usually refer to agricultural slaves, but they also show awareness that some slaves managed large estates and businesses (Mt 25:14-23; see also Mt 24:45-51; Lk 15:22; 17:7). The references to slaves in the Epistles almost always assume an urban context. In fact, every Christian slave mentioned in the New Testament lives in a city.

One of the more common tasks of urban slaves was to be *paidagogoi* to the children of the family. *Paidagogos* does not refer to a teacher, even though the English word *pedagogue* comes from it. Rather, it refers to a guardian who made sure the boys got to school and back home safely. Such a guardian is the image Paul has in mind in discussing the purpose of the law in Galatians 3:24: "So that the law was our custodian [*paidagogos*] until Christ came, that we might be justified by faith."

Like slaves in antiquity, African slaves in the Americas were mostly used in agriculture and mining. Many were used as domestics, and some were taught specialized skills. But modern African slaves rarely were trusted with the kind of responsible and highly skilled positions that many slaves performed in the Roman world. The ancients seem to have been more disposed to believe that slaves had the ability and could be trusted to act faithfully on behalf of the master in his absence. This may be in part because of racial prejudice, which simply was not a factor in ancient slavery, and in part because modern slaves did not have the incentive of earning their freedom—a strong motivating factor for many slaves in antiquity (as we shall see below).

### Attitudes Toward Slaves and Slavery

Greek thinkers like Plato and Aristotle believed that some slaves were slaves by nature and subhuman while some were simply slaves by circumstances (see the quote at the beginning of this chapter). But the Romans did not think of slaves as inferior by nature. As a result, they did not question the ability of slaves to perform high-level functions. While the Romans considered slaves as humans morally, their law regarded slaves as property. The thousands of slaves who worked as chattel gangs on ships, farms, road construction or mining typically were treated as commodities to be bought and sold at will. Jewish tradition allows for slavery, but regards the enslavement of Jews by Jews as improper because a Jew was a slave of God. The New Testament would apply to Christians this concept of God's people as his slaves (1 Cor 7:22).

Since Romans enslaved people from any ethnic group who had opposed them in war, or who were the victims of slave raiders, slavery was not tied to any specific ethnic group as was modern slavery in the American South and elsewhere. The ethnic composition of Rome's slaves changed over time as Rome took wartime captives in various locales. The ancients in general, including the Romans, did not connect skin color with issues of superiority or inferiority.[8] Although they did not consider slaves inferior by nature, they considered them inferior in status. Thus, they believed slaves *should not* perform functions that normally were performed by upper-class Romans. Roman literature and correspondence show an increasing anger at the emperors for using slaves and former slaves to carry out bureaucratic functions that senators had once performed. At times, a former slave acting in the name of the emperor might give orders to a senator. This was for some Romans the ultimate attack on their dignity. The Roman writer Petronius reflects this attitude in his depiction of a freedman risen far above his worth in "Trimalchio's Dinner" (*Satyricon* 76).

The institution of slavery was never questioned by the ancients. They did recognize that slavery negated pride and self-respect. Even Christianity, generally speaking, did not oppose the institution outright. Slaves for the most part accepted their status and did not question the existence of slavery. They certainly wanted to become free, but they saw nothing immoral about owning slaves. In fact, some slaves purchased their own slaves. These latter slaves legally belonged to the slave's free master, but masters found it a useful incentive to allow their more capable slaves to make money and buy their own property. A slave who bought other slaves instead of buying his own freedom presumably was content with his situation and probably was a good worker.

The Gospels evidence no belief that a slave is inferior to a free person. Jesus' teachings are far more in line with those Old Testament writings that speak of God's followers as his slaves. Jesus considered himself a slave of his heavenly father in that he came to do God's will and to accomplish his work (Jn 4:34; 5:30, 36; 8:28-29).

In contrast with ancient attitudes, the moral legitimacy of slavery was an issue for some Americans even before the founding of the United States. The U.S. Constitution legitimized slavery but sought to limit its spread. By the mid-nineteenth century, the American nation was sharply divided over the morality of slavery.

### Treatment of Slaves
The ancients had no concept of a just limit to what work could be required of a slave, but they did at times place limits on abuses of slaves by their masters. In the early Empire era, a court of appeal allowed abused slaves to force their

sale to a new master. Abuse serious enough to justify state intervention included physical cruelty and not providing enough food.

Slaves in the Americas also frequently were abused. Accounts by and about modern slaves make clear that masters were willing to torture slaves even when doing so caused them serious financial loss (if the slave died or was unable to work for a long time). At times this was a matter of terrorizing the other slaves into submission, but at other times it cannot be explained rationally.

Although major slave revolts were rare, individual slaves escaped frequently. Rewards of up to five hundred sesterces were sometimes offered for escaped slaves. Recaptured slaves might be flogged, kept in chains, sent to a slave prison, branded with a hot iron, or crucified. While the apostle Paul encouraged Christian slaves who could legitimately gain their freedom to do so (1 Cor 7:21), in at least one case he did not support runaway slaves (Philem 12).

### Marriage Among Slaves

Slaves had no legal right to marry and few inducements from society to maintain stable relationships. Despite all this, they regularly set up informal marriages and commemorated each other after death. The wording they used in burial inscriptions is similar to wording used by legally married citizens.

Members of the senatorial class, from the time of Augustus, were prohibited from marrying freed slaves. It may seem astonishing that any would wish to marry so far below their class in such a class-bound culture, but at times they did so. Ten percent of slaves in all categories married freeborn persons. P. R. C. Weaver estimates that nearly two-thirds of male imperial slaves and freedmen married freeborn women. A freeborn woman would marry an imperial slave or freedman because, while in some categories her status was higher (liberty, extraction), in others his might be higher (wealth, influence, perhaps education or profession), and so he could improve her position and provide an even better future for their children.

The emperor Claudius in 52 prohibited free women even from cohabiting with slaves without the knowledge of the slaveowner. Any children born to this union were slaves, and the woman, if freeborn, was reduced to freed (*libertina*) status. Such unions apparently happened often enough to deserve a special decree by Claudius and a later amendment to the decree.[9]

### Slaves and the Household

Slaves were part of the Greek or Roman household. Not that they were members of the family, although some became quite close to their masters and even at times married them and became family. Ancient families did not maintain the same physical distance from servants that modern families often do however. And yet the Romans, in legal terms, classified slaves as *instrumentum vocale* ("speaking tools"), just above the household's livestock in status. The head of the household, the *paterfamilias* in Roman terms, held great power over the slave. His power to execute slaves without just cause had diminished by the New Testament era, but he could do just about anything else.

Christian slaves are portrayed in the New Testament as part of a larger household, sometimes Christian, sometimes not. Many slaves, along with their masters, came to belief in Christ (1 Cor 1:16; 16:15; Acts 16:15, 31-34; 18:8). Others came to faith apart from their household (1 Cor 7:10-11, 21; 1 Pet 2:18-25; 3:1-2; 2 Tim 1:5). "Chloe's people" probably refers to slaves or freedmen in her household who were traveling between her home in Corinth and business in Ephesus, or vice versa (1 Cor 1:11). We cannot tell if Chloe was a Christian.

Several passages in the New Testament, often called "household codes," prescribe the proper relationships between members of the household.[10] The instructions do not challenge the institution of slavery, or the authority of master over slave, but they do seek to transform the relationships within those institutions and lines of authority.

The traditional expectations were that masters would take advantage of their power over their slaves, and that slaves would respond with deceptiveness and lack of zeal for their work. Masters are told in the New Testament to deal with their slaves in justice and fairness, knowing that God is their master (Col 4:1), and to give up threatening their slaves (Eph 6:9). Slaves are told to obey their masters not just externally but with "sincerity of heart." They should do this not to gain the approval of the master but as "slaves of Christ" and in the fear of the Lord (Col 3:22; Eph 6:5-7). They should consider their masters "worthy of all honor" in order to bring good repute to the name of God. They should respect their Christian masters and not take advantage of them (1 Tim 6:1-2).

### Slavery and Freedom

Roman citizens often freed their slaves. In urban households, this frequently happened by the time the slave reached age thirty. We know of few urban slaves who reached old age before gaining their freedom. Each freed slave became not only a *libertus* or *liberta* ("freedman" or "freedwoman") but usually also a Roman or Latin citizen. This meant that, at least for slaves in the cities of the Empire, slavery was more a process than a permanent state, a temporary condition to endure while heading toward a better way of life. In the practice of freeing slaves, ancients and moderns parted ways dramatically. While some

African slaves were bought out of slavery by others or given their freedom in their master's will, this was much less frequent than in the ancient world.

The proportion of freedmen to the total population increased greatly under the Empire since Romans freed their slaves with great frequency. During the New Testament era, a majority of the residents of the city of Rome most likely were either slaves or of slave origin. In fact, Caesar Augustus became so alarmed at the high level of emancipation that in A.D. 4 he made thirty the minimum age at which slaves could be freed and limited how many were freed each year. He was concerned that too many uneducated, non-Romans were becoming Roman citizens. But the practice of freeing slaves helped make the slave system more effective. It encouraged slaves to work hard and to maintain a positive attitude, believing that they would buy their way out of slavery one day in the not-too-distant future. Slaves in the Greek cities of the East were not freed nearly as regularly, but even Eastern masters did provide some opportunity for slaves to earn their freedom.

Figure 11.2. A mural in the temple of the cult of emperor worship, Herculaneum, Italy. Imperial slaves and freedmen maintained this cult throughout the Empire.

Many slaves, while working for a Roman master, could earn and save money toward buying their freedom. In general, female slaves engaged in female-oriented work would be freed by the mistress, and male slaves by the master, but free men often freed female slaves in order to marry them. Slaves employed in gangs on the large farms of Romans generally had little opportunity to save money for their freedom. Those in the city, who had the chance to do a little handcraft or trading on the side, were better positioned to buy their freedom. By contrast, African slaves in the United States had little incentive to work hard beyond the fear of punishment, and less cause to hope for a better life for themselves and their families.

Slaves of citizens traditionally added part of their former master's name to their own upon manumission (emancipation). The names of male Romans consisted of three parts: first came the *praenomen*, followed by the family name (the *nomen*) and the personal name (the *cognomen*; see chapter nine). Former slaves normally took the *nomen* of their former master as a prefix to their (usually Greek) slave name. For example, the author and former Jewish general Josephus prefixed Flavius to his name in response to the patronage of the imperial Flavian house.

These issues of emancipation must be remembered when looking at Paul's comments to slaves in 1 Corinthians 7. In verse 21, Paul says, "Were you a slave when called? Never mind. But if you can gain your freedom, avail yourself of the opportunity." The average slave reading this could indeed expect to gain her freedom at some point. But she had no real control over whether she would stay a slave or be emancipated. So Paul is not telling Christian slaves to stay enslaved when he says, "in whatever state each was called, there let him remain with God" (1 Cor 7:24). Rather, he is telling them not to worry about a condition they cannot control, but all things considered, it is better to be free than enslaved.

The epistle to Philemon deals with Onesimus, a runaway slave belonging to Philemon, a Christian and acquaintance of Paul. Philemon was wealthy enough to have a large house with which he hosted Christian meetings and guests, and to be a patron of Christians in other ways as well (Philem 2, 5-7, 22). Philemon probably had more than one slave. After leaving Philemon, Onesimus came to Rome, ran into Paul and became a Christian. Paul then sent Onesimus back to Philemon along with this letter (Philem 10-12). Paul says that he would have preferred to keep Onesimus with him, to aid him, but would not do so without Philemon's consent. He asks his friend to receive Onesimus back "no longer as a slave but more than a slave, as a beloved brother" (Philem 16). Paul probably is asking Philemon either to emancipate Onesimus or not to change the original timetable for emancipation, so that he might return to Paul legally as a freedman of Philemon.

### Relationship Between Freedman and Former Master

Some freed slaves found it hard to make a living in their new lives. This was in part because they were skilled at tasks performed by slaves, not free persons, and so found it hard to find work. Others earned a comfortable living by working hard at a craft or trade, either under their patron's sponsorship or with a good deal of independence. A few grew quite wealthy.

Freed slaves were legally obliged to provide service to their former master, now their patron, so long as they also had enough time to earn their own livelihood. They would often continue serving in the same occupation, only now as an employee.

Freedmen learned from their master how to run a shop he financed, how to practice a trade to which he apprenticed them and how to handle his accounts. They served in the master's place in occupations below his status. As one burial inscription of a freed silversmith put it:

> He never said an angry word in his life and did nothing except by his master's will. He always had a quantity of gold and silver by him and never coveted any of it for himself. He excelled everyone in the craft of silverwork (*Inscriptiones Latinae Selectae* 7695).[11]

Freedwomen composed a large part of the Roman working class, serving as shopkeepers and artisans or continuing in domestic service. They generally pursued the same occupations for which they had been trained as slaves.

Many freedwomen continued working for their former owners after being freed. A freed wife could not divorce without the permission of her patron, who in some cases was also her husband (*Digest* 24.2.11). Freed domestics with few skills may have welcomed the chance to remain in the security of their patron's employ and to continue living in the house rather than face the uncertainties of life among the poor.[12]

Paul probably had in mind the obligations a freedman owed his former master when he wrote, "For he who was called in the Lord as a slave is a freedman of the Lord" (1 Cor 7:22). A Christian "freedman" is not free of God but owes God a life of obedience and service in response to the master who has bought him out of spiritual bondage (1 Cor 7:23).

### Upward Mobility

Although most freed slaves lived out humble lives, those who did rise in status give us the most frequent and most dramatic examples of increase in status of any group in the Roman world. Not every freedman went from former slave to rich merchant. Theirs was in effect the social climber class. For example, in Pompeii, freedmen and their descendants made up between a third and a half of the governing aristocracy by the first century A.D.[13] Descendants of freedmen were also a major element among the local ruling classes of Pannonia and Africa. The more successful former slaves joined local urban aristocracies as ministers of the cult of emperor worship. Freedmen often took a prominent part in the city rites of the emperor cult. In local city branches of the cult, three freedmen typically shared with three freeborn citizens responsibility for maintaining a local branch of the cult.

The ruling class defined and even punished freedmen to try to prevent this kind of upward mobility. Freedmen were made a group separate from other free persons. They owed continued reverence, duties and payments to their former masters. The senate considered requiring freedmen to wear a special uniform so any dodging of duty would be noticed. At private dinners, they got the least honored seat. They could not serve in the legions or aim at municipal magistracies. They could not form a sexual relationship with a free woman of a higher class, senatorial or equestrian, without risking capital punishment. A freedman who proclaimed himself a member of the equestrian class, even if he possessed the required wealth, could be prosecuted.[14]

Some African slaves in America who gained their freedom saw their status rise dramatically. For example, a slave in North Carolina, named April, was trained by his master (and probably his father), William Ellison, to repair cotton gins. Freed by Ellison's will, April changed his name to William Ellison and eventually became the richest man of any color in his state (until the Civil War swept away the niche he had carved for himself and his family).[15]

## Imperial Freedmen

The most outstanding examples of rising social status in the early Empire come from among the freedmen of the emperor, who along with imperial slaves constituted the household of Caesar (*familia Caesaris*).[16] The *familia Caesaris* consisted of slaves and freedmen who maintained the emperor's properties and his religious cult and who supervised the revenues of the Empire (see in figure 11.2 a photograph of the temple of the emperor cult in Herculaneum). Those who rose to the top of the latter group achieved a status far above that of most people in Rome.

An imperial slave boy's civil service began with education. In school he was taught the basics necessary for those helping administer a Mediterranean empire: Latin, Greek and applied mathematics. Upon completing his training, he spent several years in domestic service. At the age of twenty, he began serving in a series of minor posts. After receiving freedom, around age thirty, he could move on to intermediate posts such as record officer, correspondent, accountant or paymaster. In his forties, he might serve in a senior post such as chief accountant, chief record officer or chief correspondent. Because of his status as a member of the imperial household, even while a slave he could marry a freeborn woman, possess his own slaves and acquire considerable wealth. His position in the imperial bureaucracy allowed him to exercise power far beyond that of any non-Roman or poor Roman citizen.

In light of the foregoing, it is not surprising that imperial freedmen enjoyed a high level of social status among the Roman lower classes, especially among its foreign groups. For example, in his *Letters* Pliny the Younger calls Claudius Aristion "the leading citizen of Ephesus, popular for his generosity" (6.31.8). Based on studies of the surviving inscriptions, imperial freedmen often dominated the leadership of Rome's private associations (for more on associations, see chapter twelve).

Marcus Antonius Felix, procurator of Judea at the time Paul was imprisoned in Caesarea in A.D. 57, was an imperial freedman of the household of Antonia, daughter of Mark Antony. His rise to equestrian status and the office of provincial governor was an extreme example of the potential upward mobility of imperial slaves. Felix was the brother of Pallas, manager of the imperial accounts under Claudius and another successful freedman. Pallas secured equestrian status (an exception to Roman law) and a series of important appointments for Felix, including the governorship of Judea (Suetonius *Claudius* 25.1, 28; Pliny *Letters* 8.6). The Roman historian Tacitus reveals the kind of anger felt toward such upstarts by the ruling class when he writes that Felix "practiced every kind of cruelty and lust, wielding the power of a king with all the instincts of a slave" (*Histories* 5.9).

Felix's brother Pallas was so wealthy that he could turn down a gift of fifteen million sesterces from the senate. He did accept from that body the honorary status of a praetor, one of the highest offices in the Empire. Freedmen reached the summit of their power under emperors Claudius and Nero. After that, their importance in the top positions of the imperial administration declined.

Paul, probably writing from Rome, sends greetings from the saints in "Caesar's household" (Phil 4:22). This is a clear reference to the *familia Caesaris*. Some of these may have had positions of authority and high relative status, but we do not know any more about them.

## The New Testament Attitudes Toward Slavery

Slaves and slavery are mentioned frequently in the New Testament. Most New Testament references to slavery accept it as a fact of life. A number of references use slavery as a metaphor, usually of the believer's relationship to God. A few references reflect a negative view of slavery. But the writers of the New Testament never condemn slavery as an institution, or call for its abolition. While they do not outright condemn slavery, neither do they provide any justification for it. Some later Christians have sought justification in the New Testament for Christian ownership of slaves. It is hard to imagine a more inaccurate understanding of the New Testament.

The absence of a call for the abolition of slavery needs to be seen in light of a number of issues. First, slavery had been a fact of life for the various peoples of the Mediterranean for many centuries. No Greek or Roman author ever attacked slavery as an institution. We know of only two groups that rejected the concept of slavery: the Essenes at Qumran in Palestine (Josephus *Jewish Antiquities* 18.18-22) and the Therapeutae of Egypt (Philo *On the Contemplative Life* 70). Second, the New Testament never counters and at times supports the general view that enslavement was to be avoided or ended whenever possible. Paul's use of slavery as a metaphor for the Christian's relationship with God indicates that he well knew how completely a slave was bound to the will of his owner. Third, while Christian slaveowners are not told to free their slaves, they are told to transform their relationship with them into one of brotherhood. This may be paternalistic, but it takes into account the reality that freed slaves often found it difficult to make a living. Fourth, none of the leading figures in the New Testament owned slaves, so far as we know. This sets an example for other Christians, even if some did not follow it. Fifth, Paul repeatedly says that before God, and thus in the church, there is no difference between slave and free (1 Cor 12:13; Gal 3:28; Col 3:11). This would have sounded like utter nonsense to the average Roman, but it reveals a revolutionary definition of identity and status.

If a slave is treated as a member of the family, as a beloved employee, does it matter whether the slave is legally free or not? Yes, in several respects. For example, a slave is not free to leave the master's household, a slave does not have legal control over his or her children, and a slave cannot legally pass property to them. In these ways a slave's situation cannot be compared to that of a modern company employee.

We have records of Christians freeing their slaves, beginning in the second century. It would take several centuries, but a Christian emperor of Rome would finally outlaw slavery. However, by then slavery had ceased to be an important factor in the economy, and its abolition involved considerably less hardship than it would have in the first century.

**For Further Reading**

Barrow, R. H. *Slavery in the Roman Empire.* New York: Barnes & Noble, 1968.

Finley, M. I. *Ancient Slavery and Modern Ideology.* New York: Penguin, 1980.

Harrill, J. Albert. *The Manumission of Slaves in Early Christianity.* Tübingen: Mohr, 1995.

Hopkins, Keith. *Conquerors and Slaves.* New York: Cambridge University Press, 1978.

Jacobs, Harriet A. *Incidents in the Life of a Slave Girl: Written by Herself,* ed. Jean Fagan Yellin. Cambridge, Mass.: Harvard University Press, 1987.

Johnson, Michael P., and James L. Roark. *Black Masters: A Free Family of Color in the Old South.* New York: W. W. Norton, 1984.

Patterson, Orlando. *Slavery and Social Death: A Comparative Study.* Cambridge, Mass: Harvard University Press, 1982.

# Chapter 12

# The Family, Women & Education

*Parents subject the still malleable characters of their children
to what will do them good. Let them cry and struggle as they will,
we swaddle them tightly lest their still immature bodies become deformed
rather than grow up straight and tall. Later we instill liberal culture
by means of terror if they refuse to learn.*
SENECA *MORAL EPISTLES* 47

*Wives, be subject to your husbands, as is fitting in the Lord.
Husbands, love your wives, and do not be harsh with them.
Children, obey your parents in everything, for this pleases the Lord.
Fathers, do not provoke your children, lest they become discouraged.
Slaves, obey in everything those who are your earthly masters,
not with eyeservice, as men-pleasers, but in singleness
of heart, fearing the Lord.*
COLOSSIANS 3:18-22

*Fathers, do not provoke your children to anger,
but bring them up in the discipline and instruction of the Lord.*
EPHESIANS 6:4

*Train up a child in the way he should go,
and when he is old he will not depart from it.*
PROVERBS 22:6

WE CAN LEARN A LOT ABOUT WHAT IT WAS LIKE TO LIVE IN THE first century from the private lives of the people of that era. In this chapter we will consider the nature of the family, the places occupied by women and attitudes toward women, and the importance to first-century families of educating children. We will seek to answer questions such as, what did marriage mean to them? What forms did marriage take? How did husbands and wives relate to each other and to their children? How and why did marriages end? What place did women have in the cities of Rome? What place in the Christian churches? Finally, we will look at the educational attitudes and practices among Jews, Greeks and Romans of that era, and how they help illuminate the New Testament.

## Marriage

Under Roman rule, only certain marriages had legal standing. Only when both partners were Roman citizens could a legal marriage *(matrimonium)* normally be formed. By the late Republic, the most common form of legal marriage was one in which the wife did not come under her husband's complete authority. Instead, her father remained her legal guardian. As a result, she did not belong to her husband's family and would usually get back her dowry if the marriage ended. This form of marriage, "without *manus*," gave Roman women more independence than they had ever known and considerably more than that of Greek women for most of Greek history.

Other marriages were informal, not governed by Roman law. This does not mean that Rome considered such unions immoral, just that the government did not offer them legal protection. Children born to an informal marriage were illegitimate and took their status from the mother. In practice, this meant that the father had no legal rights over them.

Slaves typically initiated informal marriages with other slaves, usually within their master's household. With permission, a slave could marry a slave from another household. Slave marriages involved little security since either partner or the children might be sold at any time. Despite this, many slave marriages lasted a long time, often despite changes in habitation or status from slave to freed. In the surviving epitaphs, slaves refer to each other as husband and wife.

Roman law made the minimum marriage age twelve for girls, fourteen for boys. The age of first marriage for free Roman girls normally was twelve to eighteen. Men married for the first time as late as thirty, but in Roman culture a five-year difference between man and woman seems to have been most common among both free persons and slaves. The age of first marriage for Jewish girls probably also was between twelve and eighteen.[1]

## Family Structure

The most significant feature of the Roman household *(familia)* was that its power was concentrated in the hands of the male head, the *paterfamilias.* The members of the household were those persons over whom the *paterfamilias* had power. Only the *paterfamilias* could own property under Roman law. His power was unbroken until his death.

The Roman household normally was composed of husband, wife, unmarried children, slaves, freedmen and clients (see in figure 12.1 a photograph of a re-creation of a Roman villa). Bigamy was illegal. With apparently few exceptions, sons set up their own households when they married. The first century B.C. Roman orator Cicero described the family unit as a married couple and children. Brothers and cousins formed their own households like colonies of their parents' home (*De officiis* 1.53). However, even though the younger generation lived under a different roof, they still were under the legal authority of their father as *paterfamilias*.

The Roman family tended to be small at all social levels. Few families had as many as three children who survived infancy. The epitaphs from lower-class families seldom record more than two children. Burial inscriptions also mention a number of single-parent families (only one parent is named on the inscription). The frequency of divorce and of the early death of one parent must have led to frequent remarriage and thus to stepchildren and blended families. Grandparents seem not to have been prominent in the Roman family because of a shorter life expectancy than in modern times.

We must understand that modern Western family structures differ considerably from ancient ones. Although we can talk about a Roman nuclear family, this refers more to living arrangements than to the nature of the family as a whole. The *paterfamilias* had far more influence over all of the members of his extended family, regardless of where they lived, than do most parents today. The sense of family unity and duty to preserve family honor was higher then than now. At the same time, expectations limited the freedom of members of ancient families in ways that few Americans experience.

The structure of Roman slave families did not differ substantially from that of the free populace. Many slaves in Rome in this era could hope to win their freedom. If they were owned by Roman citizens, they would normally be granted Roman citizenship as well when they were freed. In A.D. 4 the minimum age of manumission was set at thirty, but exceptions were allowed. Females were likely to be freed earlier than males, in part because masters had to free them in order to marry them. While marriage to a slave by lower-class freeborns was perfectly acceptable, it was a cause for social ostracism among the wealthy. A slave had no father in the eyes of Roman law, so when he was freed his former master was recognized as his legal father.[2]

The Hellenistic family or household (*oikos*) included members of the family by blood and marriage, as well as property "movable" (slaves, animals) and "immovable" (e.g., house, land, tools). It was more likely multigenerational than was the Roman family, with three generations of a Hellenistic family often living under the same roof. The Hellenistic husband and father never had power close to that of the Roman *paterfamilias*, but he still was the ultimate

**Figure 12.1.  Outer *peristyle* (courtyard) and the J. Paul Getty Museum, Malibu, California.** This is a re-creation of a first-century Roman villa.

authority in his family. For example, he, sometimes with the input of his wife, arranged the marriages of his children.

Unlike Roman and Hellenistic law, Jewish law allowed polygamy. But in the cities of the Greco-Roman world, the Jews typically adopted the marriage practices of the larger culture. The Jewish household probably consisted of two, sometimes three, generations of kin by blood and marriage. Most Jewish families probably did not own slaves. Unlike the Roman *familia*, those that included slaves probably did not include freedmen, since freedmen owed no continuing service to former masters who were not Roman citizens (such as most Jews).[3]

Christian families probably looked a lot like Jewish and pagan families. First-century Christian adults were either first- or second-generation converts, thus not far removed from their Jewish or pagan origins. Jewish and Christian families would have constituted weakened patriarchies. The low social status of the *paterfamilias* in these families would have undermined his power. In addition, since marriage for most Jews and Christians was not legitimate in the state's eyes, Roman law, which served to reinforce the patriarchy, would not aid Jewish or Christian men. The small size of their dwellings and their economic status would keep the household small: husband, wife, and two or three children.

### Husband-Wife Relationships

Both Roman and Jewish marriages typically were arranged by the parents of the prospective spouses, sometimes with the latter's assistance. Marriages were arranged for the sake of the entire family. A father in the upper classes took into account what social and economic benefits an alliance with another family would bring. He also considered the suitability of the prospective spouses for each other. Among the lower classes, social alliances can hardly have been much of a factor. Here the emphasis would have been on finding a spouse suitable for one's son or daughter. Faithfulness to the relationship and harmony within the marriage were ideals. In addition, the need to raise children to continue the family line was considered a basic obligation. In the absence of evidence to the contrary, it seems likely that Christian parents also arranged the marriages of their children.

The most important goal of Roman marriage was producing children, but it was not the only goal or expectation. In fact, a man who divorced his barren wife might be chastised for putting the desire for children above marital loyalty. By contrast, Palestinian Jewish custom required a husband to divorce a barren wife. The Roman concept of marriage also included the desire for compatibility, partnership and love. Literature from the time of Augustus promotes the idea that a wife should be a welcome partner in prosperity and adversity. The Roman popular ideal, strongly supported by the government, was a happy and harmonious marriage. The Roman poet Ovid celebrated a couple who were so harmonious throughout their long marriage that they wished to die together (*Metamorphosis* 8.708).

Since their marriages were arranged, one might think that Romans did not look for romance in marriage. In fact, Roman literature at times portrayed married love as passionate and romantic. Some writers felt the need to condemn men who displayed too much affection toward their wives publicly, or even privately in front of their children. The Roman senator Cato once expelled a man from the senate for publicly kissing his wife. This all suggests that married couples were at times quite passionate.

Roman wives were expected to obey their husbands in all things. During the Roman Republic, the husband had as much power over his wife as he did over his children. By the New Testament era, this power had eroded somewhat, but it still was far greater than that given to husbands in the modern Western world. In some respects, the power of husbands in fundamentalist Islamic nations today is similar to that of the ancient Romans, except that Romans could only have one wife at a time.

Hellenistic wives also were obliged to obey their husbands. The husband's power over his wife among the Hellenists was not so great as among the Romans, but it was still considerable.

Jews saw having children as an obligation, based on the command "be fruitful and multiply" (Gen 1:28). The general consensus was that this commandment was directed to men only. The expressions of sentiment in the Jewish inscriptions discovered in the city of Rome give us some insight into what qualities were expected in a spouse, parent or child: a good reputation, religious piety and devotion to family members.[4] Christians are not commanded to have children or commended for doing so in the New Testament.

*Husbands.* As noted above, the head of the Roman *familia* held almost absolute power over all the members of his household. This power, which included even the power of life and death, was called *patria potestas.* It had diminished considerably by the first century A.D., but the Roman husband and father still held total control of the family property. Even his adult sons owned nothing legally before his death. In practice, however, many adult sons lived quite independently of their fathers. In any case, many fathers did not live long into their children's adulthood. The early second-century author Plutarch, who considered himself progressive in such matters, tells newlyweds, "Every activity in a virtuous household is carried on by both parties in agreement, but discloses the husband's leadership and preferences" (*Advice on Marriage* 139A). This appears to suggest that the couple's decisions should be based on consensus but that the wife must subordinate herself to the husband's governance.

Philo, a Jewish intellectual of the upper classes in Alexandria, wrote during the early first century A.D. about the proper Jewish family. Philo said that the family was based on three features: an unbreakable bond of love and kinship, the inherent superiority of parents and a hierarchy of male and female that associates women with the senses and men with the mind (*On the Special Laws* 1.200-201).

The Christian ideal of the household in the pastoral epistles offers a strict sexual ethic, allowing one standard of behavior for men and women (1 Tim 5; Tit 2). This departs from the Roman position that, while husbands and wives both were told to avoid sexual infidelity, women were more severely chastised for it by society. For example, Plutarch cautions against sexual infidelity by husbands but suggests that the bride overlook her husband's sexual affairs (*Advice on Marriage* 144D; 143F).

First Peter tells Christian husbands to live with their wives "in an understanding way, as with a weaker vessel, since she is a woman" and to grant her honor as a fellow heir of salvation (1 Pet 3:7 NASB). This suggests a more or less traditional hierarchical relationship, softened by the recognition of the wife's equal standing before God. This would not have required much change for former pagans or Jewish Christians. This relationship is similar to that described in the Pastoral Epistles of the New Testament, in which the husband has authority over his wife, children and slaves and is responsible for their behavior.

*Wives.* Greek wives in the classical era, at least among the upper classes, lived extremely sheltered lives. They were not allowed out of doors except to attend important events, and then only when accompanied by male relatives. This meant, for example, that husbands or slaves did all of the shopping. A woman seen in public in the classical Greek city was thought to be either a slave or a prostitute. Within the home, women were confined to the women's quarters, into which no males besides family members could enter. This measure were an attempt in large part to make sure that the women stayed sexually pure, so that their children were the true descendants of their husbands and thus had the right to bear the family name and preserve its traditions. But after the wars that brought about the collapse of classical-era Greece, Greek women were able to be seen in public without scandal. By the New Testament era, Greek and Hellenistic women were able freely to take part in the public life of the cities of the Empire.

Plutarch and Juvenal told their upper-class readers how wives should and should not behave. Plutarch says that wives should not initiate love making and should accept their husbands' friends, avoid untraditional beliefs but accept their husbands' gods, be content to stay at home, and remain silent except to address their husbands (*Advice on Marriage* 140C-F; 142C, D). Writing in late first-century A.D. Rome, Juvenal gives us a portrait of the ideal wife: one who does not cheat on her spouse but puts up with his affairs, who does not reject his friends, who does not leave behind his gods for foreign religions, and who does not make a public spectacle of herself but manages his household (*Satire* 6).

Clearly, a wife's conversion to Judaism or Christianity could lead to serious conflict with her husband. First Peter devotes almost half of its section on codes of household behavior to address this problem. It tells wives to be submissive to their husbands so that those who are not Christians may be won over by their behavior. This behavior was to include being chaste and respectful and having a gentle and quiet spirit. The model for this behavior is the obedience of Sarah to her husband Abraham (1 Pet 3:1-6).

It is not clear to what degree, if at all, women in the lower classes experienced greater freedom in marriage in the New Testament era than in earlier times. The necessities of life in the lower classes would have exerted a curb on the possibilities for social freedom among lower-class women. For example, women in the lower classes did more physical labor and earned more of the family's income than women in wealthier families. On the other hand, women in nonlegal marriages had the ability to leave a relationship without interference by the state. Such women were also far more likely to get custody of their children. Many lower-class families were fatherless, requiring the mother to take full responsibility to provide for and raise her children, thus bestowing on her the rights and duties of a head of household.

Jewish wives living in the cities of Rome would have had more freedom in some respects and less in others than women who lived under Jewish law. In the cities they were more free to actively engage in the society outside their homes. They would have found it easy to divorce their husbands, whether or not their marriage was legal in the eyes of Rome. Under Jewish law, a wife could not divorce her husband unless she prosecuted him and the court ordered a divorce (*m. Nedarim* 11.12). Also under Jewish law, the wife's guardianship was transferred from her father to her husband at marriage. On the other hand, Jewish law allowed women to take legal actions without the assistance of a guardian, to own property and to control property without interference from their husbands.[5]

*Divorce.* Divorce in earliest Rome was rare, in part because only the husband could initiate divorce, and he needed a powerful reason such as adultery (*adulterium*). Divorce became easier to obtain and much more common in the late Republic. The old idea that divorce was shameful seems to have passed away by the second century B.C. By the end of the Republic, wives were able to initiate divorce as easily as husbands. Divorce was typically a matter of mutual consent. The courts became involved only if the parties failed to agree on terms such as the return of the dowry.

In the New Testament era, the procedure for divorce was simple. One need only send one's spouse a letter of intent to divorce. It was not necessary to state the reason for the divorce, and normally the reasons were not made public. Romans generally divorced for the following reasons: failure to have children (generally assumed to be the woman's fault), political reasons like those that dictated many marriages, continued adultery by the spouse and to initiate a desired new marriage.

**Figure 12.2. Burial marker from a wealthy Greek family (National Museum, Athens, Greece). The figures symbolize characteristics of the deceased and people in her life.**

We have very little evidence of wives divorcing their husbands for adultery. This may be because adultery for men applied only to affairs with married women in their social class. Affairs with slaves or lower-class free women were not considered adultery by the state. By contrast, women could be punished for affairs with slaves or men of the lower classes. It was considered a crime (which came to be called *stuprum*), though not adultery, for married or unmarried men to commit fornication with unmarried "respectable" women (the same law applied to male homosexuality). The penalty for both *adulterium* and *stuprum* was usually exile.

In 18 B.C. Caesar Augustus made adultery a criminal offense. He required a husband who caught his wife in the act of adultery to divorce her and then bring her to trial. If he only learned of her adultery secondhand, he was compelled to divorce her but not necessarily to prosecute her. A woman who divorced her husband for adultery could make on that basis more stringent demands for the restoration of her dowry (Ulpian *Digest* 6.13). Roman adultery laws were intended mainly to preserve the legitimacy of the upper-class family's children and to promote the production of legitimate children. This helps explain why such regulations focused on control of the behavior of upper-class women.

Roman divorce usually included separating a mother from her children. The children of a legal marriage belonged to the father according to Roman law. Children of a slave mother belonged to her master and so would not be taken away simply because a husband left her. Of course they might be taken away for other reasons. Children born outside legal marriage to a free woman could not legally be taken from her when the relationship dissolved since no man could lay legal claim to them. It may be that women in such situations were able to keep their children.

The Roman lower classes could divorce as easily as could the upper classes. Economic necessity may have prevented some divorces; often both spouses had to work to provide for themselves and their children. On the other hand, a number of women in the urban lower classes, because they had to work, possessed a skill that might allow them to survive apart from their husband. However, we have little evidence for divorce among the lower classes. This is primarily because many of the marriages in the lower classes in Rome were not legal, and so legal divorce was not required to break the union. Broken families among the lower classes were very common as a result of other factors: the death of a spouse, the continued slave status of at least one partner and the slave trade in children.

Since most early Christians were not wealthy or Roman citizens, they would have had little interest in most Roman laws about divorce. This would change over time, of course. Nevertheless, the New Testament's comments on divorce suggest that church leaders were dealing with converts who shared the more liberal Roman attitudes toward divorce. The Gospels refer to the Jewish practice of allowing divorce based on written notice (Mt 5:31; 19:7; Mk 10:4). Jesus opposed this practice, allowing divorce only for "unchastity" (Mt 19:9). In Mark

10:11-12, Jesus recognizes that both men and women divorce their spouses, whereas Matthew has him refer only to men. The fact that Mark includes women gives added support to the belief of many scholars that this Gospel was written for a Roman audience. Paul tells the Corinthians not to divorce their spouses, even if they are not Christians, but he says that if the unbeliever leaves, the Christian is free (1 Cor 7:10-15). The term translated "separation" here refers to divorce. The ancients had no equivalent of the modern legal concept of separation.

### Parent-Child Relationships

*Fathers.* The Roman author Seneca believed that fathers showed their love for their children by imposing structure: waking them up early to be productive, not allowing them to be idle and drawing effort from them (*De providentia* 2.5). The father is generally depicted as more strict than the mother. Seneca portrays this strictness as genuine love, because its purpose is to oversee the real interests of the child. However, Roman fathers were able to show affection and tenderness. In the literature they cherish children whether beautiful or ugly, healthy or sick. We also see them taking an interest in their sons' education.

Hellenistic fathers were expected to teach their sons a trade or otherwise give them the means to make a living. For most this meant teaching their sons to be farmers. They could expect to be cared for in old age if they did so.

The fundamental obligation of Jewish parents, according to Jewish literature, was to feed and clothe their children. Failure to do this was the worst type of neglect (*Letter of Aristeas* 248). According to Philo, the father was primarily responsible for financial support, from providing a dowry for daughters and an inheritance for sons to basic food, clothing, education and health care (*On the Special Laws* 2.233). The rabbis considered it a paternal obligation to teach a son a trade. Jewish parents, especially fathers, were expected to discipline their children. Corporal punishment was the primary means of discipline. Parents were not to play or laugh with their children or risk spoiling them (Ecclesiasticus 30:1-13). At the same time, they were not to be too harsh in disciplining their children.

*Mothers.* Romans viewed the mother as the transmitter of traditional morality. She ideally was a firm disciplinarian. Romans believed that tasks such as nursing infants were better left to others. At the same time, Roman women were encouraged to watch closely the moral development of children and grandchildren. The Roman mother was almost fully responsible for her daughter's education since daughters were educated primarily in domestic skills. The fact that daughters married earlier than sons, and tended to live closer to their husband's family than their birth family, suggests that the emotional bond between mother and son was stronger than that between mother and daughter. Ross Kraemer thinks that Jewish mothers, like Greco-Roman mothers, had closer emotional attachments to their sons than to their daughters.[6]

Philo told his Jewish readers that the physical nurturing of a child was primarily the mother's responsibility. Because of maternal affection and the physical need to breastfeed, mothers who were separated from their infants would suffer great distress, according to Philo. Jewish literature depicts motherhood as the fulfillment of a woman's life. Second Timothy begins with a commendation of Timothy's mother Eunice and grandmother Lois, indirectly crediting them with instilling strong faith in Timothy (2 Tim 1:5).

*Children.* The period of childhood was short for the lower classes since children in poorer families went to work early in their lives. The fact that many humble Roman families lived in a combined home and workshop made it impossible to focus home life on the children. Children seem to have been exposed to many influences besides that of their parents.

In a regular Roman marriage, children took their status from their father at the time of conception. In extralegal marriages, they took their status from their mother at the time of birth.

The duty children owed their parents, termed *pietas,* was associated by Romans with the duty humans owed their gods. The religious overtones of respect for and submission to parents (especially the father) reverberate throughout Roman literature. For example, the rise to power of Octavian (Caesar Augustus) was defended by propagandists as an expression of Octavian's *pietas* toward his adoptive father, Julius Caesar, since Octavian took vengeance on Caesar's enemies.

Hellenistic children were expected to honor their parents, as demanded by both nature and the gods. Parents were due honor because they had given children life and many benefits. Also, those benefits, in particular food, clothing and companionship, should be paid back to parents in their old age. For the Hellenists, honor to parents ranked either right behind honor to the gods or just behind honor to the gods and country.[7]

The obligations of Jewish children may be summed up by the command to "honor your father and mother" (Ex 20:12). Closely related to honor was the obligation to obey. Obedience to parents is a major theme in the Wisdom tradition (Prov 1:8; 6:20).

Several passages in the New Testament, often called "household codes," prescribe the proper relationships between members of the Christian household (Eph 5:21—6:9; Col 3:18—4:1; 1 Tim 6:1-2; Tit 2:9-10). Their teachings bear some similarities to patterns in the Roman household. The codes depict a husband and father who is clearly in charge. Wives are told to "be subject" to their husbands (Eph 5:22, Col 3:18), and children are admonished to obey their parents (Eph 6:1-3, Col 3:20). As with the Romans, a child's obedience is connected to his obedience to his deity. The codes include slaves in the household; Christian slaves are expected to obey their masters whether or not the masters were Christians (Eph 6:5-9; Col 3:22—4:1; 1 Tim 6:1-2; Tit 2:9-10). Also as with the Romans, adult children are expected to care for their elderly parents (1 Tim 5:4).

But we also see striking differences between the Roman model and the New Testament codes. There is a greater level of mutual responsibility and accountability in the Christian household, as there is in the church. The husband is given instructions that limit his power over his wife. He is told to love her sacrificially, on the model of Christ's sacrificial love for the Church (Eph 5:25-33; Col 3:19). Although the father is expected to have control over his children (1 Tim 3:4-5), his power over them is limited by warnings that he not provoke and thus discourage them (Eph 6:4; Col 3: 21). The Romans certainly expected slaves to obey their masters, but they did not try to make it a moral and religious obligation as does the New Testament (Eph 5:5-8; Col 3:22-24; 1 Tim 6:1-2; Tit 2:9-10). Christian masters likewise bear a responsibility to their slaves, not to threaten them (Eph 6:9) but to treat them fairly (Col 4:1), since the masters have the same heavenly master as do their slaves. We do not know how well Christians in the New Testament era lived up to these prescriptions. Apparently enough did not do so to make them worth including in several Epistles.

## Women in Greco-Roman Culture and the New Testament

One of the ways in which ancient society most differed from the modern Western world was its static nature. Things changed very slowly. Most people lived virtually the same life their parents had. We can make serious mistakes in our understanding of the New Testament world if we expect it to change as quickly as ours does. This is nowhere more true than in the case of gender roles. Women, like men, were expected to fulfill very specific roles in society. A woman who stepped outside of those roles would not have been considered courageous and forward-looking; she would have been thought selfish and decadent (see figure 12.2, a photograph of a woman's grave marker). By contrast, a man under some circumstances might be admired for stepping out of his expected roles.

Greco-Roman culture regarded women (with notable exceptions) as incapable of the level of intellectual ability achieved by men. It allotted to women the duty of childbearing and child rearing. In the New Testament era, women in the upper classes were often able to step outside of this model. Women in the urban lower classes did not experience their level of independence, but they often worked alongside their husbands in the shop or at some other occupation. If slaves, they worked as domestics in the household of their master or mistress.

*Women in the cities of the Empire.* Both Greek and Roman traditions expected women to be modest and unobtrusive and to lead uneventful and unexciting lives. Similarly, 1 Peter commends a "reverent and chaste behavior" and a "gentle and quiet spirit" in women (1 Pet 3:1-6). But we have a number of stories of strong Roman women operating behind the scenes, influencing their men to take some public action. The report in Matthew that Pilate's wife urged him in a note not to convict Jesus fits this pattern (Mt 27:19).

Ancient writers often reminded women readers of women who remained faithful to their husbands even as widows. The literary and perhaps societal ideal was the *univira,* the woman who had been married to only one husband. Legislation by the emperor Caesar Augustus, however, required every woman between twenty and fifty to be married or lose her rights of inheritance and other privileges. Augustus was seeking to stem the tide of childless aristocrats that threatened many old aristocratic families with extinction. Those who were widowed or divorced were to remarry and bear children.[8]

Although Greek and Roman traditions opposed changes in the status of women, opportunities for women to be upwardly mobile existed in the New Testament period. Women in the upper classes had the greatest opportunities to break out of traditional roles. A woman who gained wealth through inheritance or investment was in a position of influence and power, even though society expected women to have a subordinate position.

However, women did not have to be in the upper classes to gain at least some economic independence. Inscriptions show that women of lower social standing were active in commerce and manufacture. Freedwomen from the East often traded in luxury goods, such as purple dye or perfumes (e.g., Lydia in Acts 16:14). In Pompeii a woman named Eumachia used some of the money she had made in a brick-making business to donate a major building to a trade association. Also in Pompeii, a woman named Mamia financed the construction of the temple of the Genius of Augustus. Women were mentioned on coins and inscriptions throughout the Empire as benefactors and officials of cities and as recipients of municipal honors.[9]

Urban women in the New Testament era did not remain secluded in their homes. Among other things, they joined clubs—usually the same clubs as did men. In fact, associations of priestesses are about the only all-woman clubs for which we have evidence. Women appear in small numbers in the lists of Greek associations long before the Romans came east. Fairly often in imperial times, women were called upon to serve as founders or patronesses of men's associations. This typically involved providing a meeting place or giving an endowment for club expenses. For Italy and the Italian provinces, scholars estimate that 5 to 10 percent of the patrons of and donors to associations were women.[10]

Women were also active outside the home in religious matters. They took part in cults primarily practiced by women, but they also participated in private cults that attracted both sexes and in official state cults. The newer cults, before they became established, were more likely to give women the freedom to hold offices alongside men. As the cult sought respectability in the larger society, it progressively removed women from leadership.

In fact, women seem to have been attracted especially to religions of the eastern Mediterranean and Egypt. Literature of the period (written by men) often blames women for practicing a strange religion different from that of their husbands. Many women were attracted to the cult of Isis, the Egyptian goddess. The cult stressed the equality of women and men. One prayer to Isis said, "You have made the power of women equal to that of men" (Oxyrhynchus Papyrus 1380). However, priests in this cult outnumbered priestesses and may have outranked them as well.

*Women in the Christian congregations.* A number of the women among Jesus' followers seem to have had some measure of social and financial independence. They are depicted as traveling with his disciples and contributing to his ministry expenses (Lk 8:1-3). Despite their lack of presence among the apostles, women played crucial roles in Jesus' life and ministry from the beginning. Jesus' mother Mary is depicted as the first human to hear of Jesus' coming and is commended by God for her faith (Lk 1:28, 30, 42, 48). Jesus regularly taught women (Jn 4:10-26; 11:20-27) and received their acts of kindness and financial support (Lk 8:3; 10:38-42; 23:56). Joanna, the wife of Chuza, the tetrarch Herod Antipas's steward (Lk 8:3), may have been the follower of Jesus named Joanna (Lk 24:10).

Jesus apparently taught that both men and women can remain unmarried out of dedication to God (Mt 19:3-12). This teaching ran counter to most Jewish and pagan traditions, in which marriage and procreation were obligations and (for women) the principal means of achieving fulfillment. Many of his contemporaries would have considered some of Jesus' views on women radical, but he stopped short of calling for dramatic changes in existing gender relationships.

According to Acts, the women disciples joined with the men in prayer and fellowship following Jesus' resurrection (Act 1:14). They evidently helped to elect Matthias (Acts 1:15-26). They reportedly received the indwelling of the Holy Spirit and spiritual power along with male believers at Pentecost (Acts 2:1-11, 17-18). Women were often among the first believers (Acts 5:14; 12:12; 16:14-15; 17:4, 34).

Paul's teachings and descriptions of Christian women indicate a new realm of ministry activity that was denied to the typical Jewish woman, and they present a softened version of the larger society's patriarchal family structure. Many of the women mentioned in the Pauline books of the New Testament seem to have enjoyed some level of economic and social independence. The Pauline circle included women who headed households, ran businesses, had independent wealth and traveled with their own slaves and helpers. Paul led to Christ several "Greek women of high standing" in Macedonia (Acts 16:14; 17:4, 12). Some who were married converted to this new religious sect without the consent of their husbands (1 Cor 7:13). Paul allowed them to initiate divorce, though he advised against it. In addition, women took on some of the same roles as men within the congregation. Some exercised functions like public praying and prophesying (1 Cor 11:4-5). Christian women at Corinth in particular apparently experienced remarkable freedom (1 Cor 1:11; 11:5; 16:19; Acts 18:2, 18).[11]

A number of women served in positions of leadership in the Pauline congregations. Women like Lydia (Acts 16:14, 40), Priscilla (Acts 18:2-3; Rom 16:3-4; 1 Cor 16:19), Phoebe (Rom 16:1-2), the mother of Rufus (Rom 16:13) and Chloe (1 Cor 1:11) were fellow workers with Paul. They are described as evangelists and teachers, and women whose homes hosted churches. We do not know the level of leadership exerted by women in the Christian congregations. The absence of fixed, formal offices at the time makes it hard to determine the scope of their functions.

The difficulties in interpreting some of Paul's comments about women adds to this uncertainty as well. Paul considered women the spiritual equals of men in Christ (Gal 3:28) and told both Christian men and women to submit to one another (Eph 5:21). His writings permit Christian women to pray and prophesy in the church meetings (1 Cor 11:2-16; Acts 21:9). On the other hand, Paul warns women not to usurp leadership in public worship (1 Tim 2:12). Paul appears to order women to "keep silence in the churches" (1 Cor 7:34-36), but in light of his acceptance in 1 Corinthians 11 of women who pray and prophesy in public worship, this probably refers to the inappropriate interruption of speakers. The Greek author Plutarch, writing about fifty years later, warns the unlearned not to interrupt lectures (On Lectures 3). In some contexts, including the Jewish religious context, it was considered inappropriate for women to interrupt a speaker with questions.[12]

## Education in Greco-Roman Culture and the New Testament

Education in one form or another was important to all the urban social classes in the New Testament era. Formal education was an essential part of life in the upper classes, at least for males. Less formal education was important among the lower classes, especially in the cities. Jews and Christians, with their written Scriptures, may have placed greater emphasis on literacy than did their pagan counterparts in the lower classes.

*Jewish education.* Many Jews in the modern world place great importance on education. In fact, education has been a priority in Jewish society for over two millennia. The home was the setting for the earliest Jewish instruction, and festivals were probably among the primary occasions when children were taught their heritage—by instruction and observation. They learned in this manner the crucial stories that shaped the Jewish community.

Less information has survived about exactly what Jews thought a father should teach his son. The Jewish author Philo says that educating children is the task of the father, who must provide academic, philosophical, physical and moral instruction and discipline (*On the Special Laws* 2.29, 236). The father was also expected to teach his son a trade. At what age would such instruction begin? Philo says that Jewish parents teach their children about the one true God from "their earliest years" (*Embassy to Gaius* 115). Josephus says that the Jews begin to learn the law as soon as they are able to understand anything (*Against Apion* 2.18).[13]

In poorer households, especially ones in which the parents worked long hours, there would have been less time to instruct children and less money to pay for a teacher. Children in such households would have learned only the rudiments, if anything at all. There must have been differences between Jewish households in Judea and those in the Hellenistic and Roman cities. Clearly, poorer families would have found a pilgrimage to Jerusalem too expensive.

We have very little information about education in the synagogues of the Jewish dispersion. There is no indication that Hebrew was taught since the Scriptures had been translated into Greek. On the other hand, children and proselytes did clearly receive scriptural instruction; the writings of the New Testament, addressed to Christian groups in Greco-Roman cities that included Jews, clearly presuppose a knowledge of the Jewish Scriptures.

For the most part, the earliest Christians were Jews and Jewish sympathizers, who probably brought this attitude toward education into the church. This includes the study of the Greek Old Testament and later the Christian writings. Many Christian parents, perhaps most, would not have been able to afford a teacher and so themselves would have provided their childrens' education.

Education in the New Testament is mentioned in the context of the congregation, not the household. More in the Jewish tradition is *1 Clement*, written around A.D. 95. It makes instruction in the Christian faith one of the responsibilities of parents (*1 Clement* 21:6-8).

*Greek education.* Greek education stressed "discipline" *(gymnasia)* for the body and "music," a term that included literature, for the soul. The most distinctive institution of Greek cities in the New Testament era was the gymnasium. An indication that the Hellenized Jews in Jerusalem had gone to the extreme in adopting Greek customs was the building of a gymnasium (1 Macc 1:14; 2 Macc 4:9, 12). This public building, maintained by the city, usually consisted of an open courtyard surrounded by a colonnade. Along one side were rooms for bathing and meeting. Running and hurling the javelin would be practiced in the gymnasium. In some cities, parents had to pay the teachers. In others, the city paid the teachers out of special endowments.

Paul refers to this emphasis on discipline of the body when he writes, "Every athlete exercises self-control in all things" (1 Cor 9:25). First Timothy gives a nod to the Greek passion for training the body when it observes that, "bodily training is of some value" (1 Tim 4:8).

The Greek student went to school at daybreak. If his family was wealthy, he was accompanied by a slave attendant *(paidagogos)*. Schools held from 60 to 120 students. Students sat on benches with waxed writing tablets on their knees. The teacher sat on a chair on a platform. The slave attendants usually sat in the back of the classroom. Children who did not learn their lessons properly could be severely whipped by the teacher. In some times and places, girls received instruction in schools along with boys, at least for a few years, but most schools were for boys only.

Instruction relied heavily on copying and memorizing certain pieces of literature. This eventually became a standardized core curriculum, which included the epics of Homer, the tragedies of Euripides, the comedies of Menander and the speeches of Demosthenes. Other passages from more contemporary authors could also be included. This meant that the content of education was quite similar from Greek city to Greek city. Educated people had read many of the same passages. They had also copied them, recited them and memorized them. Through this they came to share a common culture. They all knew the more familiar myths, and they recognized standard quotations when they heard them in the theater, in speeches and in letters.

This emphasis on rote memory would continue to be the preferred approach to education for many centuries, not only in Europe but also in Asia. Only in the last 150 years has teaching focused less on memorization and more on analysis and evaluation. The other key principle here is the use of an approved curriculum, a classical literary canon, that could provide a common culture and set of values. Western education has taught from a generally accepted canon ever since. In recent years, however, the classical canon has come under attack and been abandoned or modified by many schools.

When a young man reached eighteen, he was freed from the care of the slave attendant. From eighteen to twenty, upper-class youth in Athens underwent a compulsory, state-sponsored course of military and athletic training. Because of the nature of Greek education, Paul is able to assume certain things about the educated among his readers. For example, he expects at least some readers and hearers to recognize his allusions to the writings of Menander (1 Cor 15:33), Epimenides (Tit 1:12) and Aratus (Acts 17:28).[14]

*Roman education.* The Roman upper classes were as well versed in Greek language and literature as they were in Latin. In fact, upper-class Romans often sent their sons to Greece for education. Quintilian (A.D. 40-118) was a great authority on Roman education and the tutor to Emperor Domitian's sons. He shows the Roman respect for Greek learning when he writes that Roman children should be taught Greek before they are taught Latin. But the Romans made some changes to the Greek approach to education. Mathematics, geometry and music were taught only insofar as they had practical applications. Rhetoric, not philosophy, was the subject that ranked supreme in higher studies. The Romans had little liking for the Greek custom of athletes performing in the nude. More to their taste were the horse races of the hippodrome and the gladiatorial games of the colosseum.

Roman classroom facilities usually were very simple. A school might be established in a rented *pergula,* or "shed," in front of a house separated from the public by a thin partition. Some schools met out of doors. Students would sit on benches, while the teacher sat on a chair. For writing they began with waxed tablets; as they progressed, they would use papyrus sheets or even the parchment of a worthless manuscript. For arithmetic the pupil would use an abacus with pebbles. Teachers were usually poorly paid; they were of low social status and had little prestige. The Romans copied the Greeks in using pedagogues for their children (often Greek slaves). Education in Rome was not compulsory, free or overseen by the state. However, the state might intercede and ban a teacher who diverged too far from the traditional curriculum (Suetonius *De grammaticis* 12).

Boys and girls in the upper classes may have been educated equally up to the time of the boy's coming of age (age fourteen), when he became a voting citizen and began preparing for a public career. Fathers in the upper classes then began taking their boys to public meetings, law courts and business meetings. The formal education of girls in the upper classes probably did not go beyond their middle teens since their arranged marriages would soon begin. A few young women were provided further education by their parents.

The traditional curriculum was based almost completely on Greek and Latin literature (usually poetry), upon which the teacher would comment. At the elementary level, children learned reading, writing and arithmetic by rote memory as they listened to dictation, memorized and recited back. Even at higher levels, this approach predominated since manuscripts were very expensive to produce.

Rome offered no formal technical education—no vocational schools, no applied fields. Its educational system would have seemed quite impractical to the lower classes even if they could have afforded it, but the lower classes could afford little or no formal education. Their children had to learn a trade by being apprenticed to an adult, usually one or both of their parents. Some slave children, especially those born into the household, were educated along with the master's children.

Children did not attend school during the summer, from July to October, or during a number of holidays in December and March. Every eighth day, the market day, was also a holiday. Children who wanted to feign illness on a school day might rub their eyes with olive oil or take cumin to make themselves appear sick.

Children attended elementary school, called *ludus* (literally "play"), from age seven to ten or eleven. The modern complaint that teachers are paid poorly is not a new one. Parents in that day demanded much from the teacher but paid him little, and at times only when ordered to do so by the courts. Children were regularly flogged by the schoolmaster as a means of discipline. Between the ages of twelve and fifteen or sixteen, the young Roman would attend a secondary or grammar school. This was called the *ludus litterarius*, and the teacher was called the *litteratus* or *grammaticus*. The main subjects were technical grammar and literature, including Homer, Virgil and Cicero.

Higher education consisted mainly of rhetoric or communications. For example, students learned the parts of a well-constructed speech. With the help of standard textbooks, they memorized model speeches and passages that could be inserted into any speech as needed. They learned lists of possible ways to say anything about any topic. The most characteristic form of instruction was the public lecture. Well-crafted public speaking was considered the sign of a polished and educated person. The lesser-educated public knew how to judge plays, recitations and public lectures. All the major philosophical schools practiced similar principles of rhetoric.

**The New Testament and Education**

The New Testament demonstrates respect for education, particularly in spiritual matters. One of the most important responsibilities of Christians expressed in the New Testament is the obligation to teach the beliefs of the Church (e.g., Mt 28:19-20; Acts 2; 1 Cor 4:17; Col 3:16; 1 Tim 4:11; 6:2; 2 Tim 2:2; Tit 2:1). The Jews in Thessalonica are commended for their nobility in studying the Scriptures to verify Paul's assertions (Acts 17:11). Although Jesus appears to have had little formal education, Paul was highly educated in both Jewish (Acts 22:3) and Greek schools.

Paul and other early Christian leaders seem to have been judged at times on their rhetorical abilities. Some of their audiences seem to have looked at them as though they were engaged in an oratorical competition. Paul's response was to label it foolishness, but to do so in a way that showed he too knew how to play the game (2 Cor 10-13). We must bear in mind that the average resident of a Greek city had a basic acquaintance with classic literature, reinforced by the plays and mimes and recitations of bards at festivals.

But we do not know the level of rhetorical training and sophistication among the Christian communities to which Paul's letters were addressed. They apparently had some knowledge of rhetoric, however, since Paul makes rhetorical and philosophical allusions throughout his letters. In fact, Paul's writings contain about thirty different rhetorical figures. F. W. Farrar suggests that Paul may have received some basic training at the famed center of learning in Tarsus.

On the other hand, the scarcity of classical allusions (except those in Acts 17:28; 1 Cor 15:33; Tit 1:2) and the limited sophistication of his use of Greek suggest that Paul did not receive advanced classical training in his home town. This may have been because he was sent to Jerusalem at age thirteen if not earlier (see Acts 22:3). Whatever his training, Paul refused to use the kind of elaborate and pompous rhetorical language commonly used by the orators of his day to gain applause (e.g., Tertullus, Acts 24:1-8).[15]

**For Further Reading**

Balsdon, J. P. V. D. *Roman Women: Their History and Habits.* Westport, Conn.: Greenwood, 1975.

Bradley, Keith R. *Discovering the Roman Family.* New York: Oxford University Press, 1991.

Cohen, Shaye J. D., ed. *The Jewish Family in Antiquity.* Atlanta: Scholars, 1993.

Foley, Helene P., ed. *Reflections of Women in Antiquity.* New York: Gordon and Breach Science, 1981.

Gardner, Jane F. *Women in Roman Law and Society.* London: Croom Helm, 1986.

Ilan, Tal. *Jewish Women in Greco-Roman Palestine.* Peabody, Mass.: Hendrickson, 1996.

Jeffers, James S. "Jewish and Christian Families in First Century Rome." In *Judaism and Christianity in First-Century Rome,* ed. Karl P. Donfried and Peter Richardson, pp. 128-50. Grand Rapids, Mich.: Eerdmans, 1998.

Osiek, Carolyn, and David L. Balch. *Families in the New Testament World: Households and House Churches.* Louisville, Ky.: Westminster John Knox, 1997.

Pomeroy, Sarah. *Goddesses, Whores, Wives, Slaves: Women in Classical Antiquity.* New York: Schocken, 1975.

Pomeroy, Sarah, ed. *Women's History and Ancient History.* Chapel Hill: University of North Carolina Press, 1991.

Rawson, Beryl, ed. *The Family in Ancient Rome: New Perspectives.* Ithaca, N.Y.: Cornell University Press, 1986.

Richlin, Amy. "Approaches to the Sources of Adultery at Rome." *Women's Studies* 8 (1981): 225-50.

Veyne, Paul, ed. *A History of Private Life.* Vol. 1, *From Pagan Rome to Byzantium,* ed. Philippe Aries and Georges Duby. Cambridge, Mass.: Harvard University Press, 1987.

# Chapter 13

## Provinces &
## Cities of the
## New Testament Era

*But all cities worship Artemis of Ephesus, and individuals hold her
in honor above all the gods. The reason, in my view,
is the renown of the Amazons, who traditionally dedicated the image,
also the extreme antiquity of this sanctuary. Three other points as well
have contributed to her renown, the size of the temple,
surpassing all buildings among men, the eminence of the city
of the Ephesians and the renown of the goddess who dwells there.*
PAUSANIAS 4.31.8

*I [Paul] am a Jew, born at Tarsus in Cilicia, but brought up in this city
at the feet of Gamaliel, educated according to the strict manner
of the law of our fathers, being zealous for God as you all are this day.*
ACTS 22:3

G ENERAL INFORMATION ABOUT THE CITIES AND REGIONS OF THE
Roman Empire only goes so far. At some point we must know
something about the unique nature of each of the provinces and of
major cities of the Empire in order to go beyond a superficial
understanding of what it was like to live during the New Testament era (see
map 7 for the locations of the provinces and major cities of the Empire).

The Romans organized their empire into provinces, ruled from capital cities
by Romans of senatorial or equestrian rank (see chapter six and appendix A for
more information). At times these provinces approximated the territory held
by the independent country they replaced. The following entries are organized
alphabetically by Roman province, then alphabetically by city. If you wish to
locate a city and do not know to which province it belonged, consult the list of
provinces and cities at the end of this chapter.

**Achaia Province**

The Roman province of Achaia, a senatorial province when Paul visited it, consisted of southern Greece, just south of the province of Macedonia. From A.D. 15 to 44, Achaia was under the jurisdiction of the governor of the province of Moesia. Under the emperor Claudius's direction, in 44 Achaia was made a separate senatorial province governed by a proconsul (e.g., Gallio in Acts 18:12), appointed by the Roman senate. This is probably when the judgment seat mentioned in Acts was set up in the center of Corinth (cf. Acts 18:12, 16-17). Achaia's capital, Corinth, was served by the seaport of Cenchrea. Athens, Sparta, Megara, Thebes and Delphi also were in Achaia (Acts 19:21; Rom 15:26; 2 Cor 1:1; 1 Thess 1:7-8). Paul talked about Christians in Achaia (principally those in Corinth, 2 Cor 9:2-4; 11:9-10).

Figure 13.1. The Parthenon temple on the Acropolis, Athens, Greece

*Athens.* Athens had been the capital of an empire that made possible the classical era of the fifth century B.C. Not long thereafter the empire was destroyed by Athen's rival, Sparta. Athens was conquered by the kingdom of Macedonia in the third century B.C. and again by the Romans in the second century B.C. In view of its prominent past, the Romans recognized Athens as a free and allied city and allowed it to continue its institutions and self-governance. In the New Testament era, Athens was known as an intellectual and cultural center. Following the A.D. 64 fire in Rome, the emperor Nero raided the city's art treasures to decorate his new palace. But Roman emperors also gave back to Athens; in the first two centuries A.D., they contributed heavily to various building projects in the city (see figures 13.1 and 13.2, the Parthenon and Mars Hill in Athens).

Paul stopped briefly in Athens on his second missionary journey. He spoke in the synagogue and in the city agora (Acts 17:17). Paul was brought by Epicurean and Stoic philosophers before the council of the Areopagus. There Paul spoke of "temples with hands," probably referring to the grand temples of the Acropolis, such as the Parthenon (Acts 17:24 NASB). Paul's reference to seeing in Athens an inscription "to the unknown god" is supported by the second-

Figure 13.2. The Areopagus (Mars Hill) as seen from the Acropolis, Athens, Greece

century A.D. Greek writer Pausanius, who reported seeing altars at Athens to "gods called unknown."

*Cenchrea.* This town was the seaport of Corinth. Paul took a ship from Cenchrea at the end of his first visit to Corinth (Acts 18:18). A Christian community existed here by the time Paul wrote his letter to the Romans, in which he refers to Phoebe, a *diakonos* ("minister") and *prostatis* (probably "patroness") of the church at Cenchrea (Rom 16:1-2).

*Corinth.* The classical-era city Corinth was established around 1000 B.C. After rising in prosperity through trade and local industry, Corinth sent colonists to establish the city of Syracuse on the island of Sicily. Corinthian pottery and bronzes were exported widely. In the second century B.C., Corinth helped lead the resistance to Roman expansion on the Greek mainland. Because of this, when the Romans conquered Greece they totally destroyed the city (146 B.C.). It remained uninhabited for many years, until the Roman dictator Julius Caesar refounded it as a Roman colony.

Caesar colonized the new Corinth largely with freedmen, according to the geographer Strabo. These freedmen became the new local aristocracy. One example is a well-known benefactor in Corinth, active in the time of Tiberius, named Gnaius Babbius Philinus. He probably was a freedman of Greek extraction. He was elevated to the office of aedile and later, "in return for his generous gifts," he was made priest of the local state cult. A second example comes from an inscription found near the theater. It tells us that an "Erastus" paved the square east of the theater's stage building "in return for his aedileship, at his own expense."[1] This may well be the same Erastus who was "city treasurer" and a member of the Christian community in Corinth (Rom 16:23). Other inscriptions record similar success stories among the freedmen and descendants of freedmen in Corinth.

By the time of Paul's visit (c. 50), Corinth once again had become a major city. In fact, it was the largest and most prosperous city in southern Greece, with over 100,000 persons. New Testament indications that Corinth had a sizable Jewish community are supported by Philo, who singles out Corinth and Argos as cities in southern Greece with Jews (Philo *Embassy to Gaius* 281-82). Much of Corinth's population was mobile (sailors, businessmen, government officials and the like).

Corinth's walls enclosed an area two and a half times that of Athens. Its twin harbors, Cenchrea on the east and Lecheum on the west, invited large crowds of travelers and merchants. It was the most important administrative and commercial center in Greece. Its government was typical of a Roman colony, with annually elected officials called *duovires* and aediles.

Not long before Paul's visit to Corinth, under Tiberius, Gaius and Claudius, extensive building projects gave Corinth more and more the appearance of a Roman city. This was most noticeable in the forum, where the lower and larger section became the forum of the people and the upper section became the administrative quarter.

Corinth's importance to trade increased as it oversaw a method of transporting smaller ships on land. This involved carting them over the narrowest point of the isthmus, about 3.5 miles wide, between the Corinthian and Saronic Gulfs, thus avoiding the sea journey around the Peloponnese. Agriculture in Corinth was poor, but its handcrafts were exported widely.

Aphrodite was worshiped with great devotion in Corinth. Strabo says that in her temple on the fifteen-hundred-foot high hill above the city, called the Acrocorinth, "there were more than a thousand temple slaves, prostitutes, whom both men and women had dedicated to the goddess" (*Geography* 8.6.20). These prostitutes were held in high regard by many in Corinth. They even had their own seats at the city theater. In contrast with Christian beliefs, few Greeks saw prostitution as immoral or shameful. Paul's attack on this attitude is addressed to Christians who apparently had, in harmony with the spirit of the locale, coined the phrase "all things are lawful for me" (1 Cor 6:12).

Members of many religious groups at Corinth, like the Christians there, met to eat a common religious meal (1 Cor 8-11). For example, followers of Dionysus met in subterranean dining rooms where six couches were cut into the rock around a stone table. Similar dining rooms at the sanctuary of Asklepios could accommodate eleven persons with small tables in front of them.[2]

The city lay about 1.5 miles south of the Corinthian gulf. As Paul approached the city, he would have to pass through a wall six miles in circumference that enclosed the city and Acrocorinth. He first would have seen the Acrocorinth towering above the city to its south, crowned with fortification walls. He would have passed through widely scattered suburbs to arrive in the forum in the north part of the city. The forum measured six hundred feet from east to west, three hundred feet from north to south. Latin inscriptions were everywhere. A temple on the western slope of the forum was dedicated to the family of the Julii, and another was dedicated to Livia, the wife of Augustus. At the eastern end, a Roman basilica accommodated the law courts, and at the southern edge, in front of a colonnaded row of shops almost five hundred feet long (the largest in the Empire) was the *bema*, the "tribunal" where the Roman governor conducted official public business and before which Paul would later appear (Acts 18:12-17). A row of shops along the side of the forum sold meat and wine (see figure 13.3). Paul probably has these shops in mind in his reference to a Corinth-

**Figure 13.3.** Remains of shops lining the northwest side of the Lower Forum in Corinth, Greece. They included the meat markets, where one could buy meat sacrificed to gods such as Apollo (cf. 1 Cor 8).

ian "meat market" (1 Cor 10:25).

Paul ministered in Corinth for eighteen months. Among the names of people connected with the church in Corinth, half are Latin (Crispus, Gaius, Fortunatus, Tertius, Quartus and Titius Justus) and half Greek (five to nine names, depending on whether one interprets some mentioned in Romans 16 as companions of Paul or residents of Corinth). Paul seems to acknowledge the preeminence of this church over the other congregations in Achaia (2 Cor 1:1).

There was money to be made by the Christians in Corinth. Some of the Corinthian Christians had an "abundance" of wealth by comparison with Christians in Macedonia and Jerusalem (2 Cor 8:14). Paul suggests that their manner of celebrating the Lord's Supper will "humiliate those who have nothing" (1 Cor 11:22).

The Isthmian games were held near Corinth every two years in honor of Poseidon, god of the sea. This event was one of the four major festivals of

Greece. If Paul was in Corinth in the spring of 49 or 51, he could have seen them. Athletic events included foot races, two-horse chariot races, the pentathlon (running, jumping, discus and javelin throwing, and wrestling) and the pankration (boxing and wrestling). The victor's crown in the time of Paul apparently was withered wild celery, a "perishable wreath" (1 Cor 9:25).

## Asia Province

The Roman senatorial province of Asia was created around 129 B.C., after King Attalus III of Pergamos willed his kingdom to Rome. Occupying the western third of Asia Minor, Asia included the lands that had been colonized by Greeks in the Bronze Age (for example, the city of Troy). It also included all or part of several former countries: Mysia, Lydia, Caria and Phrygia, plus several islands. The governor had his capital at Ephesus. Jews from Asia were present in Jerusalem for Pentecost (Acts 2:9).

Asia province contained the most enthusiastic supporters of the cult of the emperor. Whenever a new emperor took power, its cities competed for the honor of building a temple to him. Ephesus was permitted to erect two temples to Augustus, making it at the time the chief city for the emperor cult in the province. But Augustus's successor, Tiberius, would show more favor to the city of Smyrna to the north, and Gaius Caligula would favor Miletus to the south. Gaius's successor Claudius was emperor when Paul preached in Ephesus, and the Ephesians were still competing for imperial favor. The emperors Domitian and Hadrian would later name Ephesus the official warden of the emperor's temple in Asia.

On his second missionary journey, Paul was prevented from preaching in Asia (Acts 16:6), but on the third trip he ministered extensively in this province (Acts 19:10). Paul traveled through or by the region of Mysia (Acts 16:7-8). All of the cities in Asia visited by Paul were centers of trade and participated in the general prosperity of the province in the first century A.D. Revelation 1:11 lists the "seven churches that are in Asia" (Rev 1:4) as Ephesus, Smyrna, Pergamum, Thyatira, Sardis, Philadelphia and Laodicea. Included among the addressees of 1 Peter 1:1 are believers in Asia.

Most of the cities of the province had large Jewish communities. Jews in Asia seem to have been more successful than elsewhere in maintaining good relations with the local authorities. In the two places where Jews were best integrated with the larger community, Sardis and Apameia, no Pauline mission can be detected even though Paul or his associates had ministered in nearby cities. This kind of strong relationship between the Jewish community and the city at large would have made it difficult for Christian missions, at least among the

Jews, to proceed unhindered, because Paul's Jewish opponents could have more easily turned the city against Paul.

*Colossae.* Colossae was twelve miles southeast of Laodicea in the south of the province of Asia. The great trade route from Ephesus, through the Cilician Gates to Tarsus and Syria, went through Colossae and helped to make it a prosperous city long before the New Testament era. By Paul's day, the city had lost its former importance as a great Phyrgian city. Strabo called it a "small town." The elder Pliny, writing in the early first century A.D., places it in the second rank of towns in Phrygia, well below Hierapolis, Laodicea and Apameia in status.[3]

Despite the relatively early presence of a Christian community here, John did not include Colossae among the seven churches of Asia to whom he writes in Revelation 1—3. The church here may have been founded by Epaphras (Col 1:2; 4:12). Paul himself had not visited the Colossians before writing to them (Col 2:1). The church seems to have met in the home of Philemon (Philem 2). The group opposed to Paul's teachings in this area advocated "angel worship." This may reflect external influence (scholars think Persian, Gnostic or Essene) or local influence from one of the area's native cults.

*Cos.* An island off the coast of Asia Minor near Caria, Cos was famous for its fertile land and its banking. It lay on the main shipping route between Greece and the East. Herod the Great of Judea sent money every year to Cos in order to maintain his honorary position there (Josephus *Jewish War* 1.424). An inscription discovered in Cos commemorates a monument erected in honor of "Herod the Tetrarch, son of Herod the Great." This is a reference to Herod Antipas, who probably stopped at Cos some time during A.D. 6-10, when he made a donation to the temple of Apollo on the nearby island of Delos. Paul stopped briefly at Cos on his third missionary journey (Acts 21:1).

*Ephesus.* Ephesus was located at the mouth of the Cayster River on the west coast of Asia Minor. The city was founded by Greek colonists in 1044 B.C. It became a part of the province of Asia in 133 B.C. Its strategic importance for land and sea trade helped make this city the most important commercial center in Asia province. During the first century B.C., Ephesus was politically and economically weak, like many cities in Asia Minor. According to the ancient author Appian, this was the reuslt of severe extortions by Roman governors and soldiers (*Roman History* 12.7.48). Appian blames Marc Antony in particular for demanding ten times the normal tax revenue during the civil wars that followed the assassination of Julius Caesar (*Civil Wars* 5.5). When Augustus took control, peace and prosperity came to Ephesus and Asia Minor.

Ephesus was a free city, meaning that it had home rule, with a Greek constitution, instead of rule by Roman officials. It owned a very large territory extending inland from the coast.

Ephesus had a population of over 400,000 in the New Testament era. The amphitheater in which Paul's friends appeared before the people and the town clerk seated about 25,000 people (Acts 19:31; see figure 7.1). It is located on the western slope of Mount Pion and is used for occasional concerts today. The great agora (central market and business district) of Ephesus measured 360 feet

**Figure 13.4. The great library in Ephesus, Asia Minor. This was one of the most important libraries in the Hellenistic East, along with those at Alexandria, Pergamum and Tarsus.**

by 360 feet. At one end of it was the great library of Ephesus (see figure 13.4).

The Temple of Artemis outside Ephesus, the largest and most lavishly decorated temple in the Hellenistic age, was considered one of the seven wonders of the ancient world. Construction began in 350 B.C. on the temple, an edifice that Paul would have seen. It measured 340 feet long by 100 feet wide, and its hundred columns supported a roof fifty-five feet high. The Artemis worshiped at Ephesus was actually a goddess of fertility from the region of Anatolia that over time had become identified with the Greek goddess Artemis. The temple of Artemis was also a bank where people all over the Roman world deposited money. The temple also lent money and received legacies and private donations. It owned revenue-producing property, including sacred fish and herds of deer (Dio Chrysostom 31.54). It was an asylum for debtors and for the helpless (Achilles Tatius 7.13). Missionaries carried the cult of the goddess throughout the world. In Acts it is asserted that it is she "whom all Asia and the world worship" (Acts 19:27). Strabo tells how the goddess commanded a woman to take her statue along on a colonizing expedition. As a result, many cities used reproductions of her Ephesian statue in worship.

The church father Irenaeus and the church historian Eusebius claim that the apostle John spent his last five years in Ephesus and during this time wrote the five books of the New Testament ascribed to him. The churches singled out for comment in John's book of the Revelation are within easy communication range of Ephesus.

Paul passed through Ephesus several times (Acts 18:19; 19:1). He spent nearly three years here on his third missionary journey (Acts 19). No doubt he stayed so long, at least in part, because of Ephesus's position as a center of commerce and government from which the gospel could more readily spread. According to 1 and 2 Timothy, Paul's associate Timothy was later stationed in  Ephesus to give assistance to the local church leaders. The primary story in Acts 19 concerns the riot that breaks out when the makers of silver statues of Artemis—devotional aids and tourist trinkets—object to Paul's missionary activity. Archaeologists have located several silversmith shops in Ephesus. The statue was a stiff, upright figure resembling the trunk of a tree or a mummy, covered with sculptured animals and plants, including twenty-four or more rounded objects on the goddess's chest. Scholars traditionally believed that these were multiple breasts symbolizing the fertility of this goddess, but they may in fact have been ostrich eggs, which also signify fertility and are found today in many Greek village churches. Some scholars think they were fruit, also signifying fertility.[4] Hellenistic writing about Artemis of Ephesus typically concentrates on her role as a savior (Strabo *Geography* 14.1.22). Among the attributes given her was her ability to rule over cosmic powers, symbolized by the zodiacal signs on her statues (cf. Eph 1:21; 3:10; 4:8; Col 1:16; 2:8, 15, 20).

Paul came into conflict not only with exorcists and with silversmiths making silver statues of Artemis, but also with persons in the synagogue (Acts 17:17; 19:8-9, 33-34). Josephus preserves several edicts by Roman officials guaranteeing the rights of the Jews of Ephesus, including exempting from military service those Jews who were Roman citizens (and so would normally be expected to serve). On the other hand, friction between Jew and Gentile is implied in a 14 B.C. letter sent by Herod Agrippa to the magistrates and people of Ephesus. In it, he says that the Jews of Asia should be able to collect money to send to the temple in Jerusalem and that they should not have to appear in court on the sabbath (Josephus *Jewish Antiquities* 16.167-68; cf. 14.262-64).

Paul knew of several Christian households in Ephesus. He taught in the "hall of Tyrannus" (Acts 19:9). Second Timothy 1:16-18 refers to the household of an Onesiphorus, who refreshed Paul in Rome despite Paul's imprisonment (see also *Acts of Paul* 7). We learn from Ignatius that a bishop of Ephesus was named Onesimus, who was perhaps the slave referred to in the letter to Philemon.[5]

*Laodicea.* Laodicea was twelve miles northwest of Colossae in the southern part of the province of Asia. It was founded in the mid-third century B.C. by the current ruler of the Seleucid Empire, Antiochus II, and named for his sister and wife, Laodice. The city's great wealth was based on its commerce and on a locally produced, world-famous black wool. In fact, Laodicea dominated the wool-making industry of the region. When an earthquake leveled the city in A.D. 60, its citizens refused to accept an imperial subsidy and rebuilt the city on their own. Inscriptions show that associations of traders and craftsmen were numerous and important here. One of these was called "The Most August Guild of the Wool Washers."

Colossians refers to a church in Laodicea. Paul did not found this church, since he apparently had not met its members (Col 2:1). Epaphras's great concern for the church suggests that he may have helped found it (Col 4:13). Paul asks the Colossians to greet the believers in Laodicea and to exchange letters from him with them. In greeting the Laodicean church, Paul singles out Nympha, the patroness of a house church there (Col 4:15-16). Apparently the letter to the Laodiceans is lost, although some think that Ephesians was originally sent to Laodicea.

The book of the Revelation chastises the Laodiceans for their trust in riches and counsels them to use a spiritual eyesalve to improve their sight (Rev 3:17-18). This is probably intended as symbolic of "Phrygian powder," a widely used eye medicine that may have originated in Laodicea. Laodicea obtained its water from hot springs some distance away. Once the water had traveled through sealed stone conduits, it was neither hot enough for the baths nor cool enough for drinking. Perhaps Revelation's mention of lukewarm water is a reference to this water system (Rev 3:16). It would appear that by the time of the writing of the Revelation, around 95, the congregation at Laodicea had rejected mainstream Christianity (Rev 3:14-22).

*Mysia.* Mysia was a district in the northwest part of the province of Asia, which became part of the province in 133 B.C. It included the cities of Troas, Assos and Pergamum. Paul passed by (or through) this district on his way to Troas (Acts 16:7-8).

*Patmos.* Patmos is an island in the Aegean Sea, southwest of the island of Samos and west of Ephesus. It is eight miles long and five miles wide. According to the Revelation, John the Apostle received the visions recorded in this book while banished to this island (Rev 1:9). Later Christian sources say that John was exiled here by the emperor Domitian.

*Pergamum.* Pergamum lay on a high hill commanding a fertile valley. It lay eighteen miles east of the Aegean Sea and on a great north-south trade route. Laid out in hillside terraces, Pergamum was considered one of the most beautiful Greek cities. Near the lower Roman city, built in the first century A.D., was a renowned health resort dedicated to the god Asklepios and a well-known school of sculpture. Archaeologists have excavated here two agoras, several temples, the gymnasium, the world-famous library, palaces and a theater. Pergamum was the capital of a Hellenistic kingdom until the monarch willed his country to the Romans in 133 B.C. Some scholars have identified the huge altar of Zeus there with "Satan's throne" mentioned in Revelation 2:13.

In his letter to the church at Pergamum, John condemned the doctrine of Balaam, which apparently had to do with Christians marrying pagans, and the doctrine of the Nicolaitans, the belief that Christians could take part in idolatrous feasts since the heathen gods did not exist.

*Philadelphia.* This city, twenty-six miles southeast of Sardis in the Roman province of Asia, lay on the Roman imperial military route from Rome, via Troas and through Phrygia. The city was refounded around 150 B.C. by the king of Pergamum and became part of the Roman Empire in 133 B.C. An earthquake in A.D. 17 destroyed the city, but the emperor Tiberius donated a large sum to rebuild it. The city's wealth was based on its location on an important trade route and on its local wine industry. The city controlled a large rural area. Revelation's address to the church implies that a significant number of Jews lived there and had come into conflict with the small Christian community (Rev 3:7-13).

*Sardis.* Sardis commanded the great trade and military road from the Aegean islands to the interior of the Roman provinces of Asia and Galatia. The city came under Roman rule in 133 B.C. when it was incorporated into the Roman province of Asia. Destroyed in A.D. 17 by the same earthquake that destroyed Philadelphia, it also was rebuilt by the emperor Tiberius. Among the great buildings located here in the New Testament era was the temple of Artemis, with its seventy-eight columns fifty-eight feet high. Archaeologists have discovered a Jewish synagogue here dating to the third century A.D. Its size and opulence suggest a large and prosperous Jewish community at that time. Revelation addresses the church of Sardis (Rev 3:1-6).

*Smyrna.* Located on the west coast of Asia Minor in the Roman province of Asia, Smyrna lay at the base of Mount Pagus, which served as its acropolis or fortress. It was one of the larger cities of the Empire, with 200,000 residents. Its famed "Street of Gold" curved around the lower slopes of the hill and was lined with impressive buildings. At one end of the street stood a temple of Zeus, and at the other end stood a temple to the mother goddess Cybele Sipylene, the patron deity of the city. The city boasted a public library. Smyrna contested with Ephesus for recognition as the first city of Asia. In Revelation, John commends the Christians in the city (Rev 2:8-11) for enduring much suffering.

*Thyatira.* Located fifty-two miles northeast of Smyrna in the Roman province of Asia, Thyatira was a large commercial center on the river leading to Smyrna. It reached the height of its prosperity around A.D. 100. We find more evidence of trade guilds here than in any other city of Asia. Lydia, a seller of purple from Thyatira, probably represented her guild in Philippi (Acts 16:14). Presumably the purple cloth she sold was made in the region of Thyatira, which produced the well-known red dye. Inscriptions show intense activity on the part of guilds engaged in activities related to Lydia's trade, such as dyers, wool makers and linen weavers. Revelation addresses the Christians in the city (Rev 2:18-29).

*Troas.* Troas was a port city ten miles south of the strategic Hellespont, on the west coast of the Roman province of Asia. It was founded in the fourth century B.C. by the Hellenistic monarch Antigonus. Julius Caesar reportedly considered making it his imperial capital (Suetonius *Julius Caesar* 79.3). The city wall was six miles in circumference. It had a theater and received water from an elevated aqueduct. Recognizing the importance of this city, Augustus made it a Roman colony.

Troas was a pivotal point in Paul's travels. At Troas he turned to Macedonia after trying to minister to the provinces of Asia and Bithynia (Acts 16:6-10). In addition, Luke appears to have joined the missionary team in Troas. Several years later, after his long stay in Ephesus, Paul preached briefly in Troas (2 Cor

2:12-13). After a visit to Greece he returned to Troas and stayed with the Christians there for a week. The incident with Eutychus also occurs in Troas (Acts 20:9-12). Paul may have founded the Christian community here, which was still strong in the early second century when the Christian bishop Ignatius passed through the city on his way to martyrdom in Rome (Ignatius *Letter to the Philadelphians* 11:2).

### Cappadocia Province

This inland Roman province had at different times been part of the Babylonian, Hittite and Persian empires. It became a Roman province in A.D. 17. Visitors from Cappadocia were present in Jerusalem at Pentecost (Acts 2:9), and 1 Peter is addressed to it (1 Pet 1:1). The city of Caesarea here was an early center of Christianity, but we know little more about it.

### Cilicia Province

Located in southeastern Asia Minor, along the Mediterranean Sea, the Roman province of Cilicia was organized in 102 B.C. The New Testament refers to it a number of times (Acts 21:39; 22:3; 23:34; 27:5). Western Cilicia was rugged and mountainous, while the eastern part, by far the most populous part, contained fertile plains. Trade routes from the Euphrates and Syria met about fifty miles east of the city of Tarsus and then turned west across Asia Minor to Ephesus. Tarsus was the chief city of the province and Paul's birthplace. Paul most likely took this route to Derbe on his second missionary journey (Acts 15:41; 16:1).

During the time of Jesus and Paul, eastern Cilicia (including Tarsus) was under the administration of the governor of Syria. In A.D. 60 all of Cilicia was made an independent province with its own legate. This is why Luke and Paul speak of Syria and Cilicia together (Gal 1:21; Acts 15:23, 41).

Jews had settled in Tarsus and other Cilician cities after the conquests of Alexander the Great. Jews from Cilicia belonged to the so-called Synagogue of the Freedmen in Jerusalem (Acts 6:9).

*Tarsus.* Tarsus lay just twenty miles south of the Cilician Gates, the name given to the narrow gorge through which passed the only overland trade route between Syria and Asia Minor. This helped make Tarsus a prosperous city since virtually all overland trade between East and West passed through it. Tarsus lay astride the Cyndnus River, ten miles from the Mediterranean Sea. Ships usually docked at a harbor up the Cydnus, five or six miles south of the city.

With a continuous history of some six thousand years, Tarsus is one of the oldest cities in the world. It was probably the capital of ancient Cilicia in the Hittite era. Greek merchants established a colony here in the seventh century

B.C. to be near the silver and iron mines of the local mountains.

A free city under the Seleucids, Tarsus was taken by the Roman general Pompey in 64 B.C. Marc Antony made Tarsus a free city in 41 B.C. and exempted it from taxes. After A.D. 60 Tarsus was the capital of the independent province of Cilicia. It boasted a respected university and ranked with Athens and Alexandria as an intellectual center. It was the home of several well-known scholars, including Athenodorus the Stoic, two tutors to Roman emperors, and Antipater, the head of a school in Athens. Paul was born in Tarsus and probably received a Hellenized education here before being sent to Judea for a formal Jewish education (Acts 9:11).

## Crete Province

The fourth largest island in the Mediterranean, Crete played a major part in the development and distribution of culture from the fourth to the first millennia B.C. After conquering the island in 67 B.C., Rome made it a separate Roman province.

The ship carrying Paul to Rome about A.D. 60 took refuge temporarily in a small bay on the southern side of Crete (Acts 27:8). According to Titus 1:5, Paul sent Titus to Crete to organize the church there. Paul quotes from a poem by a Cretan named Epimenides (c. 600 B.C.) in both Acts 17:28 ("For we are indeed his offspring") and Titus 1:12 ("Cretans are always liars, evil beasts, lazy gluttons").

*Clauda.* Clauda is a small island twenty-three miles southwest of Crete. On his journey to Rome, Paul's ship used Clauda to shelter it from a violent wind when it was unable to reach the Cretan port of Phoenix (Acts 27:16).

*Lasea.* Little is known about the town of Lasea, located in southern Crete near the harbor of Fair Havens (Acts 27:8-12). Paul and his guard took shelter at Fair Havens on their way to Rome. The ship's owner rejected Paul's advice to remain there for the winter, wishing to make for the safer harbor of Phoenix. Consequently, the ship was blown off course by a violent storm.

## Cyprus Province

Cyprus is the third largest island in the Mediterranean, about equidistant from Asia Minor and Syria. It had been at different times settled by Phoenicians and Greeks. It was controlled at one time by the Persians, and later by the Ptolemies. The Romans took the island in 58 B.C. Augustus made it a senatorial province in 22 B.C. Jewish Christians came to Cyprus to escape persecution (Acts 11:19-20). Paul and Barnabas landed at Salamis on the eastern coast on the first journey. According to Acts 13, they crossed the island to the west, preaching as they went. From Paphos, Paul and his companions set sail for the mainland at Perga (Acts 13:13). Later, Barnabas returned to minister on Cyprus with John Mark (Acts 15:39).

*Paphos.* On the west end of the island of Cyprus lay Paphos, the capital of Cyprus under the Romans. Paphos was a well-known center of worship of the goddess Aphrodite. After traversing the island from Salamis to Paphos, Paul and Barnabas preached to the Roman proconsul (governor), Sergius Paulus. As they explained the gospel to him, a magician named Elymas opposed them. This Elymas is described as a Jewish false prophet, who may have acted as an advisor to the proconsul. The proconsul is said to have believed in Christ when he saw Elymas struck by Paul with temporary blindness (Acts 13:6-13).

*Salamis.* Situated at the east end of Cyprus, Salamis was the island's greatest port and commercial center when Paul and Barnabas landed here on their first missionary journey (Acts 13:5). The city center, a great limestone forum (750 by 180 feet), was surrounded by shops. To the south of it stood a temple to the god Zeus.

**Egypt Province**

Egypt became an imperial Roman province in 31 B.C., after Octavian's defeat of the Roman general Marc Antony and the last Ptolemaic monarch of Egypt, Cleopatra VII. Egypt's wealth and reputation as a regional power caused Octavian to make it one of the provinces under his direct control. Although Rome stationed legions in Egypt, the province was administered by a prefect of equestrian status rather than a legate. Egypt was too rich, and of too much strategic importance, for Augustus to risk letting a senator control it. Its history of supporting claimants to power in Rome, first Pompey and then Mark Antony, made Augustus understandably nervous about entrusting it to a senator. In fact, emperors usually did not leave even a prefect in charge of Egypt for too long. Egypt's importance to the Empire grew over time, in large part because of the city of Rome's increasing dependence on its grain.

*Alexandria.* Alexandria was founded by Alexander the Great in 332 B.C. following his conquest of Egypt. Located on the Mediterranean Sea near the western branch of the Nile, it became one of the largest commercial centers of the Greco-Roman world. The famed library at Alexandria was the largest in the Western world, reputedly housing 700,000 volumes. The library complex also included lecture halls, laboratories, parks and zoos. Much of the library was destroyed during Julius Caesar's siege of Alexandria. Alexandria was also known for its magnificent temple to the god Serapis and its royal tombs and for an ancient palace. By the first century A.D., Alexandria was the second largest city of the Roman Empire, with a population of over 600,000.

Alexandria was very cosmopolitan. Organized as a Greek city, it nevertheless included large numbers of native Egyptians as well as Jews, Romans and immigrants from all over the world. This meant that Alexandria played host to a multitude of religions as well. Some of them exerted influence on one another. Popular Egyptian deities in the New Testament era included the goddess Isis and the god Serapis, a deity combining the nature of the Egyptian god Osiris with the outward appearance of a Greek father-god.

The city was one of the most important ports in the world. The Pharos lighthouse at its harbor, nearly 450 feet high, was one of the seven wonders of the ancient world. From Alexandria, massive cargo ships bore to Rome Egyptian grain, as well as linen and luxury goods. In exchange, they brought the city all the products of the world. Two of the grain ships used to transport Paul to Rome came from Alexandria (Acts 27:6; 28:11).

Alexandria contained the largest Jewish population of any city in the Empire outside of Palestine, perhaps 150,000. According to Philo, two of the city's five formal divisions were called Jewish (*Against Flaccus* 55). Alexandrian Jews traditionally had equal rights with the Greeks, but tensions between the two groups appear to have been always just below the surface. Serious violence broke out in A.D. 38, 55 and 115.

The Gospel of Matthew says that Mary and Joseph took Jesus to Egypt to hide from Herod (Mt 2:13-14). It is highly likely that they stayed in Alexandria. They may even have had relatives or friends there. Because of the large Jewish population there, it seems likely that Jews traveled regularly between Alexandria and Palestine. This may explain how Jewish former slaves, who had returned from Alexandria to Jerusalem, could set up their own synagogue in Judea (Acts 6:9). Since the establishment of a synagogue generally required ten men (who would normally have been heads of families), this implies a goodly number of Alexandrian expatriates in one area. In addition, Jews from Egypt were present at Pentecost (Acts 2:10).

Alexandria was, along with Jerusalem, Antioch and Rome, one of the four great centers of Christianity from the third century on. But we do not know how Christianity came to Alexandria. Apollos, a disciple who worked with Paul at Corinth, was from Alexandria (Acts 18:24). He was eloquent and well versed in the Scriptures. There is no good historical support for the tradition that John Mark founded the church in Alexandria.

## Galatia Province

Galatia, in eastern Asia Minor, was a client kingdom of Rome from 166 B.C. to 25 B.C., when the emperor Caesar Augustus made it a Roman province. In doing so, Augustus added to the old kingdom some territory from a number of the surrounding countries. The Romans turned the cities of Lystra and Pisidian Antioch into Roman colonies.

Landowners in this province included descendants of the old native aristocracies and Roman citizens of Italian origin who had come as colonists. They also included wealthy Romans of the equestrian and senatorial orders, like the family of the Sergius Paulus, who Paul encountered as governor of Cyprus (Acts 13:7). His family is known to have had extensive landholdings in the region of Pisidia. Sergius Paulus might even have provided Paul with introductions to the aristocracy in the city of Pisidian Antioch.

Paul visited Lystra and Pisidian Antioch as well as the Roman colonies of Iconium and Derbe on his first missionary journey (Acts 13—14). He returned to these cities at the beginning of his third missionary journey (Acts 18:22-23). The letter to the Galatians was probably written to these cities, though some scholars think it was written to churches in the old former kingdom to the north, which Paul may have visited on his second journey (Gal 1:2; Acts 16:6).[6] First Peter is also addressed in part to believers in Galatia (1 Pet 1:1).

*Antioch of Pisidia.* Founded around 301 B.C. by Seleucus I Nicator, the founder of the Seleucid Empire, this was one of sixteen cities named after Seleucus's father, Antiochus. It is called Pisidian Antioch to distinguish it from the other Antiochs (such as Antioch of Syria). Recognizing its importance as a border fortress, with good views to the north, south and west, in 25 B.C. the Romans made it a Roman colony. Roman veterans were settled here, and the city became the military center of the surrounding area. Its leading citizens were descendants of Roman soldiers.

The eight districts of the city all bore Latin names. The main square was named Platea Augusta, ringed by the temple to Augustus and colonnade walls engraved with a record of Augustus's accomplishments. The gravestones of the local elite marked the resting places of Roman equestrians and a few senators. The city had a great number of priesthoods, both official and local. Roman roads connected it with the other Roman colonies, such as Lystra, founded in the area.[7]

On his first missionary journey, Paul planted a church in Pisidian Antioch (Acts 13:13-52). Its witness reportedly was heard throughout the region. Only Ephesus and Thessalonica saw comparable results. Pisidian Antioch hosted a large Jewish population from 200 B.C. on. Acts 13:43-52 places emphasis on the Jews and converts to Judaism in Antioch. Acts says that some Jews were able to turn the people against Paul and Barnabas and had them driven out of town (Acts 13:50). Second Timothy also refers to persecutions against Paul in Pisidian Antioch (2 Tim 3:11).

*Derbe.* The Roman colony named Derbe was located about sixty miles southeast of Lystra in southern Galatia. To show devotion to Rome and the emperor Claudius, the city prefixed his name to its own for a few years, making it Claudioderbe. Derbe lay on the border between the Empire and the kingdom of Commagene. It was governed from A.D. 41 to 72 by an ally of Rome. On his first missionary journey, Paul came to Derbe after having been stoned at Lystra. According to Acts 14:6, 20, he made many disciples here. Paul passed through Derbe on his way to Lystra, on his second journey (Acts 16:1), and may have visited it on his third journey (Acts 18:22-23). Gaius, one of Paul's disciples and companions, was from Derbe (Acts 20:4).

*Iconium.* An important city of Phrygia in the Hellenistic era, Iconium was made a part of the province of Galatia in 25 B.C. It stood on a plateau 3,400 feet above sea level. The emperor Claudius allowed the city to call itself Claudiconium, prefixing his name to that of the city. Paul brought the gospel here on his first missionary journey (Acts 13:51; 14:1-6, 21), returned here on his second journey (Acts 16:2), and may have returned again on his third journey (Acts 18:23). Iconium is probably one of the cities Paul had in mind when he wrote Galatians. The emperor Hadrian made it a Roman colony in the second century A.D. Second Timothy refers to persecutions suffered by Paul in Iconium (2 Tim 3:11).

*Lycaonia.* Lycaonia was a region in southern Asia Minor and part of the province of Galatia in the first century A.D. Acts 14:5-6 calls Lystra and Derbe "cities of Lycaonia." The local Lycaonian language was still in common use among the people of this region, even in the city (Acts 14:11). Apparently few Jews lived in this region since Acts makes no mention of a synagogue or local Jews (Acts 14:6-20).

*Lystra.* A city in southern Galatia about eighteen miles southwest of Iconium, Lystra was founded as a Roman colony by Augustus around 25 B.C. in order to control the mountain tribes on Galatia's southern frontier. It was built in a remote valley on a small hill. Clearly it did not function as a center of trade since it lies some distance from the great east-west trade route. Although a minor colony, Lystra had strategic significance under the early emperors. Paul established a church here on his first missionary journey and visited it on his second and third journeys (Acts 14:6-20; 16:1-5; 18:23). The people of Lystra hailed him and Barnabas as Hermes and Zeus. Later, Paul was stoned and left for dead outside the city. Paul apparently met Timothy at either Lystra or Derbe. Second Timothy refers to persecutions suffered by Paul in Lystra (2 Tim 3:11).

## Italy

The peninsula of Italy is 700 miles long and 125 miles wide. The Alps mountain range stretches along the entire length of the peninsula. Italy's primary source of wealth in ancient times was agriculture. Copper and iron mines were also important. Italy is mentioned several times in the New Testament: as Paul's final destination (Acts 27:1, 6), as the former home of Priscilla and Aquila (Acts 18:2) and as the home of Christians who send greetings with the letter to the Hebrews (Heb 13:24).

*Puteoli.* This was the harbor on the Bay of Naples where Paul landed on his journey to Rome. It was one of the best harbors on the Italian coast, having been founded centuries earlier by Greek colonists. Puteoli was at this time still the principal port of Rome, even though the emperor Claudius had begun to develop the much closer port of Ostia in the previous decade. Many Jews lived in Puteoli. A Jewish community existed here for nearly a century before Paul arrived (Josephus *Jewish War* 2.104; *Jewish Antiquities* 17.328). Christianity also had been established here before Paul landed (Acts 28:13-14). After seven days, Paul and the others followed the Appian Way 150 miles north to the city of Rome.

*Rome.* When Paul came to Rome around A.D. 60, it was a city of about one million persons that dominated an empire of about fifty million people. The city was originally built on seven small hills near the Tiber River. The Roman Forum (300 by 150 feet) was the largest of several forums at the center of the city's political, legal, commercial and religious life. The forum was lined with massive marble temples to Saturn, Vesta, the divine Julius, and Castor and Pollux. Other buildings included the residence of the Vestal Virgins, the priestesses of the Roman state religion, and the senate house. Paul's trial may have been held in the Basilica Julia, on the south side of the forum.

Just to the south of the forum, on the Palatine Hill, sat the palaces of the emperors. The great Temple of Jupiter was built on the Capitoline Hill to the west. On the north side of the Palatine was the colossal racetrack, the Circus Maximus. About fifteen years after Paul's death, the Flavian Amphitheater (nicknamed the "Colosseum" after the nearby statue of Nero called the "Colossus") was built just west of the Roman Forum. The Jewish population of Rome ranked behind only that of Alexandria among the cities of the Roman Empire outside of Palestine. Acts suggests that Paul, after speaking with Jewish leaders in Rome, focused his missionary efforts on the Gentiles.

**Judea Kingdom and Province**
Judea became part of the province of Syria in 63 B.C. It was made part of Herod's client kingdom in 40 B.C. but became a separate Roman province in A.D. 6. It remained a Roman province except during A.D. 41-44 when it was added to the

kingdom of Agrippa I. The Roman procurator governed from Caesarea and was under the authority of the governor of Syria.

*Caesarea Sebaste.* Located on the Mediterranean coast of Judea, about sixty-five miles northwest of Jerusalem, this Caesarea was the capital of the Roman Judea from A.D. 6 on. This meant a loss of civil power for the high priests in Jerusalem. Herod the Great rebuilt the city of Sebaste between 21 and 9 B.C. In an attempt to impress his Roman overlord, he renamed it for Caesar Augustus. Herod provided land here to settle six thousand colonists, including soldiers. He created a massive harbor by using the recent invention of concrete that sets underwater (hydraulic concrete) to make an artificial, circular breakwater. Called Caesarea Maritima, this became the most important harbor in the region.

The city contained magnificent palaces and lavish public buildings, all in the Hellenistic style. According to an inscription, the city theater was dedicated to the emperor Tiberius. The inscription also names Pontius Pilate as military procurator of Judea. Caesarea was largely Gentile in population, but it hosted a large and vocal Jewish minority. The Gentile and Jewish communities clashed continually. Josephus reports that all of the city's twenty thousand Jewish inhabitants were massacred at the beginning of the Jewish rebellion in A.D. 66 (*Jewish War* 2.457; 7.362).

Caesarea is mentioned a number of times in the New Testament. According to Acts, King Herod Agrippa I was struck dead by God in Caesarea (Acts 12:19-53). Philip the Evangelist (one of the first deacons, Acts 6:5) lived here with his four prophesying daughters (Acts 21:8-9). Acts reports that Peter was called in a vision to preach to a centurion in Caesarea. This centurion, named Cornelius, was a partial convert to Judaism. Peter led him to faith in Christ (Acts 10:1-2, 24; 11:11-12). Paul greeted the church at Caesarea, while on his way to Jerusalem, at the end of his second missionary journey (Acts 18:22). Later, he was imprisoned for two years under Felix and Festus in Caesarea before appealing to Caesar and being sent to Rome (Acts 23:23; 26:32). Paul also appeared in trials before Festus and Herod Agrippa II in Caesarea (Acts 26). In later centuries, the church fathers Origen and Eusebius lived and ministered here.

*Jerusalem.* Located thirty-three miles east of the Mediterranean Sea and fourteen miles west of the Dead Sea, Jerusalem was built on a hilltop ringed by higher hills. It was the capital of the united kingdom of Israel under Kings David and Solomon. After Solomon, it was the capital of the kingdom of Judah until its capture by the Babylonians in 597 B.C. After 539 B.C. Jews were allowed to rebuild Jerusalem. A new Jewish temple was completed in 516 B.C. In 168 B.C.

the Seleucid kingdom of Syria captured Jerusalem and desecrated its temple. A Jewish revolt led to freedom in 165 B.C. In 63 B.C. the Romans took control of Jerusalem and Judea.

Jerusalem was the religious center for Jews both in Palestine and throughout the Empire during the New Testament era. During the great religious festivals, Jerusalem was filled with Jewish pilgrims. The Romans responded by posting many more soldiers. At such times the city often became the scene of violence, as when Jesus was crucified and when Paul was rescued from a mob (Acts 21:30).

The Romans did not dare rule the province of Judea from Jerusalem because of the extreme sensitivity of Jews toward the sanctity of their holy city. But the Romans did keep a permanent cohort of soldiers (about six hundred) in the city, probably at the Antonia fortress. This fortress was built in the time of Nehemiah (Neh 2:8; 7:2). In the second century B.C. it was the palace of the Hasmonaean kings. Herod the Great renamed it in honor of his friend and patron, the Roman general Marc Antony. The apostle Paul was imprisoned in the barracks here until he was transferred to Caesarea (Acts 21:37; 22:24; 23:10, 16, 32). In an attempt to maintain control over this often volatile city and province, the Romans stored the garments of the high priest in the Antonia fortress. They only released them for Jewish holy festivals.

The Temple of Herod, a reconstruction of the temple completed under Ezra in 516 B.C., was begun in 19 B.C. by Herod the Great and completed in A.D. 64. Six years later, the Romans destroyed much of the city and the entire temple as they put down a four-year rebellion by the Jews. What was left of the city was leveled after a second Jewish revolt in A.D. 134 under Bar Kochba. The emperor Hadrian rebuilt it as a pagan city named Aelia Capitolina and denied Jews entrance to the city.

*Jamnia.* Jamnia, in the south of Judea, had its own harbor and territory. After the first-century war against the Romans, it became a center of Jewish learning.

*Joppa.* Simon the Maccabee conquered Joppa and added it to Judea (1 Macc 13:11). It had the best harbor on the Palestine coast until the construction of Caesarea Maritima.

*Ptolemais.* The ancient town of Accho, on the Palestine coast, was never conquered by the Israelites. It was renamed Ptolemais by Ptolemy, the founder of the Hellenistic dynasty in Egypt that bore his name. Its good anchorage made it an important port in ancient times.

Ptolemais was the only city in Palestine made a Roman colony by the Julio-Claudian emperors (31 B.C.-A.D. 69). When the emperor Claudius re-founded the city as a Roman colony, he settled in it a number of veterans from the four legions then stationed in Syria. A Latin inscription from A.D. 56 records the building of a Roman road from Antioch to the "new colony of Ptolemais." Later events make the purpose of this clear: Ptolemais was used as a staging point for military activities in southern Syria, Judea and across the frontier of the Euphrates River.[8] Paul sailed here from Tyre on his way to Jerusalem (Acts 21:7).

## Macedonia Province

Located on the northwest corner of the Aegean Sea, the kingdom of Macedonia rose to prominence under Philip II and his son Alexander the Great. The region was a crossroads of land routes from the Adriatic, the Danube and Thrace, and its ports offered access by sea to the East. Several of Paul's references to Macedonia, in his second letter to the Corinthians, suggest a playful rivalry in ministry between the churches of Macedonia and the churches of Achaia (2 Cor 8:1; 9:2-4; 11:9-10).

Macedonia was dismembered by Rome in 167 B.C. and reorganized as a Roman province twenty years later, ruled by a proconsul in Thessalonica. The Romans divided Macedonia into four regions, each a genuine subprovince with a separate ruling council. The Roman province included most of the northern part of modern Greece and portions of modern Bulgaria, Serbia, and half of Albania. Macedonia was an important land route between Asia and the West. Its principal cities included Neapolis, Philippi, Amphipolis, Apollonia, Thessalonica and Berea. Macedonia had suffered in the Roman civil wars but prospered under Augustus.

*Amphipolis.* This city was enclosed on three sides by the curving Strymon River, giving rise to its name ("surrounded city"). The Greek general and historian Thucydides was exiled for failing to rescue Amphipolis from a siege in 422 B.C. Paul passed through here as he followed the Egnatian Way from Philippi to Thessalonica on his second missionary journey. Amphipolis was thirty-four miles southwest of Philippi and twenty-one miles northeast of Apollonia.

*Apollonia.* The Apollonia mentioned in Acts 17:1, south of Lake Bolbe, was one of a number of towns of this name in the ancient world. Paul passed through this small town on his second missionary journey, as he followed the Egnatian Way from Philippi to Thessalonica. Apollonia was about twenty-one miles southwest of Amphipolis and about thirty miles east of Thessalonica.

*Berea.* A city of southern Macedonia, Berea lay in the foothills of Mount Bermium. It lay about fifty miles southwest of Thessalonica. It was a prosperous town with a Jewish population. Paul and Silas came to Berea after being forced out of Thessalonica (Acts 17:10). They left Berea for Athens, in the province of Achaia, where Timothy met them. Paul and Silas probably stayed in Berea only a few days. According to Acts, the Jews in Berea were more open to the gospel than were those in Thessalonica, and many believed. Paul and Silas were forced to leave Berea by their opponents, who stirred up the populace against them (Acts 17:11-14). Sopater, one of Paul's friends and fellow travelers, was from Berea. Later tradition states that the slave Onesimus, mentioned in Philemon, became the first bishop of the church of Berea.

*Neapolis.* Located in modern northern Greece, Neapolis served as the port of Philippi ten miles to the northwest. It is situated on a neck of land between two bays of the Aegean Sea. The Egnatian Way, the Roman military road and trade route that connected the Adriatic Sea with the Aegean Sea, met the Aegean in Neapolis. This helped make Neapolis a very important port. Paul landed here on his second missionary journey, responding to the call to come to Macedonia (Acts 16:11).

*Philippi.* In 360 B.C. Philippi was founded by and named for Philip II of the kingdom of Macedonia. Located on a Macedonian hilltop next to a broad plain, Philippi oversaw the main road from Europe to Asia Minor. The gold mines that had made it an important city were exhausted by the time the Romans took control in 168 B.C. In 42 B.C., after defeating the assassins of Julius Caesar here, Antony made Philippi a Roman colony and populated it with veterans of the battle. After his victory over Antony eleven years later, Octavian also settled some of his veterans here, as well as a number of Antony's supporters. This double colonizing of the city, and the frequent passages of troops through it in the following years, made Philippi one of the most Roman cities in the East.

Philippi was in many respects a miniature Rome. The plan of the city was distinctively Roman: the famed east-west route, the Egnatian Way, passed through the center of the city and formed its main axis. The *bema,* from which Paul and Silas were judged, is on the north side of the 300-by-150-foot forum at the center of the city. The town's 1,000-foot high acropolis towered over the forum. A large Greek theater was built into its eastern slope. Latin, not Greek, was the language of the city: 86 percent of the inscriptions found here dating to this era are in Latin. Augustus granted it the *ius Italicum,* meaning that the colonists enjoyed the same rights of ownership as if their land was on Italian soil. But a strong local population remained.

Political officials in Paul's day were for the most part descendants of the original Roman colonists. Some may have come from the few native families whose loyalty to Rome and influence had gained them Roman citizenship and a share in governing.

Luke correctly observes that Philippi, a Roman colony, was a city in the first district of Macedonia (Acts 16:12). This is the only city whose Roman colonial status is mentioned in the New Testament, and the only city whose technical status is introduced in Acts. This may be because Paul's treatment here related directly to the city's special status (see chapter seven on Roman law).

Paul ministered here on his second missionary journey, speaking first to some devout Jews at a prayer meeting by the side of the river Gangites (Acts 16:3). Lydia of Thyatira was the first convert (Acts 16:14). The conversion of a slave "fortune teller" led her masters to stir up a riot against Paul and Silas (Acts 16:16-40). The church at Philippi was the first established by Paul in Europe. It frequently sent gifts to Paul (Phil 4:14-17; 2 Cor 11:9). The letter to the Philippians is in part written to thank them for this assistance. Paul later visited the Philippian Christians and observed Passover here (Acts 20:6).

*Thessalonica.* Founded in 315 B.C., Thessalonica was named for the half sister of Alexander the Great. The city was of great strategic importance, situated on important trade routes and possessing a fine harbor. In Paul's day it was, along with Corinth, one of the two most important centers for trade in Greece.

The Romans made Thessalonica the capital of the province of Macedonia. The Roman general Pompey made it his headquarters in his civil war against Octavian. Later the city went over to Octavian, and after his victory he made it a free city. This meant that it could retain a Greek republican form of government and the right to mint coins. Further, Rome could not put a military garrison within its walls. Other sources confirm the accuracy of the comment in Acts that the town's rulers (known to have numbered five or six) were known by the unusual title *politarchoi*, "city authorities" (Acts 17:6, 8).[9]

Only a handful of cities in the Roman world surpassed its population of around 200,000. Its inhabitants included handworkers, traders and orators from Greece, Asia Minor, Egypt and Italy, but Greek culture predominated. The two Thessalonian delegates who helped Paul take their donations to Jerusalem seem to reflect this diversity: one had a Latin name, Secundus, and one a Greek name, Aristarchus (Acts 20:4). We know little about the Jewish residents of Thessalonica, except that Paul found a synagogue here (Acts 17:1).

Paul commends the believers here for rejecting "idols" in order to serve the true God (1 Thess 1:9-10). Dionysus was worshiped both in a public cult with a state-appointed priest and in private associations. In addition, devotees of the Egyptian cult of Isis and Serapis, including wealthy Romans of high status, met in a house for religious and social purposes. Paul ministered here with considerable success on his second missionary journey. A "great multitude" of converts to Judaism became Christians, along with some Jews and some prominent women (Acts 17:4 NASB). Paul left Thessalonica after the city officials took a pledge from Jason (Acts 17:9). Later, Paul wrote two letters to the city.

## Pamphylia-Lycia Province

This Roman province occupied the southwest tip of Asia Minor. It became Roman territory in 188 B.C. but was not made a province until A.D. 43. Its chief importance to the Romans was its harbors, two of which are mentioned in the New Testament. Paul changed ships at the harbor of Patara, probably to make better time on his last journey to Jerusalem (Acts 21:1-2). Later, on his trip to Rome, he was transferred to an Alexandrian grain ship bound for Italy at the port of Myra (Acts 27:5-6).

*Myra.* A city of Lycia on the southern coast of Asia Minor, Myra was built near a navigable river two miles from the Aegean Sea. It boasted a large (360-foot diameter) theater. In Paul's day its port was an important stop for Egyptian grain ships, which often had to sail first to Asia Minor on their way to Rome. This was because at certain times of the year, the winds on the Mediterranean changed from westerly to northwesterly. Paul transferred here to an Alexandrian grain ship bound for Italy (Acts 27:5-6).

*Pamphylia.* This region lay south of Galatia, northeast of Lycia and west of Cilicia. It was part of the combined province of Lycia-Pamphylia when Paul passed through it (Acts 13:13; 14:24; 15:38). Roman generals and emperors modified the way in which this area was governed several times. For example, Pamphylia was made part of the Roman province of Cilicia in 67 B.C. In 36 B.C. Marc Antony made it a part of Galatia. Claudius joined it with Lycia in A.D. 43. In A.D. 69 Nero reunited Pamphylia and Galatia. The emperor Vespasian united Lycia and Pamphylia a few years later. According to Acts 2:10, Jews from Pamphylia were present at Pentecost. Christianity in this region was established only slowly.

*Patara.* Patara was a seaport of the province of Lycia on the southwest coast of Asia Minor. Local mythology held that the city was founded by Patarus, legendary son of the god Apollo. Its temple and oracle to Apollo Patareus was famous. Extensive remains have been uncovered, including a theater and baths. An arch discovered here reads, "Patara, capital of the Lycian nation." In this port, Paul changed ships on his trip to Jerusalem near the end of his third missionary journey (Acts 21:1-2).

*Perga.* Perga was the capital of the district of Pamphylia, twelve miles inland from its port city of Attalia. Perga successfully resisted the influences of Greek culture. Paul seems to have passed through Perga, without stopping, on his first missionary journey. Some scholars believe that malaria was rampant when Paul passed through and that he might have contracted the fever himself (Acts 13:13-4; Gal 4:13). Paul preached in Perga at the end of his first journey (Acts 14:25), but later history suggests that his ministry bore little fruit.

### Pontus and Bithynia Province

On the northern coast of Asia Minor, facing the Black Sea, lay the two kingdoms of Pontus and Bithynia. The Romans combined them into a single senatorial province under a proconsul.

The kingdom of Pontus, founded around 300 B.C., was situated on the Black Sea between Armenia and the Halys River. In 66 B.C. Pompey conquered it and eliminated its perceived threat to Roman rule. Rome controlled its western regions for the next century. In A.D. 64 it was made a senatorial province. Jews from Pontus were present in Jerusalem on Pentecost (Acts 2:9). Aquila, a member of Paul's ministry group, was a native of Pontus (Acts 18:2).

The Roman senatorial province of Bithynia, established in 27 B.C., was located in northwest Asia Minor. Its capital was Nicomedia. Bithynia is mentioned twice in the New Testament. Paul, on his second missionary journey, was prevented from entering Bithynia by the "Spirit of Jesus" (Acts 16:7). First Peter addresses Christians in Pontus and Bithynia (1 Pet 1:1).

Pontus and Bithynia became an imperial province when Pliny the Younger came as legate in A.D. 111. We get a fascinating glimpse into the growth of early Christianity from surviving correspondence between Pliny and the Roman emperor Trajan. Pliny reported that Christianity "has spread not only in the cities, but in the villages and rural districts as well." Pliny reports that among the Christians were a number of prominent Roman citizens, and that many of Bithynia's pagan temples were "almost deserted" (*Letters* 10.96). The Christian movement here was strong in both city and country.

### Sicily Province

The island of Sicily was Rome's first province, so designated in 227 B.C. Caesar Augustus made it a senatorial province governed by a propraetor.

*Syracuse.* Syracuse, a city in Sicily, was founded by the Greek city-state of Corinth in the eighth century B.C. It fought off a massive attack by the Athenian Empire in 415-413 B.C. but fell to the Romans in 241 B.C. The city suffered terribly during the Roman civil wars of the first century B.C. Paul stopped here on his way to Rome. His ship lay in the harbor of Syracuse for three days, awaiting favorable winds (Acts 28:12). We are not told that Paul preached here. Christianity probably spread to Sicily from the Italian mainland.

## The Provinces of Spain

Called Hispania by the Romans, most of Spain came under Roman control when Rome conquered Carthage in the second Punic War (218-202 B.C.; cf. 1 Macc 8:3). Rome did not conquer northwest Spain until the time of Augustus. Augustus divided the region into three provinces. Several famous contemporaries of Paul were Romans born in Spain: Gallio, Seneca and Lucan. Paul wished to preach in Spain (Rom 15:24, 28; cf. 2 Cor 10:16), but we have no firm evidence that he did so. The late first-century Christian work *1 Clement* suggests that Paul went to Spain (*1 Clement* 5), as does later tradition. Christianity was present in Spain from at least the second century.

## Syria Province

Syria was an imperial province. At the time Octavian took full control of the Empire, the province of Syria was Rome's only direct presence in the Near East. Like the other provinces acquired in the imperial era, Syria was a military area. The higher officials who operated in this region were, without exception, personal appointees of the emperor, serving until recalled. The position of Legate of Syria was very important. So far as we know, all those to hold this position were ex-consuls. The senatorial commanders of the legions in Syria, also called legates, served under them. By the latter part of Augustus's reign, three regular legions were stationed in Syria (over eighteen thousand Roman soldiers with an unknown number of auxiliary soldiers). By A.D. 23 the number of legions in Syria had increased to four. These officials and soldiers represented almost the entire Roman presence in the Near East. Rome sent very few civilian administrators. We know of only one: a procurator of equestrian rank who oversaw taxation and payment of the troops.

In essence, Syria was a sphere of military activity, and the Roman presence there was essentially a military one. The role of these forces was to defend against the kingdom of Parthia across the Euphrates river and to maintain order both in Syria and over independent kingdoms, such as Judea, in the sphere of Roman influence. The Romans seem to have virtually ignored certain areas of Syria throughout the first century, such as the barren steppe to the east of the Orontes river ruled by the kings of Emesa. At some point in the early first century A.D., the Romans conducted full-scale military operations against the Ituraeans of Mount Lebanon, technically within the region of Syria. These were mountain people who regularly plundered the surrounding farmland. In 15 B.C. Augustus established Colonia Iulia Augusta Felix Berytus (modern Beirut) to help control them.

Syria's prosperity reached its height in the second century A.D. Chief industries included leather, linen and wine. Much trade flowed through Syria by land and sea. Syria's large cities were centers of Hellenistic culture in the Near East. Besides Antioch and Damascus, Syria's important cities included Berea, Laodicea, Epiphania, Heliopolis with its magnificent temples, Palmyra and Apamea. The ancient writer Strabo says that Apamea's commercial importance in the region was second only to that of Ephesus. It also was an administrative center and played host to a large Jewish population. The territory it controlled was quite large and prosperous.[10]

A first-century A.D. Roman poet of equestrian status, Juvenal, gives in exaggerated form the attitude of many Romans toward other cultures. He says: "For years now Syrian Orontes has poured its sewage into our native Tiber—its lingo and manners, its flutes and outlandish harps."[11] Paul tells the Galatians that he visited the "regions of Syria and Cilicia" after his visit with Peter in Jerusalem (Gal 1:21; cf. Acts 15:41). The thousands of villages in the Syrian countryside were little touched by Hellenistic or Roman influences.

*Antioch of Syria.* Founded in 301 B.C. by Seleucus I Nicator, the founder of the Seleucid Empire, Antioch was one of sixteen cities named after Seleucus's father, Antiochus. In fact, the Syrian Antioch mentioned in the New Testament was one of five Antiochs in Syria alone. In the first century A.D. this Antioch was the third largest city in the Roman Empire (behind Rome and Alexandria) with a population estimated at 500,000. It was called "the Queen of the East" and "the Beautiful and the Golden" city. Seleucus laid out the city on the gridiron plan common to Hellenistic cities. One quarter was given to Greeks and another to native Syrians. Each quarter was surrounded by walls. Antioch controlled the land routes connecting Asia Minor, the Euphrates and Egypt. It had a good water supply and was surrounded by fertile farmland. It was far enough from the Mediterranean to protect it from attack by sea, but still within a day of one of the region's best harbors. Its major disadvantage was the winter rains that often caused the nearby Orontes River to flood.

Syrian Antioch was the capital of the Seleucid Empire when it fell to the Roman general Pompey. Pompey occupied Antioch in 64 B.C. and made it a free city. This meant that it could have its own constitution, be free of a military garrison and be exempt from paying tribute. Julius Caesar undertook a comprehensive building program. Under Augustus, Antioch became the capital of the imperial province of Syria and the headquarters of the legate of Syria. Augustus visited the city twice in 31-30 B.C.

Antioch remained for many years an important center of government, a respected intellectual center and a center for travel and commerce. Retired government officials often spent their fortunes in Antioch, gambling on the chariot races, relaxing in the public baths and indulging in exotic delicacies. A racetrack was built in Antioch in the first century A.D. Villas, baths and aqueducts have been found in abundance in Antioch and her suburbs.

*Jews and Antioch.* The Jewish quarter in Antioch was called the Kerateion, and was located in the southeastern quadrant of the city. Jewish power and influence in Antioch can be seen in the great central street, paved with marble by Herod the Great in honor of Augustus. Two Roman miles long, the street was one of Antioch's claims to fame. Antioch may have included Jewish residents from the beginning. The first Jews here may have been former mercenaries who had served Alexander the Great (Josephus *Against Apion* 1.192, 200). As their wealth increased, the Jews of Antioch sent expensive offerings to Jerusalem. If the first Jewish Christians shared in this prosperity, it may explain how they were able to send famine relief to Christians in Judea under Claudius (Acts 11:27-30). Jews in Antioch had some influence on the Gentiles around them. Josephus reports that a number of Gentiles were attracted to the synagogue and to the Jewish way of life (*Jewish War* 7.45).

The influence and wealth of the Jews in Antioch declined significantly around the middle of the first century A.D. Around 40 a persecution in Antioch led to the deaths of many Jews and the destruction of synagogues. This may have been a reaction to Jewish resistance in Antioch to Emperor Gaius Caligula's decree in 39-40 that a statue of himself be placed in the Jerusalem temple. It may also have had been connected to the persecution two years earlier in Alexandria. About this time, Jewish Christians began to preach to and eat with pagans in Antioch (Acts 11:19-20; Gal 2:11-13).

Several works of antiquity focus on Jew-Gentile relationships in Antioch: Galatians 2:11-13, Acts 11:19-20, Matthew 15 (probably written from Antioch), 4 Maccabees and Ignatius's *Letter to Philippians* 5—9 (c. A.D. 100).

*Christianity and Antioch.* Syrian Antioch was extremely important to early Christianity. Nicholas, one of the original deacons, was a believer from Antioch (Acts 6:5). Many Christians fled to Antioch to escape the persecutions in Jerusalem following the death of Stephen. They preached here to Gentiles and Greek-speaking Jews and to Gentiles (Acts 11:20). A leader in the church at Antioch, Barnabas, strengthened ties with the mother church in Jerusalem (Acts 11:22-30) and brought Paul to the Antioch church as a teacher (Acts 11:27-30). The followers of Jesus were first called "Christians" at Antioch according to Acts 11:26. This is probably because believers in Antioch, for the first time, stood out enough from Jews to be nicknamed "Christus-people" by the local pagans. Foreign missions originated with the Christian community at Antioch, in its sponsorship of Paul's three missionary journeys (Acts 13:1-4; 15:35-36; 18:22-

23). Acts 13:1 lists some of the leaders in the church at Antioch: Barnabas, Symeon the Black, Lucius the Cyrenaean, Manaean the childhood companion of Herod Antipas, and Saul.

Controversy developed early over the initiation of Gentiles into the church (Acts 15; Gal 2:11-13). The tension centered on whether these Gentiles needed to accept the central cultural-religious Jewish symbols, especially circumcision and dietary laws. Paul insists that he never accepted any compromise of his "freedom" from these sectarian customs. In the Jerusalem Council, where the need to make Gentile converts follow the requirements of Jewish law was discussed, the broader view of Antioch prevailed over the narrower view of many in Judea (Acts 15; cf. Gal 2:4-14).

Antioch continued to be a major center of Christianity for centuries. It produced a number of church leaders in later years, notably the apologist Theophilus and the preacher John Chrysostom.

*Berytus.* The Romans established a colony at Berytus (modern Beirut) on the Mediterranean coast, called Colonia Iulia Augusta Felix Berytus. It was populated by the veterans from two legions. This city sent fifteen hundred men to aid the legions from Syria in putting down the revolts in Judea in 4 B.C. following the death of Herod the Great. This city also was a source of Roman soldier and officer recruits for many years.

*Caesarea Philippi.* Located north of the Sea of Galilee on the southwest slope of Mount Hermon, this city was named Caesarea by Herod Philip the tetrarch, son of Herod the Great, in honor of Tiberius Caesar (Josephus *Jewish Antiquities* 18.28). The name Philippi was added to distinguish it from the Caesarea on the coast (see Caesarea Sebaste under Judea Province). It was an important center of Hellenistic civilization and culture. Its population was mostly Gentile. Peter gave his famous confession of who Jesus is in this city (Mt 16:13-20; Mk 8:27).

*Damascus.* This ancient city was already two thousand years old in the New Testament era. Damascus was at times a part of the Decapolis, the multicity region to the east and north of Palestine. The Romans made Damascus part of their sphere of influence when they defeated the Seleucid Empire in 64 B.C. But Rome's control of Damascus was more theoretical than actual. Damascus was bordered by the independent kingdoms of Emesa to the north, Palmyra to the east and the realms of the Herodian dynasty to the south. Only to the west, in the city of Sidon, did direct Roman rule exist in the first century. Rome seems to have intervened rarely in local Damascene rule. The present East Gate of the old city dates to Roman times. The street leading from this gate to the bazaars of the city is called "Straight Street" today and probably follows the same course as the "street called Straight" of Acts 9:11.

The kingdom of Nabataea may have gained some control over Damascus in the late 30s. Paul visited synagogues here after his conversion (Acts 9:8-25). He had to escape over the city wall when troubles arose. The danger Paul faced in Damascus came not from Rome but from the Jewish community and from an official serving King Aretas of Nabataea (Acts 9:1-25; 22:3-16; 26:12-20; 2 Cor 11:32). This official, called an ethnarch, may have exercised authority in Damascus on behalf of Aretas. Paul returned to Damascus after spending time in Arabia (Gal 1:17).

*Decapolis.* The name Decapolis (literally "ten cities"; Mt 4:25; Mk 5:20; 7:31) refers to region occupied by a collection of cities. It lay east of Galilee and north of Peraea on the east side of the Jordan River. It used to be thought that these cities formed a political confederacy, but now most scholars see "Decapolis" as simply a loose geographical term. Most of the original ten cities were built by the followers of Alexander the Great. The cities were rebuilt to a degree by the Romans after 64 B.C. and extended special privileges, such as minting coins, conducting courts of law and establishing armies. The Roman general Pompey liberated all the cities of the Decapolis from Jewish rule (they had been conquered by the Hasmonaeans) and added them to the province of Syria.

The Decapolis at one point included eighteen cities. The cities normally included in the fluctuating lists of Decapolis members are Scythopolis, Abila, Pella, Philadelphia, Gerasa, Dium and Adraa. Gadara and Hippos joined the Decapolis league after Augustus freed them from Herodian control in 4 B.C. The Decapolis also probably included, at certain times, Damascus, Canatha and Raphana. These cities formed a stronghold of Hellenistic culture in the midst of a region that was often hostile toward Greeks and later toward Romans. It is not surprising that the Romans helped renovate such outposts of Hellenistic civilization.[12] The town of Jerash, perhaps the New Testament Gerasa, in the time of Jesus included a theater and temples to Zeus, Artemis and the emperor Tiberius.

In 20 B.C. Augustus visited Syria and, according to Josephus, heard accusations from the people of Gadara against Herod the Great (the city was at that time a part of Herod's kingdom). The Gadarans accused Herod of robbery and destruction of temples in the hope of being taken from Herod's jurisdiction and attached to the province of Syria. Augustus refused to do so (Josephus *Antiquities* 15.354-59). After the death of Herod, Augustus did honor their request (Josephus *Jewish War* 2.97).

The Gospels report two contacts between Jesus and the Decapolis. Multitudes came to him from Decapolis in the beginning of his ministry (Mt 4:25). The Gadarene demoniac related the story of his healing to people in the Decapolis (Mk 5:20). On more than one occasion, Jesus traveled through this region (e.g., Mk 7:31). The fourth-century church historian Eusebius reports that at the beginning of the Jewish war with Rome, the Christian community in Jerusalem fled to the Decapolis town of Pella (*History of the Church* 3.5.2-3).

*Seleucia.* This name was given to nine cities of the Seleucid Empire by Seleucus I Nicator. Only one of these, Seleucia Pieria, is mentioned in the New Testament. Built by Seleucus in 300 B.C., it sat near the mouth of the Orontes River and served as the port of Syrian Antioch. The city was built against the foothills of Mount Pieria. The lower part of the city contained the harbor and warehouses, while the upper city perched on a higher shelf of the mountain. Paul and Barnabas left on their first missionary journey from this port (Acts 13:4) and probably returned to it at the end of the trip.

*Tyre.* The city of Tyre, in the first century A.D., was on an island one-fourth mile from the mainland. Alexander the Great conquered the city in 332 B.C., killing or selling into slavery most of its population. The Greeks immediately rebuilt the city, but little of the ancient culture remained. The Romans made Tyre a Roman colony. Tyrian purple dye and cloth brought Tyre some prosperity under the Romans. Paul stopped for a week in Tyre at the end of his third missionary journey (Acts 21:3-4).

**For Further Reading**

Levick, Barbara. *Roman Colonies in Southern Asia.* Oxford: Clarendon, 1967.

Millar, Fergus. *The Roman Near East*, p. 66. Cambridge, Mass.: Harvard University Press, 1993.

**Achaia Province**
Athens
Cenchrea
Corinth

**Asia Province**
Colossae
Cos
Ephesus
Mysia
Patmos
Pergamum
Philadelphia
Sardis
Smyrna
Thyatira
Troas

**Cappadocia Province**

**Cilicia Province**
Tarsus

**Crete Province**
Clauda
Lasea

**Cyprus Province**
Paphos
Salamis

**Egypt Province**
Alexandria

**Galatia Province**
Antioch of Pisidia
Derbe
Iconium
Lycaonia
Lystra

**Italy**
Puteoli
Rome

**Kingdom of Judea**
Caesarea Sebaste
Jerusalem
Jamnia
Joppa
Ptolemais

**Macedonia Province**
Amphipolis
Apollonia
Berea
Neapolis
Philippi
Thessalonica

**Pamphylia-Lycia Province**
Myra
Pamphylia
Perga

**Pontus and Bithynia Province**

**Sicily Province**
Syracuse

**The Provinces of Spain**

**Syria Province**
Antioch of Syria
Berytus
Caesarea Philippi
Damascus
Decapolis
Seleucia
Tyre

**Table 13.1. Selected provinces and cities of the Roman Empire**

# Appendix A

## A Summary of Greco-Roman History

*[The study of history] is the best medicine for a sick mind;*
*for in history you have a record of the finite variety of human experience*
*plainly set out for all to see; and in that record you can find for yourself*
*and your country both examples and warnings;*
*fine things to take as models, base things,*
*rotten through and through, to avoid.*
LIVY *HISTORY OF ROME* 1.1

WHY SHOULD SOMEONE INTERESTED IN THE NEW TESTAMENT study the history of the Greco-Roman world? This history is important because the key to understanding the New Testament is *context*. The various books of the New Testament were written to real people who knew their own history and culture. If we do not try to put ourselves into the context of the original readers of the Scriptures, we can very easily read our own culture into a passage and reach wrong conclusions about what it meant to the author and therefore what it should mean to us. The New Testament world did not just spring into existence overnight. The forces that created it and maintained it had been in motion for centuries. The values that the Greeks and Romans brought to the governing of their empires, for example, were deeply embedded in their own concept of what it meant to be a Greek or Roman. A brief look at history helps us to see how and why the Greeks and Romans acted as they did in the time of Jesus and Paul. We can then much better understand the opportunities and challenges facing Christianity, its members and its potential converts.

## The Hellenistic Kingdoms

By the New Testament era, the influence of Greek-speaking peoples in the Near East went back nearly a millennium as trade, migration, and tourism brought an interchange of customs and ideas. This influence became dominant with Alexander the Great's conquest of the Near East in the late fourth century B.C. Alexander was the young king of Macedonia, a country north of Greece that was heavily influenced by Greek culture. His father had conquered the various city-states of Greece, which had been worn out by years of constant warfare among themselves. Alexander used the expanded Macedonian Empire to supply him with the army that would once and for all end the menace of the Persian Empire. Between 332 and 323 B.C., he won a series of victories over the Persians and others in the Near East and beyond, extending his empire to Egypt in the south and to western India in the east.

As Alexander conquered a land, he established Greek cities as centers of governance and Greek culture. At the same time, he sought to gain the willing allegiance of the peoples he conquered by retaining many of their cultural norms. He even ordered his top officers to marry local women as a symbol of the integration of Hellenistic and local ways. Alexander died in 323, before he had the chance to consolidate his conquests and establish a stable government. He also died without an heir, but the generals who carved up his empire among themselves continued his policies of setting up outposts of Hellenistic civilization while embracing some local customs. This process of "Hellenization" would continue to have a strong impact on the Near East up to and past the New Testament era.

Four major kingdoms emerged from Alexander's empire (see map 2 for the kingdoms of Alexander's successors). Antigonus took control of the original kingdom of Macedonia, and exercised control over the Greek city-states to his south. Ptolemy took Egypt and established the Ptolemaic dynasty that would last until the rise of Caesar Augustus and Roman control of the Mediterranean. Seleucus took control of Syria and Middle East, and for a short time the Seleucid Empire included the lands east of Syria (which would later form the independent Parthian Empire). The small kingdom of Pergamum was controlled by the Attalids in western Asia Minor (modern Turkey) from its capital at Pergamum. The history of these four kingdoms is in large part the history of the continued integration of Hellenistic culture with local culture, at least in the cities. It is also a history nearly constant internecine warfare. For example, the Seleucids and Ptolemies frequently fought over Palestine.

These Hellenistic kingdoms, with the exception of Macedonia, governed peoples who had nothing in common with their rulers. The leaders sought to address this by continually founding and expanding Hellenistic cities, some on the foundations of older cities (see chapter three). The Greek language became the language of governance, trade and education. Those who wanted or needed to have ongoing contact with the new rulers understood that they had to learn Greek ways. As a result, the closer one was to the seats of power in the Near East, the more one was influenced by Hellenization. That means that the most Hellenized people could be found in the upper classes, among those living in cities (especially in Hellenized ones) and among those involved in trade, commerce, education and the arts. Local farmers in the countryside, who had little or no reason to visit a city, were not as strongly influenced by Hellenization. Consequently, while Jesus' early followers spoke the local language of Judea, Aramaic, the books of the New Testament, addressed for the most part to Christians in the cities, were written in Greek.

## Early Rome

*Origins.* Rome's origin is shrouded in fable. Romans believed that their society arose after the fall of the city of Troy in the Trojan War (twelfth century B.C.) when the Trojan prince Aeneas escaped west and settled in Italy. Two of his descendants, the twins Romulus and Remus, were fathered by Mars, the god of war. They were abandoned at birth, then nursed by a she-wolf and raised by a shepherd. Romulus killed his brother in anger and then established the city of Rome in 753 B.C. as a refuge for fugitives. He organized the kidnapping of women from the Sabine people, just to their northeast, to supply wives for his followers. Some years later, Romulus was supposedly taken up by the gods and was worshiped from that time on as the god Quirinus. We can only confirm, from archaeological evidence, that the seven hills of Rome harbored settlements from the eighth century B.C. and that these settlements formed one city around 600 B.C.

While the rest is probably fable, its repetition tells us something about how the Romans saw themselves: war-like by nature, as descendants of the god of war; empowered with the strength and cunning of the wolf who nursed their founders; and established by desperate men who successfully fought everyone around them for survival. Many Romans believed that just as it was the fate of the Greeks to bring culture to the world, it was the fate of the Romans to bring order to the world. It is important for us to note that the Romans from a very early period believed they were destined to rule. They believed that they were better suited by nature and ability for rule than were other peoples. And they believed that the gods had selected them for this task. Perhaps this way of looking at the world underlay their actions somewhat like the concepts of "manifest destiny" and the assumed superiority of Europeans underlay the movement westward by European immigrants in the nineteenth-century United States.

Early Roman authors believed that Romulus was the first of seven kings to rule over Rome, before the founding of the Republic in 509 B.C. We cannot be sure that these kings indeed ruled Rome, but we do know that Rome during this time came under the influence or perhaps domination of the Etruscan Empire. The Etruscans, north of Rome in the north-central part of the Italian peninsula, had achieved prosperity, a developed culture and a successful military. Roman art, religion, military science and politics show the influence of the Etruscans. For example, the Romans adopted the Etruscan practice of raising armies from among their property-owning citizens rather than using the common but inefficient practice of requiring each clan to raise a certain number of troops.[1]

*Government under the Republic.* The kings were assisted in their rule by the senate, an assembly of the heads of families of the aristocracy. Roman tradition holds that the seventh king, Tarquin the Proud, was a tyrant whose activities motivated the people to revolt and establish a republic. The elimination of the monarchy would become a heroic theme of liberation for later philosophers and dramatists. In fact, the monarchy was overthrown by Roman aristocrats chafing for more power, with the help of the ruler of the Etruscans.

Nevertheless, the Republic (509-31 B.C.) did mark a major shift in Roman history. The Romans had learned a strong distaste for monarchy, and they were determined never to be ruled by a single powerful leader again. Into the vacuum left by the toppled monarchy came the army, controlled by the local aristocracy. The Romans set up the Centuriate Assembly, their main deliberative body, on the model of their army. The assembly made laws and oversaw the courts and elections. The senate continued as an advisory body made up of approximately three hundred current and former elective officeholders (who also were the heads of the Roman aristocratic families). Initially, the chief elected officers were the *praetors,* who ruled as a group (see table A.1). Later, two members of the group came to be seen as preeminent and would be called consuls. Over time, a constitution was devised to define the powers and limits of the governing bodies.

We should not think of a modern representative democracy when we think of the Roman Republic. The senate dominated the state in this era. While it lacked any constitutionally recognized powers, it controlled all the official forms of government. Only members of the senate were elected to the highest offices. The senate, most of the time, could block efforts by official bodies, such as the Centuriate Assembly, from taking actions it opposed.

All state offices were unpaid, honorary positions. Most positions lasted only one year. Although unpaid, they offered the officeholder a variety of ways to line his purse and increase the honor of his family. The most important office under the Republic was that of consul. The two consuls elected each year conducted foreign policy and oversaw the general administration of Roman society. They were the closest thing republican Rome had to a chief executive. Most of the time a consul refrained from making broad use of his powers, knowing that at the end of the year he would have to face as a simple senator any enemies he had made. The office next in importance was that of praetor. The positions of general or governor of a province were filled by current or former praetors or consuls. Next were the aediles, who supervised the markets and business centers located near temples. They also supervised the great games and festivals of Rome, a financially burdensome but reputation-building duty. They normally paid for the games and festivals out of their own pockets, and men like Julius Caesar went heavily into debt in the process. Below them in status were the quaestors, administrative officials typically attached to the staff of a general or a governor.

The officeholders had no bureaucracy to assist them. They were served only by very small staffs of scribes, messengers and honor guards (called lictors). Most officeholders looked to their family and friends, and especially to their clients, for administrative assistance.

Two other posts were filled only when needed: dictator and censor. The dictator was elected to a six-month term to deal with a crisis, usually military in nature. The office was rarely invoked until the time of Sulla and Julius Caesar, who used the title to give legitimacy to their totalitarian regimes. Censors typically were appointed every five years to do a census of the people and verify that everyone was in his proper social class or *ordo*. In later years, some Roman emperors would use this office to add or delete senators as they wished.

Even by 200 B.C., when Rome had become in effect a large and complex empire, all governing was in the hands of ten senior and eighteen junior magistrates. All were elected annually, and fully half of them were devoted exclusively to affairs within the city of Rome. What is the significance of the complex division of powers devised by the Romans? They did not trust one person with all of this authority, and they established this division of powers to make sure that no one person could easily assume total authority.

*The ladder of honor, or* cursus honorum, *from highest to lowest:*

**Proconsul**
  Governor of a major province
  City prefect

**Consul**
  Republic: two elected annually as executives of Roman government
  Empire: two selected annually by the emperor

**Prefect**
  Overseer of a state treasury
  Governor of a lesser province

**Legate**
  Commander of legion
  Governor of a lesser province (also called propraetor)

**Praetor** (age thirty minimum)
  Urban
  Foreign

**Aedile**
  Supervised markets and business centers

**Tribune of the Plebs** (plebians only)
  Veto power over legislative decisions

**Quaestor**
  Admission to senate (about age twenty-five)
  Administrative assistant to general or governor

**Military Tribune**
  Commander of a cohort
  Assistant to the legionary commander

---

**Table A.1. Offices and their functions in the system of Roman government**

*The patron-client relationship in the Republic.* Rome was a highly structured society, controlled by a few families. Not surprisingly, those at the top believed that societal stability was based on everyone knowing and accepting his or her place in the social order. This heavy emphasis on order affected all of Rome's institutions, leading to tight discipline in the Roman army, unusual powers given to the head of the Roman family and strict barriers between social classes. These barriers were particularly strong between the aristocracy and the rest of the citizenry. Intermarriage with members of the lower classes usually was not tolerated. These patricians, as they were originally called, formed clans that were bound by blood, marriage and religious rituals unique to each clan. The plebians, as the rest of the citizenry was called, represented all economic levels from rich to poor.

From earliest times the patricians, for self-preservation and to increase their power, assumed the position of patron to clients from among the lower classes. The clients were free Roman citizens who for various reasons had become dependent economically and socially on their patrons. Clients were to recognize their dependence on the patron, and the patron was to protect the weaker client. The client had to appear publicly with his patron when called upon, as a sign to the society of his patron's power and influence. In turn, the patron defended his client at court, an important service. In fact, in the early days of the Republic, commoners found it difficult to gain justice at court without the support of a patron. The patron-client relationship was permanent and hereditary, but its hold on many client families weakened over time, especially if their descendants gained wealth and status. Some early patricians had many clients. For instance, the patrician family of Fabius (479 B.C.) had 306 members and 4,000 to 5,000 clients.[2]

As Rome expanded, the notion of clienthood changed. Often, the citizens of a city conquered by a Roman general became his clients *en masse*. The general was then to act in their interests back in Rome. This mass clientage gave him great power to pursue his own interests. All of the powerful generals of the late Republic, such as Marius, Sulla, Pompey and Julius Caesar, used this power to great advantage. The senate did nothing to oppose this practice since it was not prepared to commit the resources of Rome to the support of non-Romans. However, the rise of these powerful generals would contribute to the fall of the Republic, and the patron-client relationship began to lose the personal nature it once possessed. Toward the end of the Republic, only the generals and strong political leaders truly benefited from the patron-client system, and during the Empire it would come to be dominated by the emperor. The rise of the great generals illustrates how even those at the highest levels of society can be short-sighted and not do what is in their best interests. If the senate had provided to Roman soldiers all the benefits they received from their generals, it would have broken the patron-client relationship thus established between the generals and their armies. In doing so, it might have prevented the rise of emperors who were selected and placed on the throne by the army. But the senate was at heart a conservative institution and could not bring itself to do things it had never done before: for example, paying soldiers and settling retired landless soldiers on conquered land.

The patron/client institution in Rome established power along lines of personal relationships. This is often true today as well, but we more frequently

Figure A.1. Close-up of a model of the city of Rome in the fourth century A.D., showing at bottom the Circus Maximus. Used mainly for horse and chariot races, the Circus Maximus could accommodate 300,000 spectators.

see power attached to positions or offices. The person in a position automatically has the power that goes with that position. This was less true for Rome. Even those in official positions brought into those positions much of the power they would be able to exercise, based on the power relationships (such as the number of clients, the favors owed to them) they had established before taking office.

*The struggle of the orders.* The fall of the monarchy had been a triumph for the patricians, who through their control of the army and their clients controlled the state. But during the fifth century B.C., conditions in Italy and constant infighting among the patricians created a poor economy and increasing indebtedness among the plebians. This led to the so-called Struggle of the Orders, as the plebians took measures to protect themselves from the patricians. According to tradition, in 494 B.C. the plebians literally left the city of Rome, refusing to serve in the army or obey the patricians. They forced the patricians to accept the establishment of a new office, called the tribune of the plebs, in opposition to the patrician-dominated Centuriate Assembly and the senate.

The persons of the tribunes were declared sacrosanct, meaning that any person who harmed them would be given over to the vengeance of the gods and could in practice be killed by anyone as an instrument of the gods' judgment. This was done to protect the tribunes from retribution by the powerful patricians. Further, tribunes could veto any action by a patrician magistrate in order to protect the interests of the plebeians.

Over time, the patricians were forced to make more concessions to the far more numerous plebeians. For example, the Tribal Assembly, governed by the tribunes of the plebs, was set up as a permanent assembly alongside the Centuriate Assembly. By the end of this era, the tribunes had been incorporated into the republican constitution as officers of the state.

But the richest plebeians wanted more. They believed that they had been denied their rightful share of power based solely on their lack of aristocratic ancestry. Eventually the patricians agreed to share governing powers with the descendants of Rome's oldest and wealthiest plebeian families. For instance, in 367 B.C. the state gave plebeians a right long held by patricians: to make personal use of land taken in war by Rome. In the same year, patricians gave plebeians the right to hold the highest offices in Roman government. Certain important positions were created that could only be held by plebeians. Plebeians gradually came into the senate, and a new aristocracy, based on a patrician-plebeian alliance, emerged. Historians usually place the end of the Struggle of the Orders in 287 B.C., when the Tribal Assembly became the main law-making body and could operate without the approval of the senate. Around the same time it also gained the power to ratify treaties with foreign governments.

However, by this time the plebeians who controlled the Tribal Assembly were members of the senate as well. In other words, they had been brought into the ruling class and came to share the attitudes and values of the patricians. This struggle demonstrates how the Romans had learned a valuable tool for overcoming opposition, which they would use over and over in the coming centuries. First, they convinced the ruling class of a people they had absorbed that the Roman system benefited their class more than did independence. Then they used that group to keep its people in check. Later we will see how the Romans co-opted the ruling elite of Judea, the Herodians, as a way to keep the Jewish people pacified.

In this era, Roman aristocrats began learning how to share power. In a sense, they were learning how to change their notions of "us" and "them," allowing their definition of "us" to expand. First it would expand from Roman patricians to include wealthy and honorable Roman plebians. Later it would expand to include other Italian aristocrats, and eventually aristocrats from around the Empire. This worked for them because by the time a former outsider was elevated to the senate, he had absorbed the values of Rome. Because he had truly become Roman, the decisions he made were the same ones a Roman patrician would have made in his place. This is in fact a mark of a strong society: its values are so persuasive, and so firmly held by its long-time members, that new members adopt these values fully and without reservation. Once a society can no longer do this, it is headed for decline.

### Rome as Conqueror

*Conquest of Italy.* No one who saw Rome around 500 B.C. would have predicted its incredible rise to dominance. What motivated the Romans to invest enormous amounts of money and energy and the lives of its young men in an unending quest for expansion? Romans always claimed that their wars were purely wars of self-defense. They believed that some wars were not just, so they looked for ways to justify their wars. Some of their wars were responses to clear threats. Others resulted from the fear that if they did not attack first, they would be attacked. Still others were justified as aid to a town or region in a distant land that had an alliance with them, and thus they were in reality defensive wars. These rationalizations for wars often stretched credulity. At times it is hard to accept that the Romans themselves believed them.

In the beginning of the Republic, Rome was only one of many towns and villages that populated the wide-open plains of the region of central Italy called Latium. Feeling the need for mutual defense against the dominant powers of Italy (Etruscans, Gauls, Samnites and Greeks), they had formed the Latin League some years earlier. In this league, Rome learned how to incorporate non-Romans into its society. Citizens of one city in the league could move to Rome and become citizens there. Legal contracts that involved citizens from other Latin cities, including marriages and wills, were honored at Rome. As Rome expanded, it would gradually make these advantages available to the peoples it absorbed (see map 1).

But in 390 B.C. Rome suffered the first of many setbacks when the city itself was overcome and sacked by the Gauls. The Gauls were actually Celts from northern Europe who had migrated to Gaul (modern France) many years before and had then invaded northern Italy. The Gauls had raised havoc throughout the Etruscan Empire. The shock of this sack may have helped create in Romans the need to expand in search of safe frontiers. Of course, the wealth in land, slaves and gold taken by a victorious Rome also provided a strong motivation.

An attempt by Latin League members to rebel from Roman control ended in 338 with Rome victorious. Rome abolished the league, but instead of harshly punishing the rebellious cities, Rome realized the need to address their complaints about unequal treatment. It granted the peoples of four of the cities full Roman citizenship and left their municipal governments intact. Citizens of those towns could henceforth be elected to office in Rome. Those in other towns were given citizenship, but without the right to vote or hold office. People in still other towns were allowed to remain independent and were given certain rights (the so-called Latin citizenship), but they were not given Roman citizenship. As Rome expanded its control into less populated areas, it set up Latin colonies. These colonies were cities populated by Roman citizens who accepted the reduction to Latin citizenship in exchange for large grants of land. Where military garrisons were needed to secure strategic points, the Romans set up Roman colonies: small towns, often composed of former soldiers, whose inhabitants retained full Roman citizenship rights. The model of the Roman colony would be used extensively as Rome expanded overseas. Just as Roman patricians had learned how to share power with the plebeians, so Romans were learning how to share power with the upper classes among the Latins. The settlement in 338 increased Rome's territory by more than one-third and its population by over 200,000.[3]

Not long after this, Rome began a series of bloody wars with the Samnites, then the most powerful state in the Italian peninsula. The Romans saw the Samnites in their mountain fortresses as a threat to the cities and farmlands of the central Italian plains. After losing a major battle in 321, the Romans methodically began surrounding Samnium with fortresses. In 295 Rome defeated a combined force of Samnites, Etruscans and Gauls. By 290 Rome controlled all of central Italy and was the dominant power in the Italian peninsula. Soon after, the Romans founded new colonies and built new roads to allow their troops to move quickly to areas of conflict.

Rome's wars with the Samnites put it for the first time in direct contact with the Greek cities of southern Italy. These cities had been established by Greek colonists many years earlier. Like other Greek colonies, they were independent cities with no formal ties to their mother cities back in Greece. Rome involved itself in the politics of these towns as early as 326 B.C. when the Greek city of Neapolis (modern Naples) threw out its Samnite protectors and placed itself under the protection of Rome. The Greek city of Tarentum, in southern Italy, maintained a kind of protectorate over other cities in the region. When in 282 B.C. Rome accepted the invitation of one of these cities, Thurii, to help it defend itself against attacking Oscans, Tarentum felt its position threatened and attacked a Roman fleet. Tarentum also called on Pyrrhus, king of Epirus in northwest Greece, to help battle the Romans. Pyrrhus defeated the Romans twice, beginning in 280, but his army sustained heavy losses and could not persuade any of Rome's allies to defect. As in the past, Rome came back from its losses and decisively defeated Pyrrhus in a third battle. Pyrrhus was forced to return to Greece, and in 272 Rome conquered Tarentum. This gave Rome control of all of southern Italy. On the Italian peninsula, only the Gauls in the far north remained outside Rome's control (see map 1 for Italy in the second century B.C.). As a result of Rome's defeat of Pyrrhus, whose army was highly regarded, many in the eastern Mediterranean took notice of Rome as a rising power. Rome showed that it did not fear confrontations with the old powers of the Mediterranean East.

*Rome and Carthage.* Rome's expansion into southern Italy brought it into conflict with its long-time ally, the city-state of Carthage on the North African coast (see map 7). Up to that point, Rome and Carthage had common enemies and no competing interests, but both had expanded rapidly since their first treaty, in 509 B.C. Carthage dominated North Africa, and its fleets of trading ships plied the seas from Egypt to Spain. When one faction on the island of Sicily appealed to Carthage for support, and another appealed to Rome, both decided to intervene. The Carthaginians did so to maintain their influence there, and the Romans did so to prevent Carthaginian influence from becoming control. Thus began the First Punic War.

In the First Punic War (264-241 B.C.), Rome fought a land battle on Sicily and was successful at pushing Carthage back into the western part of the island. It also won several victories at sea. Rome came back, after losing a fleet of ships, to force Carthage to give up its claims to Sicily in 241. Rome built on this victory three years later by forcing the surrender of the islands of Sardinia and Corsica. This first war with Carthage demonstrated on the one hand the lack of consistent strategy and uneven quality of leadership that resulted from Rome's system of appointing military officers to one-year terms. On the other hand, it revealed the tremendous resources in human resources and wealth, not to mention resolve, that allowed the Romans to endure great losses and still emerge victorious.

For the next two decades, Rome worked to strengthen its connections in Greece by putting down the pirates of Illyria (modern Yugoslavia and Albania) that for years had threatened trade in the Adriatic Sea. Meanwhile, the Gauls mounted an assault on Rome that ended in 225 B.C. with another Roman victory. Rome began establishing colonies in Gallic homelands in northern Italy.

While Rome was pacifying northern Italy, Carthage was busy extending its control in Spain. The Second Punic War (218-201 B.C.) broke out when Carthage attacked Saguntum, a city in Carthaginian Spain under Roman protection. Accepting Rome's superiority at sea, the Carthaginians decided to fight this war on land. Hannibal, son of the Carthaginian leader in Spain, marched on Rome with an army of twenty thousand infantry, six thousand calvary and a number of elephants. He skirted Roman defenses by marching his army out of Spain, through Gaul, across the Alps and south into Italy. Although he lost most of the elephants on this trek, it was a successful strategy. An accomplished general leading a professional army, Hannibal defeated one Roman army after another. He was supported in this by the Gauls of northern Italy, who saw a chance to throw off Roman control. Roman losses were so great that they recruited sixteen-year-olds and slaves into the army. A number of cities in the south surrendered to Hannibal without combat after his resounding victory over Roman forces at Cannae in 216; others had seen enough of Rome's resilience to believe that it would eventually defeat the Carthaginians. Hannibal was unable to lay siege to the city of Rome, and the Roman fortresses through-out Italy held out. The cities Hannibal took were always retaken eventually by the Romans. For years, Hannibal ravaged the Roman countryside but could not force the Romans either to surrender or to fight a final battle.

The emergence of a Roman general to rival the ability of Hannibal helped turn things around for Rome. P. Cornelius Scipio, commanding Roman forces in Spain, was able to drive out the Carthaginians by 205 B.C. Scipio was sent to attack Carthage, in hopes that Hannibal would be forced to leave Italy and defend his homeland. This indeed happened; in 203 Hannibal returned to Africa and lost a pitched battle to Scipio at Zama, in modern Tunisia.

In the aftermath of this war, Rome began the practice of severely punishing peoples who betrayed it. Massive tracts of land in the north and south of Italy were seized by Rome and became part of its "public lands," owned by the state but generally used by the upper class for farming and grazing at little or no cost. The rebellious cities in the south came back into the Roman fold quickly, but the Gauls in the north were subdued only after another twenty years of fighting, which ended around 180 B.C. A city that refused to surrender to the Romans would find itself not only conquered, but all its men killed and its women and children sold into slavery. Spain came under Roman domination as well, although Rome would have to devote many years and much expense to its subjugation. Rome divided Spain into two provinces, Nearer and Further Spain. These provinces joined ones set up earlier in Sicily, Sardinia and Corsica. Rome continued its policy of setting up Latin and Roman colonies in conquered areas. But as it found fewer and fewer citizens willing to accept reduced citizenship in exchange for land, it was forced to set up more Roman colonies and fewer Latin ones. From this era on, Rome would teach the world that you might win a battle against it, or rebel from it successfully for a time, but the Roman response, when it came, would be terrifying and without mercy.

*Rome and the Hellenistic East.* Rome's early interventions in the East showed that it felt it could rule others better than they could rule themselves. Rome also showed that its concept of "national interest" was expanding. The Carthaginians had been assisted in their war against Rome by the kingdom of Macedonia. As a counter to Macedonia, Rome established an alliance with the Greek city-states of the Aetolian League, just south of Macedonia. Rome attacked Macedonia in 200 B.C., officially on behalf of the Greek states, after Macedonia refused to vacate its Greek possessions. The Romans did not seek to destroy Macedonia; they simply wanted to weaken it and thus eliminate it as a threat to Rome's interests. Rome won a decisive victory against Macedonian forces in 197 B.C., and by the next year the Macedonians had pulled out of Greek lands. The Roman general Flamininus then announced an Act of Liberation at the Isthmian Games outside of Corinth, making the Greek cities free (under the protection of Rome, of course). This caused the Greeks to see Rome as their liberator.

Rome's intervention in Greece posed a threat to the Seleucid Empire. Its ruler, Antiochus III, had his own interests in Greece, and arrived with an army of liberation in 192 B.C. The Romans returned, however, and forced him to leave Greece. In 190 B.C. a Roman army defeated Antiochus in Asia Minor. The decline of Seleucid power in the East, which had been underway for a number of years, was accelerated by the terms forced on Antiochus. Neither of the other Hellenistic kingdoms, the Ptolemaic Empire of Egypt or the kingdom of Pergamum, had the desire to challenge Rome at this time, so they left it to consolidate its gains.

Although Rome was just beginning to have influence in the Middle East, major changes rocked the region at the beginning of the second century B.C. As we shall see, Judea had been under foreign domination long before the Romans came along. In fact, by the 140s B.C. the Jews were ready to give Roman overlordship a try.

The Ptolemaic kingdom of Egypt controlled Judea until 198 B.C., when the Seleucid Empire won a war and added Judea to its domain. Judea would remain a part of the Seleucid Empire for the next fifty years. Under both of these monarchies, the Judeans were generally free to order their internal affairs as they saw fit. Palestine was ruled by a governor chosen by the emperors, and it had to pay taxes to its overlord. But Judea itself, which consisted only of a several-mile radius around Jerusalem, had a bit more independence. It was a temple-state under the rule of the Jewish high priest, always drawn from the ancient family of the Zadok who had been high priest under King Solomon (1 Chron 9:11).

The Roman defeat of the Seleucids, only a few years after they had taken control of Judea, had serious consequences for internal Jewish politics. The Romans took some of the Seleucid Empire's wealthier provinces and demanded a huge annual tribute. The need for money to pay these taxes drove the Seleucids to accept bribes in exchange for backing candidates for high priest in Judea. Antiochus IV (175-163 B.C.) first took a bribe to support Jason against his brother Onias III. A few years later Antiochus agreed to support Menelaus, who was not a member of the Zadok family, against Jason.[4]

Antiochus IV had nearly succeeded in his attempt to conquer Egypt when Rome intervened and defeated his forces in 168 B.C. Back in Judea, this loss led Jewish leaders to remove Menelaus and install Jason as high priest. Antiochus took this as an act of rebellion. As punishment he and his army destroyed the walls of Jerusalem and looted the temple treasury. Since the temple cult had been the focus for dissension, Antiochus turned the temple into a shrine to the Greek god Zeus, banned the practice of Judaism and attempted to turn Jerusalem into a Hellenistic city. For three years (167-164 B.C.) this "abomination of desolation" dominated the temple.

Many Jews took up arms against Antiochus IV rather than submit to such changes. Their leaders were an old priest of the Hasmonean family, Mattathias, and his five sons. One of the sons, Judas Maccabaeus, proved to be a genius at guerrilla warfare. The Jews were able to defeat a succession of larger and better-armed Seleucid armies. Now more interested in territory beyond the Euphrates, Antiochus came to terms with the Judeans. Judea would once again become a quasi-independent Jewish temple-state and would remain in the Seleucid Empire.

However, the Hasmonean leaders, the Maccabees and their supporters were not content with this, and Judea finally won national independence in 142 B.C. under Simon, the last surviving son of Mattathias. The people in gratitude recognized Simon in 143 as high priest and founder of a new hereditary high priesthood. To protect against reconquest by the Seleucids, Simon made a far-reaching agreement with the Roman authorities. Rome recognized the Jewish religion as a legitimate religion within Rome, giving all Jews in Roman territory the right to worship freely according to the dictates of their religion.[5]

Suspicious that Macedonia was preparing once again to threaten Roman interests, the Roman army finally destroyed the Macedonian kingdom in 168 B.C. Unquestionably, Roman aggressiveness was motivated also and increasingly by the desire of competing generals for glory and wealth. For example, in a single day, the Romans destroyed over seventy villages and towns in Macedonia and enslaved their entire populations. Rome divided Macedonia into four free but impotent states. The Roman armies returned home laden with great wealth in gold and slaves. Rome's policy of allowing cities and regions internal independence, while denying them the freedom to conduct foreign policy, would lead to a number of limited wars until Rome decided to incorporate Greece fully into its growing empire.

Rome had shown that it could tolerate independent states in its orbit, so long as they appeared to pose no threat to its ultimate control over whatever it deemed its sphere of influence. States that threatened would lose their independent identity as provinces of greater Rome.

This happened to Macdonia in 148 B.C. when it attempted to throw off Roman overlordship. The Romans not only thwarted this rebellion, but they established the province of Roman Macedonia, the first Roman province in Greece. Two years later, Greek actions considered overly independent by Rome led to a savage object lesson for Greece: the complete sack and destruction of the ancient city of Corinth. As practiced increasingly by the Romans from this time on, a "sack" consisted of either taking or destroying everything of value in the city, including the killing of the men and enslavement of many if not all of its women and children. Greece was put under the supervision of the Roman governor of Macedonia. In the same year, Rome concluded a three-year siege of Carthage with the sack and destruction the capital city of its old rival. The North African lands formerly controlled by Carthage were turned into the Roman province of Africa. The capital city was completely destroyed and its land sowed with salt to prevent farming and thus the reestablishment of the city.

By 146 B.C. Rome emerged as the dominant power in the entire Mediterranean region. Besides controlling Italy, it had established the following provinces: Sicily, Sarinia-Corsica, Nearer and Further Spain, Macedonia and Africa. It would soon add provinces in Asia Minor and southern Gaul. In addition, it had established patron-client relations with the reduced Seleucid Empire, Egypt, Pergamum, Rhodes and many other smaller states and cities. The Romans now referred to the Mediterranean simply as "Our Sea."

**Social Revolution in Rome**
*Territorial expansion and the Roman economy.* The seemingly endless succession

of wars fought by the Romans gradually changed the nature of the Roman economy. The principal change, as we shall see, was to make the Roman economy dependent on slavery. Slavery would become so much a part of the Roman way that the society could not have eliminated slavery, even if it had wished to, without destroying its economy. For most of the Republic, Roman soldiers were citizens drafted to serve, on a temporary basis, at their own expense. They supplied their own weapons and equipment, and even their own food. The burden this produced on the average Roman farmer was tremendous. Without slaves to work while he was away, he depended upon whatever meager cash reserves he had and the usually small booty he gained in victory over his enemy to keep his family fed in his absence. But one-year campaigns became multiyear, and men by the thousands never returned home alive. As a result, these farms were often forfeited to the state for nonpayment of taxes or taken by a wealthy neighbor to repay defaulted loans. Still others were sold outright to wealthy farmers, who increasingly used slaves captured in the wars to farm their expanding holdings. Because slaves could not be drafted, they provided an uninterrupted source of labor in wartime. In addition, the wealthy landowner could depend upon his poorer neighbors, now serving in the army, to bring back with them slaves captured in battle to help him farm the land he had acquired from them in their absence. So, as soldiers brought back their replacements in chains, the Roman economy was gradually transformed from one of subsistence citizen farmers to one of large plantations owned by the wealthy and farmed by gangs of slaves.[6]

What happened to the subsistence farmers? Of those who did not die in battle, some made a career out of military service and at times were awarded land or money by their general. This served as a basis for the burgeoning independence of Roman generals since their soldiers came to see them, not Rome, as their true leaders. Some former soldiers returned to farming, to work as tenant farmers perhaps on land they once owned. Over time, however, fewer and fewer wealthy farmers used tenant farmers. Other displaced farmers, in ever increasing numbers, moved to the major cities of the Roman world to try to find some means of livelihood. They came especially to the capital, where the government provided grain at low, subsidized rates in order to keep the poor citizenry pacified. They found very little work in the city since much of the labor there, by the late republican era, was performed by slaves. Some found day work unloading ships or on construction projects, and some tried to start their own businesses.

**Figure A.2. Bronze statue of Caesar Augustus (National Museum, Athens, Greece). This statue originally was mounted on a bronze horse.**

*The Gracchan Revolution.* The rapidly changing social and economic conditions of Rome led to a great deal of unrest. Revolts and insubordination among Roman soldiers took place in 198, 190 and 189 B.C. Riots against the military draft occurred in 151 and 138 B.C. To address dissatisfaction among lower-class Romans, greater guarantees of the personal rights of citizens were written into law, use of the death penalty against citizens became very rare and secret balloting was introduced into the voting process. Tribunes began to use their powers on behalf of groups or persons who they felt were not receiving justice from the state. In all of this, we can see the deterioration of the old social bonds, such as those between patron and client.

Despite these attempts at reform, Rome continued to evolve from a society of peasant citizen farmers into an empire of massive, slave-run plantations and cities overflowing with impoverished citizens. A group of men in the senate, led by the brothers Tiberius and Gaius Gracchus, became concerned by the disappearance of the peasant farmer and the consequent implications for Rome's economy and military. The Gracchans believed that they could do Rome a service, and increase their family's status and power, by dividing up some of Rome's "public lands" among landless citizens. The public lands were lands taken in conquest by Rome and owned only by the state. The fortunate citizens would thus be available to serve in the army, which by law could only recruit landowners, and the new landowners would feel beholding to the Gracchans. Tiberius Graccus, as a tribune of the plebs in 133 B.C., proposed this land distribution.

The main problem with this plan was that many wealthy and powerful Romans were farming this public land, either as legal lessors or as squatters, and had come to think of it as their property. But Tiberius received surprising help from the huge number of lower-class citizens who flooded Rome to support his proposals. After the reforms passed the assembly, these citizen farmers went home, and Tiberius lost his supporters. An attempt to co-opt the equestrian class to his cause failed, and he was assassinated by his opponents in the senate. His reforms were not carried out.

In 123 B.C. Tiberius's younger brother Gaius was elected tribune of the plebs. He intended to reinstate Tiberius's reforms while avoiding his mistakes. He began by enacting legislation appealing to equestrians and the lower classes. One of his lasting reforms established a monthly ration of grain for poor citizens at below-market prices. He was elected tribune again in 122 and gained the support necessary to pass his reform legislation. But by 121 Gaius was out of office, his coalition had collapsed, and he was killed by his enemies. Only a few of his reforms, not including the distribution of land, succeeded.[7]

In the struggle over land and power, the Roman aristocrats set themselves up against the commoners. In doing so they set the stage for powerful individuals, such as military leaders, to use the commoners' resentment against them.

*The Roman Revolution: Marius and Sulla.* In terms of land distribution and other reforms, the generals of the first century B.C. were to succeed, at least to a degree, where the tribunes of the second century had failed. Gaius Marius, elected consul in 108 B.C. to fight the Numidians of North Africa, changed the nature of the Roman army. Under Marius, landless citizens were admitted to the army for the first time and had all of their expenses paid by the state. This provided the military with a new source of soldiers, Roman peasants with a source of employment and Marius with lifelong supporters. The success of his army proved to his opponents that landless peasants would fight for Rome. His fully professional army became the model for the armies of later generals.

Marius's power reached its height when he beat back an invasion by several German tribes. The Germans defeated a series of Roman generals until Marius decisively overcame them in 103-102 B.C. Marius attempted to get land for his retired soldiers, and even marched them illegally into the Roman assembly to force passage of his measure, but only a relative handful actually received land.

Meanwhile, discontent continued to stir Rome's Italian allies. They no longer were willing to tolerate Rome's policy of using them to fight its wars but not allowing them to share in the governance of the state. When a 91 B.C. attempt to give Italians Roman citizenship was defeated, many of them revolted from Roman rule and established an independent Italian state. In 90 Rome extended full Roman citizenship to all Italians who had not joined the revolt and in 89 offered it to all who would lay down their arms. By 89 the war was effectively over. By 80 all of peninsular Italy was united under a single political and legal system.

The leading Roman general to emerge from this "Social War" was Lucius Cornelius Sulla, who had served under Marius. In 88 he was selected to conduct the war against Mithridates VI, king of Pontus, a nation east of Asia province (modern Turkey). Earlier, Rome had prevented Mithridates from placing puppet rulers on the thrones of neighboring Cappadocia and Bithynia, nations that were independent but lay within the Roman sphere of influence. An attack on Pontus by the Roman-sponsored ruler of Bithynia led Mithridates to fight. He overran Bithynia and Cappadocia and occupied the Roman province of Asia in 88 B.C. He ordered the native peoples of the province to massacre all Roman citizens living there, and reportedly they killed eighty thousand Romans in one day. This massive demonstration showed the rage felt by many in Asia against Roman rule.

Marius felt that he should have been given this command and tried to take it away from Sulla. Sulla took a page from his mentor's playbook and marched on Rome at the head of his army. He drove Marius out of Rome and then headed to Roman Asia. By 85 B.C. he had forced Mithridates to leave Asia. Two years later, he once again used military force to control Rome. In order to raise funds and also eliminate his enemies, he published a list of names and rewards for the death of each. By this method, he killed about 200 senators and 1,600 members of the next order, the equestrians. In assuming the office of dictator from 82-79 B.C. he sought to give the senatorial aristocracy the powers it had lost over the years. He added to the 150 members of the senate who had survived his purges an additional 400 men. This broadened the composition of the senate and weakened the power of the old families.

*The Roman Revolution: Pompey, Crassus and Julius Caesar.* Despite Sulla's restoration of senatorial powers, the senate remained unable to control its military leaders. After Sulla's death in 78 B.C., two of his generals, Pompey the Great and Crassus, were the first to prove this point. They rose to prominence by leading armies against revolts: Pompey in Italy and Spain, and Crassus against the escaped slaves under Spartacus (73-71 B.C.). The two served as fellow consuls in 70 B.C., and together they dismantled Sulla's reforms. In 67 a young Julius Caesar allied with them and helped convince the senate to give Pompey extraordinary powers to eliminate the pirates who had made trade in the eastern Mediterranean so risky.

Pompey did an amazing job of clearing the Mediterranean of pirates. This helped him gain command of a new war against Mithridates. Fighting between Pontus and Rome had broken out once again when Rome declared Bithynia, near Pontus, a province of Rome. Mithridates invaded Bithynia as the champion of a member of the former royal house. Between 66 and 62, Pompey defeated Mithridates and toppled his empire. Mithridates retreated from Pontus and committed suicide in 63 B.C. Pompey virtually redrew the map of the eastern Mediterranean, founding seven new Roman provinces and making treaties. Pontus was made a Roman province, as was Syria. Tigranes, king of Armenia, kept his kingdom independent only by acknowledging Pompey as conqueror and becoming an ally of Rome.[8]

Needing allies for his fight with the senate over his treaties and decisions in the East, Pompey helped Caesar win election as consul for 59 B.C. Caesar in his political campaigns allied with the remnants of Marius's followers and so gained the hatred of the senate. The mutual support system that Pompey, Crassus and Caesar developed has been called the First Triumvirate. Between 58 and 52 B.C. Caesar served as governor of Gaul and carried out a series of spectacular conquests. He brought most of western Europe into the Roman fold during these years.

Crassus was killed in 53 B.C. in a battle against the Parthian Empire, east of Syria and Palestine. Over the next two years, the relationship between Pompey and Caesar deteriorated. When Caesar refused the order of a nervous senate to relinquish command in Gaul and return to Rome, Pompey agreed to champion the senate against Caesar.

*The Roman Revolution: Civil war and the fall of the Republic.* In the civil war that followed Pompey's denunciation of Caesar (49-45 B.C.), Caesar returned from Gaul with his army and took control of Italy. He then pursued and defeated Pompey and the other generals who opposed him. When Caesar returned to Rome in 45, he showed clemency to his former enemies in the senate. Between 47 and 44, he initiated building programs, began to distribute land to his veterans, reformed the calendar that had become months out of synchronization with the seasons and addressed the problem of debt. Caesar made it clear that for him the old Republic was finished. When he had himself appointed "dictator for life" in 44 B.C., some senators reportedly feared that he would next have himself proclaimed king so they assassinated him.

Before his death, Caesar adopted his great-nephew Gaius Octavius (Octavian) as his heir. The eighteen-year-old and sickly Octavian, regarded by Caesar's veterans as their true leader, became part of a new ruling triumvirate along with Caesar's old lieutenants, Marc Antony and Lepidus. By 42 B.C. these three had taken vengeance on all of Caesar's murderers. This show of devotion *(pietas)* to the memory of his adoptive father endeared Octavian to Romans, especially to the soldiers who had fought for Caesar. In 36 B.C. Lepidus was dropped from the triumvirate. Octavian and Antony had a parting of the ways, and began building separate power bases: Antony in the east, Octavian in the west. Since Octavian controlled Italy, the only place Antony could go for the money and military support he needed was Egypt.

Though under Roman patronage, Egypt was still ruled by the dynasty established by Alexander the Great's general, Ptolemy. The Ptolemies were Macedonian in origin. They kept the conquered native peoples of Egypt under their control by assuming many of the traditional forms of Egyptian culture and by using only Macedonians and Greeks in their army. Most important, Rome had not yet raided its royal treasury. Antony struck up an alliance with the ruling Ptolemy, Cleopatra VII. To what degree their alliance was personal and romantic is uncertain, but Octavian played up the alliance as traitorous and immoral to drum up support in Italy for a war. In 31 B.C. he declared war, not on Antony but on Egypt, in order to avoid the stigma of civil war. Octavian's forces won a complete victory against Antony and Cleopatra that year at Actium on the western coast of Greece, and the two vanquished leaders committed suicide. Finally, Octavian, or Caesar Augustus as he would come to be known, was left undisputed ruler of the Roman world.

Thus by the time of Jesus, Rome was firmly in control of the Mediterranean and everyone in it. Its culture was poised to spread throughout the eastern Mediterranean.

## The Roman Empire

*Caesar Augustus (emperor, 31 B.C.-A.D. 14).* Octavian knew that a return to the Republic was neither possible nor desirable. The empire of Rome had become too far-flung and too complex to be governed by the old system (see map 7). At the same time, he attempted to avoid Julius Caesar's fate by retaining the offices and terminology of the Republic. He showed respect for the senate and maintained a modest personal lifestyle. Knowing that the senate needed him, in 27 B.C. he announced that, having restored the Republic, he was relinquishing his powers. A frantic senate persuaded him to retain the consulship and control of the military. It gave him the title *princeps* (literally, "first person" or "first among equals"), a term applied in the past to former consuls regarded as preeminent in honor and status. This is the origin of the English word *prince*. In the same year, the senate gave him the name Augustus ("enlarged one"). In 23 B.C. he resigned the consulship and was given by the senate extraordinary proconsular powers that allowed him to intervene in provincial government at his discretion (see in figure A.2 a photo of a statue of Caesar Augustus).

With the return of political stability, Augustus reduced the size of the army from sixty to twenty-eight legions. This involved settling over 100,000 veterans in colonies from Italy to Syria. Augustus paid for this out of Egypt's treasury, which he had seized after the defeat of Antony and Cleopatra.

Much of the legendary grandeur of the city of Rome resulted from Augustus's ambitious and nearly constant building programs. His buildings were enormous and opulent, a reflection of Rome's current great wealth. He nearly doubled the water supply volume by adding several aqueducts. He built the first permanent amphitheater in Rome. His buildings used marble on a large scale for the first time. According to the biographer Suetonius, Augustus said that he found Rome a city of brick and left it a city of marble. Meanwhile, Roman voices were beginning to complain that wealth and power were destroying the values that had made Rome great.

Roman conquests during the late Republic were consolidated and expanded under Augustus. Rebels in Spain were completely subdued, and Caesar's conquests in Gaul were organized into three provinces. Over a period of years, the southern part of central and eastern Europe fell to the Romans. But in A.D. 9 Rome suffered its worst defeat in many years when it lost three entire legions in an attempt to conquer Germany east of the Rhine. Augustus chose not to replace these legions and to give up on his goal of capturing Germany. Rather than try to defeat Rome's old enemy to the east of Syria, the Parthians, Augustus used the independent state of Armenia as a buffer against Parthia. The client kingdoms of Judea and Cappadocia served a similar function. From this point on, Rome rarely attempted territorial expansion; it began to focus more on maintaining its frontiers.

Augustus inaugurated what is known as the *principate* (rule of *princeps*, "first citizen"), an arrangement in which the ruler was to be viewed as first citizen of the Empire rather than dictator. In practice, however, the princeps enjoyed increasing power either because he took it or because the senate granted it to him.

*Tiberius Caesar (emperor, A.D. 14-37).* In A.D. 4, childless and near the end of life, Augustus made his stepson Tiberius his heir. By the time Augustus died in A.D. 14, the senate and people of Rome were fully ready to accept Tiberius as the new leader of Rome. Tiberius thus became the second emperor in what became the Julio-Claudian dynasty, named for the two families that composed it.

Tiberius proved to be an able administrator. He cut in half the state sales tax, which had been 1 percent, and left a large surplus in the treasury at his death. His greatest difficulty as emperor was getting along with the senate.

In 19 Tiberius responded to a public scandal by ordering the expulsion of all Jews from Rome. Reportedly four Jews from Rome had persuaded a wealthy Roman convert to contribute a large sum of money to the Jewish temple and then kept the money. Four thousand Roman Jews were drafted into military service in Sardinia.[9] However, either the expulsion edict was soon allowed to lapse or was never enforced, because within a few years the Roman Jewish community was as large as ever.

*Gaius Caligula (emperor, A.D. 37-41).* The year before his death, Tiberius appointed as joint heirs his grandson, Tiberius Gemellus, and his grandnephew, Gaius. Gaius when a little boy had been nicknamed Caligula, "little boots," by the troops of his father Germanicus. With the support of the Praetorian Guard, Gaius proclaimed himself emperor. He murdered Gemellus and used treason trials to confiscate the wealth of rich senators.

With Gaius a new era of Roman control over the Near East began. The period of rule through client kings began to give way to more direct rule by Rome. In 40 the Jewish author Philo led a delegation of Jews from Alexandria to the emperor. They protested their treatment at the hands of pagan Gentiles in the city, who had murdered a number of Jews in the process of setting up statues of the emperor in Alexandrian synagogues. The Jews explained that, while their beliefs prevented them from sacrificing to the emperor, they were always willing to sacrifice for him. Gaius responded that the failure of the Jews to recognize his divinity seemed not so much criminal as lunatic. Meanwhile, Gaius learned that, in the Judean town of Jamnia, Jews had destroyed an altar to the emperor set up by the town's Greeks. Gaius responded by ordering the legate (governor) of Syria to convert all places of worship in Judea, including the temple in Jerusalem, into shrines of emperor worship. This action was completely untypical of Roman attitudes and rule. The legate collected three legions and marched on Judea, but he delayed enforcing the order, fearing it would cause a general uprising. While he waited, word arrived that Gaius was dead, and the order was not carried out.[10]

Many stories of Gaius's mental instability have survived, for example his plan to make his horse a senator and his declaration that he was the incarnation of the god Jupiter. Anthony Barrett says that "while he was not clinically mad he was so obsessed with a sense of his own importance as to be practically devoid of any sense of moral responsibility."[11] Gaius lived a lavish lifestyle beyond even his extensive means. Rather than appear to rule simply as the first among equals, as had Augustus, he preferred to be seen as an absolute monarch. In 41 the Praetorian Guards, his personal guards who were supposed to protect him, murdered him and replaced him with his uncle, Claudius.

*Claudius (emperor, A.D. 41-54).* Claudius had never sought to rule the Empire. He lived for years in the shadow of his Julio-Claudian relatives, writing books and conversing with scholars. As emperor he attempted some well-meaning reforms, but he was too dependent on his freedmen advisors to give strong guidance to reforms. Under his direction, military leaders finally completed the conquest of Britain, which Julius Caesar had begun many years before. Claudius pursued an extensive program of public works, in particular the construction of a new port at Ostia, a few miles south of Rome.

During Claudius's reign, hostilities broke out once again between the Greeks and Jews of Alexandria. Rather than try to determine which side was at fault, he threatened to punish whichever side renewed the conflict in the future. He affirmed the traditional rights of Jews and criticized Gaius's "madness" in humiliating the Jews. Josephus tells us that Herod Agrippa I convinced Claudius to speak in favor of Jewish rights in Alexandria and elsewhere.[12]

Several sources tell us that Claudius ordered the expulsion of Jews from Rome during his reign. Suetonius says the Jews were expelled "because they were persistently rioting at the instigation of Chrestus." Orosius, referring to a passage in Josephus that we do not possess today, dates this edict to 49. If "Chrestus" refers to Christ, then this expulsion may have resulted from a dispute between Jews and Jewish converts to Christianity. *Chrestus* was indeed a variant spelling for the name of Christ *(Christus)*, and in both Tacitus and Tertullian we find the terms *Chrestianos* and *Chrestianer* used for Christians. This interpretation of the edict finds support in Acts 18, according to which the Jew

Aquila and his wife Priscilla flee Rome for Corinth as a result of this edict (Acts 18:1-3). Since Paul probably came to Corinth sometime in 50, a date of 49 for the edict makes sense. The context of Acts implies that Aquila and Priscilla were Christians before they met Paul; thus, it is reasonable to think that they were Christians before they left Rome. Paul, in writing to the Romans in the second half of the 50s, also indicates that Christians were present in Rome by the 40s when he says that he has wanted "for many years" to visit the Roman Christians (Rom 15:23).

This edict is evidence that the first Roman Christians were Jewish converts to Christianity who came into conflict with the Roman Jewish community. This conflict may have led to the kind of violence portrayed by Acts in cities visited by the apostle Paul. Because of the constant disturbances, the Roman government ordered the expulsion of all Jews from Rome. But since there were so many Roman Jews, and since some were Roman citizens and some were slaves belonging to citizens, probably not all Jews actually left. In any case, the edict would have lapsed upon the death of Claudius in 54. We find Aquila and Priscilla once again in Rome when Paul writes the letter to the Romans in the late 50s (Rom 16:3).

*Nero (emperor, A.D. 54-68).* Claudius was succeeded by his adopted son, Nero. Nero's rule can be divided into two periods: the early period, until 62, when he allowed himself to be guided by the philosopher Seneca and by the head of the Praetorian Guard, the Praetorian Prefect Burrus; and the later period, when he ruled on his own. The early period saw a more balanced, enlightened rule, including several positive reforms. The later era was characterized by the eccentric rule of a despot who believed he was above all an artist, and who left the Empire in the hands of freedmen while he conducted a concert tour through Greece. Out of his love for Greek culture, on his own initiative he declared all of Greece free. But out of fear for his position, he viciously murdered anyone who seemed to threaten him. Reportedly among his victims were his mother, his wife and his stepbrother.

A fire in July of 64 ravaged most of the center of Rome. Nero quickly began rebuilding the city and provided for the immediate needs of the victims. But the Roman historian Tacitus says that his efforts could not "banish the sinister rumor and belief" that the fire was intentional (*Annals* 15.44). Although Tacitus seems to believe the rumors that Nero ordered the fire, there is no hard evidence for this. At any rate, Nero needed to remove blame from himself in the minds of the angry Roman public. He found appropriate scapegoats, according to Tacitus, in the Christians. Thus began the Neronian Persecution.

Hundreds of Roman Christians, perhaps several thousand, lost their lives in this persecution. Tacitus says that "an immense multitude" was convicted (*Annals* 15.44). Clement uses a similar phrase when he says that "a great multitude" was put to death at this time (*1 Clement* 6.1). The unanimous testimony of later Christian tradition is that Peter and Paul were both put to death under Nero. Tacitus's description of the persecution suggests that the Roman Christians were mostly noncitizens. A citizen could not have been put to death in the ways Tacitus describes: dismemberment by wild dogs, crucifixion and death by fire. The persecution probably lasted until 66.

Apparently the Christians were chosen for this role because of their unpopularity. Tacitus calls them "a class hated for their abominations" (*Annals* 15.44). Christians were disliked for rejecting the Roman gods and following strange practices. They were a new group in Rome and so were more distrusted even than the Jews. Their strangeness was compounded by the fact that they acted like a nation but lacked both ethnic unity and a single place of origin. Another reason for their unpopularity and perhaps for their selection as scapegoats was the belief among many Christians that the world would soon end by fire.

In 66 dissatisfaction with Roman rule finally led to a general revolt in Judea. Rome sent an army under the Roman general Vespasian to put it down. Vespasian had almost completed the restoration of peace when Nero died and civil war broke out over the succession.

*Vespasian (emperor, A.D. 69-79).* Nero's death was followed by a year of civil war, in which three men (Galba, Otho and Vitellius) each served as emperor for a brief period. In mid-69, the Roman general Vespasian, then still in the middle of putting down the Jewish rebellion, decided to use his influence with the legions in the Mediterranean to challenge Vitellius for the throne. He succeeded in making his relatively obscure family, the Flavians, the new imperial dynasty even though they were not related by blood or marriage to the only dynasty Rome had yet known, the Julio-Claudians. Despite his public claim to rule after the manner of Augustus, Vespasian assumed from the beginning all the various offices and powers that Augustus, Tiberius and Claudius had taken years to accept. Vespasian served as a consul each year, appointed his son Titus as praetorian prefect, and publicly stated that one of his sons would succeed him as emperor.[13]

Vespasian brought stability to the Empire. He put down rebellions, reformed the army, built extensive fortifications for the defense of Rome and raised numerous public buildings in the capital. Most important of all, he restored the Roman economy, which had been in a terrible state when he took power. His son Titus took over command of the war in Judea when Vespasian went to Rome to assume power. Titus destroyed Jerusalem and its temple in A.D. 70. A triumphal arch eventually was erected next to the Roman Forum to commemorate the victory.

*Titus (emperor, A.D.79-81).* Titus was the first natural son to succeed his father as emperor. During the reign of Titus, Mount Vesuvius in southern Italy erupted, burying the Roman towns of Pompeii and Herculaneum. Titus marked the completion of the Flavian Amphitheater (Colosseum), which had been begun by Vespasian, with a hundred-day-long festival. We have no evidence that Christians were ever martyred in this arena. Built on the site of Nero's obnoxiously opulent palace grounds, the Colosseum was intended from the first to generate good will for the Flavians, and it succeeded in doing so. Titus died of apparently natural causes only two years into his reign.

*Domitian (emperor, A.D. 81-96).* After Titus's death in 81, his younger brother, Domitian, became emperor. Domitian was an able administrator and rebuilt extensively following a major fire in Rome in 80. The Empire prospered under his administration. Domitian soon gained the undying hostility of the senate by his autocratic ways. After 86 he apparently required officials of his household to address him as "Lord and God." A persecution of Jews occurred about 90 and soon engulfed Christians.

Domitian grew increasingly suspicious of those around them and had several important people executed. This led to his assassination in A.D. 96. Christian tradition says that the apostle John was exiled to the Isle of Patmos around 90 but returned to Ephesus after Domitian's death.

**For Further Reading**

Christ, Karl. *The Romans.* Trans. Christopher Holme. Berkeley: University of California Press, 1984.

Grant, Michael. *History of Rome.* New York: Charles Scribner's Sons, 1978.

Nagle, D. Brendan. *The Ancient World,* p. 283. Englewood Cliffs, N.J.: Prentice Hall, 1989.

Rostovzeff, M. I. *The Social and Economic History of the Roman Empire.* 2 vols. 2nd ed. Rev. P. M. Fraser. Oxford: Clarendon, 1963.

# *Appendix B*

## Chronology
## of Events

| Date | Rome | Judea | Palestine Outside Judea | Christianity |
|------|------|-------|-------------------------|--------------|
| 50 B.C. | Dictatorship of Caesar (48-44) | Antipater helps Caesar in Egypt (48) | | |
| | | Antipater's sons made joint rulers of Judea (42) | | |
| 40 B.C. | Rome retakes Parthia (37) | Herod the Great (37-34) | | |
| | Emperor Caesar Augustus (31 B.C.-A.D. 14) | | | |
| 30 B.C. | Deaths of Antony & Cleopartra (30) Egypt a province (30) Achaea a province (30) Galatia a province (25) Cyprus a province (22) | | | |
| 20 B.C. | | Herod begins rebuilding temple (19) | | |
| 10 B.C. | | Death of Herod (4 B.C.) Archelaus ethnarch of Judea, Samaria & Idumea (4 B.C.-A.D. 6) | Philip tetrarch of Iturea & Trachonitis (4 B.C.-A.D. 34) | Birth of Jesus (7 or 6 B.C.) |
| A.D. 6 | | Judea made a Roman province; census under Quirinius (6) | Herod Antipas tetrarch of Galilee/ Perea (4 B.C.-A.D. 39) | |
| | Varus loses 3 legions in Germany (9) | Prefect Coponius (6-9) Prefect Marcus Ambivius (9-12) | | |

| Date | Rome | Judea | Palestine Outside Judea | Christianity |
|---|---|---|---|---|
| A.D. 10 | | Prefect Annius Rufus (12-15) | | |
| | Emperior Tiberius (14-37) Sejanus's rise to power (17) | Prefect Valerius Gratus (15-26) Joseph Caiaphas high priest (18-36) | | |
| A.D. 20 | | Prefect Pontius Pilate (26-36) | Herod Antipas leaves wife for Herodias (c. 29) | Beginning of John's ministry (26) |
| A.D. 30 | Cappadocia a province (??-??) | Pilate's massacre of Samaritans (36) Prefect Marullus (37-41) | | Crucifixion of Jesus (Passover 30) Conversion of Paul (32 or 35) |
| A.D. 40 | Emperor Gaius (37-41) Alexandrian Jews meet with Gaius (40) Gaius's order to desecrate temple (failed) (40) Murder of Gaius (41) Emperor Claudius (41-54) Expulsion of Roman Jews by Claudius (49) | King Herod Agrippa I (41-44) Procurator Cuspius Fadus (44-46) Procurator Cumanus (48-52) | | Martyrdom of James (44) Famine relief visit of Paul/ Barnabas to Jerusalem (46) Paul's first missionary journey (47-48) Jerusalem Council (49) Second missionary journey (49-52) |
| A.D. 50 | Gallio proconsul of Achaia (51-52) Death of Claudius Jews return to Rome (54) | Procurator Antonius Felix (52-59) | Herod Agrippa II king of Iturea & Trachonitis (53-94) | Paul's eighteen months in Corinth (summer 50-spring (52) Third missionary journey (52-56) Paul's three months in Corinth (winter 55/56) Paul's arrest in Jerusalem (spring 56) Caesarean imprisonment of Paul (56-58) |

| Date | Rome | Judea | Palestine Outside Judea | Christianity |
|---|---|---|---|---|
| | | Procurator Festus (c. 57-60) | | Voyage to Rome shipwreck (late fall/winter 58) |
| A.D. 60 | | Procurator Albinus (62-64) | | |
| | | | | Roman imprisonment of Paul (59-61) |
| | | Procurator Gessius Florus (64-66) | | Release & final travels of Paul (61-63) |
| | | Revolt in Judea (66-73) | | |
| | | | | Persecution under Nero (64) |
| A.D. 70 | Year of the Four Emperors (68/69) | Conquest of Jerusalem; destruction of temple (70) | | |
| | Emperor Vespasian (69-79) | | | |
| | Mount Vesuvius erupts (79) | | | |
| A.D. 80 | Emperor Titus (79-81) | | | |
| | Completion of Colosseum (81) | | | |
| | Emperor Domitian (81-96) | | | |
| | German "Limes" built (88) | | | |
| A.D. 90 | | | | Domitian's persecution (90) |

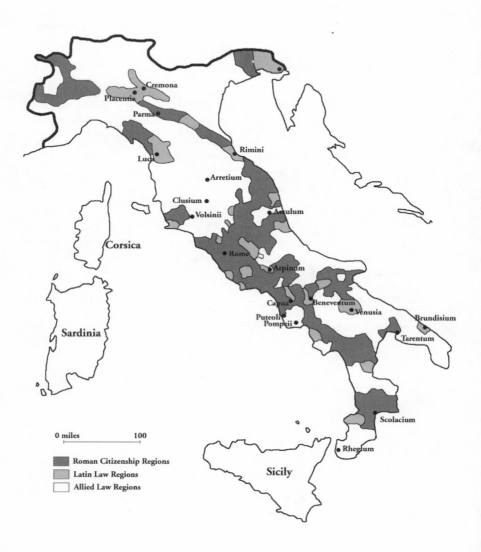

**Map 1.  Italy in the second century** B.C.

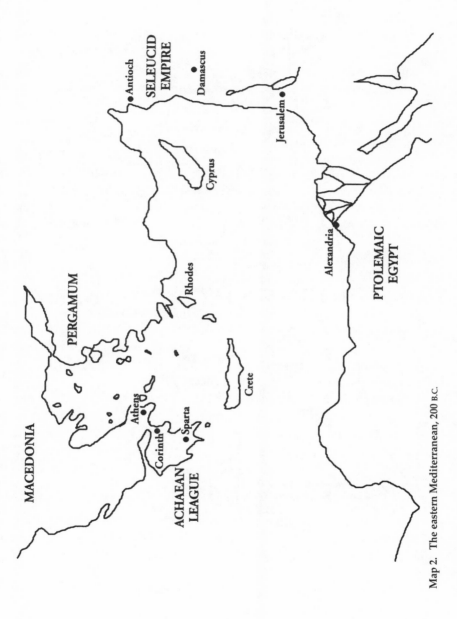

Map 2. The eastern Mediterranean, 200 B.C.

**Map 3. Palestine in the New Testament era**

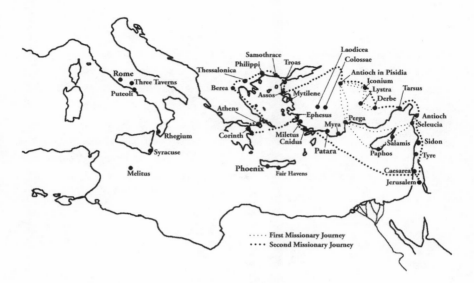

Map 4. Paul's first and second missionary journeys

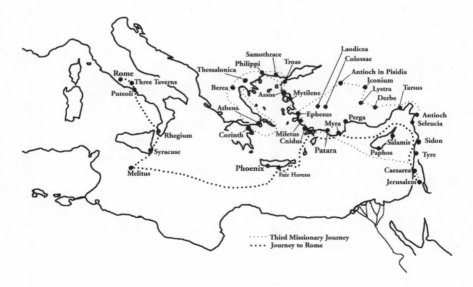

Map 5. Paul's third missionary journey and journey to Rome

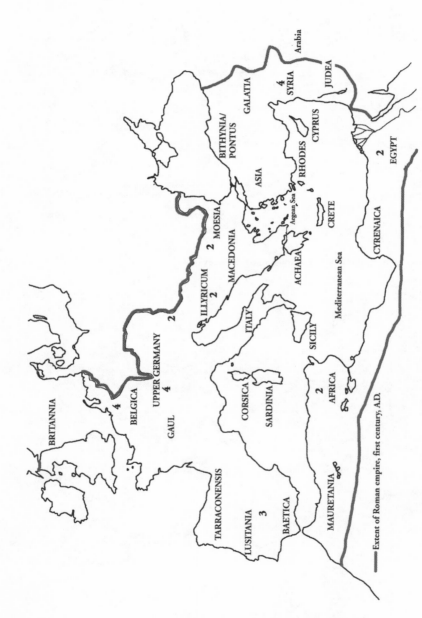

Map 6. Location and number of the Roman legions, A.D. 23

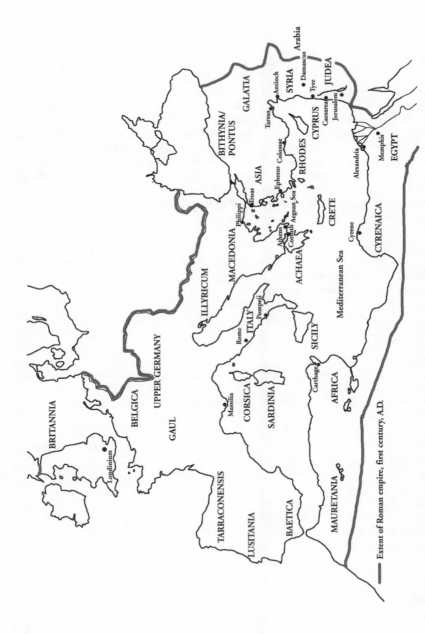

Map 7. Provinces and major cities of the Roman Empire, first century A.D.

BRITANNIA
Londinium

BELGICA
UPPER GERMANY
GAUL

TARRACONENSIS
LUSITANIA
BAETICA

MAURETANIA

MASSILIA
CORSICA
SARDINIA

ITALY
Rome
Pompeii

SICILY

AFRICA
Carthage

ILLYRICUM

MACEDONIA
Philippi

ACHAEA
Athens
Corinth
Aegean Sea

CRETE

Mediterranean Sea

Cyrene
CYRENAICA

ASIA
Troas
Ephesus Colossae

RHODES

CYPRUS

BITHYNIA/
PONTUS

GALATIA

Tarsus
Antioch
SYRIA
Damascus
Tyre
Caesarea
Jerusalem
JUDEA
Arabia

Alexandria
Memphis
EGYPT

—— Extent of Roman empire, first century, A.D.

# Notes

### Chapter 1: Historical Background to the New Testament Era
[1]See appendix A for a fuller treatment of the historical background of the New Testament.

[2]The following character is imaginary, based on how a relatively contented member of a local ruling class may have perceived the great powers of his day. I chose a Jewish leader because of the focus of this book, but much of what he says could just as easily have come from a leading Greek, Syrian or Egyptian. These people had sold out to Rome (or believed they had taken the best deal they could on behalf of their people). I imagine here a leader who is not entirely comfortable with the deal he has made and so seeks to justify it. Of course, real persons had many motivations for assimilating into the Roman system and accepting it to varying degrees.

### Chapter 2: Life & Death in the First Century
[1]John E. Stambaugh and David L. Balch, *The New Testament in Its Social Environment* (Philadelphia: Westminster Press, 1986), p. 69.

[2]John Crook, *Law and Life of Rome* (Ithaca, N.Y.: Cornell University Press, 1967), pp. 232-33.

[3]Stambaugh and Balch, *New Testament*, p. 117.

[4]Ronald F. Hock, *The Social Context of Paul's Ministry: Tentmaking and Apostleship* (Philadelphia: Fortress, 1980), pp. 32-33.

[5]Ibid., pp. 22-25.

[6]Ibid., pp. 37-39.

[7]Karl Christ, *The Romans*, trans. Christopher Holme (Berkeley: University of California Press, 1984), pp. 110-17.

[8]J. P. V. D. Balsdon, *Romans and Aliens* (London: Duckworth, 1979), pp. 244-329.

[9]Hock, *Social Context*, p. 27.

[10]Stambaugh and Balch, *New Testament*, p. 38.

[11]Wayne A. Meeks, *The First Urban Christians: The Social World of the Apostle Paul* (New Haven, Conn.: Yale University Press, 1983), pp. 16-17.

[12]Ibid., p. 18.

[13]Christ, *Romans*, pp. 108-9.

[14]Balsdon, *Romans and Aliens*, pp. 222-23.

[15]Ugo Enrico Paoli, *Rome: Its People, Life and Customs*, trans. R. D. Macnaghten (New York: David McKay, 1963), p. 89.

[16]Balsdon, *Romans and Aliens*, p. 224.

[17]Peter Garnsey and Richard Saller, *The Roman Empire: Economy, Society, and Culture* (Berkeley: University of California Press, 1987), pp. 116-17.

[18]Christ, *Romans*, pp. 106-8.

[19]Balsdon, *Romans and Aliens*, pp. 214-16.

[20]Ibid.

[21]Ibid., p. 254.

[22]Iino Kajanto, "On Divorce Among the Common Peoples of Rome," *Revue des études latines: mélanges Marcel Durry* 47 (1970): 99-113.

[23]Beryl Rawson, "The Roman Family," in *The Family in Ancient Rome: New Perspectives*, ed. Beryl Rawson (Ithaca, N.Y.: Cornell University Press, 1986), p. 13.

[24]Ronny Reich, "Caiaphas' Name Inscribed on Bone Boxes," *Biblical Archaeology Review* 18 (1992): 38.

## Chapter 3: The City in the Greco-Roman World

[1]Juvenal on life in the city of Rome. Juvenal, *The Sixteen Satires*, trans. Peter Green (Baltimore: Penguin, 1967), pp. 235-37.

[2]See chapter thirteen for descriptions of the major cities of the Empire that have some relationship to early Christianity and the New Testament.

[3]John E. Stambaugh and David L. Balch, *The New Testament in Its Social Environment* (Philadelphia: Westminster Press, 1986), pp. 107-10.

[4]Ramsay MacMullen, *Roman Social Relations* (New Haven, Conn.: Yale University Press, 1974), p. 60.

[5]Dio Chrysostom *Orationes* 34.21-23, quoted in MacMullen, *Roman Social Relations*, p. 59.

[6]John Crook, *Law and Life of Rome* (Ithaca, N.Y.: Cornell University Press, 1967), p. 243; MacMullen, *Roman Social Relations*, pp. 57-67.

[7]James S. Jeffers, *Conflict at Rome: Social Order and Hierarchy in Early Christianity* (Philadelphia: Fortress, 1991), pp. 3-7.

[8]Frederick W. Danker, *Benefactor: Epigraphic Study of a Graeco-Roman and New Testament Semantic Field* (St. Louis: Clayton, 1982), p. 122; Stambaugh and Balch, *New Testament*, pp. 74-76.

[9]A. N. Sherwin-White, *Roman Law and Roman Society in the New Testament* (Oxford: Oxford University Press, 1963), pp. 139-40.

[10]Emil Schürer, *The History of the Jewish People in the Age of Jesus Christ*, ed. Geza Vermes and Fergus Millar, trans. T. A. Burkill, 5 vols. (Edinburgh: T & T Clark, 1973), 2:23.

[11]A. H. M. Jones, *The Cities of the Eastern Roman Provinces*, 2nd ed. (Oxford: Clarendon, 1971), pp. 276.

[12]Gal 1:21; cf. Gal 2:1-14; Acts 11:25-26; 13:1. This could be as many as fourteen years if Galatians 2:1 does not include the three years in Arabia, or eleven years if it does.

## Chapter 4: Influences on Christian Organization

[1]Letter about Christians in the Roman province of Bithynia, written by Pliny the Younger to the emperor Trajan in the early second century A.D.; Betty Radice, trans., *The Letters of the Younger Pliny* 10.33 (New York: Penguin, 1963), p. 272.

[2]Letter from the emperor Trajan to Pliny the Younger, governor of Bithynia province, early second century A.D.; Radice, *Letters of the Younger Pliny* 10.34, p. 272.

[3]John E. Stambaugh and David L. Balch, *The New Testament in Its Social Environment* (Philadelphia: Westminster Press, 1986), pp. 124-27.

[4]For more on this, see James S. Jeffers, *Conflict at Rome: Social Order and Hierarchy in Early Christianity* (Minneapolis: Fortress, 1991), chap. 3.

[5]Stambaugh and Balch, *New Testament*, pp. 140-41.

[6]Scriptores Historiae Augustae *Severus Alexander* 49.6.

[7]E. A. Judge, "The Early Christians as a Scholastic Community: I and II," *Journal of Religious History* 1 (1960): 4-15; 2 (1961): 125-37.

[8]Wayne A. Meeks, *The First Urban Christians* (New Haven, Conn.: Yale University Press, 1983), pp. 77-80; Stambaugh and Balch, *New Testament,* pp. 140-41.

[9]Meeks, *First Urban Christians,* pp. 77-80.

[10]Ibid.

[11]Stambaugh and Balch, *New Testament,* pp. 140-41.

[12]Ibid., pp. 124-27.

[13]Meeks, *First Urban Christians,* pp. 75-77.

[14]Eva Cantarella, *Pandora's Daughters,* trans. Maureen B. Fant (Baltimore: Johns Hopkins University Press, 1987), pp. 113-14. See also John Crook, *Law and Life of Rome* (Ithaca, N.Y.: Cornell University Press, 1967), chap. 4; Pierre Grimal, *The Civilization of Rome,* trans. W. S. Maguinness (New York: Simon and Schuster, 1963), p. 119.

[15]Meeks, *First Urban Christians,* pp. 75-77.

[16]Fathers and children are not mentioned in the 1 Peter passages.

[17]Quoted in Carolyn Osiek and David L. Balch, *Families in the New Testament World: Households and House Churches* (Louisville: Westminster John Knox, 1997), p. 119.

[18]David E. Aune, *The New Testament in Its Literary Environment* (Philadelphia: Westminster Press, 1987), p. 196. See also David L. Balch, *Let Wives Be Submissive: The Domestic Code in 1 Peter* (Chico, Calif.: Scholars, 1981).

[19]The comment in 1 Peter 3:7 about a woman as a weaker vessel probably refers to her generally weaker physique, though this has been disputed. In any case, this passage does not appear to indicate inferiority.

## Chapter 5: Religion in the Greco-Roman World

[1]F. F. Bruce, *Paul: Apostle of the Heart Set Free* (Grand Rapids, Mich.: Eerdmans, 1977), p. 170. We are not certain to what writing Paul refers. For several ideas, see F. F. Bruce, *The Acts of the Apostles,* 3rd ed. (Grand Rapids, Mich.: Eerdmans, 1990), pp. 384-85.

[2]See Ronald H. Nash, *Christianity and the Hellenistic World* (Grand Rapids, Mich.: Zondervan, 1984), pp. 115-48.

[3]Ibid., chaps. 7-11.

[4]Everett F. Harrison, *The Apostolic Church* (Grand Rapids, Mich.: Eerdmans, 1985), pp. 12-13.

[5]Peter Garnsey and Richard Saller, *The Roman Empire: Economy, Society, and Culture* (Berkeley: University of California Press, 1987), p. 163.

[6]Ibid., pp. 164-65.

[7]John E. Stambaugh and David L. Balch, *The New Testament in Its Social Environment* (Philadelphia: Westminster, 1986), pp. 130-32.

[8]Wayne A. Meeks, *The First Urban Christians: The Social World of the Apostle Paul* (New Haven, Conn.: Yale University Press, 1983), p. 20.

[9]Garnsey and Saller, *Roman Empire,* pp. 169-70.

## Chapter 6: Governing of the Provinces & Palestine

[1]D. Brendan Nagle, *The Ancient World* (Englewood Cliffs, N.J.: Prentice Hall, 1989), pp. 288-92.

[2]A. N. Sherwin-White, *Roman Law and Roman Society in the New Testament* (Oxford: Oxford University Press, 1963), pp. 6-8.

[3]Karl Christ, *The Romans,* trans. Christopher Holme (Berkeley: University of California Press, 1984), p. 85.

[4]John E. Stambaugh and David L. Balch, *The New Testament in Its Social Environment* (Philadelphia: Westminster Press, 1986), pp. 155-56.

[5]F. F. Bruce, *New Testament History* (Garden City, N.Y.: Doubleday, 1980), p. 19.

[6]J. P. V. D. Balsdon, *Romans and Aliens* (London: Duckworth, 1979), pp. 132-33.

[7]Fergus Millar, *The Roman Near East* (Cambridge, Mass.: Harvard University Press, 1993), p. 53.

[8]Ibid., pp. 39-41.

[9]Stambaugh and Balch, *New Testament*, pp. 23-30.

[10]Bruce, *New Testament History*, p. 13.

[11]For a thorough and very readable study of Herod and his line, see Peter Richardson, *Herod: King of the Jews and Friend of the Romans* (Columbia, S.C.: University of South Carolina Press, 1996).

[12]The alternative, that Mark is using this term for the benefit of its Roman readers, does not seem as likely to me.

[13]Millar, *Roman Near East*, p. 45.

[14]See chap. 7 for a discussion of the census mentioned in Luke 2:1.

[15]Philo *On the Embassy to Gaius* 302. Quoted in Steve Mason, *Josephus and the New Testament* (Peabody, Mass.: Hendrickson, 1992), p. 105.

[16]Millar, *Roman Near East*, p. 60.

[17]Acts 12:1-19. Acts here calls him "Herod the king" and refers to his son, Agrippa II, as "Agrippa the king" in 25:13.

[18]Bruce, *New Testament History*, p. 355; Mason, *Josephus*, p. 107.

[19]Mason, *Josephus*, p. 108.

[20]Millar, *Romans Near East*, p. 63.

[21]A. H. M. Jones, *The Cities of the Eastern Roman Provinces*, 2nd ed. (Oxford: Clarendon, 1971), pp. 256, 260.


**Chapter 7: Tools of Governance**

[1]A. N. Sherwin-White, *Roman Law and Roman Society in the New Testament* (Oxford: Oxford University Press, 1963), pp. 125-26.

[2]D. Brendan Nagle, *The Ancient World* (Englewood Cliffs, N.J.: Prentice Hall, 1989), pp. 290-91.

[3]F. F. Bruce, *New Testament History* (Garden City, N.Y.: Doubleday, 1980), p. 32.

[4]Oxyrhynchus Papyrus 255 in George Milligan, *Selections from the Greek Papyri* (Cambridge: Cambridge University Press, 1910), pp. 44-47.

[5]See Keith Hopkins, "Taxes and Trade in the Roman Empire," *Journal of Roman Studies* 70 (1980): 126; Fergus Millar, *The Roman Near East* (Cambridge, Mass.: Harvard University Press, 1993), pp. 49-52; Tenney Frank, ed., *Rome and Italy of the Empire*, An Economic Survey of Ancient Rome 5 (Baltimore: Johns Hopkins Press, 1933), p. 7.

[6]John E. Stambaugh and David L. Balch, *New Testament in Its Social Environment* (Philadelphia: Westminster Press, 1986), pp. 79-81; Sherwin-White, *Roman Law*, pp. 124-25; Michael H. Crawford, "Money and Exchange in the Roman World," *Journal of Roman Studies* 60 (1970): 40-48.

[7]Sherwin-White, *Roman Law*, pp. 13-15.

[8]For more on crucifixion, see Martin Hengel, *Crucifixion in the Ancient World and the Folly of the Message of the Cross* (Philadelphia: Fortress, 1977).

[9]Wayne Meeks, *The First Urban Christians* (New Haven, Conn.: Yale University Press, 1983), p. 66.

[10]For more on the options, see R. A. Kearsley, "The Asiarchs," in *The Book of Acts in Its Greco-Roman Setting*, ed. D. W. J. Gill and C. Gempf (Grand Rapids, Mich.: Eerdmans, 1994), pp. 363-76.

[11]Tacitus *Annals* 15.73.4; see also Dio Cassius 61(60).35.2-4; 62.20.1.

[12]Bruce, *New Testament History*, p. 254, Sherwin-White, *Roman Law*, pp. 99-107.

[13]F. F. Bruce, *Paul: Apostle of the Heart Set Free* (Grand Rapids, Mich.: Eerdmans, 1983), p. 361.

[14]Sherwin-White, *Roman Law,* pp. 108-19.

[15]Karl Christ, *The Romans,* trans. Christopher Holme (Berkeley: University of California Press, 1984), pp. 74-76.

[16]Ramsay MacMullen, *Roman Social Relations* (New Haven, Conn.: Yale University Press, 1974), pp. 94-95; based in part on conjecture. See B. Dobson, "Legionary Centurion or Equestrian Officer? A Comparison of Pay and Prospects" *Ancient Society* 3 (1972): 198.

[17]Suzanne Dixon, *The Roman Family* (Baltimore: Johns Hopkins University Press, 1992), pp. 55-58.

[18]Millar, *Roman Near East,* p. 85.

[19]Sherwin-White, *Roman Law,* p. 110.

## Chapter 8: Social Class & Status in the Empire

[1]Cicero, quoted in Ramsay MacMullen, *Roman Social Relations* (New Haven, Conn.: Yale University Press, 1974), p. 116.

[2]D. Brendan Nagle, *The Ancient World* (Englewood Cliffs, N.J.: Prentice Hall, 1989), p. 278.

[3]Karl Christ, *The Romans,* trans. Christopher Holme (Berkeley: University of California Press, 1984), pp. 66-70; Richard Duncan-Jones, *The Economy of the Roman Empire: Quantitative Studies* (London: Cambridge University Press, 1974), pp. 17-32.

[4]MacMullen, *Roman Social Relations,* p. 89.

[5]Christ, *Romans,* pp. 70-72.

[6]MacMullen, *Roman Social Relations,* p. 105.

[7]John E. Stambaugh and David L. Balch, *The New Testament in Its Social Environment* (Philadelphia: Westminster Press, 1986), p. 66.

[8]Naphtali Lewis, "A Veteran in Quest of a Home" *Transactions and Proceedings of the American Philological Association* 90 (1959): 140.

[9]MacMullen, *Roman Social Relations,* p. 105.

[10]Gerd Theissen, *The Social Setting of Pauline Christianity: Essays on Corinth* (Philadelphia: Fortress, 1982), pp. 145-74.

[11]Seneca *On Benefits* 1.4.2. Cf. Richard P. Saller, *Personal Patronage Under the Early Empire* (New York: Cambridge University Press, 1982), p. 119 n. 1. See also Juvenal *Satires* 1.46; 7.142; Ludwig Friedländer, *Roman Life and Manners Under the Early Empire,* trans. L. A. Magnus, 4 vols. (New York: Dutton, 1908-1913), 2:195-202.

[12]Christ, *Romans,* p. 97; H. G. Pflaum, *Abrégé des Procurateurs Equestres* (Paris: E. de Boccard, 1974), p. 19; Friedländer, *Roman Life,* p. 197.

[13]P. A. Brunt, *Social Conflicts in the Roman Republic* (New York: Norton, 1971), p. 48. P. R. C. Weaver, *Familia Caesaris* (Cambridge: Cambridge University Press, 1972), pp. 5-6; chap. 22.

[14]Dio Chrysostom *Orationes* 7.125, quoted in MacMullen, *Roman Social Relations,* p. 118.

[15]*Corpus inscriptionum latinarum* 4.9839b, quoted in MacMullen, *Roman Social Relations,* p. 119.

[16]Wayne A. Meeks, *The First Urban Christians: The Social World of the Apostle Paul* (New Haven, Conn.: Yale University Press, 1983), p. 73.

[17]Ibid., p. 53.

## Chapter 9: Citizenship

[1]Karl Christ, *The Romans,* trans. Christopher Holme (Berkeley: University of California, 1984), pp. 81-83; A. N. Sherwin-White, *Roman Law and Roman Society in the New Testament* (Oxford: Oxford University Press, 1963), pp. 172-93.

[2]John Crook, *Law and Life of Rome* (Ithaca, N.Y.: Cornell University Press, 1967), pp. 255-57.

[3]John E. Stambaugh and David L. Balch, *The New Testament in Its Social Environment* (Philadelphia: Westminster Press, 1986), pp. 31-32.

[4]Though most scholars accept that Paul was a Roman citizen, some dispute Paul's citizenship, based largely on questions about the accuracy of Acts. For the latter, see Calvin Roetzel, *Paul: The Man and the Myth* (Columbia, S.C.: University of South Carolina Press, 1998), and Jerome Murphy-O'Connor, *Paul: A Critical Life* (N.Y.: Oxford University Press, 1996).

[5]Crook, *Law*, pp. 46-47.

[6]See the introduction to *Corpus inscriptionum latinarum* 16 for examples.

[7]J. P. V. D. Balsdon, *Romans and Aliens* (London: Duckworth, 1979), pp. 146-49.

[8]Sherwin-White, *Roman Law*, p. 162.

[9]Ibid., pp. 144-71.

[10]William F. Arndt and F. Wilbur Gingrich, *A Greek-English Lexicon of the New Testament and Other Early Christian Literature*, 4th ed. (Chicago: University of Chicago Press, 1952), p. 693.

## Chapter 10: The Jews in the Cities

[1]George La Piana, "Foreign Groups in Rome During the First Centuries of the Empire," *Harvard Theological Review* 20 (1927): 183-403, esp. 189.

[2]Everett F. Harrison, *The Apostolic Church* (Grand Rapids, Mich.: Eerdmans, 1985), pp. 5-6.

[3]Wayne A. Meeks, *The First Urban Christians: The Social World of the Apostle Paul* (New Haven, Conn.: Yale University Press, 1983), pp. 32-39.

[4]Wolfgang Wiefel, "The Jewish Community in Ancient Rome," in *The Romans Debate*, rev. ed., ed. Karl P. Donfried (Peabody, Mass: Hendrickson, 1991), pp. 86-94.

[5]Cicero *Pro Flacco* 69; Juvenal *Satires* 3.14; 6.542-48; 14.105-6.

[6]Meeks, *First Urban Christians*, pp. 32-39.

[7]Schmuel Safrai and Moses Stern, eds., *The Jewish People in the First Century*, 2 vols. (Philadelphia: Fortress, 1974), 1:488, 500; Victor Tcherikover, *Hellenistic Civilization and the Jews*, trans. Shimon Applebaum (New York: Atheneum, 1970), pp. 302-3.

[8]Meeks, *First Urban Christians*, pp. 80-81.

## Chapter 11: Slavery

[1]For more on modern-era slavery, see Orlando Patterson, *Slavery and Social Death: A Comparative Study* (Cambridge, Mass.: Harvard University Press, 1982).

[2]P. A. Brunt, *Social Conflicts in the Roman Republic* (New York: W. W. Norton, 1971), p. 124.

[3]For an excellent study of this passage in light of slavery, see S. Scott Bartchy, *Mallon Chresai: First-Century Slavery and the Interpretation of 1 Corinthians 7:21* (Atlanta: Scholars, 1985).

[4]Richard A. Horsley, *Jesus and the Spiral of Violence* (San Francisco: Harper & Row, 1987), pp. 254-55.

[5]J. P. V. D. Balsdon, *Romans and Aliens* (London: Duckworth, 1979), pp. 80-81.

[6]Gillian Clark, "Roman Women," *Greece and Rome* 28 (1981): 193-212, esp. 198; Sarah Pomeroy, *Goddesses, Whores, Wives, Slaves: Women in Classical Antiquity* (New York: Schocken, 1975), pp. 191-92.

[7]Ramsay MacMullen, *Roman Social Relations* (New Haven, Conn.: Yale University Press, 1974), p. 95.

[8]Frank M. Snowden, *Before Color Prejudice: The Ancient View of Blacks* (Cambridge, Mass.: Harvard University Press, 1983).

[9]Suzanne Dixon, *The Roman Family* (Baltimore: Johns Hopkins University Press, 1992), p. 90.

[10]Eph 5:21-6:9, Col 3:18—4:1, 1 Tim 6:1-2, and Tit 2:9-10.

[11]Quoted in Karl Christ, *The Romans*, trans. Christopher Holme (Berkeley: University of

California Press, 1984), pp. 78-79.

[12]Pomeroy, *Goddesses*, pp. 201-2.

[13]Beryl Rawson, "Family Life Among the Lower Classes at Rome in the First Two Centuries of the Empire," *Classical Philology* 61 (1966): 82.

[14]John Crook, *Law and Life of Rome* (Ithaca, N.Y.: Cornell University Press, 1967), p. 51.

[15]Michael P. Johnson and James L. Roark, *Black Masters: A Free Family of Color in the Old South* (New York: W. W. Norton, 1984).

[16]P. R. C. Weaver, *"Familia Caesaris": A Social Study of the Emperor's Freedmen and Slaves* (New York: Cambridge University Press, 1972), p. 4; T. M. Finn, "Social Mobility, Imperial Civil Service and the Spread of Early Christianity," *Studia Patristica* 17 (1982): 31-37.

### Chapter 12: The Family, Women & Education

[1]Richard P. Saller, "Men's Age at Marriage and Its Consequences in the Roman Family," *Classical Philology* 82 (1987): 21-34.

[2]Richard P. Saller and Brent D. Shaw, "Tombstones and Roman Family Relations in the Principate: Civilians, Soldiers and Slaves," *Journal of Roman Studies* 74 (1984): 124-56, esp. 145-51.

[3]Adele Reinhartz, "Parents and Children: A Philonic Perspective," in *The Jewish Family in Antiquity,* ed. Shaye J. D. Cohen (Atlanta: Scholars, 1993), p. 87.

[4]O. Larry Yarbrough, "Parents and Children in the Jewish Family of Antiquity," in *The Jewish Family in Antiquity,* ed. Shaye J. D. Cohen (Atlanta: Scholars, 1993), p. 41.

[5]David C. Verner, *The Household of God: The Social World of the Pastoral Epistles* (Chico, Calif: Scholars, 1983), pp. 45-46. See also Tal Ilan, *Jewish Women in Greco-Roman Palestine* (Peabody, Mass.: Hendrickson, 1996).

[6]Ross S. Kraemer, "Jewish Mothers and Daughters in the Greco-Roman World," in *The Jewish Family in Antiquity,* ed. Shaye J. D. Cohen (Atlanta: Scholars, 1993), p. 94; Suzanne Dixon, *The Roman Mother* (Norman: University of Oklahoma Press, 1988), pp. 233-35.

[7]Yarbrough, "Parents and Children," pp. 53-54.

[8]John E. Stambaugh and David L. Balch, *The New Testament in Its Social Environment* (Philadelphia: Westminster Press, 1986), pp. 111-12. On the *univira,* see Marjorie Lightman and William Zeisel, "Univira: An Example of Continuity and Change in Roman Society," *Church History* 46 (1977): 19-32.

[9]Wayne A. Meeks, *The First Urban Christians: The Social World of the Apostle Paul* (New Haven, Conn.: Yale University Press, 1983), p. 24.

[10]Ramsay MacMullen, "Women in Public in the Roman Empire," *Historia* 29 (1980): 208-18, esp. 211.

[11]Meeks, *First Urban Christians,* pp. 70-71.

[12]For more information on this and related issues, see Craig S. Keener, *Paul, Women and Wives: Marriage and Women's Ministry in the Letters of Paul* (Peabody, Mass.: Hendrickson, 1992).

[13]Reinhartz, "Parents and Children," p. 87; Yarbrough, "Parents and Children," pp. 42-45, 87.

[14]Stambaugh and Balch, *New Testament,* p. 122.

[15]Anthony J. Tambasco, *In the Days of Paul: The Social World and Teaching of the Apostle* (New York: Paulist, 1991), p. 7.

### Chapter 13: Provinces & Cities of the New Testament Era

[1]Inscription 232 in J. H. Kent, *Inscriptions 1926-1960, Corinth: Results,* American School of Classical Studies at Athens 8 (Camden, N.J.: Princeton University Press, 1966), pp. 99-100 and plate 21. Kent thinks that Erastus was a freedman who had become wealthy in commerce (p. 100).

[2]John E. Stambaugh and David L. Balch, *The New Testament in Its Social Environment* (Philadelphia: Westminster Press, 1986), p. 158.

[3]Joseph Barber Lightfoot, *Saint Paul's Epistles to the Colossians and to Philemon* (New York: Macmillan & Co., 1890; reprint, Grand Rapids, Mich.: Zondervan, 1959), p. 16.

[4]Robert M. Grant, *Gods and the One God* (Philadelphia: Westminster Press, 1986).

[5]Stambaugh and Balch, *New Testament*, pp. 149-52.

[6]Everett F. Harrison, *Introduction to the New Testament* (Grand Rapids, Mich.: Eerdmans, 1971), pp. 257-59.

[7]Barbara Levick, *Roman Colonies in Southern Asia* (Oxford: Clarendon, 1967), pp. 42-46.

[8]Fergus Millar, *The Roman Near East* (Cambridge, Mass.: Harvard University Press, 1993), p. 66.

[9]A. N. Sherwin-White, *Roman Law and Roman Society in the New Testament* (Oxford: Oxford University Press, 1963), p. 96.

[10]A. H. M. Jones, *The Cities of the Eastern Roman Provinces*, 2nd ed. (Oxford: Clarendon, 1971), p. 70.

[11]Juvenal, *The Sixteen Satires*, trans. Peter Green, (New York: Penguin, 1967), satire 3, 89.

[12]Millar, *Roman Near East*, p. 39.

**Appendix A**

[1]D. Brendan Nagle, *The Ancient World* (Englewood Cliffs, N.J.: Prentice-Hall, 1989), p. 251.

[2]Karl Christ, *The Romans*, trans. Christopher Holme (Berkeley: University of California Press, 1984), p. 11.

[3]Nagle, *Ancient World*, p. 265; Arnold J. Toynbee, *Hannibal's Legacy* (London: Oxford University Press, 1965), 1:134.

[4]F. F. Bruce, *New Testament History* (Garden City, N.Y.: Doubleday, 1980), p. 3.

[5]Everett F. Harrison, *The Apostolic Church* (Grand Rapids, Mich.: Eerdmans, 1985), p. 4.

[6]Christ, *Romans*, p. 38.

[7]Nagle, *Ancient World*, pp. 304-9.

[8]Bruce, *New Testament History*, p. 9.

[9]Josephus *Jewish Antiquities* 18.81-84.

[10]Michael Grant, *The Roman Emperors* (New York: Charles Scribner's Sons, 1985), p. 27; Josephus *Jewish War* 2.201-2.

[11]Anthony A. Barrett, *Caligula: The Corruption of Power* (New Haven, Conn.: Yale University Press, 1989), p. 240.

[12]Josephus *Jewish Antiquities* 19.279-91.

[13]Christ, *Romans*, 53.

# Subject Index

Achaia, 114-15, 117, 155, 260, 264, 281-82

Alexandria, 32, 38, 46, 57, 116, 121, 133, 212-13, 215-17, 273-75, 278, 316-17

Amphipolis, 281, 292

Antioch of Pisidia, 156, 276, 292

Antioch of Syria, 276, 287, 292

Antipater, 121-22, 273

apartment, 25, 40, 55-56, 59-62

Aphrodite, 92, 95, 263, 274

Apollonia, 37, 281, 292

appeal to Caesar, 112, 119, 168-70, 199, 207, 210

Aquila, 26-27, 83-85, 195, 206, 211-12, 217, 278, 285, 318

Archelaus, 124, 127-29, 149

aristocrat, 21-23, 112, 115, 159, 174, 182, 184, 186, 189, 191-93, 250, 296, 301-2, 311

army, 43, 92, 118-19, 145, 153, 157, 171-74, 178-79, 188, 190, 203, 205, 208, 221, 296, 298-301, 304-9, 312, 315

auxiliary legion, 185

Artemis, 27, 74, 92-95, 117, 163, 259, 268-69, 271, 290

Asia, 9, 27, 37-38, 41, 66, 70, 111, 114, 117, 145, 148, 155, 163, 166-67, 199, 207-9, 211, 213, 254, 265-73, 275, 277, 281-85, 287, 291-92, 294, 306, 308, 312, 329

Athens, 67, 94, 117, 255, 260-62, 273, 292

bankers, banking, 23-24, 64, 266

baths, 29, 41, 51-53, 58, 60, 62-63, 69, 284, 288

Berea, 164, 194, 281-82, 287, 292

Berytus, 177, 286, 289, 292

burial, burial association, 40, 44-46, 73-76, 78-79, 149, 245

Caesarea, 38, 66, 102, 121, 123-25, 128-30, 138-39, 150, 168, 177-78, 279-80, 289, 292

Cappadocia, 114, 148, 272, 292, 312, 315

Cenchrea, 38, 260, 262, 292

census, 129, 143, 146-48, 202, 297, 325

child, children, childhood, 44, 60, 82, 85, 86-87, 132, 175, 177, 184, 204, 222 226, 237-44, 246-50, 253-56, 289. *See also familia;* father; mother; parents

Chloe, 195, 229, 252

Christ, 66, 84-86, 126, 132, 144, 249, 274, 317

church, 12, 45, 56, 62, 71, 75, 77-81, 83-88, 108-9, 195, 212, 235, 252-53, 257, 264, 275-77, 279, 282-83, 288-89

organization, 71-88

Cilicia, 27-28, 114, 166, 272-73, 284, 287, 292

citizen, citizenship, 17, 31, 42, 57, 107, 112, 115-17, 137, 153, 161-62, 166, 168, 173, 175, 177, 182, 188, 190-92, 196-202, 204-9, 255, 299, 302-3, 306, 311-12

city, cities, 23, 25-29, 31-38, 48-70, 74-76, 81, 84-85, 91, 94, 97, 100, 102-3, 105, 107, 112, 114-17, 120-26, 128, 133, 139-42, 144, 146, 154-59, 163-66, 188-91, 193-95, 207-9, 211-13, 215-18, 250, 259, 294-95, 297, 299-300, 302-3, 308

Clauda, 273, 292

Claudius, Emperor, 34, 75, 105, 133-34, 136-38, 140, 165, 170-71, 212, 214-15, 228, 260, 263, 265

Claudius Lysias, 114, 166, 175, 185-86, 202, 205-6, 209

client, 17, 36, 60, 82, 172, 182-83, 192, 297-99

clothing, 26, 42-44, 54, 61, 189

Cognomen, 202-6, 231

coins, 9, 24, 126, 134, 148-54, 250, 283, 290

colony, Roman, 52, 59, 115-16, 157, 160, 165, 202, 209, 262, 271, 276-77, 280, 282-83, 291, 303

Colossae, 54, 266, 269, 292

Corinth, 31-32, 62, 75, 83-84, 93, 112, 115-16, 149, 164-66, 194-96, 208, 212, 252, 262-65, 285, 292, 308

Cornelius, 25, 206, 279, 305, 312

craftsmen, 54, 95, 142, 188, 193, 214, 269

Crete, 114, 273, 292

crime, 33, 89, 131, 154-58, 160-62, 164, 169,

# Scripture Index